The
ENCYCLOPEDIA
of ASTROLOGY

The ENCYCLOPEDIA of ASTROLOGY

RECEIVE WISDOM AND
UNDERSTANDING WITH THIS
ASTROLOGICAL GUIDE

SARAH CHRISTENSEN FU

Thorsons

Thorsons
An imprint of HarperCollins*Publishers*
1 London Bridge Street
London SE1 9GF

www.harpercollins.co.uk

HarperCollins*Publishers*
Macken House, 39/40 Mayor Street Upper
Dublin 1, D01 C9W8, Ireland

First published by HarperCollins*Publishers* 2025

3 5 7 9 10 8 6 4 2

© HarperCollins*Publishers* 2025

Sarah Christensen Fu asserts the moral right to be identified as the author of this work

Author: Sarah Christensen Fu
Astronomy consultant: Mary McIntyre
Cover designer: Ros Saunders and e-Digital Design
Cover illustrator: Maria Brzozowska
Editors: Caitlin Doyle and Sianez Osman
Illustrator: Andrew Paciorek
Typesetter: Amnet and e-Digital Design

A catalogue record of this book is available from the British Library

ISBN 978-0-00-875772-4

Printed and bound in Malaysia

All rights reserved. No part of this publication may be reproduced, stored in a retrieval system, or transmitted, in any form or by any means, electronic, mechanical, photocopying, recording or otherwise, without the prior written permission of the publishers.

Without limiting the author's and publisher's exclusive rights, any unauthorised use of this publication to train generative artificial intelligence (AI) technologies is expressly prohibited. HarperCollins also exercise their rights under Article 4(3) of the Digital Single Market Directive 2019/790 and expressly reserve this publication from the text and data mining exception.

This book contains FSC™ certified paper and other controlled sources to ensure responsible forest management.

For more information visit: www.harpercollins.co.uk/green

Contents

Letter of Introduction	3
Astrological Concepts and Basic Definitions	9
Astrological Terms	19
Western Astrology	77
Western Astrology Birth Charts	121
Western Zodiac Houses	134
Centers of Learning in Western Astrology	156
Key Texts of Western Astrology	157
Notable Figures of Western Astrology	159
Astrology Around the World	171
Chinese Astrology	173
Cultural Variations in Asia	197
Japanese Astrology	197
Korean Astrology	201
Mongolian Astrology	205
Tibetan Astrology	208
Vietnamese Astrology	213
Egyptian Astrology	216
Greek Astrology	225
Hellenistic Astrology	231

Islamic Astrology	241
Jyotish Astrology (Indian)	252
Mesoamerican Astrology	267
Aztec Astrology	275
Mayan Astrology	281
Mesopotamian Astrology (Babylonian)	287
North American Indigenous Astrology	296
Cherokee Astrology	308
Norse Astrology	311
Roman Astrology	317
Planets and Celestial Bodies	325
Celestial Events	369
Almanac of Upcoming Celestial Events	379
Timeline of Astrology	429
Astrology and Spiritual Practices	449
Astrological Tools and Techniques	473
Modern Astrology: Technology and New Adaptations	485
Applications of Astrology	497
Resources	517

INTRODUCTION

Letter of Introduction

Dear fellow seekers,

Several years ago, I embarked on a cosmic journey into the study of astrology. Armed with a healthy dose of skepticism and a penchant for snark, I did a deep dive into sun signs to write a book called *Bad Birthdays: The Truth Behind Your Crappy Sun Sign*. It was a tongue-in-cheek exploration of astrology's darker side, and I threw myself into research. I started with a visit to the Body, Mind, Spirit Festival in Denver, Colorado, where I talked with celebrated local astrologers, and then I voraciously read the most famous and established books on the subject. I explored the websites that can run instant birth charts based on your place and time of birth and downloaded a half-dozen apps. I probably watched hundreds of hours of astrologers on YouTube explain their art. In short, I went down the astrological rabbit hole.

As I immersed myself, I learned that while scientific principles and tools guide and lend structure to astrological studies, the interpretation of the study of the stars is truly an art. The promise of being seen, known, and understood on a cosmic level is powerful to people today, and has been for all of human history. To paraphrase many of the histories I've read: the first human who noticed that the Sun rose and set every day was the first astronomer, and the first human who created meaning for him or herself out of that was first astrologer. Of course this is over-simplified, but the idea helps to demonstrate how ancient and deeply ingrained the urge to relate the cosmos to our daily lives can be.

Astrology emerged all over the world as humanity evolved—in Mesopotamia, an ancient tablet, the *Enuma Anu Enlil*, attributed omens to the movement of Venus, while in Denmark, burial sites from around 1400 BCE were oriented to face the rising Sun during the winter solstice. In other parts of the world, early astrologers were making oracle bone inscriptions in China featuring constellations, and in India around 1000 BCE, the *Vedas* were penned, mapping and interpreting the night sky. The search for meaning and understanding of oneself is primal, and so is developing that meaning through the study of the cosmos. Early astrologers had a concept that I found repeated in different ways across many different studies: "As above, so below" (first attributed to the *Emerald Tablet*, thought to be written around the 8th or 9th century CE in modern-day Egypt). It means that whatever is playing out in the sky above us is repeated here on Earth in our daily lives and relationships.

As I researched the history of astrology, I also realized that it has a great deal in common with religion. In addition to ancient roots and creation stories, many of the debates around astrology overlap with questions about religion—for example, free will versus determinism: if the planets guide the ups and downs of people's lives, then how much control do people have over their own outcomes? The deep questions that surfaced in my study of astrology provided lots of food for thought!

In conversations with friends I found that while some people's interest in astrology stops at the infamous pick-up line, "What's your sign?" (and don't forget to waggle the eyebrows while asking!), others truly use insight from their birth chart and their sun sign horoscopes to influence their work and major life decisions. And that divide didn't stop with my friends! Many famous modern figures have truly found comfort and guidance in astrology. For example, Carl Jung, the father of analytical psychology, was an avid student of astrology, and Nancy and Ronald Reagan, former first lady and U.S. president, consulted astrologers during his time in office according to the memoir of former White House Chief of Staff Donald Regan.

While I am a self-taught student of astrology, there are scholars in the field who I admire greatly and would like to recommend for anyone who desires deeper study. Carole Taylor, author of *Astrology: Using the Wisdom of the Stars in Your Everyday Life*, and Sue Tompkins, author of *The Contemporary Astrologer's Handbook*, are both important voices in astrological studies.

This encyclopedia gives information and interpretation of each of the zodiac signs, or sun signs, and also defines and explains rising signs, astrological houses, aspects, birth charts, and more. There is also a listing of cultures, a timeline, and an overview of tools that astrologers have used throughout history to try to better understand what drives and dictates how humans behave.

I have also included information on celestial bodies and how they are thought to impact behavior, from the star we call the "Sun" to the mysterious, broody Pluto, downgraded by astronomers but still greatly important to astrologers. Each planet and celestial phenomenon has its own personality and effect, from eclipses to the cosmic scapegoat "Mercury in retrograde," and this book attempts to define them in a simple-to-understand way.

The book is organized by topic and then alphabetically, with an index in the back that should make it simple to find each term or reference. Because this encyclopedia is authored by a Western student of astrology and will be published in the West, its primary focus will be on Western astrology. There is a list of key texts in each cultural section, plus a full list of sources

The Encyclopedia of Astrology

at the end of the book to help readers further their knowledge and learning about astrology.

My great hope is that each reader who picks up this book will use the information to understand the art and science behind astrology, while also getting to know him- or herself better. I see astrology as a mirror that can be held up to gain a deeper understanding of one's habits, hidden desires, and the obstacles that may block the way. Astrology can be a tool that will serve readers throughout their lifetime and enrich their relationships with family and friends, careers, and lives.

Happy reading, stars!

Sincerely,
Sarah Christensen Fu

The Encyclopedia of Astrology

ASTROLOGICAL CONCEPTS & BASIC DEFINITIONS

What Is Astrology?

Astrology is the ancient and contemporary practice of interpreting the movements and positions of celestial bodies to understand and interpret their influence on the daily life of humans. The word derives from the Greek *astrologia*, combining *astron* (star) and *logia* (study of), reflecting its origins as an organized system of tracking the stars and planets, and the perceived meaning of each. While there are many different astrological systems, they all have one thing in common: each system maps the relationship between the cosmos and earthly life, examining how planetary placements at specific moments correlate with an individual's personality traits, relationships, and life events.

Astrology is used in many ways to understand all aspects of life, including:

- **Personality Insights:** Understanding core traits, emotional needs, and interpersonal tendencies.
- **Career Guidance:** Identifying strengths, passions, and best career paths.
- **Relationship Analysis:** Exploring compatibility and dynamics in partnerships through synastry.
- **Life Transitions:** Navigating major milestones, such as the Saturn Return or Uranus Opposition.
- **Self-reflection:** Using the chart as a tool for introspection and personal development.
- **Health and Wellness:** Examining the planetary influences on potential health

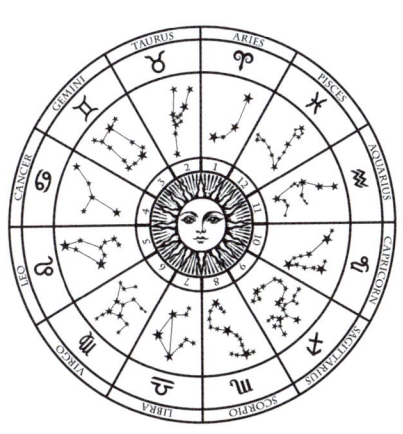

The Encyclopedia of Astrology

conditions and courses of treatment, or preventative care and habits that can sustain a healthy lifestyle.
- **Spiritual Growth:** Aligning life choices with the soul's purpose and higher aspirations.
- **Family Dynamics:** Analyzing ancestral patterns and parent-child relationships through house placements.

Of course, at any cocktail party in the Western world, bringing up astrology will get a number of predictable reactions. Some people will be thrilled to talk about their sun sign and how accurate daily horoscope apps can be, while others will glaze over, declare it all ridiculous, and find any opportunity to escape the conversation. Many people see it as an outdated set of beliefs with no tie to science. After reading this book, readers should be able to appreciate, engage in, and discuss astrology at a more nuanced level, with an advanced understanding of the terms used in astrology, and an overview of astrological practices at different points in time and at different places around the globe.

While there are a number of debates and critiques in the field of astrology, what can't be denied is the prevalence around the globe of astrological beliefs and how formative these beliefs were in creating modern culture. This book aims to define, classify, and explain the history and evolution of modern astrological practices. It focuses on Western astrology but also includes significant entries for cultures around the world.

DEBATES AND CRITIQUES OF ASTROLOGY

To begin an overview of astrology, it's helpful to look at some of the critiques and debates commonly held against the field of study. Some of these debates are ancient, stretching back to the earliest astrological studies, while some are more contemporary, focusing on more modern occurrences or interpretations.

Age of Aquarius and Age of Pisces Timing

The song "Age of Aquarius," by the band The 5th Dimension celebrates an era marked by trust, harmony, and understanding. But has humanity entered this magical age yet? The timing of the Age of Aquarius remains highly debated, with estimates ranging from the late 1800s to beyond 2600 CE. Some astrologers point to the 1960s cultural revolution as its beginning, while traditionalists calculate it will begin between 2100 and 2160 CE, based on precession measurements. Others link it to specific celestial alignments like the 2020 Jupiter–Saturn conjunction or the influence of stars like Alpha Aquarii.

The Age of Pisces, which precedes the Age of Aquarius, began around 1 BCE–100 CE, coinciding with the rise of major religions—particularly Christianity, whose fish symbol aligned with the Piscean age. Most astrologers agree we are currently in a transition period between the Age of Pisces and the Age of Aquarius, though the exact timing remains the subject of debate.

Astronomical Precession

Astronomical precession, or the precession (slow change of direction) of equinoxes, is the gradual shift in Earth's rotational axis over an approximately 26,000-year cycle, causing the apparent position of stars and constellations to drift relative to Earth's seasonal markers.

This means that the zodiac has shifted gradually since astrologers made their first divisions and mapped the constellations due to Earth's axial precession. In fact, constellation positions have shifted approximately 24 degrees since Babylonian times. This creates questions about how astrologers reconcile the difference between what was historically mapped and the current astronomical reality.

Free Will Versus Determinism

One of the most interesting debates around astrology is the

The Encyclopedia of Astrology

ASTRONOMICAL PRECESSION

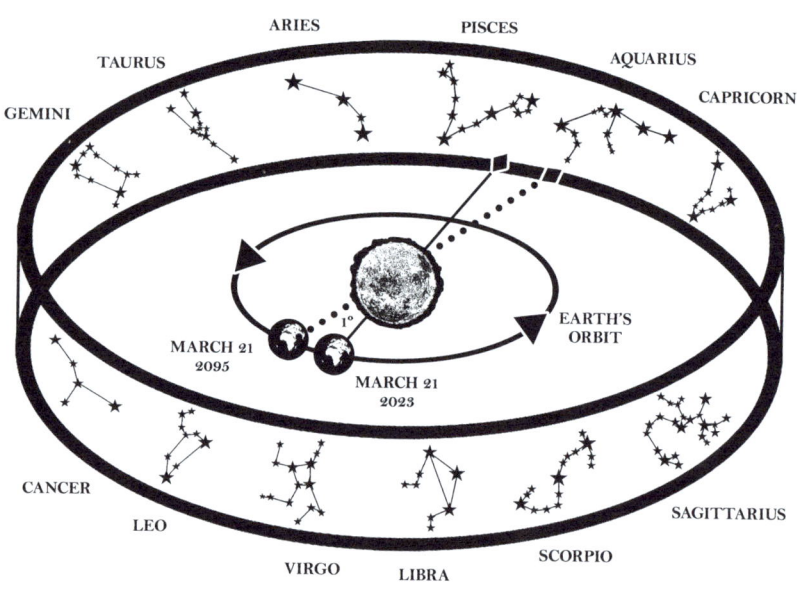

philosophical debate about free will and determinism. Do all astrologers believe that celestial influences absolutely determine fate, or do some believe that the movement of the cosmos simply suggest tendencies or possibilities? This question touches on fundamental issues of human agency and cosmic influence.

Hemispheric Differences
Astrologers debate how interpretations should differ between northern and southern hemispheres. The traditional meanings associated with signs and houses arise from Western astrologers and from the northern hemisphere and may need significant adaptation when crossing the equator. While the seasonal cycles and viewable constellations differ between the northern and southern hemispheres, the Earth's relationship to the skies remains consistent no matter where an

individual is located on the planet. Most Western astrologers maintain consistent interpretations regardless of location, because the system primarily relates to the Earth's relationship with celestial bodies rather than the seasons.

Historical Accuracy

Scholars continue to examine whether ancient astrological predictions and techniques demonstrated reliable results.

This investigation includes analyzing historical records, examining documented predictions, and evaluating the evolution of astrological methods across different cultures.

House System Validity

One of the most confusing parts of studying astrology is that different house systems produce varying chart interpretations, particularly at extreme latitudes where some systems become mathematically unstable.

The choice between Placidus, Koch, Equal House, and other systems significantly impacts chart interpretation. For instance, a planet near the cusp of the seventh house in the Placidus system might appear in the sixth house in the Equal House system, leading to different emphases in chart interpretation.

Most of the time, while the choice of house system can affect the interpretation of planetary positions within houses, it does not alter the fundamental placements of the ascendant or the sun sign in an individual's natal chart.

Modern Versus Traditional Rulerships

The discovery of outer planets (Uranus, Neptune, and Pluto) sparked ongoing debate about whether those planets should be assigned rulership over signs traditionally governed by classical planets.

This conversation touches on broader questions about how and when astrology should incorporate new astronomical discoveries.

The Encyclopedia of Astrology

Newspaper/App Horoscopes

The widespread publication of simplified sun sign horoscopes raises questions about astrology's public perception and credibility.

While these columns make astrology accessible, they often oversimplify complex natal chart interpretations.

Ophiuchus, the 13th Zodiac Sign

Ophiuchus is referred to as the "13th zodiac sign" and sometimes appears in contemporary astrology discussions, though it's not recognized in traditional Western astrology. It represents the constellation of the "Serpent Bearer" positioned between Scorpio and Sagittarius.

In astronomical terms, Ophiuchus is a large constellation through which the Sun actually passes from approximately November 29 to December 17. When NASA pointed this out in 2011, it created confusion since traditional Western astrology uses a fixed zodiac system of 12 signs rather than tracking the actual constellations, which have shifted due to Earth's axial precession over centuries.

Planetary Hours Calculation

Methods for calculating planetary hours vary, particularly in locations experiencing extreme differences in daylight duration. These calculations become especially complex near the poles, where traditional timing systems may break down.

Professional Standards

The astrological community continues to debate what qualifications or certifications should be required for professional practice. Different organizations and groups propose varying standards for education, testing, and certification.

Religious Opposition

Many religious traditions, particularly monotheistic faiths, have historically opposed astrological practice as challenging divine sovereignty. This theological tension continues to influence modern debates about astrology's spiritual validity.

The Encyclopedia of Astrology

Scientific Falsifiability

The question of whether astrological claims can be tested using scientific methods remains contentious. The complex, multifaceted nature of astrological interpretation presents challenges for traditional scientific methodology.

Statistical Studies

Research attempting to prove or disprove correlations between celestial patterns and human behavior produces mixed results. Methodological challenges include accounting for multiple variables and defining measurable outcomes.

Sidereal Versus Tropical Zodiac

The choice between sidereal calculations based on fixed stars and tropical calculations based on seasonal points remains actively debated. Each system offers different advantages and philosophical justifications.

Time Zones and Birth Time Accuracy

Modern time standardization through zones and daylight saving time creates questions about precise birth time calculation. These artificial time boundaries may affect traditional astrological timing techniques.

Twins Paradox

The observation that individuals born at nearly identical times and locations can experience different life paths challenges simple astrological determinism. This phenomenon suggests the need for more nuanced understanding of celestial influences.

The Encyclopedia of Astrology

ASTROLOGICAL TERMS

Astrological Terms: A–Z

These terms are in alphabetical order, with some supporting terms nested under central terms.

AGES OF MAN

The Ages of Man concept assigns different life stages to the rulership of specific planets, each governing distinct developmental periods. This is related to the time-lords concept developed as an innovation under Hellenistic astrology.

> **Moon:** Birth to age 4, representing infancy and early growth.
> **Mercury:** Ages 5 to 14, associated with education and learning.
> **Venus:** Ages 15 to 22, linked to emotional development, friendships, and romantic relationships.
> **Sun:** Ages 23 to 42, reflecting adulthood and career pursuits.
> **Mars:** Ages 43 to 57, signifying ambition and assertiveness.
> **Jupiter:** Ages 58 to 69, connected to reflection and wisdom.
> **Saturn:** Ages 70 to 99, representing resignation and life's later stages.

The perspective of planetary influences corresponding to human developmental phases is rooted in ancient astrological traditions.

ALMANAC, CELESTIAL ALMANAC

An almanac is a yearly calendar that tracks astronomical and astrological events, including Moon phases, planetary movements, eclipses, and seasonal changes. Traditional almanacs also included weather predictions, planting guides, and tide tables, serving as essential reference guides for farmers, sailors, and astrologers. These publications have evolved from ancient Babylonian clay tablets to modern digital formats, and they

The Encyclopedia of Astrology

maintain their core purpose of documenting cyclical patterns in the sky and their earthly correspondences.

Popular almanacs over the ages have included:

The Babylonian Almanacs, dating from 1800–750 BCE, were among the first systematic recordings of celestial events, containing detailed observations of planetary movements and eclipses, and their correlation with earthly omens.

The medieval ***Alfonsine Tables***, commissioned by Alfonso X of Castile in 1252, became the most widely used astronomical/astrological reference in Europe for over three centuries, offering more precise calculations of planetary positions and eclipses.

The Astronomical Almanac (originally the *American Ephemeris* and *Nautical Almanac*), published continuously since 1767, has bridged both astronomical and astrological uses with its precise planetary positions. It includes detailed astronomical calculations, planetary ingress, and eclipse data calculated for the Western hemisphere.

Raphael's Almanac, first published in 1820, remains one of the longest-running purely astrological almanacs still in publication today.

The Rudolfine Tables published in 1627 were far more precise than previous tables. This set of astronomical tables was compiled by Johannes Kepler and refined planetary positions, significantly improving astronomical accuracy.

ANTISCIA AND CONTRA-ANTISCIA

Antiscia, derived from the Greek term for "shadow," are pairs of zodiac signs that mirror each other across the solstitial axis—also known as the Cancer–Capricorn axis (0° Cancer to 0° Capricorn).

The Encyclopedia of Astrology

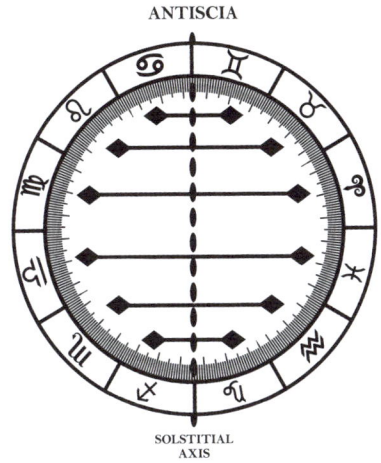

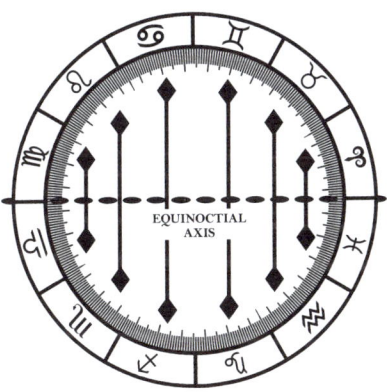

This symmetry is believed to create a subtle connection between planets positioned at these mirrored degrees, offering additional insights into astrological chart interpretations.

ARMILLARY SPHERE

An armillary sphere is a tool designed for visualizing the apparent motions of celestial bodies around the Earth. It looks like a skeletal celestial globe made of rings and hoops, which represent major celestial circles—the equator, ecliptic, and meridians. The armillary sphere emerged in ancient Greece during the 3rd century BCE, though similar models may have existed earlier in ancient China and Babylon.

Contra-antiscia points are pairs of degrees in the zodiac that are equidistant from the solstitial axis of Cancer and Capricorn, but on opposite sides of it—creating a mirror reflection across the solstice points.

The Encyclopedia of Astrology

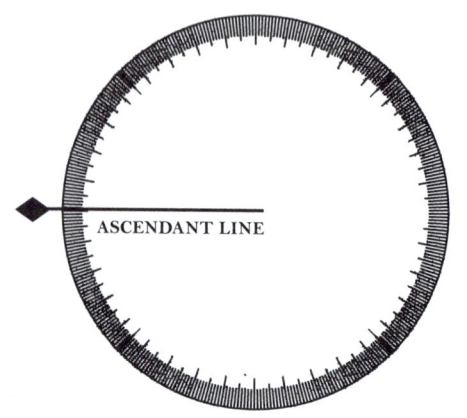

impact on first impressions, physical appearance, and a person's approach to life. While a person's sun sign represents core identity, the ascendant is thought to act as a lens through which that identity is expressed to the world, influencing everything from mannerisms to the way a person approaches challenges.

ASCENDANT

The ascendant, also known as the rising sign, is the zodiac sign that was rising on the eastern horizon at the exact time of a person's birth. The ascendant is believed to have a significant

ASPECT

An aspect in astrology refers to the angular relationship between two planets in a birth chart, which is measured in degrees along the zodiacal cir-

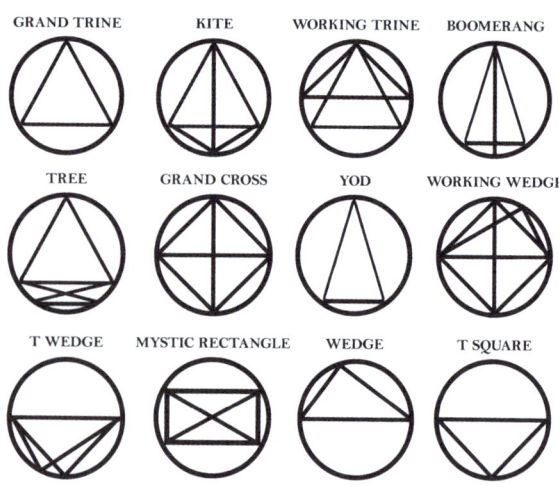

The Encyclopedia of Astrology

cle. These angles are believed to create specific energy patterns that influence how the planets' energies interact and manifest in a person's life.

- Major aspects (conjunction, sextile, square, trine, opposition)
- Minor aspects (semi-sextile, quincunx, etc.)
- Orbs and aspect patterns
- Grand trines, T-squares, yods

See more in **Aspects and Relationships**.

ASTROCARTOGRAPHY

Astrocartography, also known as astrolocality or relocational astrology, is a branch of astrology that examines how different locations on Earth may influence a person's life based on their birth chart. It was developed in the 1970s by American astrologer Jim Lewis, who created a system of mapping planetary lines across the world.

ASTROLOGICAL AGES

Astrological ages, also known as the Great Ages, are approximately 2,160-year periods defined by the Earth's slow backwards movement through the zodiac constellations, with a complete cycle—a Great Year—taking about 25,920 years.

Today, the ages are currently transitioning from the Age of Pisces to the Age of Aquarius. This shift is called the Great Turning, though there is significant debate among astrologers about the exact timing of this shift.

Each age is believed to bring distinct themes that influence human civilization and consciousness.

Age of Aquarius

The Age of Aquarius is characterized by revolutionary changes in consciousness, technological innovation, humanitarian values, and a shift from hierarchical structures to collective, networked ways of thinking and organizing society.

The Encyclopedia of Astrology

AQUARIUS

Age of Pisces

The Age of Pisces was marked by the rise of organized religion, mysticism, and faith-based belief systems that shaped human civilization through spiritual and institutional authority.

PISCES

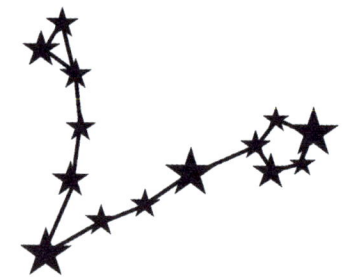

ASTRONOMY

Astronomy is the scientific study of celestial objects, phenomena, and the universe as a whole. It encompasses the observation and analysis of stars, planets, moons, comets, galaxies, and cosmic events like supernovae and black hole mergers. Using tools such as telescopes, satellites, and spacecraft, astronomers investigate the physical and chemical properties of celestial bodies, their movements, and their interactions. As one of the oldest sciences, astronomy bridges theoretical and observational techniques to address questions about the origins of the universe, the nature of space and time, and the potential for life beyond Earth.

AUTUMNAL EQUINOX

The autumnal equinox functions as both a moment in time and a point in space—it occurs where the Sun crosses the celestial equator moving southward, marking 180 degrees of celestial longitude and the beginning of Libra in the tropical zodiac.

AXIS (AXES)

An axis on an astrological birth chart represents a pair of opposite houses or points in the

The Encyclopedia of Astrology

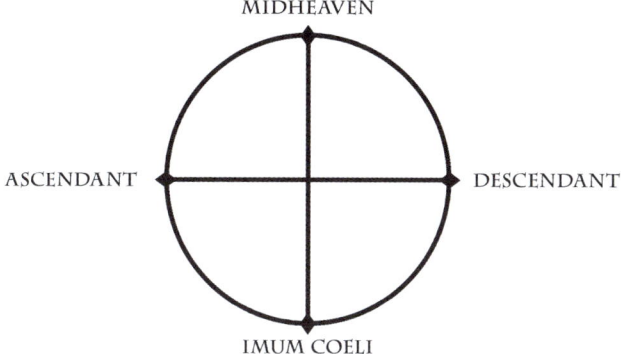

zodiac wheel that work as complementary forces, creating a dynamic polarity in a person's birth chart.

The main axes include the Ascendant–Descendant axis, representing self versus relationships, and the Midheaven–Imum Coeli axis, representing public life versus private life.

Ascendant–Descendant (ASC–DESC) Axis

The Ascendant–Descendant Axis, denoted on a birth chart with "ASC" on the left side and "DESC" on the right, connects the eastern and western horizons at birth, with the ascendant representing the self, and the descendant representing relationships. This axis highlights the interplay between personal identity and how a person relates to others.

The ascendant, or rising sign, is the zodiac sign and degree rising on the eastern horizon when a person was born, symbolizing the way a person projects themselves outwardly.

Opposite the ascendant, the descendant marks the zodiac sign setting on the western horizon at the exact moment of birth, reflecting themes of relationships and the qualities a person seeks in others to balance their own nature.

The Ascendant–Descendant Axis runs across the birth chart, while the MC–IC Axis runs straight up and down.

Midheaven–Imum Coeli (MC–IC) Axis

The Midheaven–Imum Coeli Axis is the vertical axis of an astrological birth chart. The midheaven point is also known as the Medium Coeli and is abbreviated as "MC" at the top of a birth chart, while the Imum Coeli is "IC" at the bottom. This axis highlights the relationship between a person's external achievements and internal foundations, and indicates how personal background influences public endeavors.

The midheaven point—also known as Medium Coeli, abbreviated to "MC"—located at the cusp of the tenth house, signifies one's public life, career aspirations, and reputation. It is the highest point in an astrological birth chart, marking the zodiac degree that is at the intersection of the ecliptic (the apparent path that celestial bodies trace across the sky from Earth), with the local meridian (the imaginary line that arches across the sky from the northern point of the horizon) traveling directly overhead, and then down to the southern point of the horizon.

The Imum Coeli, at the cusp of the fourth house, pertains to one's private life. Literally meaning "bottom of the sky" in Latin, it represents the deepest, most private point in a birth chart. Located directly opposite the Midheaven or Medium Coeli, this point marks where the ecliptic intersects with the meridian *below the horizon*, symbolizing one's roots, family background, and emotional foundation. The IC acts as a gateway to understanding childhood experiences, ancestral patterns, and the internal source from which a person draws their strength.

Nodal Axis

The Nodal Axis, formed by the North and South Nodes of the Moon, indicates our soul's journey in this lifetime. The South Node represents familiar patterns and innate talents from past experiences, while the North Node points to qualities and experiences we need to develop for spiritual growth.

NODAL AXIS

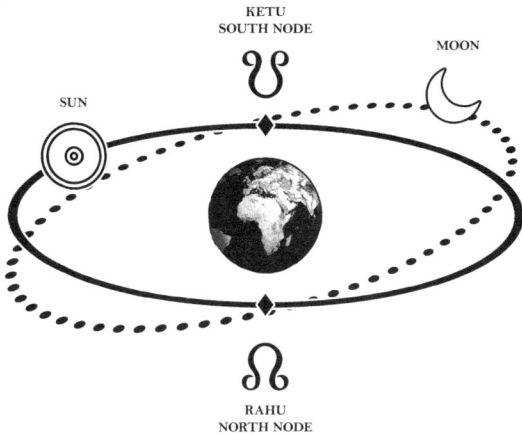

The lunar nodes are two calculated points where the Moon's orbit intersects the ecliptic, which is the apparent path of the Sun through the sky. These points, known as the North Node and South Node, carry deep symbolic significance in astrology, offering insights into the soul's karmic journey and purpose.

The North Node signifies the qualities, experiences, and lessons that an individual is meant to develop and embrace in this lifetime. It represents the path of growth and spiritual evolution, often requiring movement beyond familiar territory. Though its themes may feel unfamiliar or challenging, aligning with the North Node fosters fulfillment and purpose.

The South Node reflects traits, habits, and experiences carried over from past lives or early life. It represents areas of comfort, natural talents, and ingrained patterns. While these qualities can provide a strong foundation, an over-reliance on the South Node may lead to stagnation or repetition of old patterns. Balancing the South Node's gifts with the lessons of the North Node encourages growth.

A nodal return occurs when the transiting North Node returns to its natal position, often aligning with a renewed sense of purpose or direction.

The Encyclopedia of Astrology

The nodal cycle spans approximately 18.6 years, with key milestones marking significant periods of personal and spiritual development.

BENEFIC PLANETS

Benefic planets are considered favorable influences in astrology, traditionally associated with bringing positive qualities and outcomes. In classical Western astrology, Venus and Jupiter are regarded as the primary benefic planets.

VENUS

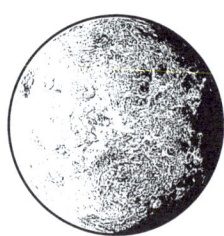

These planets are thought to ease challenges, promote opportunities, and enhance the beneficial aspects of life, especially when well-aspected or positioned in a birth chart. Their influence can bring balance, optimism, and a sense of well-being to the areas of life they govern.

JUPITER

BIRTH CHART

A birth chart, also known as a natal chart, is a personalized map of the sky at the exact moment and location of a person's birth. It represents the positions of the planets, the Sun, the Moon, and other celestial points within the 12 astrological houses, each governing specific areas of life. The chart is divided into zodiac signs, and the alignment of these elements is believed to influence personality, life path, strengths, challenges, and relationships. The earliest surviving horoscopic chart for an individual is from Babylon and dates to 410 BCE.

An astrologer needs a person's birth date and birth time

to pinpoint the placement of the stars and other celestial bodies at the exact time and place of birth. A few options exist for people who don't have their birth time and location: the first is to estimate to the best of one's ability and create a birth chart based on the estimation. The second would be to research the birth charts of individuals who have similar qualities and work backwards to claim the chart details that best fit. Neither of these methods provide accuracy, but both offer some opportunity for astrological investigation and potential insights.

See more in **Birth Chart**.

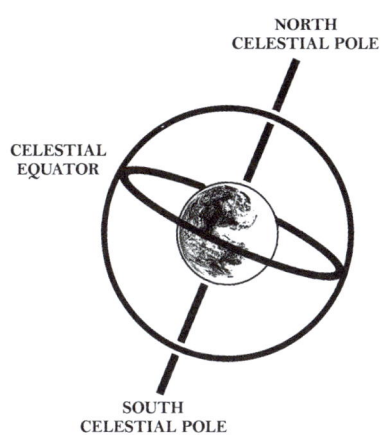

CELESTIAL EQUATOR

The celestial equator is like a projection of Earth's equator onto the celestial sphere, dividing it into northern and southern hemispheres. This imaginary line serves as a reference in the equatorial coordinate system, aiding in the precise positioning of celestial objects.

CELESTIAL LONGITUDE

Celestial longitude is a coordinate used to specify the positions of objects in the sky. It measures the angular distance eastward along the ecliptic—the path the Sun appears to take across the sky—from the vernal equinox, which serves as the zero point.

CELESTIAL SPHERES

The celestial spheres were an ancient cosmological model that envisioned the universe as a series of concentric, transparent spheres centered around a stationary Earth, with each sphere carrying celestial bodies such as the Moon, Sun, planets, and stars.

The Encyclopedia of Astrology

CELESTIAL SPHERES

This geocentric framework, developed by Greek philosophers such as Aristotle and Ptolemy, was used to explain the apparent motions of these bodies across the sky until it was replaced by the heliocentric model during the Scientific Revolution of the 16th and 17th centuries.

CHALDEAN ORDER
The Chaldean order originated from ancient Babylonian astronomers who organized the visible planets based on their apparent speed of motion across the night sky. The slower the planet appeared to move, the higher and more distant it was believed to be in the celestial spheres.

The Encyclopedia of Astrology

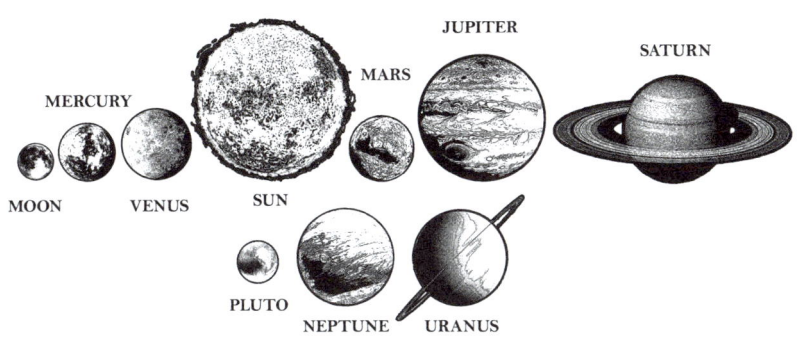

The Chaldean order is:
- Saturn
- Jupiter
- Mars
- Sun
- Venus
- Mercury
- Moon

The Chaldean order was used to assign planetary rulership to the days of the week and hours of each day, creating a system that astrologers still reference today. Each day begins with its namesake planet ruling the first hour, then following the Chaldean sequence hour by hour, creating a continuous cycle.

See more in **Planetary Days** and **Planetary Hours**.

CHART PATTERNS

Chart patterns in birth charts occur when planets form distinct geometric shapes or configurations that create significant meaning. These patterns tell a story of how planetary energies interact and flow within a person's life, with each shape suggesting different dynamics, some harmonious and some filled with tension.

Some chart patterns include: Grand Trine, T-Square, Yod, Bowl, Bundle, See-saw, Locomotive, Splash, and Bucket.

See more in **Chart Patterns**.

CHIRON RETURN

Chiron is a small planetary body classified as both an asteroid and

The Encyclopedia of Astrology

a comet that orbits between Saturn and Uranus in our solar system. The Chiron Return is a transit where the celestial body Chiron returns to the house where it was at the time of a person's birth. This takes place in a person's life at around age 50, marking a time of deep healing and the ability to transform personal wounds into wisdom that can help others.

See more in **Transits**.

COMBUSTION

Combustion refers to a condition where a planet is in close proximity to the Sun on a birth chart, typically within 8.5 degrees, causing its influence to be weakened or overpowered by the Sun's intense energy. This proximity diminishes the planet's visibility and its ability to express its inherent qualities effectively.

COSMOLOGY

Cosmology is the scientific study of the origin, structure, evolution, and ultimate fate of the universe. It seeks to understand the large-scale properties of the cosmos by examining phenomena such as the big bang, cosmic inflation, dark matter, dark energy, and the distribution of galaxies.

Rooted in both theoretical physics and observational astronomy, cosmology combines mathematical models and empirical data to explore fundamental questions about the nature of space, time, and matter. It also intersects with philosophy, metaphysics, and astrology, reflecting humanity's enduring quest to comprehend the universe's beginnings and its overarching purpose.

CUSPS

People whose birthday falls within one day of the boundary between two adjacent zodiac signs fall on the cusp, or transition, between the two signs and are sometimes said to have traits of both signs.

See more in **Cusps**.

The Encyclopedia of Astrology

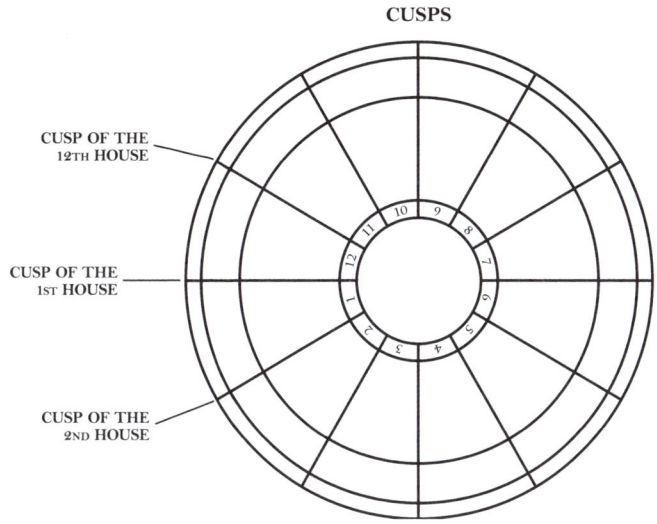

CYCLES

A cycle is a sequence of events or processes that repeat in a specific order, often returning to the initial state. The zodiac itself is a cycle, and other examples of important and influential cycles in astrology include:

- Lunar phases of the Moon
- Planetary returns and transits
- Retrograde periods
- Astrological ages

Other fundamental cycles include:

- The 19-year **Metonic Cycle**—where the Moon's phases align with the same calendar dates.
- The 54-year **Triple Conjunction Cycle** of Jupiter and Saturn that is used to track major societal shifts.
- The **Saros Cycle**, spanning 18 years and 11 days, that predicts when eclipses will repeat in similar geographical locations.
- The 780-year **Great Mutation Cycle** tracks how Jupiter–Saturn conjunctions shift through elements, traditionally marking pivotal changes in civilization.

The Encyclopedia of Astrology

DECANS

A decan is a division of an astrological sign into three equal parts, each spanning 10 degrees of the 30-degree zodiac sign. Each decan is associated with a planetary ruler and adds nuance to the characteristics of the sign, blending its traits with the influence of the decan's ruler.

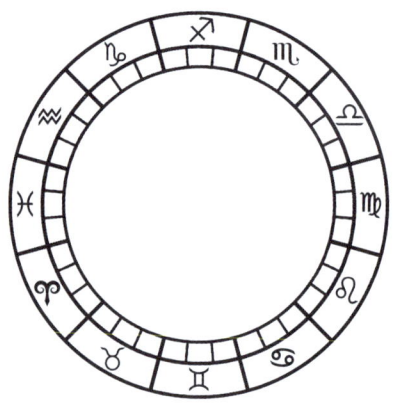

DECLINATION

Declination measures a celestial body's angular distance north or south of the celestial equator, akin to Earth's latitude. Astrologers analyze declinations to understand planetary positions relative to Earth, considering aspects like parallels—when two planets share the same declination—which can influence the interpretation of planetary relationships.

DEGREE

A degree is a specific point within the 360-degree zodiac wheel. These degrees help astrologers pinpoint the exact position of planets, stars, and other celestial bodies at any given moment, allowing for more precise astrological interpretations.

The degree placement is particularly important in birth charts, where even a difference of a few degrees can significantly impact the interpretation of planetary positions and their relationships to each other.

DEVELOPMENTAL PHASES

The zodiac signs represent a natural progression of personal and spiritual development, and this progression is called developmental phases. The phases begin with Aries as the initial spark of self-discovery and individual identity and advances from basic self-awareness to emotional understanding and relationships, then to deeper connections with others, and finally to universal consciousness and wisdom. Each sign builds upon the lessons of the previous ones, creating a complete cycle of growth that mirrors human psychological and spiritual evolution.

- Aries
- Taurus
- Gemini
- Cancer
- Leo
- Virgo
- Libra
- Scorpio
- Sagittarius
- Capricorn
- Aquarius
- Pisces

See more in **Zodiac Seasons**.

DIGNITY

Dignity, or essential dignity, in astrology refers to the relative strength or weakness of a planet based on its position in the zodiac.

A planet is considered dignified, or strong, when it is placed in a zodiac sign where it can express its nature effectively—its domicile or exaltation. Conversely, a planet is considered debilitated, or weak, when it is in a sign that makes it difficult to express its qualities, such as being in its detriment, fall, or unfavorable house position.

Accidental Dignity: The strength a planet gains due to its specific position and conditions within an astrological chart, independent of its inherent qualities. Factors contributing to accidental dignity include:

Almuten: From Arabic *al-mateen*, adopted into Western medieval astrology, refers to the planet with the most essential dignity in a particular degree or chart position. Still used in traditional Western practice.

Angular Houses: Planets located in angular houses (first, fourth, seventh, tenth) are considered more potent, with the first and tenth houses offering the greatest strength.

Aspects and Conjunctions: Beneficial aspects with favorable planets like Venus or Jupiter enhance a planet's accidental dignity. Challenging aspects with malefic planets like Mars or Saturn can diminish it.

Cadent Houses: Cadent houses (third, sixth, ninth, twelfth) are seen as weaker positions for planets.

Combustion: Refers to a condition where a planet is in close proximity to the Sun on a birth chart, causing its influence to be weakened or overpowered by the Sun's intense energy.

Detriment: A detriment in astrology occurs when a planet is positioned in the zodiac sign opposite to the one it rules, creating a challenging or uncomfortable energy for that planet to express itself.

Domicile: The zodiac sign where a planet feels most naturally powerful and expressive, similar to being in its own home. Its energies and influences can manifest most effectively and positively.

Exaltation: Exaltation refers to a specific zodiac sign where a planet's energy is heightened and expressed in its most positive, beneficial form. When a planet is in its sign of exaltation, its inherent qualities are amplified and can manifest more freely, allowing its influence to reach its fullest potential.

Fall: Fall refers to the zodiac sign where a planet's energy is at its weakest or most challenged, positioned exactly opposite to its sign of exaltation. When a planet is in its fall, its natural qualities and influences become muted or distorted, making it harder for that planet's energy to express itself effectively.

The Encyclopedia of Astrology

Planet	Domicile	Detriment	Exaltation	Fall
Sun ☉	Leo	Aquarius	Aries	Libra
Moon ☾	Cancer	Capricorn	Taurus	Scorpio
Mercury ☿	Gemini Virgo	Sagittarius Pisces	Virgo	Pisces
Venus ♀	Taurus Libra	Aries Scorpio	Pisces	Virgo
Mars ♂	Aries Scorpio	Taurus Libra	Capricorn	Cancer
Jupiter ♃	Sagittarius Pisces	Gemini Virgo	Cancer	Capricorn
Saturn ♄	Capricorn Aquarius	Cancer Leo	Libra	Aries

Planetary Speed and Motion: A planet moving direct and swiftly is deemed stronger, whereas retrograde motion or slower-than-average speed can weaken its influence.

Succedent houses: Succedent houses (second, fifth, eighth, eleventh) provide moderate strength for planets.

DIRECT

Direct refers to the normal or forward motion of a planet in the zodiac, moving from west to east as viewed from Earth. This is in contrast to "retrograde" motion, where a planet appears to move backward. A planet is considered direct when it resumes its regular path after a period of retrograde or has not undergone retrograde motion recently. Direct motion is associated with clarity, progress, and ease in the areas of life governed by the planet.

DISPOSITOR

A dispositor is a planet that has rulership over the zodiac sign where another planet is currently placed, forming a chain of influence and responsibility.

For example, if Mars is in Taurus, Venus (the ruler of Taurus) becomes Mars's dispositor, meaning Venus has influence over how Mars expresses its energy.

These relationships create a network of planetary connections called dispositorship chains,

The Encyclopedia of Astrology

which help astrologers understand how planets work together and influence each other within a birth chart.

DIURNAL ARC

The diurnal arc is the segment of a celestial body's apparent daily path that lies above the observer's horizon—from the point of rising to setting. This arc represents the duration the celestial body is visible in the sky during a 24-hour period.

ECLIPTIC

The ecliptic is the apparent path that the Sun, Moon, and planets trace across the sky over the course of a year, as viewed from Earth. This circular path forms the foundation of the zodiac, as it's divided into the 12 astrological signs that we use to track the Sun's movement. The ecliptic is particularly important in astrology because all major planetary movements are measured in relation to this path, and it serves as the reference plane for calculating celestial positions in birth charts.

ELEMENTS

The four elements—fire, earth, air, and water—represent fundamental energies that shape the zodiac signs' core qualities and behaviors.

Fire

The element of transformation and spirit, fire represents creative force, enthusiasm, and dynamic energy. Aries, Leo, and Sagittarius approach life with passion and confidence, inspiring others through their natural warmth and leadership abilities. Their challenges can include impulsiveness and burning out quickly.

Earth

The element of form and manifestation, earth represents stability, practicality, and material resources. Taurus, Virgo, and Capricorn excel at turning ideas into reality, creating lasting structures and reliable systems. Their challenges can include inflexibility and excessive materialism.

Air

The element of thought and connection, air represents intelligence, communication, and social bonds. Gemini, Libra, and Aquarius thrive on mental stimulation and exchanging ideas, naturally connecting people and concepts. Their challenges can include overthinking and emotional detachment.

Water

The element of emotion and intuition, water represents feeling, empathy, and subconscious wisdom. Cancer, Scorpio, and Pisces navigate life through emotional understanding and instinctive knowing, offering deep healing and emotional support. Their challenges can include mood swings and emotional overwhelm.

The Encyclopedia of Astrology

EPHEMERIDES, EPHEMERIS

Ephemerides are astronomical tables that list the exact positions of planets and celestial bodies every day. The term comes from the Greek word *ephemeros* meaning "daily," as they typically show positions for each day of the year, used much like a celestial almanac. This is used to track the movement of the planets and is essential in creating astrological birth charts.

Raphael's Ephemeris is one of the longest-running and most trusted astrological reference guides, though there are others published on websites such as astro.com. Example table can be found opposite.

EQUINOX

An equinox occurs twice a year when the Sun is directly above Earth's equator, resulting in nearly equal day and night lengths worldwide. These events mark the start of spring around March 21 and autumn around September 23 in the northern hemisphere.

Equinoxes embody powerful moments of transition and equality—times when the solar masculine principle and lunar feminine principle achieve tem-

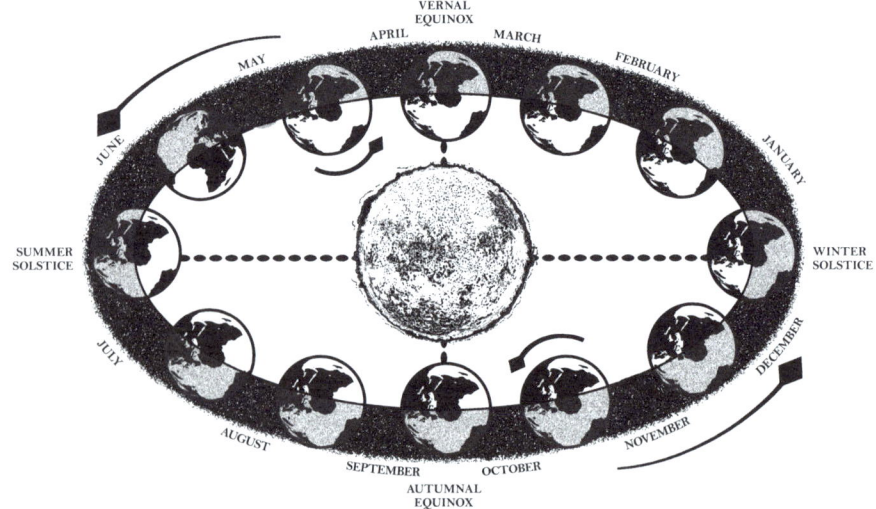

SOLSTICE AND EQUINOX DIAGRAM

The Encyclopedia of Astrology

EPHEMERIS CHART

JANUARY 1970 — 00:00 UT

Day	Sid.t	☉	☽	☿	♀	♂	♃	♄	♅	♆	♇	☊	☊	⚸	⚷	Day
T 1	6 40 55	10♑ 9'23	10♎42	29♑ 1	4♑27	12♓14	2♏20	2°R 4	8♎43	29♏53	27°R24	14°R 4	15♓17	2♌46	2♈31	T 1
F 2	6 44 52	11°10'32	23°26	29°31	5°43	12°59	2°28	2♉ 3	8°44	29°55	27♍23	14♓ 3	15°14	2°53	2°32	F 2
S 3	6 48 49	12°11'42	6♏37	29°50	6°58	13°44	2°36	2° 3	8°45	29°57	27°23	14° 0	15°11	2°59	2°33	S 3
S 4	6 52 45	13°12'52	20°17	29°R59	8°14	14°28	2°44	2°D 3	8°45	29°59	27°23	13°55	15° 8	3° 6	2°34	S 4
M 5	6 56 42	14°14'03	4♐27	29°58	9°29	15°13	2°51	2° 3	8°46	0♐ 0	27°23	13°47	15° 5	3°13	2°36	M 5
T 6	7 0 38	15°15'13	19° 5	29°44	10°45	15°58	2°59	2° 4	8°46	0° 2	27°23	13°38	15° 1	3°19	2°37	T 6
W 7	7 4 35	16°16'24	4♑ 6	29°19	12° 0	16°43	3° 6	2° 4	8°46	0° 4	27°23	13°29	14°58	3°26	2°38	W 7
T 8	7 8 31	17°17'35	19°19	28°42	13°16	17°27	3°14	2° 4	8°47	0° 5	27°22	13°20	14°55	3°33	2°39	T 8
F 9	7 12 28	18°18'45	4♒35	27°54	14°31	18°12	3°21	2° 5	8°47	0° 7	27°22	13°13	14°52	3°39	2°41	F 9
S 10	7 16 24	19°19'55	19°42	26°55	15°47	18°57	3°28	2° 5	8°47	0° 9	27°22	13° 8	14°49	3°46	2°42	S 10
S 11	7 20 21	20°21'05	4♓32	25°48	17° 2	19°41	3°35	2° 6	8°47	0°10	27°21	13° 6	14°45	3°53	2°44	S 11
M12	7 24 18	21°22'14	18°59	24°35	18°18	20°26	3°42	2° 7	8°47	0°12	27°21	13°D 6	14°42	3°59	2°45	M12
T 13	7 28 14	22°23'22	3♈ 0	23°17	19°33	21°11	3°48	2° 8	8°R48	0°14	27°20	13° 7	14°39	4° 6	2°47	T 13
W14	7 32 11	23°24'30	16°36	21°58	20°49	21°55	3°55	2° 9	8°48	0°15	27°20	13° 8	14°36	4°13	2°48	W14
T 15	7 36 7	24°25'37	29°49	20°39	22° 4	22°40	4° 1	2°10	8°47	0°17	27°19	13°R 8	14°33	4°19	2°50	T 15
F 16	7 40 4	25°26'43	12♉41	19°24	23°20	23°24	4° 7	2°12	8°47	0°18	27°19	13° 6	14°30	4°26	2°52	F 16
S 17	7 44 0	26°27'49	25°17	18°14	24°35	24° 9	4°13	2°13	8°47	0°20	27°18	13° 2	14°26	4°33	2°54	S 17
S 18	7 47 57	27°28'53	7♊39	17°10	25°50	24°54	4°19	2°14	8°47	0°21	27°18	12°56	14°23	4°39	2°55	S 18
M19	7 51 53	28°29'57	19°50	16°15	27° 6	25°38	4°25	2°16	8°47	0°22	27°17	12°49	14°20	4°46	2°57	M19
T 20	7 55 50	29°31'01	1♋53	15°28	28°21	26°23	4°31	2°18	8°46	0°24	27°16	12°40	14°17	4°53	2°59	T 20
W21	7 59 47	0♒32'03	13°50	14°51	29°37	27° 7	4°36	2°20	8°46	0°25	27°16	12°32	14°14	4°59	3° 1	W21
T 22	8 3 43	1°33'05	25°43	14°23	0♒52	27°51	4°41	2°22	8°45	0°26	27°15	12°24	14°11	5° 6	3° 3	T 22
F 23	8 7 40	2°34'06	7♌33	14° 4	2° 7	28°36	4°46	2°24	8°45	0°28	27°14	12°17	14° 7	5°13	3° 5	F 23
S 24	8 11 36	3°35'06	19°23	13°54	3°23	29°20	4°51	2°26	8°44	0°29	27°14	12°13	14° 4	5°20	3° 7	S 24
S 25	8 15 33	4°36'06	1♍13	13°D52	4°38	0♈ 5	4°56	2°28	8°44	0°30	27°13	12°10	14° 1	5°26	3° 9	S 25
M26	8 19 29	5°37'05	13° 6	13°59	5°54	0°49	5° 1	2°31	8°43	0°31	27°12	12°D10	13°58	5°33	3°12	M26
T 27	8 23 26	6°38'03	25° 6	14°12	7° 9	1°33	5° 5	2°33	8°42	0°33	27°11	12°10	13°55	5°40	3°14	T 27
W28	8 27 22	7°39'00	7♎16	14°32	8°24	2°18	5° 9	2°36	8°42	0°34	27°10	12°12	13°51	5°46	3°16	W28
T 29	8 31 19	8°39'57	19°40	14°59	9°40	3° 2	5°14	2°38	8°41	0°35	27° 9	12°14	13°48	5°53	3°18	T 29
F 30	8 35 16	9°40'53	2♏22	15°31	10°55	3°46	5°17	2°41	8°40	0°36	27° 8	12°15	13°45	6° 0	3°21	F 30
S 31	8 39 12	10♒41'48	15♏27	16♑ 8	12♒10	4♈30	5♏21	2♉44	8♎39	0♐37	27♍ 7	12°R15	13♓42	6♌ 6	3♈23	S 31

porary harmony before beginning their eternal dance of waxing and waning throughout the year.

ETHNOASTROLOGY

Ethnoastrology is the study of how different cultural groups incorporate astrological practices into their beliefs, traditions, and daily lives. It explores the diverse ways astrology is used across societies, such as for decision-making, life guidance, and ritual practices. For example, Vedic astrology in India deeply influences choices regarding marriage and career, while Chinese astrology integrates the zodiac animals and Five Elements to align personal and business activities. Ethnoastrology highlights the intersection of astrology with cultural values, historical contexts, and collective identities.

FIXED STARS

Fixed stars are celestial objects that maintain relatively constant positions relative to each other in the night sky, unlike planets, which move noticeably over time. Historically, they were believed to be attached to a celestial sphere surrounding Earth, appearing stationary due to their immense distances. In astrology, fixed stars are considered to influence human affairs when they form close alignments with planets or significant points in a natal chart, with each star traditionally associated with specific traits or outcomes.

A royal fixed star, also known as a Behenian fixed star or a medieval fixed star, belongs to a group of 15 stars considered especially powerful in traditional astrology and medieval magic. These stars were documented in medieval Arabic and European texts, with Aldebaran, Regulus, Antares, and Fomalhaut positioned near the ecliptic at approximately 90-degree intervals, being particularly significant as they mark the four royal gates of heaven.

FORECASTING

Forecasting examines upcoming planetary movements and celestial events to anticipate potential influences and energies. Astrologers analyze transits (where planets are currently positioned) in relation to a person's birth chart or to general astrological patterns. This practice includes studying planetary returns, progressions, and significant alignments to understand cycles and predict possible trends in different areas of life.

GEOCENTRIC

Geocentric refers to a perspective or system in which Earth is the central point of observation. In the context of astrology, a geocentric chart is drawn from Earth's vantage point, depicting the apparent movements and positions of celestial bodies as seen from the Earth's surface. This perspective highlights how the planets, Sun, and Moon appear to orbit around us, rather than reflecting their actual positions in relation to the Sun (as in a heliocentric model). It emphasizes the human experience of the cosmos, grounding interpretations in the observable sky from Earth's unique point of view.

GIBBOUS

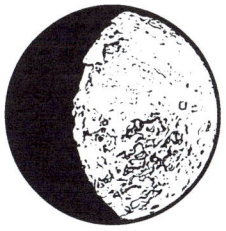

WAXING GIBBOUS

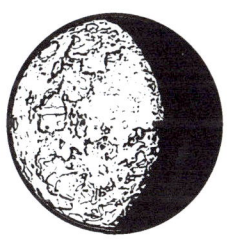

WANING GIBBOUS

(Waxing gibbous and waning gibbous) A gibbous moon appears when the Moon is more than half illuminated but not yet full, occurring both as the Moon waxes toward full (waxing

The Encyclopedia of Astrology

gibbous) and wanes from full (waning gibbous). In astrological interpretation, the waxing gibbous phase represents a time of refinement and fine-tuning of goals as they near completion, while the waning gibbous phase symbolizes sharing wisdom gained from recent experiences. The term comes from the Latin *gibbosus* meaning "humpbacked," referring to the Moon's convex shape during these phases.

See more in **Phases of the Moon**.

GLYPHS

A glyph is a symbolic character or pictograph that represents an element of astrology, such as a planet, zodiac sign, or aspect. These simplified drawings evolved from ancient astronomical notations and sacred symbols, allowing astrologers to efficiently record complex cosmic information. Rather than writing out "Jupiter in opposition to Mars," an astrologer can quickly mark ♃ ☍ ♂, making birth charts and other astrological documents more concise and universally readable regardless of language barriers.

See more in **Astrological Symbols**.

GREAT AGES
See **Astrological Ages**.

GREAT TURNING

The Great Turning refers to the monumental shift between astrological ages, specifically the current transition from the Age of Pisces to the Age of Aquarius. This gradual process spans several hundred years and is marked by fundamental changes in human consciousness, societal structures, and global paradigms. Astrologers view this period as a cosmic catalyst for transformation, where old systems and beliefs dissolve while new, progressive ideals emerge—much like a slow-moving dawn that takes centuries to fully brighten.

The Encyclopedia of Astrology

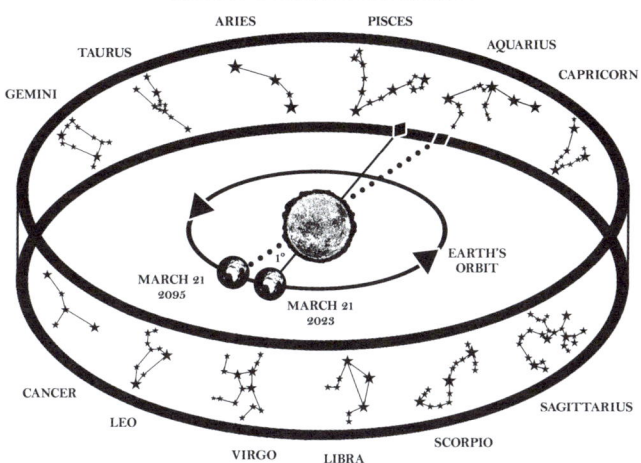

ASTRONOMICAL PRECESSION

The astrological Great Turning is characterized by increasingly rapid technological advancement, growing focus on collective welfare, and radical departures from traditional hierarchies, mirroring themes associated with Aquarian energy.

HELIACAL RISING

The heliacal rising occurs when a star or planet first becomes visible above the eastern horizon just before sunrise, after a period of being hidden by the Sun's glare.

Ancient civilizations used these appearances to mark important seasonal changes and create calendars, with the heliacal rising of Sirius being particularly significant in Egyptian culture for predicting the annual Nile flood.

The term comes from the Greek *helios* (Sun) and was vital for early astronomical timing and predictions, as it helped track planetary cycles and seasonal patterns.

HELIOCENTRIC

Sun-centered astrological calculations. Some modern astrologers might reference heliocentric positions for additional insight, but the traditional birth chart is

The Encyclopedia of Astrology

inherently geocentric since it represents the unique cosmic snapshot from the exact location where someone took their first breath.

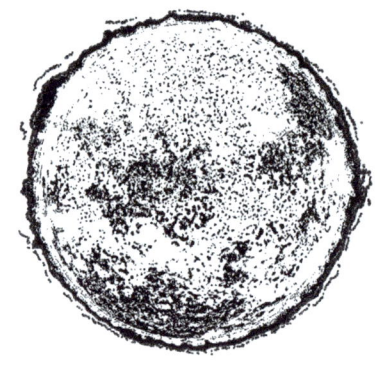

HERMETIC STUDIES

Hermetic studies explore ancient philosophical and spiritual teachings based on texts attributed to Hermes Trismegistus, a legendary Egyptian sage. These writings combine mystical wisdom, practical magic, and early scientific understanding—particularly focusing on the interconnection between cosmic and earthly realms through the principle "as above, so below." The tradition encompasses three main practices: astrology (understanding celestial influences), alchemy (transforming matter and consciousness), and theurgy (divine magical practices).

HOROSCOPE

A horoscope is a detailed interpretation of celestial positions and their influence on human affairs, typically focused on a specific period or moment in time. The term comes from the Greek words *hora* (time) and *skopos* (observer), literally meaning "observer of the hour."

Personal horoscopes are calculated using the exact positions of celestial bodies at someone's birth time and location, providing insights into personality traits, relationships, and life events. Over time, this complex practice evolved into the familiar newspaper columns that began in the 1930s with R.H. Naylor's predictions for Princess Margaret in the *Sunday Express*, and led to the popularization of sun-sign astrology.

Modern horoscopes appear in various forms, from detailed yearly forecasts to daily predictions in magazines and apps.

The Encyclopedia of Astrology

While traditional astrologers create personalized horoscopes using complete birth charts that consider multiple planetary positions and aspects, most mass-media horoscopes focus solely on sun signs, offering general guidance to broad audiences based on the Sun's position in the zodiac at the time of birth.

HOUSE SYSTEMS

A house system is a method of dividing the celestial sphere into 12 distinct sections, with each approach offering a different way to calculate these divisions. The choice of house system can significantly impact the placement of planets within houses, which is why astrologers often select a specific system based on their training, experience, or the type of astrology they practice.

See more in **House Systems**.

HOUSES

There are 12 houses in the zodiac. As the Earth rotates, the planets and stars in each house shift. Each house represents a specific area of our lives—it's a section of the sky as we see it from Earth and mapped in a birth chart.

See more in **Western Zodiac Houses**.

INGRESS

An ingress refers to the moment when a planet enters a new zodiac sign. For example, the Aries Ingress occurs when the Sun enters Aries at the spring equinox. Astrologers traditionally use this chart to forecast political and social trends for the coming year.

In predictive astrology, ingresses serve as powerful forecasting tools, with different emphases depending on the planet involved. Each planetary ingress opens a new era of influence that lasts until the next ingress of that planet.

The most frequently used ingress charts are:

The Encyclopedia of Astrology

Solar Ingresses (seasonal):
The Sun entering cardinal signs (Aries, Cancer, Libra, and Capricorn) forecasts themes for the next three months.

Jupiter Ingresses (yearly):
Jupiter moving into a new sign approximately once a year shows areas of growth and opportunity.

Saturn Ingresses (2.5 years):
Saturn moving into a new sign indicates areas of restriction, responsibility, and structural changes in society.

Outer Planet Ingresses (Uranus, Neptune, Pluto):
These rare events spanning years or decades correlate with major cultural and generational shifts.

INTERCEPTED SIGNS
An intercepted sign occurs when one zodiac sign is completely contained within a house, without touching either the beginning or ending cusp of that house. This creates an unusual situation where the intercepted sign's ruling planet may have difficulty fully expressing its energy, since the sign doesn't have direct access to a house cusp. Because of this arrangement, the signs ruling the cusps of the intercepted house will each rule two houses instead of one, creating a concentrated area of energy in the chart.

JUPITER RETURN
The Jupiter return is a transit which occurs every 12 years, bringing cycles of growth, opportunity, and expansion—many people experience significant breakthroughs or lucky breaks during these periods.

JUPITER

See more **Transits**.

The Encyclopedia of Astrology

KOCH TABLES

Koch tables, developed by the German astrologer Walter Koch in the 1960s, provided a specialized house system calculation method. These tables offered a mathematical approach to determining house cusps that was particularly useful for locations at extreme latitudes.

See more in **House Systems**.

LUMINARIES

Shorthand for the Moon and the Sun, derived from the Latin word *luminare* meaning "light-giving body." Together, they represent the two most visible and influential celestial bodies in traditional astrology, with the Sun ruling conscious, outer expression and the Moon governing inner emotions and subconscious patterns.

The term acknowledges their special status among celestial bodies, as they are the only ones that appear to give off their own light from Earth's perspective, though we now know the Moon reflects the Sun's light.

LUNAR NODES

The lunar nodes are two calculated points where the Moon's orbit intercepts the ecliptic.

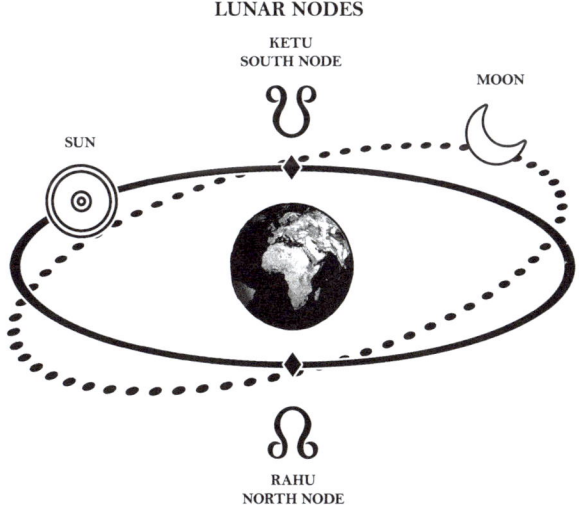

The Encyclopedia of Astrology

See **Nodal Axis, North Node** and **South Node** under the heading **Axis**.

LUNAR PHASES

The lunar phases are the changing appearances of the Moon as observed from Earth, resulting from the Moon's orbit around Earth and the varying angles of sunlight illuminating its surface. This cycle, known as a synodic month, lasts approximately 29.5 days and includes eight distinct phases:

New Moon: The Moon is positioned between Earth and the Sun, making it invisible from Earth.

NEW MOON

Waxing Crescent: A thin sliver of the Moon becomes visible as it moves away from the Sun's alignment.

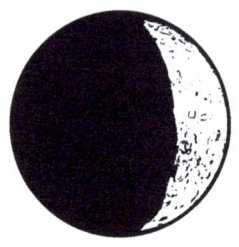

WAXING CRESCENT

Waxing Quarter: Half of the Moon's surface facing Earth is illuminated.

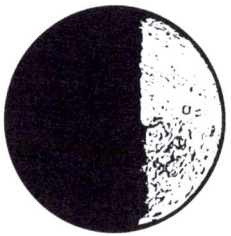

WAXING QUARTER

Waxing Gibbous: More than half of the Moon is illuminated as it approaches full illumination.

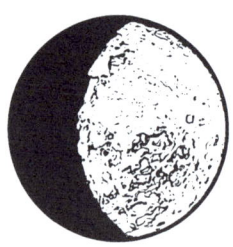

WAXING GIBBOUS

The Encyclopedia of Astrology

Full Moon: The entire face of the Moon visible from Earth is illuminated.

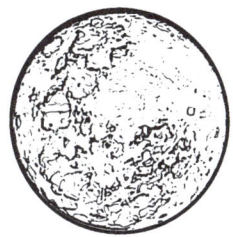

FULL MOON

Waning Gibbous: The illuminated portion begins to decrease after the full moon.

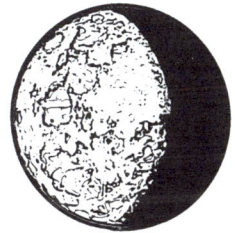

WANING GIBBOUS

Waning Quarter: Again, half of the Moon's face is illuminated, but the opposite half compared to the first quarter.

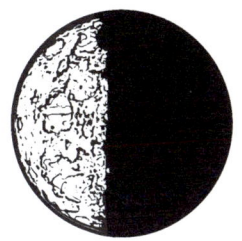

WANING QUARTER

Waning Crescent: Only a small crescent remains illuminated before transitioning back to the new moon.

WANING CRESCENT

These phases are a result of the relative positions of the Moon, Earth, and Sun, affecting the portion of the Moon's sunlit side that we can observe.

LUNISOLAR CALENDAR

A lunisolar calendar is a timekeeping system that combines

the Moon's phases and the Sun's annual cycle. It divides the year into lunar months, each corresponding to a complete cycle of the Moon's phases, while periodically adding an extra month to align the calendar with the solar year and maintain consistency with the seasons. This intercalation ensures that the calendar reflects both lunar and solar phenomena.

The lunisolar calendar remains in active use, particularly in East and South Asian countries including India, Nepal, China, South Korea, and Vietnam for traditional festivals and holidays. The Hebrew calendar, which is also lunisolar, guides Jewish religious observances and holidays throughout the year.

MALEFIC PLANETS

Malefic planets in astrology are traditionally considered to bring challenges, difficulties, or disruptive influences. The two classical malefics are Mars, associated with aggression, conflict, and impulsiveness, and Saturn, linked to restriction, delay, and hardship. These planets often signify obstacles or tests, but approached constructively they can encourage growth, resilience, and discipline. In modern astrology, outer planets such as Uranus, Neptune, and Pluto are sometimes seen as malefics due to their intense and transformative effects. Their influence is nuanced, depending on their placement, aspects, and rulerships in a birth chart.

MELOTHESIA

Melothesia refers to the concept of associating parts of the human body with celestial bodies, zodiac signs, or musical notes. The term originates from ancient Greek, meaning "limb assignment" or "division of the body." This idea was often explored in ancient and medieval astrology, medicine, and music theory.

In astrology and medicine, melothesia links specific body parts to astrological signs and planets, forming the basis for medical astrology.

Aries: Head
Taurus: Neck and throat
Gemini: Arms, shoulders, and lungs
Cancer: Chest and stomach
Leo: Heart and spine
Virgo: Digestive system and intestines
Libra: Kidneys and lower back
Scorpio: Reproductive organs
Sagittarius: Hips and thighs
Capricorn: Knees and skeletal system
Aquarius: Ankles and circulatory system
Pisces: Feet

This framework was used historically in diagnosing and treating illnesses by observing astrological influences.

MERCURY RETROGRADE

The most well-known and most-referenced retrograde is Mercury retrograde, which is traditionally associated with communication mishaps and technological difficulties. It occurs three or four times yearly for about three weeks each, affecting communication, technology, and travel.

See more in **Retrograde**.

MERIDIAN

The meridian, also known as the local meridian or celestial meridian, is the imaginary line that arches across the sky from the northern point of the horizon, traveling directly overhead, and then down to the southern point of the horizon. A geographic meridian means a line of longitude running from pole to pole, but in astrology, we're specifically concerned with the celestial meridian—that arc running from north to south through our zenith.

MOON SIGN

While the sun sign symbolizes core identity, the moon sign delves deeper into the inner world, revealing emotional instincts, subconscious reactions, and patterns of nurturing and seeking comfort. It is considered a key indicator of emotional needs, intuition, and the ways feelings are processed and expressed, offering insight into aspects of personality that are often hidden from view.

MODALITIES

Modalities, also known as modes or quadruplicities, represent three distinct ways that zodiac signs express and channel their energy throughout the seasons.

Cardinal (Initiating)

Cardinal signs each begin at the start of a season and initiate transformation, bringing leadership and innovative energy at pivotal points during each year. These signs carry remarkable energy to create change.

- Aries, starts March 21
- Cancer, starts June 21
- Libra, starts September 23
- Capricorn, starts December 22

Fixed (Stabilizing)

Fixed signs maintain and stabilize energy in the middle of seasons, providing consistency and determination. These signs help ease transitions throughout the zodiac cycle, possessing flexible energy that can bridge between different states and perspectives.

- Taurus, starts April 20
- Leo, starts July 23
- Scorpio, starts October 23
- Aquarius, starts January 20

Mutable (Adapting)

Mutable signs conclude each season with adaptable energy that prepares for transition. These signs possess a natural flexibility that helps them gather and process information, making them skilled at seeing multiple perspectives and finding creative solutions.

- Gemini, starts May 21
- Virgo, starts August 23
- Sagittarius, starts November 22
- Pisces, starts February 19

NATAL ASTROLOGY

Natal astrology is the practice of creating and interpreting

The Encyclopedia of Astrology

birth charts based on the exact time, date, and location of birth.

This type of reading reveals personality traits, life patterns, and potential challenges and opportunities by examining the position of celestial bodies at the moment of birth.

Practitioners analyze aspects, house placements, and planetary relationships to provide insight into career paths, relationship patterns, and life purpose.

NATAL CHART
Another term for "Birth Chart."

See more in **Birth Charts**.

OBLIQUE ASCENSION
Oblique ascension is the measurement of time that it takes for the celestial equator to rise above the horizon when viewed from any latitude other than the equator. The concept is particularly important in calculating house cusps and determining how planetary positions may influence different areas of life in astrological interpretations.

PART OF FORTUNE
The Part of Fortune, also called Fortuna or Lot of Fortune, is a calculated point in an astrological birth chart that represents where a person might find happiness, success, and prosperity. It's determined by the mathematical relationship between the positions of the Sun, Moon, and ascendant at the time of birth. Ancient astrologers considered this point particularly fortunate, believing it indicated areas of life where things might come easily or naturally to a person.

PHASES OF THE MOON
See Lunar Phases.

PLANETARY DAYS
In astrology, each day of the week carries specific energetic qualities that astrologers consider favorable for different types of activities and intentions.

The Encyclopedia of Astrology

The concept of planetary days traces back to ancient Mesopotamia and was later adopted by Greek and Roman astrologers, who assigned each day of the week to a ruling planet. These planetary rulers were so culturally significant that they became the basis for naming the days of the week in Latin-based languages. In English, some names derive directly from the Roman planets and their gods while others come from Old English names for Germanic or Norse equivalents.

Sunday, ruled by the Sun, brings vitality and confidence, deriving from the Old English *Sunnandæg*, and is perfectly suited for setting intentions and connecting with your authentic self.

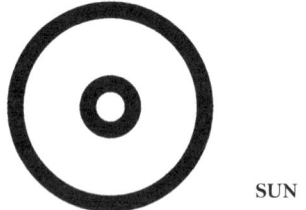
SUN

Monday, ruled by the Moon and stemming from *Monandæg*, carries lunar energy ideal for emotional work, intuition, and domestic matters.

MOON

Tuesday, Mars's day, sparks motivation and courage, making it powerful for taking action and starting new ventures. The English word is from *Tiwesdæg*, honoring the Germanic god Tiw, a war god equivalent to Roman Mars.

MARS

Wednesday, Mercury's day, enhances communication and mental agility, perfect for writing, learning, and making connections. The English word is from *Wodnesdæg*, after the Germanic god Woden, another

The Encyclopedia of Astrology

war god whom Roman historians equated to Mercury.

MERCURY

Thursday, Jupiter's day, expands possibilities and brings good fortune, supporting growth and spiritual development. The English word is from *Þunresdæg*, honoring the Germanic god Thunor, god of sky and thunder, equivalent to Jupiter.

JUPITER

Friday, Venus's day, harmonizes relationships and beauty, ideal for creative projects and nurturing connections. The English word is from *Frigedæg*, named for the goddess Frigg, equivalent to Venus.

VENUS

Saturday, Saturn's day, from *Sæternesdæg*, provides grounding energy for completing tasks, setting boundaries, and reflecting on life's structure.

SATURN

PLANETARY HOURS

The ancient practice of planetary hours divides each day and night into 12 equal parts, with each hour ruled by one of the seven classical planets. The first hour of each day is ruled by that day's governing planet (for example, the Sun rules the first

PLANETARY HOURS

Legend: ☉ Sun ♂ Mars ♃ Jupiter ♄ Saturn
　　　　　☽ Moon ☿ Mercury ♀ Venus

Hour	1 (sunrise)	2	3	4	5	6	7	8	9	10	11	12
Sunday	☉	♀	☿	☽	♄	♃	♂	☉	♀	☿	☽	♄
Monday	☽	♄	♃	♂	☉	♀	☿	☽	♄	♃	♂	☉
Tuesday	♂	☉	♀	☿	☽	♄	♃	♂	☉	♀	☿	☽
Wednesday	☿	☽	♄	♃	♂	☉	♀	☿	☽	♄	♃	♂
Thursday	♃	♂	☉	♀	☿	☽	♄	♃	♂	☉	♀	☿
Friday	♀	☿	☽	♄	♃	♂	☉	♀	☿	☽	♄	♃
Saturday	♄	♃	♂	☉	♀	☿	☽	♄	♃	♂	☉	♀

Hour	13 (sunset)	14	15	16	17	18	19	20	21	22	23	24
Sunday	♃	♂	☉	♀	☿	☽	♄	♃	♂	☉	♀	☿
Monday	♀	☿	☽	♄	♃	♂	☉	♀	☿	☽	♄	♃
Tuesday	♄	♃	♂	☉	♀	☿	☽	♄	♃	♂	☉	♀
Wednesday	☉	♀	☿	☽	♄	♃	♂	☉	♀	☿	☽	♄
Thursday	☽	♄	♃	♂	☉	♀	☿	☽	♄	♃	♂	☉
Friday	♂	☉	♀	☿	☽	♄	♃	♂	☉	♀	☿	☽
Saturday	☿	☽	♄	♃	♂	☉	♀	☿	☽	♄	♃	♂

hour of Sunday), creating a continuous cycle that influenced many cultures' understanding of time and celestial rhythms.

Planetary hours are considered in birth charts, which is why the exact time of birth is necessary for the full picture.

PLANETARY POSITIONS

Planetary positions indicate where celestial bodies are located within the zodiac at any given moment, measured in degrees along the 360-degree zodiac wheel. These positions can be mapped in relation to the zodiac signs, the 12 houses, and in aspects, or geometric relationship to each other. The placement of planets at the time of birth forms the foundation of a birth chart, while their ongoing movements through the zodiac create what astrologers call transits.

The Encyclopedia of Astrology

PLANETARY SECT

Planetary sect refers to the ancient classification system that matches planets with either daytime or nighttime births, based on the Sun's position relative to the horizon.

A planet functioning in its preferred sect—day or night—was thought to express its most positive qualities, while planets operating contrary to their sect nature were considered more challenging or problematic.

The Sun, Jupiter, and Saturn prefer day charts, expressing their benefic qualities more purely when birth occurs during daylight hours, while the Moon, Venus, and Mars operate more harmoniously in night charts.

POLARITIES

Polarity in astrology can also refer to the alternating positive, yang/masculine/active, and negative, yin/feminine/receptive, qualities assigned to each zodiac sign in sequence.

This creates a natural rhythm through the zodiac, with each sign's energy either expressing outwardly (positive) or drawing inward (negative).

Positive/Yang/Masculine/Active:

Aries (+)
Gemini (+)
Leo (+)
Libra (+)
Sagittarius (+)
Aquarius (+)

Negative/Yin/Feminine/Receptive:

Taurus (-)
Cancer (-)
Virgo (-)
Scorpio (-)
Capricorn (-)
Pisces (-)

The Encyclopedia of Astrology

PRECESSION OF THE EQUINOXES

The precession of equinoxes is the gradual shift in Earth's rotational axis over time, completing a full cycle approximately every 26,000 years. Because the tropical zodiac system used in most Western astrology pinpoints the vernal (spring) equinox, which occurs every year on April 21 as the starting point of the division of houses, the slow shift causes the apparent position of the stars and constellations to drift relative to Earth's seasons and calendar.

Today, due to precession, these alignments have shifted by about 24 degrees—meaning the constellation Aries now appears in what was originally the zodiacal division of Taurus. The signs shift approximately 1 degree every 72 years. The precession of the equinoxes is a major distinction between tropical astrology (based on the seasons and zodiacal divisions) and sidereal astrology (based on the actual positions of the constellations).

RETROGRADE (RX)

Retrograde motion occurs when a planet appears to move backward through the zodiac from

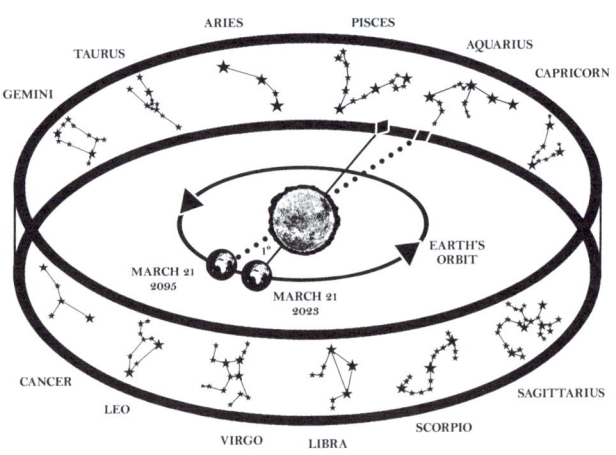

PRECESSION OF THE EQUINOXES

The Encyclopedia of Astrology

Earth's perspective, though it's actually an optical illusion caused by differences in orbital speeds. This perceived backward movement is believed to influence the areas of life associated with that planet, often leading to periods of review, reflection, and revision.

The most well-known example is Mercury retrograde, which occurs about three times per year and is traditionally associated with communication mishaps and technological difficulties.

- **Mercury Retrograde:** 3-4 times yearly for about 3 weeks each, affecting communication, technology, and travel.
- **Venus Retrograde:** Every 18 months for about 40 days, influencing love, beauty, relationships, and values.
- **Mars Retrograde:** Every 2 years for about 2.5 months, impacting drive, energy, and assertiveness.
- **Jupiter Retrograde:** Annually for about 4 months, relating to luck, growth, wisdom, and expansion.
- **Saturn Retrograde:** Yearly for about 4.5 months, concerning structure, responsibility, and life lessons.
- **Uranus Retrograde:** Yearly for about 5 months, affecting innovation, rebellion, and sudden changes.
- **Neptune Retrograde:** Yearly for about 5-6 months, influencing dreams, intuition, and spiritual matters.
- **Pluto Retrograde:** Yearly for about 5-6 months, relating to transformation, power, and deep psychological change.

RIGHT ASCENSION OF MIDHEAVEN (RAMC)

The Right Ascension of Midheaven (RAMC) represents the zodiacal degree that crosses the local meridian at the exact time of birth, marking the highest point in the birth chart. This celestial coordinate measures the angular distance eastward along the celestial equator from

The Encyclopedia of Astrology

the vernal equinox to the meridian. The RAMC is essential for calculating house cusps and determining planetary positions in a birth chart, acting as a kind of celestial timestamp of the moment we enter the world.

RISING SIGN
See **Ascendant**.

RULERSHIP
Rulership describes the natural affinity between planets and zodiac signs, where a planet is said to express its energy most purely through its ruled sign. Each planet traditionally rules one or two signs where its influence is strongest and most harmonious.

For example, Mars rules Aries, where its energetic and assertive qualities align perfectly with the sign's pioneering spirit. Ancient astrologers developed this system by observing the qualities shared between planets and signs, creating a cosmic web of relationships that helps interpret astrological charts.

See more in **Planets and Celestial Bodies**.

SATURN RETURN
The Saturn return is a transit that occurs approximately every 29.5 years—first around age 29–30 in a person's life, then again at 58–59, and 87–88—as Saturn completes its orbit and returns to its position at the time of birth. During this transit, Saturn's themes of structure, responsibility, and maturity come into sharp focus, often bringing major life transitions like career changes, serious relationships, or questioning long-held beliefs.

SATURN

See more in **Transits**.

The Encyclopedia of Astrology

SOLSTICE AND EQUINOX DIAGRAM

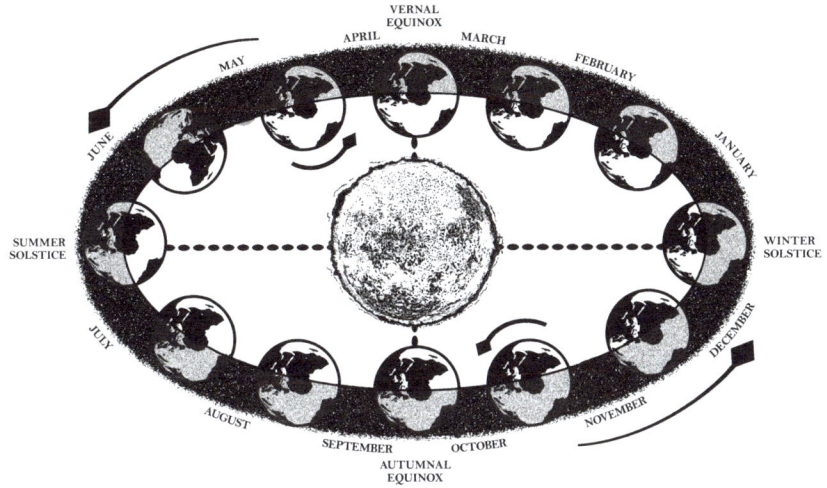

SOLSTICE

The word "solstice" comes from the Latin *solstitium*, meaning "sun standing still," as the Sun appears to pause in its seasonal journey across the sky. During a solstice, the Sun reaches its highest point in summer, or lowest point in winter, in relation to the celestial equator, marking the longest and shortest days of the year in each hemisphere.

These powerful turning points represent the Sun's ingress into the cardinal signs of Cancer and Capricorn, initiating new seasonal cycles and periods of energetic shift.

STELLIUM

A stellium is a chart pattern that occurs when three or more planets are grouped together in the same zodiac sign or astrological house, creating a concentrated area of energy in the birth chart. This configuration amplifies the themes and characteristics of that specific sign or house, often

STELLIUM

The Encyclopedia of Astrology

making it a dominant influence in the individual's personality, life focus, and experiences.

A stellium signifies a heightened emphasis on the traits, lessons, and challenges associated with the sign or house, often compelling the individual to deeply engage with those aspects of life.

See more in **Chart Patterns**.

SUN SIGN

The zodiac sign that the Sun appeared in at the time of a person's birth symbolizes their identity and how they appear in the world, giving insight into what makes them unique and influencing their personality, health, relationships, career, and hobbies.

Sun signs gained widespread popularity in the 1930s when British astrologer R.H. Naylor began writing newspaper horoscopes for the masses, leading to the overly simple horoscopes seen today in magazines and online. While the sun sign represents vital aspects of a person's core identity and ego expression, it's just one piece of a complex astrological puzzle that includes the moon sign (emotions), ascendant (outward personality), and the intricate relationships between all planets at their birth moment—professional astrologers consider numerous other factors like the houses planets occupy, their aspects to each other, and current planetary transits to create meaningful, personalized interpretations rather than generic sun sign predictions that apply generically to roughly one-twelfth of the population.

See more in **Birth Charts**.

SYNODIC MONTH

A synodic month measures the time between one new moon and the next new moon, averaging 29.53059 days. This lunar cycle forms the basis for many ancient calendars and marks the Moon's complete journey through all its visible phases from Earth's perspective. The word "synodic" comes from the Greek *synodos*, meaning "meeting" or "conjunction," referring to the Moon's alignment with the Sun at the new moon.

TABLES OF HOUSES

Tables of Houses are reference books showing how the astrological houses align at different latitudes and times. They help determine the exact degrees of house cusps based on location and birth time, essential for accurate chart creation.

THEOSOPHY

Theosophy represents a spiritual movement that emerged in the late 19th century, blending Eastern and Western mystical traditions to seek universal wisdom and understanding of divine nature. Theosophy helped revive interest in astrology by connecting astrological concepts with ideas about spiritual evolution, karma, and the development of human consciousness.

TIME LORDS

The term "time lords" refers to a concept used in certain traditional techniques, particularly Hellenistic astrology, to determine which planets have rulership over specific periods in a person's life. These techniques assign planetary rulers (or "lords") to time periods, influencing the themes, events, and experiences during those intervals.

The concept of time lords focuses on personal destiny and timing, using techniques like zodiacal releasing to understand when specific planetary energies might manifest in someone's life.

TRANSITS

Transits describe the ongoing dance between current planetary positions and the fixed snapshot of celestial bodies in a birth chart. Each transit brings its own energy pattern, duration, and significance based on the planets involved and the geometric angles they form.

Major transits include:

Saturn Return
- Ages 29–30, 58–59.
- A profound period of maturation, restructuring, and accepting adult responsibilities.

Jupiter Return
- Every 12 years.
- Brings opportunities for growth, abundance, and expansion in life areas ruled by its natal house position.

Chiron Return
- Age 50.
- Often marks a healing crisis or breakthrough regarding core wounds.

Pluto Square Pluto
- Age 36–37.
- Forces transformation through intense circumstances or power dynamics.

Uranus Opposition
- Age 40–42.
- The classic "midlife crisis" transit bringing sudden changes and awakening.

Neptune Square Neptune
- Age 40–42.
- Creates fog around identity and previously held beliefs.

Progressed Moon Return
- Every 27–28 months.
- Marks the completion of an emotional cycle.

Mars Return
- Every 2 years.
- Brings renewed energy and initiative.

Venus Return
- Every year.
- Highlights themes of love, creativity, and values.

Mercury Return
- 3–4 times yearly.
- Affects communication and thinking patterns.

Lunar Return
- Monthly.
- Influences emotional patterns and basic needs.

Solar Return
- Yearly/birthday.
- Sets the tone for the year ahead.

The Encyclopedia of Astrology

TRANSLATION OF LIGHT

The "translation of light," also known as "transfer of light," refers to a situation where a faster-moving planet (often called a "light" planet) separates from an exact aspect with one planet and then immediately applies to an exact aspect with another. In this process, the intermediary planet is considered to "transfer the light" or influence from the first planet to the second, effectively linking two planets that are not in direct aspect with each other. This technique allows astrologers to interpret how influences are carried across the chart, providing insights into the unfolding of events or the interactions between different factors in a given situation.

URANUS OPPOSITION

Uranus Opposition is a significant astrological transit that occurs when Uranus, the planet associated with disruption, innovation, and awakening, moves to the position directly opposite its placement in an individual's natal chart. This event typically happens around age 42, marking the halfway point of Uranus's 84-year orbit around the Sun. During this time, individuals often experience a heightened desire for freedom, personal reinvention, and authenticity. It can coincide with the phenomenon commonly referred to as a "midlife crisis," where sudden changes or breakthroughs may emerge in areas such as career, relationships, or personal identity.

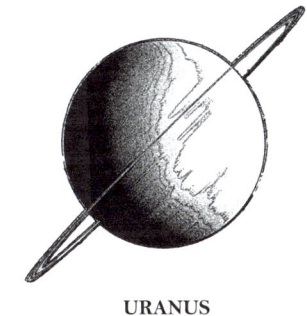

URANUS

VERNAL EQUINOX

The vernal equinox represents both a specific moment in time and a crucial point in space along the ecliptic—specifically the location where the Sun crosses the celestial equator moving northward each year.

The term "equinox" comes from the Latin *aequus* (equal) and *nox* (night), referring to the equal length of day and night that occurs when the Sun reaches this position around March 19–21 each year.

WHEEL OF LIFE

The wheel of life, also known as the zodiac wheel, represents the continuous cycle of the 12 astrological signs as they move through the sky. This circular diagram maps the Sun's apparent path through the constellations over the course of a year, with each sign occupying a 30-degree segment of the 360-degree circle. The wheel begins with Aries at the spring equinox and progresses counterclockwise through the developmental phases of each sign, reflecting not only the seasonal changes but also the developmental journey of human consciousness from basic self-awareness to universal understanding.

ZODIAC

The zodiac is a belt-like section of the sky that follows the annual path of the Sun as it appears from Earth (called the ecliptic). This belt extends about 8 degrees on either side of the ecliptic and is divided into 12 equal 30-degree sections. Each section of the zodiac is named after the major constellation that historically appeared within it, though due to the precession of equinoxes, these constellations no longer align exactly with their namesake sections.

ZODIAC DIVISION

The zodiac circle is divided into 12 equal 30-degree divisions, creating a 360-degree wheel that maps the apparent path of the Sun through the constellations over the course of a year. Each division corresponds to one of the twelve zodiac signs, starting with Aries at the spring equinox (0 degrees) and moving counterclockwise through Pisces. These divisions were first established by the Babylonians around 1000

BCE, though they drew from even earlier Sumerian observations of celestial patterns.

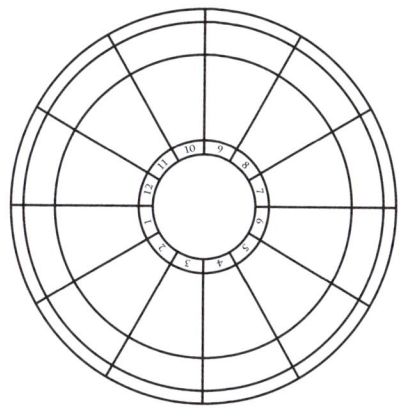

ZODIAC SEASON

A zodiac season refers to the roughly 30-day period when the Sun appears to travel through a specific zodiac constellation. Each season carries distinct energies and themes that can influence daily life, relationships, and personal growth during that time. The zodiac year begins with Aries at the spring equinox, following the Sun's journey through all 12 signs and completing a full cycle through Pisces.

ZODIAC SYSTEM

A zodiac system refers to one of three distinct methods for measuring and dividing the ecliptic—tropical, which is based on the Earth's seasons and begins at the spring equinox; sidereal, which is aligned with fixed star positions and accounts for precession; and constellational, which uses the actual varying-sized star patterns rather than equal divisions.

Constellational Zodiac

The constellational zodiac system follows the actual star patterns along the ecliptic. The system reflects what we actually see in the night sky, with planets moving through both the star patterns and the empty space between them. This system includes 13 constellations of varying sizes rather than 12 equal divisions.

Sidereal Zodiac

The sidereal zodiac, primarily used in Jyotish and Vedic astrology, bases zodiac sign placements on the actual current positions

The Encyclopedia of Astrology

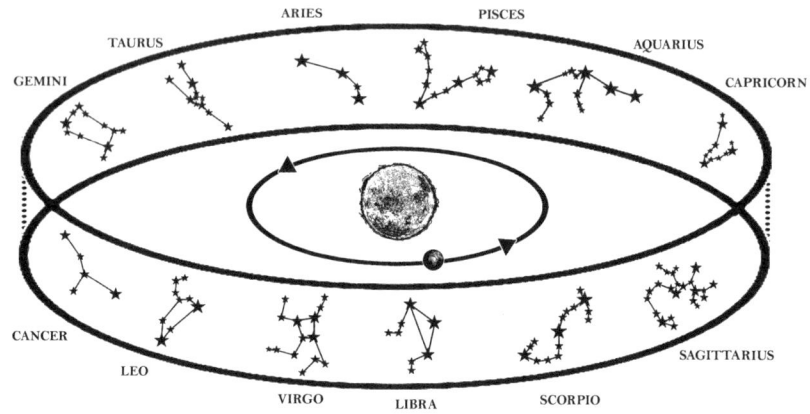

CONSTELLATIONAL ZODIAC

of the constellations, accounting for the precession of the equinoxes over time. This creates a shift between tropical and sidereal calculations, meaning your sun sign and other planetary placements might shift backward by about one sign when calculated in the sidereal system.

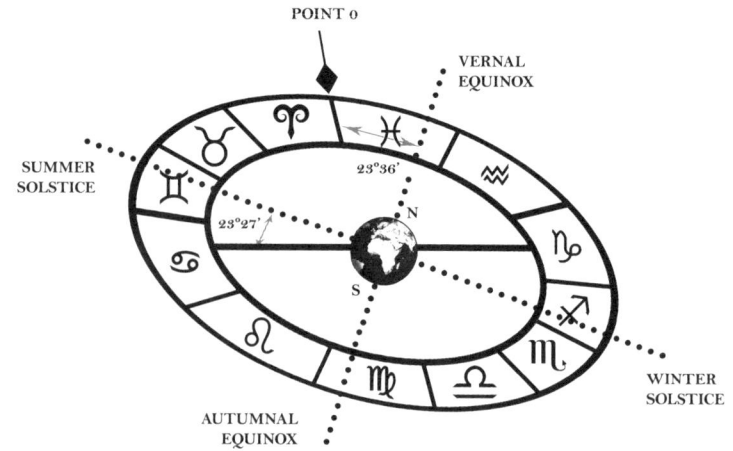

SIDEREAL ZODIAC

The Encyclopedia of Astrology

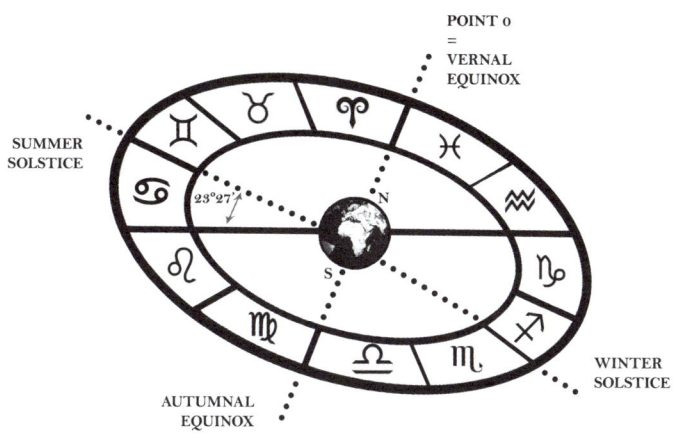

TROPICAL ZODIAC

Tropical Zodiac

Tropical astrology is a zodiac system that defines the 12 signs of the zodiac based on the Earth's seasonal cycles and the Sun's apparent movement relative to Earth's equator, rather than the fixed positions of the constellations. This system begins with the vernal equinox, marking the start of the astrological year and the zodiac sign Aries. The zodiac signs are divided into equal 30-degree segments along the ecliptic, the Sun's apparent path through the sky, creating a framework tied to Earth's relationship with the Sun and the changing seasons.

ZODIAC WHEEL

The zodiac wheel, also known as the wheel of life, represents the continuous cycle of the 12 astrological signs as they move through the sky. This circular diagram maps the Sun's apparent path through the constellations over the course of a year, with each sign occupying a 30-degree segment of the 360-degree circle. The wheel begins with Aries at the spring equinox and progresses counterclockwise through the developmental phases of each sign, reflecting not only the seasonal changes but also the evolutionary journey of human consciousness from

The Encyclopedia of Astrology

basic self-awareness to universal understanding. While astrology traditionally represents this motion counterclockwise, some visual depictions of the zodiac wheel are arranged clockwise, often for artistic or cultural readability rather than astrological accuracy.

ZODIACAL RELEASING

Zodiacal releasing is a time-lord technique in Hellenistic astrology used to map out significant periods in a person's life by dividing their lifespan into chapters and sub-chapters based on the motion of the Lot of Spirit or Lot of Fortune through the zodiac. By assigning planetary rulers to these periods according to the signs the Lots occupy, this method highlights themes, opportunities, and challenges in areas such as career, personal development, or external circumstances. The technique reveals shifts in focus and turning points, offering a structured way to interpret life's unfolding narrative.

WESTERN ASTROLOGY

Introduction to Western Astrology

Ancient Babylonians laid the foundation for what we now know as the Western Zodiac, with the Egyptians, Greeks, Romans, and Islamic schools adding their own cultural touches over time. In this system, the 12 zodiac signs each bear the name of a constellation that marks the Sun's yearly journey across the celestial sphere and the core concept is that the movement of the Earth, the Moon, other planets, and celestial bodies all send energy through people. In astrological tradition, each sign is associated with particular personality traits, elements, and ruling planets.

The zodiac is used to create horoscopes and make astrological predictions based on the positions of celestial bodies within these divisions at specific times, such as a person's birth. This relationship between the Sun's path and these star patterns forms the basis of modern sun sign astrology, the simplified form of astrology most people are familiar with today.

Western astrology has served diverse purposes throughout history and continues to evolve in its modern applications. Ancient physicians used it to guide medical treatments and surgeries based on planetary positions, while court astrologers advised rulers on matters of state including military campaigns and diplomatic missions. Farmers relied on astrological almanacs for agricultural timing, and sailors used celestial knowledge for navigation and weather prediction.

Today, the practice has largely shifted toward psychological insight and self-development, with practitioners using birth charts to explore personality traits, emotional patterns, and life cycles. Business leaders consult astrologers about project timing and investments, while couples explore relationship compatibility through chart comparison. Career astrologers offer guidance about professional opportunities, event planners consider astrological timing for significant occasions, and some financial analysts incorporate planetary cycles into market analysis.

Astrology continues to adapt to contemporary needs while preserving its ancient roots in celestial observation and symbolic interpretation.

THE WESTERN ZODIAC

A zodiac sign is the identity associated with one of 12 30-degree divisions of the ecliptic, the apparent path of the Sun, Moon, and planets across the celestial sphere over the course of the year. Each sign is named after a constellation and carries specific symbolic meanings that astrologers use to interpret personality traits, life events, and relationships. Each zodiac sign embodies unique characteristics shaped by its ruling planet, element, and mode.

The zodiac signs described in this section are also known as sun signs, which represent the constellation the Sun was traveling through at the time of birth. While experienced astrologers examine numerous planetary positions and mathematical points in a complete birth chart, the sun sign serves as a strong entry point for self-discovery since it shines a light on core personality and traits.

The 12 signs of the zodiac, along with their associated date ranges, are:

♈ Aries	March 21–April 19
♉ Taurus	April 20–May 20
♊ Gemini	May 21–June 20
♋ Cancer	June 21–July 22
♌ Leo	July 23–August 22
♍ Virgo	August 23–September 22
♎ Libra	September 23–October 22
♏ Scorpio	October 23–November 21
♐ Sagittarius	November 22–December 21
♑ Capricorn	December 22–January 19
♒ Aquarius	January 20–February 18
♓ Pisces	February 19–March 20

The signs also have associations with the elements.

The Encyclopedia of Astrology

Fire signs (Aries, Leo, Sagittarius) represent spirit and inspiration.

Earth signs (Taurus, Virgo, Capricorn) represent physical manifestation.

Air signs (Gemini, Libra, Aquarius) represent mental development.

Water signs (Cancer, Scorpio, Pisces) represent emotional depth.

Each sign also has a modality.

Cardinal signs (Aries, Cancer, Libra, and Capricorn) represent the ushering in of a new season.

Fixed signs (Taurus, Leo, Scorpio, and Aquarius) are thought to be stabilizing and grounding. They represent the essence and peak expression of each season.

Mutable signs (Gemini, Virgo, Sagittarius, and Pisces) conclude each season and are thought to be more naturally flexible and open.

WESTERN ZODIAC SIGNS

Aries
March 21–April 19

Introduction to Aries

Aries, a cardinal fire sign ruled by the planet Mars and symbolized by the Ram, is known for its energy, confidence, and zest for life. People born under this sign embody new beginnings and the initial spark of creation, preferring to take action rather than spend time thinking things through.

In Love
Aries individuals are prone to love at first sight and have a strong desire to be desired. They possess a magnetic charm and are naturally attracted to others, though this can sometimes lead to infidelity.

Family and Friends
While Aries may not excel at household chores, their enthusiasm and curiosity make them exciting companions. They bring a fresh energy to relationships, though their outspoken nature may occasionally ruffle feathers.

At Work
Aries possess natural leadership skills and thrive in roles where they can initiate projects. Their confidence and ability to "fake it till they make it" often leads to success, though they may struggle with spontaneous spending.

In Conflict
Aries individuals may be quick to anger, with explosive but short-lived tempers. Their fast reactions and preference for action over contemplation can sometimes escalate conflicts unnecessarily.

How They Shine
Aries shine through their raw manifestation power, serving as the backbone of many endeavors. Their courage, enthusiasm, and ability to lead by example often inspires others to action.

The Dark Side
The dark side of Aries can manifest in their tendency to act without thinking, potentially leading to rash decisions. Their spontaneous nature, while often a strength, can sometimes result in neglecting important details or responsibilities.

Relationships

Aries is good in relationships with:
 Aries
 Leo
 Libra

Aries may find relationships challenging with:
 Virgo
 Taurus
 Cancer

Specifications
 Symbol: Ram
 Element: Fire
 Ruled by: Mars
 Mode: Cardinal

Physical Correspondences
Aries is associated with the **head**.

Aries Constellation

Location: Northern sky, between Pisces and Taurus.
Visibility: Visible from July to March.
Brightness: Relatively dim, with only four bright stars.
Size: Mid-sized, ranking 39th in overall size.

This constellation, while not as bright or prominent as some others, is notable for its three main stars forming a curved line representing the ram's horns. Aries is the first sign of the zodiac and lies between Pisces to the west and Taurus to the east, marking the beginning of spring in the northern hemisphere.

The Aries-Taurus Cusp, the Cusp of Power

The Cusp of Power refers to the transition period between Aries and Taurus, between April 16 and April 22. The connection to "power" stems from the combination of Aries's dynamic force and leadership with Taurus's strength and determination, creating individuals who blend assertive drive with steadfast persistence.

The Encyclopedia of Astrology

Taurus
April 20–May 20

Introduction to Taurus
Taurus, a fixed earth sign, ruled by the planet Venus and symbolized by the Bull, is associated with patience, stability, and the enjoyment of simple pleasures. This sign represents the first emergence of crops, embodying the qualities of sustenance, commitment, and abundance.

In Love
People with a Taurus sun sign are sensual and cuddly, seeking comfort, stability, and someone they can rely on in relationships. They value trust and intimacy, emphasizing physical touch and the importance of a strong, lasting connection.

Family and Friends
As the strong, silent rocks of the zodiac, Taurus individuals are trustworthy and unchanging in their relationships. They excel at creating a comfortable, stable environment for their loved ones, often indulging in good food and luxuries together.

At Work
Taurus possess an immovable force of will, allowing them to resist distractions and commit fully to their tasks. Their patience and ability to remain calm under pressure make them reliable and steady workers.

In Conflict
While Taureans appear calm on the surface, they feel things deeply. Their strong will can make them stubborn in conflicts, but their patience often helps them navigate disagreements without escalating tensions.

How They Shine
Taurus shine through their ability to create and appreciate

abundance in life. They excel at relaxation and know how to indulge in life's pleasures, bringing a sense of comfort and stability to those around them.

The Dark Side
The dark side of Taurus can manifest in their tendency towards hedonism and overindulgence. Their resistance to change and strong will can sometimes turn into inflexibility or stubbornness, making it difficult for them to adapt to new situations.

Relationships
Taurus is good in relationships with:
  Capricorn
  Cancer
  Scorpio

Taurus may find relationships challenging with:
  Sagittarius
  Gemini
  Aquarius

Specifications
  Symbol: The Bull
  Element: Earth
  Ruled by: Venus
  Mode: Fixed

Physical Correspondences
Taurus is associated with the **neck** and **throat.**

Taurus Constellation

Location: Northern celestial hemisphere.
Visibility: Visible from August to April.
Best Viewing: December–January.
Brightness: Contains several bright stars, including Aldebaran (magnitude 0.87).
Size: 15th-largest constellation.

This constellation is easily recognizable due to its V-shaped

The Encyclopedia of Astrology

pattern of stars, with the bright red giant Aldebaran forming the bull's eye. Taurus is part of the zodiac and lies between Aries to the west and Gemini to the east, featuring the prominent Pleiades star cluster.

The Taurus-Gemini Cusp, the Cusp of Energy

The Cusp of Energy marks the transition from Taurus to Gemini, between May 17 and May 23. People born during this period blend Taurus's grounded stability with Gemini's quick-moving intellectual energy, often resulting in individuals who can both generate and sustain momentum in their pursuits. This cusp brings together earth and air elements, creating personalities that combine practical sensuality with mental agility—they might express this through artistic endeavors, engaging conversation, or an uncanny ability to make abstract ideas tangible.

Gemini
May 21–June 20

Introduction to Gemini:

Gemini, a mutable air sign, ruled by the planet Mercury and symbolized by the Twins, is characterized by a quick pace, innovative ideas, and a light, carefree curiosity. Geminis are natural social butterflies with a gift for communication, a thirst for knowledge, and a penchant for taking risks.

In Love

The quickest way to woo a Gemini is through the mind, with witty banter, shared learning, and intellectual debates. They appreciate words of affirmation and love poems, with flirting coming naturally to them due to their adaptable and bubbly nature.

The Encyclopedia of Astrology

Family and Friends
Geminis are drawn to new people and enjoy a good gossip session, making them entertaining and engaging companions. Their intelligent and adaptable nature allows them to connect easily with various personalities within their social circles.

At Work
In the workplace, Geminis shine with their innovative ideas and quick thinking. They thrive on variety and novelty, making them excellent at tackling diverse tasks and adapting to new situations.

In Conflict
Geminis should be careful not to use words as weapons during conflicts, as their quick wit can sometimes hurt others. Their mood can change rapidly, which may lead to unpredictable reactions in tense situations.

How They Shine
Geminis shine through their intelligence, adaptability, and ability to gather and share knowledge. Their natural curiosity and communication skills make them excellent at networking and bringing fresh perspectives to any situation.

The Dark Side
A bored Gemini can become unpleasant and unpredictable, revealing their "dark twin" side. While they feel things deeply, they're not typically interested in deep self-reflection, which can sometimes lead to a lack of emotional awareness or consistency.

Relationships
Gemini is good in relationships with:
- Aquarius
- Pisces
- Leo

Gemini may find relationships challenging with:
- Scorpio
- Gemini
- Taurus

Specifications
Symbol: The Twins
Element: Air
Ruled by: Mercury
Mode: Mutable

Physical Correspondences

Gemini is associated with the **arms, shoulders,** and **lungs**.

Gemini Constellation

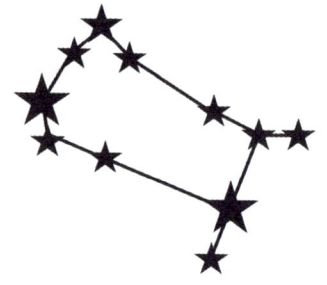

Location: Northern celestial hemisphere.
Visibility: Visible from September until May.
Size: 30th-largest constellation.

The Gemini-Cancer Cusp, the Cusp of Magic

The Cusp of Magic marks the transition from Gemini to Cancer, typically occurring between June 17 and June 23. These individuals blend Gemini's gift for communication with Cancer's deep intuition and emotional intelligence, creating a unique ability to express feelings and perceptions in ways that seem almost enchanted. Those born on this cusp often possess both intellectual curiosity and psychic sensitivity. They can articulate complex emotional experiences with remarkable clarity while maintaining an almost mystical connection to their inner world.

Cancer
June 21–July 22

Introduction to Cancer

Cancer, a cardinal water sign, ruled by the Moon and symbolized by the Crab, ushers in the season of summer. This sign is associated with introspection, reflection, and emotions. Cancers are known to value comfort, safety, and security, often focusing on nesting and creating a secure environment.

The Encyclopedia of Astrology

In Love
Cancers crave intimate connections, desiring one-on-one time, date nights, and physical affection. They prioritize emotional bonds and seek partners who can provide a sense of security and understanding.

Family and Friends
Cancer places high importance on who and what makes them feel safe, often maintaining strong boundaries to protect their emotional well-being. They value close relationships and tend to be nurturing and protective of their loved ones.

At Work
Cancers bring their emotional intelligence and intuition to the workplace, often excelling in roles that require empathy and care. They may struggle with maintaining professional boundaries due to their nurturing nature.

In Conflict
Cancers tend to be conflict-avoidant, often sidestepping issues like their crab symbol. This can lead to passive-aggressive behavior as they struggle to directly address problems.

How They Shine
Cancer's strength lies in their emotional depth and ability to create comfortable, nurturing environments. Their intuition and empathy allow them to connect deeply with others and provide emotional support.

The Dark Side
Cancers can become overly focused on the past, potentially spiraling into regret and dwelling on painful memories. Their sensitivity can sometimes lead to moodiness or emotional manipulation.

Relationships
Cancer is good in relationships with:
Taurus
Capricorn
Scorpio

Cancer may find relationships challenging with:
Aquarius

The Encyclopedia of Astrology

Sagittarius
Libra

Specifications
Symbol: The Crab
Element: Water
Ruled by: The Moon
Mode: Cardinal

Physical Correspondences
Cancer is associated with the **chest** and **stomach**.

Cancer Constellation

Location: Northern celestial hemisphere, between Gemini to the west and Leo to the east.
Visibility: Visible from September to May.
Size: 31st-largest constellation.

The Cancer-Leo Cusp, the Cusp of Oscillation
The Cusp of Oscillation occurs between Cancer and Leo, typically from July 19 to July 25, marking a transition from water to fire energy. These individuals navigate between Cancer's nurturing introspection and Leo's dramatic self-expression, often experiencing profound emotional depths while maintaining a magnetic public presence. The term "oscillation" perfectly captures their natural rhythm of moving between private, reflective periods and moments of bold, creative expression—making them uniquely equipped to understand both the heart's quiet whispers and life's grand performances.

Leo
July 23–August 22

The Encyclopedia of Astrology

Introduction to Leo

Leo, a fixed fire sign, ruled by the Sun and symbolized by the Lion, embodies the majestic and radiant energy of its ruling planet. Natural-born leaders and performers, Leos bring warmth and dramatic flair to everything they do.

In Love

Leo's expressions of love are as spectacular as fireworks, with grand gestures and theatrical displays of affection. They want their partners to recognize and appreciate their inner light, making every romantic moment feel like a spotlight moment.

Friends and Family

Leos bring warmth and energy to their relationships, feeling energized and inspired by connections with loved ones. They're generous with their affection and attention, though they do expect the same level of devotion in return.

At Work

Natural leaders in the workplace, Leos thrive when given opportunities to shine and take center stage. They excel in positions where their creativity and charisma can be put to use, though they may feel constant pressure to perform.

In Conflict

During disagreements, Leos must be careful not to make mountains out of molehills or let their dramatic nature take over. Their tendency toward theatricality can sometimes escalate minor issues into major dramas.

How They Shine

Leos shine brightest when they align with their heart's desires and express themselves authentically through dazzling displays of creativity and leadership. Their natural charisma and generous spirit make them magnetic to others.

The Dark Side

Despite their confident exterior, many Leos struggle with receiving compliments and can be self-centered in their approach to life. Their need for attention and

The Encyclopedia of Astrology

validation can sometimes overshadow their better qualities.

Relationships
Leo is good in relationships with:
 Sagittarius
 Gemini
 Libra

Leo may find relationships challenging with:
 Scorpio
 Leo
 Capricorn

Specifications
 Symbol: The Lion
 Element: Fire
 Ruled by: The Sun
 Mode: Fixed

Physical Correspondences
Leo is associated with the **heart** and **spine**.

Leo Constellation
 Location: Leo is positioned between Cancer and Virgo.
 Visibility: Visible from October until May.
 Size: 12th-largest constellation.

Leo is one of the more recognizable constellations, with its sickle-shaped pattern forming the lion's head.

The Leo-Virgo Cusp, the Cusp of Exposure
The Cusp of Exposure marks the transition from Leo to Virgo, between August 19 and August 25, when the Sun's warmth begins to mellow into harvest season. These individuals blend Leo's natural radiance with Virgo's analytical precision, creating personalities that can both illuminate and examine life's details with remarkable clarity. This cusp position combines Leo's dramatic flair and Virgo's dedication to improvement—making them natural reformers who aren't afraid to shine a spotlight

on issues that need attention while also having the practical skills to implement solutions.

Virgo
August 23–September 22

Introduction to Virgo
Virgo, a mutable earth sign, ruled by Mercury and symbolized by the Virgin, brings precision and analytical prowess to everything they touch. They possess a remarkable eye for detail and practical methodology, naturally excelling at breaking down complex systems into manageable parts while maintaining high standards.

In Love
Virgos express love through small, meaningful gestures rather than grand displays, finding passion in subtle moments like brushing hands or gentle hugs. They seek to blend their lives holistically with their partners', creating shared routines that become sacred rituals.

Family and Friends
Harmony in the household and meaningful conversations are paramount to Virgos' relationships. They value being listened to and show their care through acts of service and attention to detail.

At Work
Virgos excel in roles that require attention to detail, analysis of information, and organizational skills. Their meticulous nature and desire to be of service make them invaluable team members.

In Conflict
During disagreements, Virgos can become caught in cycles of overthinking and self-criticism, often analyzing situations from every angle. Mercury's influence can make them prone to excessive analysis of conflicts.

The Encyclopedia of Astrology

How They Shine
Virgos shine brightest when they're helping others and engaging in self-improvement activities, finding magic in transforming everyday routines into meaningful rituals. They excel at turning small ripples of change into powerful waves of transformation.

The Dark Side
Virgos can become weighed down by negative self-talk and excessive self-criticism. Their perfectionist tendencies can lead to analysis paralysis and difficulty accepting things as they are.

Relationships
Virgo is good in relationships with:
- Pisces
- Virgo
- Taurus

Virgo may find relationships challenging with:
- Aries
- Sagittarius
- Libra

Specifications
Symbol: The Virgin or Maiden
Element: Earth
Ruled by: Mercury
Mode: Mutable

Physical Correspondences
Virgo is associated with the **digestive system** and **intestines**.

Virgo Constellation

Location: Virgo is positioned between Leo and Libra.
Visibility: Visible from December until June.
Size: 2nd-largest constellation—Virgo covers a significant portion of the sky.

The Virgo-Libra Cusp, the Cusp of Beauty
The Cusp of Beauty marks the transition from Virgo to Libra,

The Encyclopedia of Astrology

between September 19 and September 25, when summer gives way to autumn's equilibrium. These individuals blend Virgo's attention to detail with Libra's sense of harmony, often expressing their dual nature through artistic pursuits, design, or the cultivation of beautiful spaces and relationships. The influence of both Ceres and Venus creates personalities who understand that true beauty emerges from the intersection of perfect function and elegant form—they possess both the practical skills to perfect their craft and the aesthetic sensitivity to make it shine.

Libra
September 23–October 22

Introduction to Libra
Libra, a cardinal air sign, ruled by Venus and symbolized by the Scales of Justice, symbolizes balance and harmony. Libras are known for their inclination toward equity and justice that, when combined with their love of beauty and art, make them natural diplomats and aesthetes.

In Love
Libras can be surprisingly detached and breezy in matters of the heart, taking on their air element's characteristics. They seek partnerships that offer both intellectual stimulation and emotional harmony.

Family and Friends
Libras thrive on getting input and perspectives from their loved ones, often seeking advice from those they trust. They create harmony in their relationships by balancing everyone's needs and maintaining peaceful connections.

At Work
With varied interests and a creative mindset, Libras excel in

The Encyclopedia of Astrology

environments that allow them to express their artistic and intellectual abilities. They make excellent mediators and team players, always striving for fairness and balance in the workplace.

In Conflict
During disagreements, Libras use their natural diplomatic abilities to find middle ground and restore harmony. They may sometimes avoid conflict altogether, preferring to maintain peace even at the cost of their own preferences.

How They Shine
Libras radiate when they're absorbing and creating beauty in any form, whether through art, music, literature, or style. Their curious nature and love for inspiration make them natural explorers of creative and intellectual pursuits.

The Dark Side
Despite their reputation for being superficial, Libras possess great depth and understanding of both light and shadow. They can sometimes get lost in chasing future ideals of happiness rather than living in the present moment.

Relationships
Libra is good in relationships with:
  Gemini
  Aquarius
  Leo

Libra may find relationships challenging with:
  Cancer
  Capricorn
  Aries

Specifications
  Symbol: The Scales
  Element: Air
  Ruled by: Venus
  Mode: Cardinal

Physical Correspondences
Libra is associated with the **kidneys** and **lower back**.

Libra Constellation
  Location: The Libra constellation lies between Virgo and Scorpius.

The Encyclopedia of Astrology

Visibility: Visible from January to June.
Constellation Size: 29th-largest constellation in the night sky. While not among the largest constellations, its distinctive pattern makes it recognizable despite its relatively faint stars.

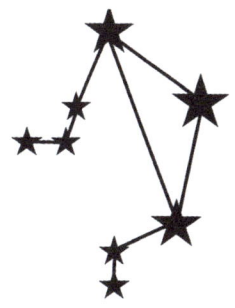

The Libra-Scorpio Cusp, the Cusp of Drama and Criticism
The Cusp of Drama and Criticism blends Libra's diplomatic grace with Scorpio's penetrating intensity for people born between October 19 and October 25. These individuals possess a unique ability to deliver hard truths with tact, combining Libra's gift for seeing all sides with Scorpio's unwavering commitment to exposing what lies beneath the surface. The name of this cusp reflects their natural talent for both dramatic expression and incisive analysis—they often excel in fields where both performance and critique are valued, whether in the arts, psychology, or investigative work.

Scorpio
October 23–November 21

Introduction to Scorpio
Scorpio, a fixed water sign, ruled by Pluto (modern) or Mars (traditional) and symbolized by the Scorpion, is known for their intense emotional depth, magnetic personality, and transformative nature.

In Love
Scorpios love deeply and passionately, seeking soul-deep

connections and unwavering loyalty from their partners while offering the same fierce devotion in return. Scorpios may prefer to merge completely in relationships—sharing resources, secrets, and transformative experiences—which can create either powerful, lasting unions or intense endings when trust is broken.

Family and Friends
In close relationships, Scorpios are fiercely protective and loyal, creating unbreakable bonds with those who earn their trust while maintaining an air of mystery.

At Work
Determined and focused, Scorpios excel in challenging roles that require investigative skills, strategic thinking, and the ability to transform difficult situations into successes.

In Conflict
When challenged, Scorpios rarely react immediately but observe carefully, storing information until they decide whether to use their powerful "stinger" or show mercy.

How They Shine
Scorpios' greatest strength lies in their ability to transform themselves and others, using their emotional intelligence and intuitive wisdom to help heal and empower those around them.

The Dark Side
Their tendency toward jealousy, obsession, and holding grudges can lead Scorpios down destructive paths if they don't learn to harness their intense emotions constructively.

Relationships
Scorpio is good in relationships with:
Cancer
Pisces
Capricorn

Scorpio may find relationships challenging with:
Leo
Aquarius
Gemini

The Encyclopedia of Astrology

Specifications
Symbol: Scorpion
Element: Water
Ruled by: Pluto (modern), Mars (traditional)
Mode: Fixed

Physical Correspondences
Scorpio is associated with the **reproductive organs**.

The Scorpio Constellation

Constellation Location: Located in the southern sky between Libra to the west and Sagittarius to the east.
Visibility: Visible from February to August—only partially visible in the northern hemisphere.
Constellation Size: 33rd-largest constellation in the night sky.

The Scorpio-Sagittarius Cusp, the Cusp of Revolution
The Cusp of Revolution marks the transition from Scorpio's transformative depths to Sagittarius's expansive, between November 18 and November 24. Individuals born during this period combine Scorpio's intensity and strategic thinking with Sagittarius's philosophical breadth and boldness, creating natural revolutionaries who can both envision and implement profound change. The mix of water and fire elements manifests as emotional intelligence paired with passionate action—they not only see what needs to change in systems or societies but possess the charismatic force and deep conviction to inspire others to join their cause.

The Encyclopedia of Astrology

Sagittarius
November 22–December 21

Introduction to Sagittarius
Sagittarius, a mutable fire sign, ruled by Jupiter and symbolized by the Archer, is always ready for the next adventure. With the luck of Jupiter and the light of the fire within, Sagittarians approach life with infectious enthusiasm and an insatiable hunger for knowledge.

In Love
While fiercely protective of their independence, Sagittarians are passionate and devoted partners once they commit to a relationship. They bring their characteristic warmth and optimism into romance, seeking a partner who will join them on life's grand adventures.

Family and Friends
Generous to a fault and armed with a playful sense of humor, Sagittarians make entertaining and loyal friends who bring excitement to any gathering. They maintain strong bonds while respecting everyone's need for space and independence.

At Work
Natural teachers and leaders, Sagittarians excel in roles where they can inspire others and tackle new challenges. They can struggle with mundane tasks and rigid authority structures, preferring to chart their own course and innovate freely.

In Conflict
Though generally optimistic, Sagittarians can be blunt with their honesty and enjoy a spirited debate, sometimes accidentally wounding others with their direct approach. They particularly bristle when their intelligence or capabilities are questioned.

The Encyclopedia of Astrology

How They Shine
With their lucky streaks, boundless optimism, and genuine curiosity about the world, Sagittarians excel at starting new ventures and inspiring others to join their quests. Their curiosity, love for learning, and enthusiasm for life are contagious.

The Dark Side
Their rebellious nature and distrust of authority can lead to unnecessary conflicts, while their tendency to spend impulsively can create financial instability. Despite their luck, their restlessness can leave projects unfinished once the initial excitement wears off.

Relationships
Sagittarius is good in relationships with:
 Leo
 Libra
 Gemini

Sagittarius may find relationships challenging with:
 Scorpio
 Cancer
 Virgo

Specifications
Symbol: The Archer
Element: Fire
Ruler: Jupiter
Mode: Mutable

Physical Correspondences
Sagittarius is associated with the **hips** and **thighs**.

The Sagittarius Constellation

Constellation Location: The Sagittarius constellation is located in the southern celestial hemisphere, positioned along the plane of the Milky Way between Scorpius and Capricornus.
Visibility: Visible from July to December.
Constellation Size: 15th-largest constellation.

The Encyclopedia of Astrology

The Sagittarius-Capricorn Cusp, the Cusp of Prophecy

The Cusp of Prophecy occurs between Sagittarius and Capricorn, from December 18 to December 24, as the free-spirited archer's wisdom converges with the grounded mountain goat's practicality. Individuals born during this period blend Sagittarius's far-reaching vision with Capricorn's ability to manifest ideas into reality, making them particularly gifted at recognizing patterns and predicting future trends or outcomes. The fusion of Jupiter's expansive wisdom and Saturn's disciplined approach creates natural teachers and leaders who can both inspire with grand visions and provide practical steps for achieving them.

Capricorn
December 22–January 19

Introduction to Capricorn

Capricorn, a mutable earth sign, ruled by Saturn and symbolized by the mystical Sea-Goat, is a natural initiator who combines practicality with tireless ambition. Capricorns are known to display a maturity and sophistication that makes them seem like old souls even in their youth.

In Love

In matters of the heart, Capricorns move with careful deliberation and tend to keep their feelings private until they're sure of their footing. Once committed, they reveal themselves to be surprisingly passionate, understanding partners who are devoted to making relationships work for the long haul.

Family and Friends

Conventional and reliable, Capricorns make steadfast friends and family members who show their love through practical support and unwavering loyalty. Their high expectations can make them seem demanding, but this comes from a place of wanting the best for their loved ones.

At Work

Known as the zodiac's hardest worker, Capricorn approaches their career with a methodical determination to reach the top. They excel in roles requiring analytical thinking and sales acumen, always willing to learn new skills and follow through on their carefully crafted plans.

In Conflict

When facing challenges, Capricorns maintain their composure and approach problems with pragmatic solutions rather than emotional reactions. Their patient, strategic nature helps them navigate difficulties with grace and wisdom.

How They Shine

Capricorns radiate excellence through their impeccable taste, disciplined approach to goals, and ability to maintain sophisticated composure in any situation. Their practical wisdom combined with natural leadership abilities makes them reliable guides for others.

The Dark Side

Their relentless drive for success and high standards can make Capricorns seem overly rigid or judgmental, while their reticent nature might be interpreted as emotional unavailability. They may struggle with accepting anything less than perfection.

Relationships

Capricorn is good in relationships with:
    Cancer
    Scorpio
    Taurus

Capricorn may find relationships challenging with:
    Sagittarius
    Aries
    Gemini

The Encyclopedia of Astrology

Specifications
Symbol: The Goat
Element: Earth
Ruler: Saturn
Mode: Cardinal

Physical Correspondences
Capricorn is associated with the **knees** and **skeletal system**.

Capricorn Constellation

Location: The Capricornus constellation is located in the southern hemisphere of the sky, positioned between Aquarius and Sagittarius.
Visibility: Visible from July to October.
Constellation Size: 40th-largest constellation.

The Capricorn-Aquarius Cusp, the Cusp of Mystery and Imagination
The Cusp of Mystery and Imagination occurs between January 17 and January 23, blending Capricorn's earthbound pragmatism with Aquarius's innovative spirit. Individuals born during this period combine Saturn's discipline with Uranus's revolutionary insight, often manifesting as practical visionaries who can translate abstract concepts into concrete achievements. The name of this cusp reflects their ability to peer into both the depths of tradition and the mysteries of the known world—they may be uniquely equipped to bridge the gap between established structures and revolutionary ideas, whether through art, science, or social reform.

The Encyclopedia of Astrology

Aquarius
January 20–February 18

Introduction to Aquarius
Aquarius, a fixed air sign, ruled by Uranus and symbolized by the Water-Bearer, embodies the paradox of an air sign symbolized by water, representing Aquarians' role as vessels of wisdom and change. Their progressive nature and humanitarian spirit make them natural innovators and visionaries who pour their energy into making the world a better place.

In Love
Aquarians approach romance with curiosity and intellectual engagement, often maintaining an air of mystery that others find intriguing. Though they can be skeptical of traditional notions of love and sometimes feel awkward about emotional expression, they bring excitement and unconventional thinking to their relationships.

Family and Friends
Highly social yet selective about their inner circle, Aquarians make fascinating friends who keep their deeper emotional connections reserved for a chosen few. They thrive in group settings while maintaining their distinctive individuality, often becoming the unique voice in their social circle.

At Work
Rather than pursuing traditional career paths or financial success, Aquarians are driven by their desire to revolutionize and improve whatever field they enter. Their entrepreneurial spirit and problem-solving mindset make them natural innovators, though they may change careers several times in pursuit of new challenges.

In Conflict
While open-minded in principle, Aquarians can be surprisingly

stubborn once they've formed an opinion, making conflict resolution challenging. Their logical approach and emotional detachment can make them appear cool or distant during disagreements.

How They Shine
Aquarians excel through their inventive thinking, technological aptitude, and ability to envision and create better systems and structures. Their unique style and forward-thinking nature often make them natural trendsetters and pioneers.

The Dark Side
Their stubborn streak and tendency to prioritize logic over emotion can leave Aquarians feeling isolated or misunderstood. They may struggle with emotional intimacy and can appear aloof or detached, even when they care deeply.

Relationships
Aquarius is good in relationships with:
  Libra
  Leo
  Aquarius

Aquarius may find relationships challenging with:
  Taurus
  Scorpio
  Cancer

Specifications
  Symbol: The Water-Bearer
  Element: Air
  Ruler: Uranus
  Mode: Fixed

Physical Correspondences
Aquarius is associated with the **ankles** and **circulatory system**.

Aquarius Constellation

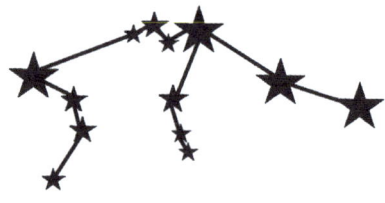

Constellation Location: The Aquarius constellation is located in the southern hemisphere of the sky, positioned between Capricornus and Pisces.
Visibility: Visible from July to December.

The Encyclopedia of Astrology

Constellation Size: The 10th-largest constellation in the night sky. Despite its size, it contains relatively few bright stars, making it a subtle but expansive presence in the night sky.

Pisces
February 19–March 20

The Aquarius-Pisces Cusp, the Cusp of Sensitivity

The Cusp of Sensitivity marks the transition from Aquarius to Pisces, occurring between February 15 and February 21, as intellectual air energy dissolves into intuitive water. Individuals born during this window merge Aquarius's humanitarian vision with Pisces's boundless empathy, creating personalities that can both conceptualize and deeply feel the interconnectedness of all things. The influence of both Uranus and Neptune often manifests as an ability to translate abstract concepts into emotional understanding—making them natural healers, artists, or innovators who can bridge the gap between rational thought and intuitive wisdom.

Introduction to Pisces

Pisces, a mutable water sign ruled by Neptune (modern) and Jupiter (traditional), and symbolized by the Fish, is a deeply spiritual and imaginative sign, characterized by their incredible sensitivity and creative nature. Their ability to surrender and trust allows them to release limiting beliefs and negative energy, opening them to their full potential.

In Love

Pisceans often idealize their romantic partners, falling in love with their perception of someone rather than the real person. They carry a persistent belief that their perfect soulmate exists somewhere, reflecting their

The Encyclopedia of Astrology

symbol of two fish swimming in different directions.

Family and Friends
As natural empaths and excellent listeners, Pisces make for deeply caring friends and family members whom others trust with their secrets. Their generous nature means that Pisces are always available to lend a sensitive ear or shoulder to cry on.

At Work
Creativity flows naturally through Pisces, manifesting in poetry, music, and artistic endeavors, though they may be hesitant to share their work publicly. Their relationship with money can be challenging, as their generous spirit often leads to them giving more than they receive.

In Conflict
Pisces individuals tend to avoid confrontation and may struggle with accepting hard truths, preferring to swim away from difficult situations. Their sensitive nature can make conflict particularly challenging for them to navigate.

How They Shine
Pisces individuals possess a unique ability to find and appreciate true beauty in the world, coupled with an extraordinary creative gift. Their empathetic nature and spiritual connection make them natural healers and artists.

The Dark Side
Pisces can become comfortable in their melancholy, sometimes choosing to dwell in sadness rather than seek change. Their tendency to avoid reality and live in a fantasy world can lead to escapist behaviors.

Relationships
Pisces is good in relationships with:
- Scorpio
- Virgo
- Cancer

Pisces may find relationships challenging with:
- Aries

The Encyclopedia of Astrology

Gemini
Leo

Specifications
Symbol: The Fish
Element: Water
Ruler: Neptune (modern) and Jupiter (traditional)
Mode: Mutable

Physical Correspondences
Pisces is associated with the **feet**.

Pisces Constellation

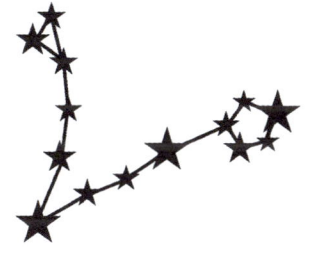

Location: The Pisces constellation is located in the northern sky, positioned between Aquarius and Aries in the zodiac.
Visibility: Visible from July to February.
Constellation Size: 14th-largest constellation.

The Pisces-Aries Cusp, the Cusp of Rebirth
The Cusp of Rebirth occurs between March 17 and March 23, marking the profound transition point where the zodiac wheel completes one cycle and begins anew. Individuals born during this period blend Pisces's deep spiritual awareness with Aries's pioneering spirit, often manifesting as creative innovators who can both dream and take decisive action. Neptune's mystical influence combined with Mars's dynamic energy creates personalities who understand both endings and beginnings—making them naturally gifted at transformative work, whether through artistic expression, spiritual leadership, or spearheading new ventures.

WESTERN ZODIAC SEASONS

A zodiac season is the 30-day window when the Sun is said to be moving or traveling through a specific zodiac sign. Regardless of the specifics of an individual's birth chart, when the Sun is in a particular zodiac sign, many astrologers believe influences of that season may show up in relationships, work, family, and other aspects of daily life.

Because the zodiac signs follow a cycle through each season and year, they also represent a story of growth and a sequence from one sign to the other. This concept is called the developmental phases.

Starting in Aries there is an explosion of growth across the northern hemisphere—a new beginning/birth, an awakening with fresh energy like a seed breaking through soil. Next comes Taurus and a settling down and a grounding with attention to material resources, and then a blossoming of communication, curiosity and learning in Gemini.

Focusing on the self, in Cancer, roots deepen and there's an awareness around our feelings and the need for security. Once secure, Leo roars in, full of confidence, creativity, and self-awareness. Virgo follows, also full of self-awareness, constantly analyzing, refining and perfecting.

Moving into a focus on relationships, Libra is most concerned with balance and finding harmony. Scorpio deepens the focus, honing in on intimate relationships, seeking transformation and depth. Sagittarius broadens the focus on relationships with a fascination on culture and travel and an intellectual curiosity and philosophical interest in making meaning.

Then, the last three signs of the Western zodiac are focused most on ideas—with Capricorn's fascination with responsibility, systems and structures, Aquarius's innovative vision and humanitarian leanings. The zodiac then completes the spiritual journey with Pisces, the most spiritual of all the signs, the dissolution of ego and a desire for connection to universal consciousness.

This progression moves from basic self-awareness and growth in Aries through increasingly complex stages of development, ultimately reaching universal consciousness in Pisces. Each sign builds upon the lessons and experiences of the previous signs, creating a complete cycle of growth and evolution.

Each season in the year has its own energy tied to what's happening in the natural world and tides of celestial bodies.

Aries Season
March 21–April 19

As Aries season dawns, aligned with the spring equinox, the astrological year begins anew. Like nature's own awakening, this season introduces bold, transformative energy. The Ram awakens dormant potential by revealing untapped reserves of strength and courage that eclipse fear-based limitations. This influx of cardinal fire energy kindles our inner spark, inspiring bold actions and vibrant transformations that might have previously felt out of reach. The surge of Aries energy creates an expansive space for embodying our most fearless and authentic selves, making this time ripe for new ventures and personal breakthroughs.

During this period between March 21 and April 19, look out for signs of the season:
- A sudden urge to clear and clean stagnant or cluttered spaces.
- Heightened physical energy, especially in the morning hours.
- Spontaneous bursts of creativity and innovative thinking.
- A magnetic pull toward new beginnings and fresh starts.
- An increased desire to lead rather than follow.
- A natural boldness in speaking up and being assertive.
- Rising competitive spirit in work and play.
- Restless dreams filled with symbols of movement and transformation.

The Encyclopedia of Astrology

Aries Season Celestial Events:

The spring equinox/vernal equinox, marking the first day of Aries. This powerful transition point represents spiritual awakening and the return of vital energy.

The new moon in Aries presents the ultimate fresh start in the zodiacal calendar. This time reminds us that prioritizing our own growth and desires isn't selfish, but essential for our development and ability to serve others later.

The full moon in Libra creates a dynamic tension with the Aries sun. This celestial opposition helps us integrate our personal ambitions with relationship needs.

Taurus Season
April 20–May 20

As Taurus season unfolds, nature settles into its steady rhythm of growth. This period grounds us in earthly pleasures and material abundance. Taurus season can bring a deeper connection to physical sensations. People may find themselves better able to listen to and pick up cues from their bodies. They may also awaken their appreciation for life's simple pleasures—an extra few minutes in bed, a delicious meal, or a nice long hug from a loved one.

During this period from April 20 to May 20, look out for signs of the season:

- A stronger desire to create an environment filled with comfort and beauty.
- Enhanced appreciation for music and artistic pursuits
- Increased focus on financial security and resource management.
- Natural gravitation toward routine and ritual.
- Heightened sensory awareness and pleasure.
- Greater patience and persistence.

The Encyclopedia of Astrology

- Strong connection to nature and the Earth.
- Dreams filled with symbols of abundance and natural beauty.

Taurus Season Celestial Events

The Sun's movement into Taurus marks a period of grounding and manifestation, when spiritual energy takes physical form.

The new moon in Taurus offers perfect conditions for setting intentions related to material abundance, self-worth, and sensual pleasure.

The full moon in Scorpio can bring drama and illuminates the balance between material and spiritual wealth.

Gemini Season
May 21–June 20

As Gemini season arrives, mental energy quickens and curiosity awakens. As the summer solstice gets closer, the days get longer—this period sparkles with intellectual vitality and social connection. Those who tune into this season's influences may find enhanced communication skills and sharper mental acuity. They may find themselves soaking up new information like a sponge, sharing what they have learned with others, and having long, enjoyable conversations.

During this period from May 21 to June 20, look out for signs of the season:

- Increased desire for social interaction and communication.
- Enhanced ability to multitask and adapt.
- Spontaneous urges to learn new skills.
- A natural pull toward writing and speaking.
- Heightened interest in local community.
- Rising curiosity about diverse topics.

The Encyclopedia of Astrology

- Active dreams filled with symbols of movement and connection.
- Enhanced synchronicities and meaningful coincidences.

Gemini Season Celestial Events

The Sun's entrance into Gemini activates mental realms and social connections, bringing a breath of fresh air to consciousness.

The new moon in Gemini presents optimal conditions for setting intentions around communication, learning, and connection.

The full moon in Sagittarius balances detail-oriented thinking with broader philosophical understanding.

Cancer Season
June 21–July 22

As Cancer season begins with the summer solstice, nurturing instincts grow stronger and a greater depth becomes apparent. Emotional intelligence and intuition can feel sharper during this season, and people might find themselves opening up and being more vulnerable in their conversations. Relationships with family and friends might feel more rewarding, with strengthened bonds and more trust.

During this period from June 21 to July 22, look out for signs of the season:
- Strong desire to create and maintain sanctuary spaces.
- Enhanced emotional sensitivity and empathy.
- Lessened FOMO (fear of missing out) and increased focus on home and family matters.
- Natural pull toward nurturing self and others.
- Heightened intuition and psychic awareness.
- Stronger connection to ancestral wisdom.

The Encyclopedia of Astrology

Cancer Season Celestial Events

The summer solstice marks the Sun's entrance into Cancer, representing peak light and emotional illumination.

The new moon in Cancer offers perfect conditions for setting intentions around emotional well-being and family connections.

The full moon in Capricorn balances emotional needs with practical responsibilities.

Leo Season
July 23–August 22

As Leo season blazes forth, creative expression and authentic self-expression take center stage. People who tune into this season's influences may find that it awakens their creative energy. It's a great time to take on new projects, lean into leadership roles, and join new networking groups. Personal magnetism and confidence may peak during this window. Also, enjoy the spice and find opportunities to play—romantic relationships may simmer a little hotter during Leo season!

During this period from July 23 to August 22, look out for signs of the season:
- Increased desire for creative expression.
- Enhanced charisma and confidence.
- Spontaneous urges to perform and share.
- Natural pull toward leadership roles.
- Heightened romantic energy.

Leo Season Celestial Events

The Sun's entrance into Leo amplifies creative energy and personal power.

The new moon in Leo presents optimal conditions for setting intentions around self-expression and creativity.

The Encyclopedia of Astrology

The full moon in Aquarius balances individual expression with collective connection.

Virgo Season
August 23–September 22

As Virgo season arrives, practical wisdom and the desire for refinement come to the forefront. This season on the brink of autumn reveals areas that are ready for improvement and refinement, and creates space for practical problem-solving. People might find that their analytical abilities and attention to detail are tuned—this is a terrific time to review progress for the year so far and start planning for the fall and winter. A desire for service and learning or skill-building may surface during this season as well.

During this period from August 23 to September 22, look out for signs of the season:
- Strong desire to organize and create systems.
- Enhanced focus on health and wellness.
- Increased attention to daily routines.
- Natural pull toward service and helping others.
- Heightened discrimination and discernment.

Virgo Season Celestial Events
The Sun's entrance into Virgo activates practical wisdom and the drive for improvement.
The new moon in Virgo offers perfect conditions for setting intentions around health and service.
The full moon in Pisces balances practical details with spiritual connection.

The Encyclopedia of Astrology

Libra Season
September 23–October 22

As Libra season begins with the autumn/fall equinox, balance and harmony become central themes. Those who tune into this season's influences may find themselves with a renewed deep appreciation for beauty and harmony, both in the world and in the home and office. It's also an opportune moment to evaluate friendships and romantic relationships to make sure they are balanced, supportive, and healthy. Diplomatic abilities and negotiation skills may also be stronger during this season.

During this period from September 23 to October 22, look out for signs of the season:
- Increased focus on relationships and partnerships.
- Enhanced appreciation for art and beauty.
- Natural pull toward social harmony.
- Heightened sense of justice and fairness.
- Stronger connection to the art of compromise and cooperation.

Libra Season Celestial Events

The autumn/fall equinox marks the Sun's entrance into Libra, representing perfect balance between day and night. **The new moon in Libra** presents optimal conditions for setting intentions around relationships and harmony. **The full moon in Aries** balances relationship needs with personal independence.

Scorpio Season
October 23–November 21

The Encyclopedia of Astrology

As Scorpio season descends, depths of transformation and mystery reveal themselves. People may find themselves with more capacity and openness for transformation. This is the season when truths or hidden meanings come out of the woodwork, and a little bit of digging and investigation can reveal major insights about oneself. This can carry through to psychological healing and recovery from trauma as layers of obfuscation are peeled away.

During this period from October 23 to November 21, look out for signs of the season:
- Strong pull toward depth and investigation.
- Enhanced psychic sensitivity.
- Increased interest in mysteries and occult.
- Natural ability to see beyond surfaces.
- Heightened emotional intensity.
- Stronger connection to shadow work.

Scorpio Season Celestial Events
The Sun's entrance into Scorpio activates transformative energy and deep psychological insight.
The new moon in Scorpio offers perfect conditions for setting intentions around transformation and healing.
The full moon in Taurus balances seeking depth with staying grounded.

Sagittarius Season
November 22–December 21

As Sagittarius season ignites, the quest for meaning and adventure takes flight. People who feel this season's influences may find that it reveals new possibilities and perspectives, and lights up their spirit of adventure! The season of the Archer can also create room for philosophical ideas to take root, grow, and mature. There is a joy and curiosity that infuses this season.

During this period from November 22 to December 21, look out for signs of the season:
- Increased desire for travel and exploration.
- Enhanced interest in higher learning and philosophy.
- Natural pull toward spiritual quest.
- Heightened optimism and faith.
- Deeper connection to universal wisdom.

Sagittarius Season Celestial Events
The Sun's entrance into Sagittarius activates the quest for meaning and truth.
The new moon in Sagittarius presents optimal conditions for setting intentions around expansion and adventure.
The full moon in Gemini balances big-picture thinking with detailed information.

Capricorn Season
December 22–January 19

As Capricorn season begins with the winter solstice, structure and ambition come into focus. During this season, people's ambition, resolve and determination may feel stronger than ever, so it's a great time to hone habits and set goals. New pathways to mastery and achievement may be revealed, while that nagging imposter syndrome may seem quieter.

During this period from December 22 to January 19, look out for signs of the season:
- Drive toward achievement.
- Enhanced ability to plan long-term.
- Increased focus on career and status.

The Encyclopedia of Astrology

- A craving for authority and responsibility.
- Bouts of determination and focus.

Capricorn Season Celestial Events

The winter solstice marks the Sun's entrance into Capricorn, representing the return of light.
The new moon in Capricorn offers perfect conditions for setting intentions around career and long-term goals.
The full moon in Cancer balances ambition with emotional needs.

Aquarius Season
January 20–February 18

As Aquarius season dawns, innovative thinking and collective consciousness expand. Those who tune into this season's influences may find that it awakens their innovation potential and reveals new solutions to old problems. This season can surface a need for authenticity in both self and relationships, and create a pull towards humanitarian efforts and charitable work or donations.

During this period from January 20 to February 18, look out for signs of the season:
- Increased interest in social causes.
- Enhanced ability to think outside the box.
- Natural pull toward group activities.
- Heightened desire for freedom.
- Rising revolutionary spirit.
- Dreams filled with symbols of future possibilities.
- Stronger connection to collective consciousness.

Aquarius Season Celestial Events

The Sun's entrance into Aquarius activates innovative thinking and group consciousness.

The Encyclopedia of Astrology

The new moon in Aquarius presents optimal conditions for setting intentions around innovation and community. **The full moon in Leo** balances collective needs with individual expression.

Pisces Season
February 19–March 20

As Pisces season flows forth, spiritual awareness and universal love deepen. This season can reveal an awareness of the interconnectedness of all things and launch creativity and imagination to extreme heights. This season can also deepen spiritual connections and create space for divine inspiration and a renewed connection with the holy and mystical.

During this period from February 19 to March 20, look out for signs of the season:
- Increased artistic inspiration.
- A desire for more meditation and personal reflection.
- Heightened empathy and compassion.
- Enhanced spiritual sensitivity and connection to the divine.

Pisces Season Celestial Events
The Sun's entrance into Pisces activates spiritual awareness and dissolution of boundaries.
The new moon in Pisces offers perfect conditions for setting intentions around spiritual growth and artistic expression.
The full moon in Virgo balances spiritual flow with practical grounding.

WESTERN ASTROLOGY BIRTH CHARTS
Introduction to Birth Charts
A birth chart is a map of the sky at the exact moment of birth. It shows the placement of all the

The Encyclopedia of Astrology

celestial bodies including the Sun, the Moon, and the planets. Astrologers use birth charts to interpret the energy, influence, and relationship between celestial bodies.

It's necessary to have a person's location and time of birth in order to create an accurate birth chart. While people who do not have that information will not be able to have the same in-depth astrological insights, they could either estimate their time and place of birth or they could study the birth charts of individuals who they feel have similar attributes and claim the data they feel best fits them.

In Western astrology using the tropical zodiac system, a birth chart is a circle divided into 12 parts. The zodiac signs run counterclockwise starting at the vernal equinox, 0 degrees Aries. The ascendant starts the chart and determines where the first house begins, and then the houses are numbered 1–12 counterclockwise around the chart. The Midheaven (MC), often located at the top of the chart, signifies the highest point the Sun reaches relative to the birthplace and is associated with career and public life. The sign on the Midheaven varies with each individual chart and is not fixed to Aries or the vernal equinox.

On a birth chart, the celestial bodies impact personality traits in different ways based on where they are placed in the sky. The Sun's location represents a person's primary identity, while the Moon's represents emotions and instincts. The zodiac sign rising on the eastern horizon at birth is the rising sign or ascendant, and the location of each of the planets is represented on the birth chart.

An astrologer measures the aspects, or geometric angles, between the celestial bodies to trace their relationships in order to predict or define influences and energies in a person's life.

How to Create a Birth Chart: Step by Step

In ancient times before digital tools, astrologers used a combination of mathematical tables,

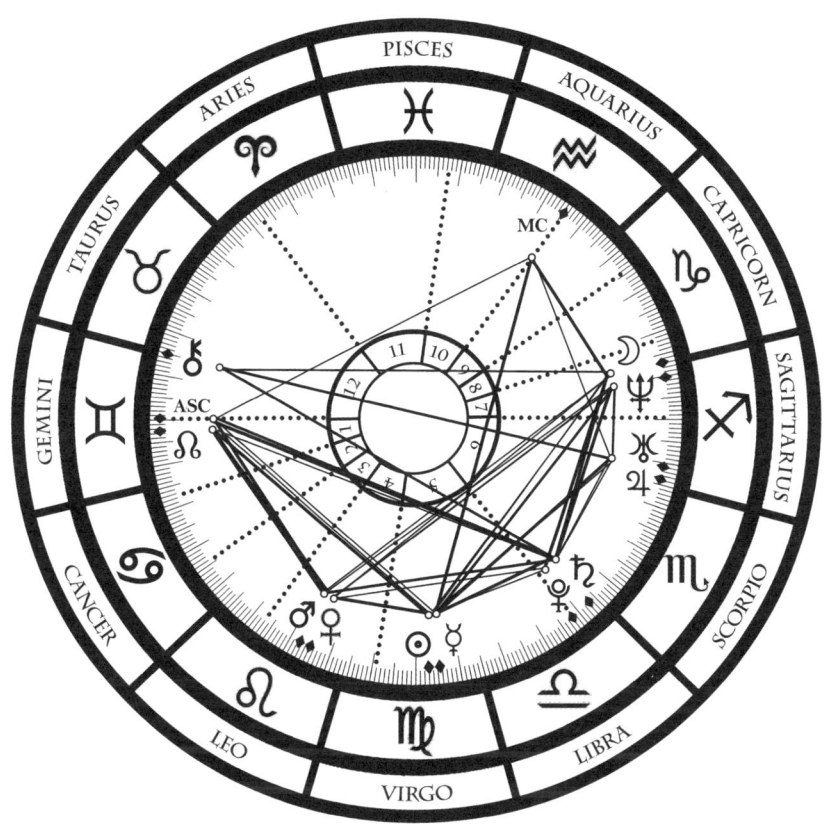

specialized equipment, and complex manual calculations to create birth charts. The primary tool was an ephemeris—a book of pre-calculated planetary positions for each day of the year—along with tables of houses that showed how they aligned at different latitudes and times.

Astrologers would use these references along with tools like the astrolabe and the armillary sphere, which helped measure the positions of celestial bodies, and slide rules specifically designed for astronomical calculations.

The Encyclopedia of Astrology

Ancient (Pre-computer) Birth Chart Calculation Process, Tropical Zodiac

Required materials:
- Ephemeris (astronomical almanac)
- Tables of houses
- Pre-printed chart wheel
- Protractor
- Aspect grid
- Mathematical tables
- Color-coding tools

Step 1: Information Gathering
- Record exact birth time, date, and location

Step 2: Core Calculations
- Calculate the ascendant degree using tables of houses
- Choose a house system
- Determine house cusps

Step 3: Start Plotting
- Draw or use pre-printed wheel divided into 12 houses and 12 signs
- Mark ascendant on left horizon (9 o'clock position)
- Place Midheaven (MC) at top of chart
- Number houses counterclockwise from ascendant

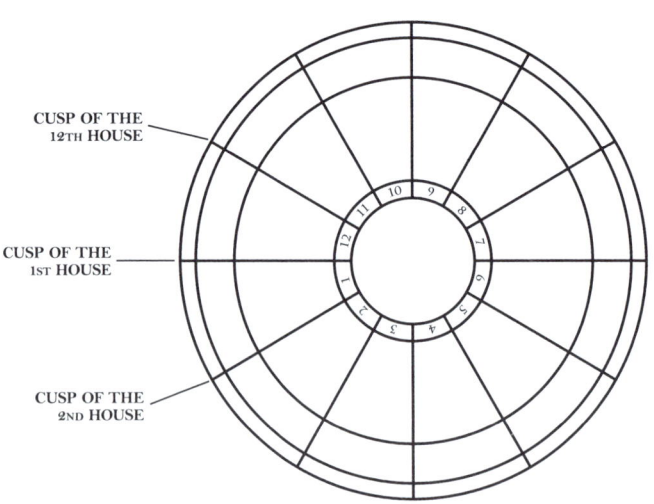

The Encyclopedia of Astrology

Step 4: Plot the Chart
- Using the ephemeris to find planetary positions and plot celestial bodies on the birth chart:
  - Sun
  - Moon
  - Mercury
  - Venus
  - Mars
  - Jupiter
  - Saturn
  - Uranus
  - Neptune
  - Pluto

Step 5: Aspect Calculation
- Use protractor to measure angles between planets
- Mark major aspects:
  - Conjunction (0°)
  - Sextile (60°)
  - Square (90°)
  - Trine (120°)
  - Opposition (180°)
- Color-code aspects for clarity:
  - Red: Challenging aspects (squares, oppositions)
  - Blue: Harmonious aspects (trines, sextiles)
  - Green: Growth aspects (conjunctions)

Step 6: Final Details
- Note retrograde planets with Rx symbol
- Double-check all calculations
- Add final annotations and interpretative notes

This meticulous process required significant expertise and time, explaining why professional astrologers were highly valued for their technical skills as well as their interpretative abilities.

In modern times, the process of calculating a birth chart is much faster—almost instant—and much more precise, though

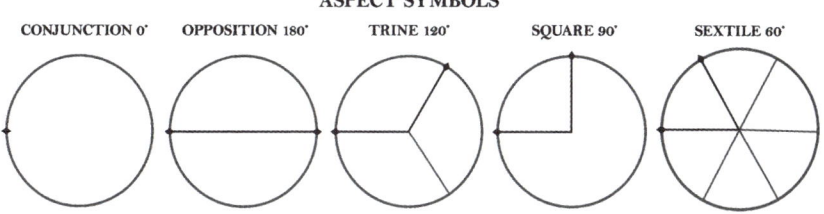

The Encyclopedia of Astrology

some of the magic, art and beauty of using ancient tools like the astrolobe and armillary spheres may be lost for the sake of convenience.

There is a plethora of online tools that modern astrologers can use to create accurate birth charts, including free websites, fee-based software, and mobile apps.

How to Create a Birth Chart with Modern Tools

The steps for creating a birth chart with modern tools are much simpler than using ancient calculations.

Step 1: Information Gathering

Record exact birth time, date, and location.

Step 2: Choose a Website or Software

Several important factors come into play when selecting a birth chart calculation website. The site should allow precise input of birth time down to the minute and specific location coordinates, not just city names, as even small differences can affect house placements and aspects. A quality birth chart generator should clearly indicate which house system it uses (such as Placidus, Whole Sign, or Koch) or allow you to choose between different systems for comparison. It's recommended to use a well-reviewed website or software and use caution when entering personal information anywhere on the Internet.

The chart should also include aspects between all major celestial bodies and provide detailed information about planetary placements within both signs and houses, rather than just basic sun/moon/rising sign information.

How to Read a Birth Chart

Interpreting a birth chart involves analyzing the positions and relationships of celestial bodies at the time of an individual's birth to gain insights into their personality and life path. Here's a step-by-step guide to reading a birth chart:

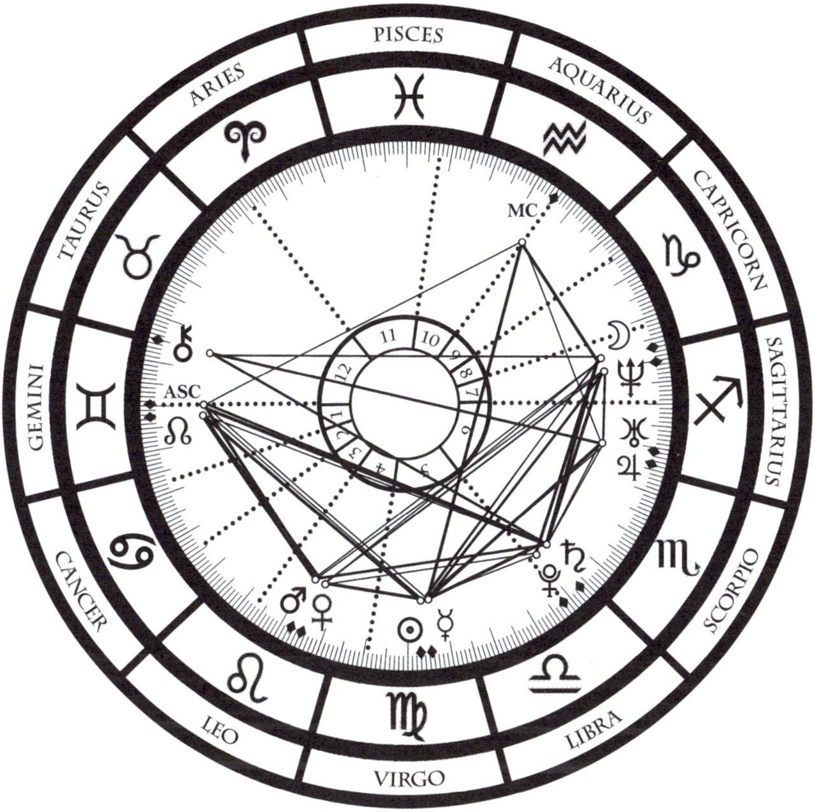

Step 1: Identify the Ascendant (Rising Sign)

The ascendant, or rising sign, is the zodiac sign that was on the eastern horizon at the exact time of birth. It influences outward behavior and first impressions. Located at the 9 o'clock position on the chart, it marks the cusp of the first house.

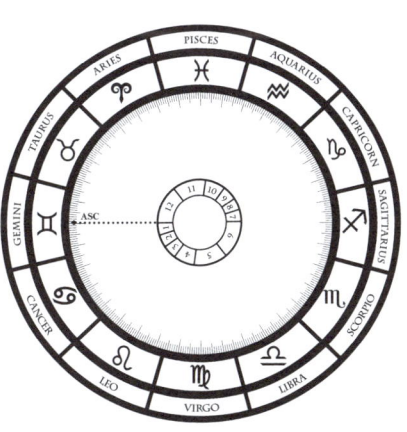

The Encyclopedia of Astrology

Step 2: Determine the Sun and Moon Signs

The sun sign represents core identity and ego, indicating fundamental personality traits.

The moon sign reflects emotional nature and subconscious patterns, revealing inner emotional responses.

Step 3: Analyze Planetary Positions

Examine the placement of each planet in the zodiac signs and houses. For example, Venus in Aquarius in the seventh house may suggest unconventional approaches to relationships.

Step 4: Interpret the Houses

The birth chart is divided into 12 houses, each representing different life areas such as self-identity, finances, communication, and relationships. The sign on the cusp of each house and any planets within provide insights into those life sectors.

Step 5: Examine Aspects

Aspects are the angles between planets that indicate how they interact.

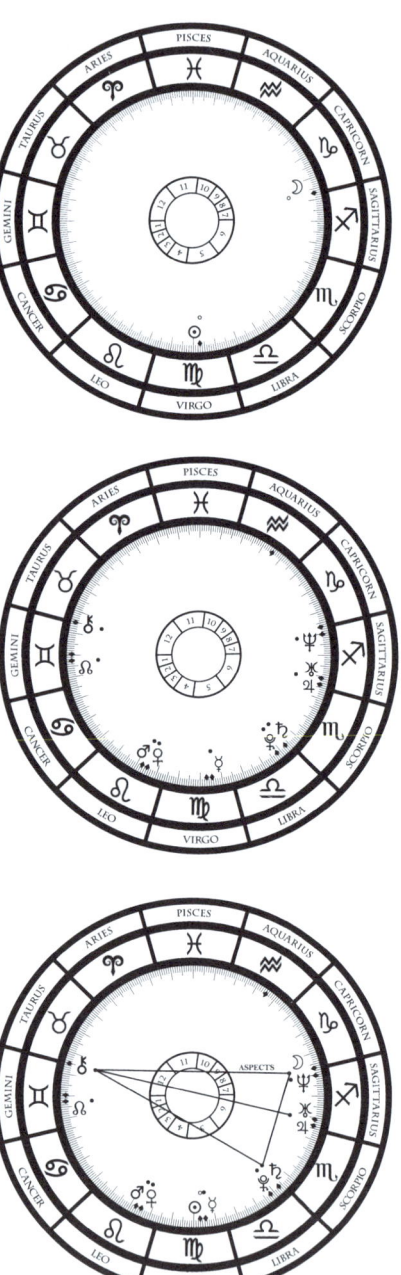

The Encyclopedia of Astrology

Major aspects include:
- **Conjunction (0°):** Planets are aligned, merging their energies.
- **Opposition (180°):** Planets are opposite each other, creating tension that requires balance.
- **Trine (120°):** Planets are 120 degrees apart, facilitating harmonious interactions.
- **Square (90°):** Planets are 90 degrees apart, indicating challenges and dynamic tension.
- **Sextile (60°):** Planets are 60 degrees apart, offering opportunities for cooperation.

Step 6: Synthesize the Information
Combine insights from the ascendant, sun and moon signs, planetary positions, house placements, and aspects to form a comprehensive understanding of the individual's character, strengths, challenges, and potential life path.

SYMBOLS AND GLYPHS
Astrologers developed an elegant system of symbols—called *glyphs*—to efficiently map the complex web of planetary positions and relationships in birth charts. These ancient symbols, many dating back to classical antiquity, represent everything from zodiac signs and planets to aspects and points of cosmic significance.

Much like musical notation allows composers to write complex scores on a single page, these astrological glyphs enable practitioners to create detailed cosmic maps that would otherwise require pages of written explanation. These glyphs are used in ephemerides and other charts that track astrological data.

Zodiac Signs
Aries

Taurus

The Encyclopedia of Astrology

Gemini

Cancer

Leo

Virgo

Libra

Scorpio

Sagittarius

Capricorn

Aquarius

Pisces

Planets and Celestial Bodies
Sun

Moon

The Encyclopedia of Astrology

Elements

Fire

Air

Earth

Water

Aspects

Conjunction *Trine*  *Sextile*

Opposition  *Square*

The Encyclopedia of Astrology

Lunar Phases

New Moon

Full Moon

Waxing Crescent

Waning Gibbous

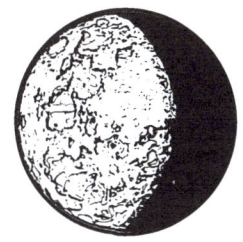

Waxing Quarter

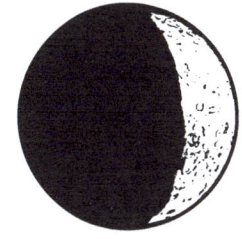

Waning Quarter

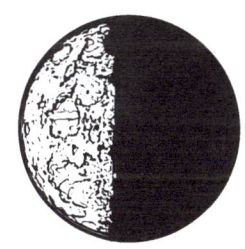

Waxing Gibbous

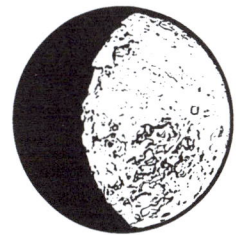

Waning Crescent

The Encyclopedia of Astrology

Other Celestial Points and Concepts
North Node

South Node

Part of Fortune

Retrograde

Vertex

WESTERN ZODIAC HOUSES
Zodiac House

A zodiac house is one of twelve 30-degree divisions of the sky that represents different areas of life, such as relationships, career, or spirituality. The zodiac wheel stays fixed like numbers on a clock face, while the houses rotate through the day based on the Earth's 24-hour rotation—creating a dynamic map of planetary positions that changes throughout the day. A person born at sunrise would have their Sun in the first house of self and identity, while someone born at noon would have their Sun near the tenth house of career and public image. Those born at sunset would find their Sun in the seventh house of partnerships, and midnight births place the Sun in the fourth house of home and family roots.

Each house has a specific focus—for example, the first house governs identity and appearance, while the tenth house relates to career and public image—creating a framework for understanding how celestial

The Encyclopedia of Astrology

energies might manifest in various aspects of someone's life.

The Twelve Houses

The zodiac is divided into 12 signs, each spanning 30 degrees, for a total of 360 degrees. Each 30-degree section is called a house. These degrees represent the sky as it curves around the Earth.

Mapping the position of the planets located within a house at any given moment gives insight into the energies at play. In a birth chart, a person's reading will change depending on which planets appear in which houses, and its exact position within the house.

The houses provide a framework for understanding how

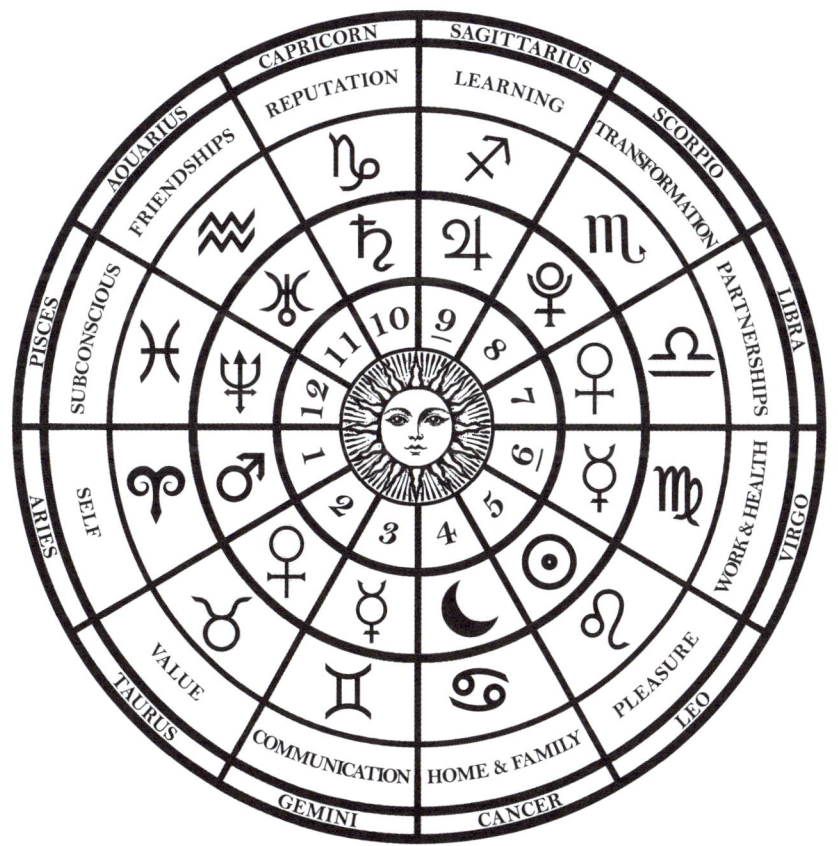

The Encyclopedia of Astrology

planetary energies might manifest in different areas of a person's life according to astrological interpretations. Each celestial body also has a home house, noted below.

The 12 houses and their primary areas of influence are seen in the chart below.

House cusps

The house cusp marks the beginning degree of each astrological house in a birth chart, acting like a doorway between houses. These sensitive points help determine which house a planet falls into and how strongly that house's themes influence the planet's expression. The degree of each cusp depends on factors like birth time and location, as well as which house system is being used in the chart calculation.

House signs

House signs refer to the zodiac sign that appears on the cusp, or the starting point, of each astrological house in a birth chart. Each of the 12 houses begins at a specific degree within a zodiac sign, creating a unique relation-

House #	Primary Areas of Influence	Home Sign	Home Planet or Constellation
1	Self and identity, appearance and life force	Aries	Mars
2	Possessions and values	Taurus	Venus
3	Communication, daily life	Gemini	Mercury
4	Parents, home, and foundation	Cancer	Moon
5	Creativity, pleasure, children	Leo	Sun
6	Work and health	Virgo	Mercury
7	Long-term partnerships and marriage	Libra	Venus
8	Mental health, death, and shared resources	Scorpio	Mars
9	Philosophy, travel, and higher learning	Sagittarius	Jupiter
10	Career and public image	Capricorn	Saturn
11	Friendships and social groups	Aquarius	Saturn
12	Secrets, loss, hidden matters	Pisces	Jupiter

The Encyclopedia of Astrology

ship between that house's themes and the sign's characteristics. For example, if Aries appears on the cusp of the tenth house of career, it suggests an enterprising, pioneering approach to professional matters.

House Systems

The concept of houses requires the sky to be broken into 12 sections, but there are several different ways that astrologers divide the celestial sphere. The choice of house system can significantly affect the placement of planets within houses, especially for locations far from the equator. Astrologers often have preferences based on their training, experience, or the specific type of astrology they practice, and the systems can be cross-referenced for a more robust reading.

Alcabitius

The Alcabitius house system, developed by 10th-century Arabic astrologer Al-Qabisi (Latinized as Alcabitius), was widely used throughout medieval Europe and remained popular until the 17th century when it was gradually replaced by the Placidus system. It uses a time-based method of house division similar to Placidus, but calculates the cusps by trisecting the diurnal and nocturnal semi-arcs in a different way, resulting in houses that can vary significantly in size. While rarely used in modern Western astrology, the system still maintains some following among traditional astrologers and those studying medieval astrological techniques, particularly those interested in working with historical source materials from the medieval period.

Campanus

Campanus, developed by 13th-century mathematician Johannes Campanus, divides the celestial sphere using the prime vertical—an imaginary great circle passing through the east point, zenith, west point, and nadir. This creates houses of varying sizes but maintains mathematical elegance. Astrological research organizations often use Campanus for its geometric precision.

The Encyclopedia of Astrology

Equal House

The equal house system divides the zodiac wheel into 12 mathematically equal 30-degree segments, starting precisely from the ascendant degree. Unlike whole sign houses, which align with full zodiac signs, equal house segments may cut across signs, maintaining the ascendant degree as the starting point of the first house. For example, if the ascendant is at 15 degrees Leo, the second house begins at 15 degrees Virgo, the third at 15 degrees Libra, and so on. This system, dating back to ancient Egypt, is valued for its simplicity and is widely used on modern astrology websites.

Koch

Developed in the 1960s by German astrologer Walter Koch, the Koch house system uses a trisection of the quadrants of the ecliptic. The system relies more on a person's physical location at the time of birth to calculate houses in the zodiac wheel. The system is thought to work well in middle latitudes but, like Placidus, becomes problematic near the poles.

Meridian

Meridian divides the celestial sphere into 12 equal sectors using the local meridian as the starting point. The houses are created by great circles that pass through the north and south points of the horizon, similar to Regiomontanus, but using the meridian as the primary reference. This system is less commonly used but provides consistent results at all latitudes.

Morinus

Morinus, named after 17th-century French astrologer Jean-Baptiste Morin, projects the celestial equator onto the ecliptic rather than using space-time relationships. The house cusps are spaced equally along the equator, creating a system that works consistently at all latitudes. This makes it especially valuable for readings in polar regions where other systems may fail.

Placidus

The most widely used system in Western astrology. Placidus divides the ecliptic by time, calculating how long it takes a point to travel from the horizon to the midheaven. Developed by 17th-century Italian mathematician Placidus de Titis, it's particularly accurate for locations between 40 degrees north and 40 degrees south latitude. The system becomes less reliable in extreme northern or southern latitudes, where planets can sometimes skip houses entirely.

Porphyry

A simple system that trisects the space between the angles in the ecliptic. Porphyry, named after the 3rd-century Greek philosopher Porphyry of Tyre, creates houses by taking the space between major angles (Ascendant, Midheaven, Descendant, and Imum Coeli) and dividing each quadrant into three equal parts. This means house sizes may vary within the chart depending on the spacing between these angles.

Regiomontanus

Regiomontanus, created by 15th-century German astronomer Johannes Müller von Königsberg, divides the celestial equator into 12 equal parts through great circles intersecting at the north and south points of the horizon. This system was widely used during the Renaissance and remains popular in horary astrology for its precision in timing events. The houses vary in size but maintain mathematical consistency around the equator.

Topocentric

Topocentric, developed in the mid-20th century by Hungarian-Argentinian astrologer Vendel Polich and British mathematician and astrologer Anthony Page, accounts for the observer's exact location on Earth's surface rather than just the center of the Earth. This system attempts to correct the distortions that occur in other house systems at extreme latitudes, making it particularly useful for readings in places like Alaska or southern Argentina. Topocentric closely resembles Placidus but uses a more complex mathematical formula.

Whole Sign

Whole sign, originating in Hellenistic astrology, assigns entire zodiac signs to each house, with the rising sign occupying the first house. The remaining houses follow in zodiacal order, creating clean, clear boundaries between houses. This system has seen a revival in recent years for its simplicity and historical accuracy.

ASPECTS AND RELATIONSHIPS

Aspects

Aspects are the relationships that two or more planets or points have with one another. Just like all relationships, some are easy and uplifting, while others are difficult and discouraging. Aspects fall into three categories: gifts, challenges, and mergers. They are measured in degrees. Also known as Ptolemaic aspects, these are the five principal angular relationships between planets recognized by the ancient Greek astronomer Claudius Ptolemy in his influential work, the *Tetrabiblos*.

Conjunction (0°)
Opposition (180°, Challenge)
Sextile (60°, Gift)
Square (90°, Challenge)
Trine (120°, Gift)

Conjunction

CONJUNCTION 0°

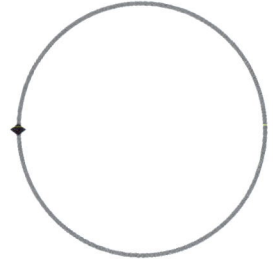

A conjunction occurs when two celestial bodies align at the same degree within a zodiac sign, resulting in a 0-degree angle between them. This alignment merges their energies, leading them to function in unison. The nature of a conjunction's influence—whether harmonious

ASPECT PATTERNS

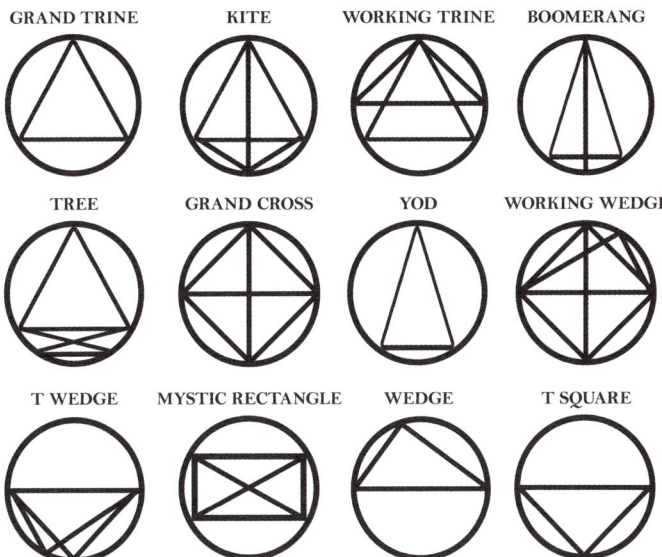

or challenging—depends on the characteristics of the involved planets and their specific positions in the natal chart.

The Gifts

Planets and luminaries that are two or four houses away from each other can manifest positive energy and impact in day-to-day life.

Sextile (60°, Gift)

SEXTILE 60°

A sextile is an astrological aspect that occurs when two planets are approximately 60 degrees apart in the birth chart. This aspect is generally considered harmonious

The Encyclopedia of Astrology

and supportive, though it requires some effort or awareness to activate its potential. The planets in a sextile are usually in complementary elements: fire and air (e.g., Aries and Gemini), or earth and water (e.g., Taurus and Cancer).

A sextile from Venus is considered the strongest sextile, and a trine from Jupiter is the strongest trine. Example: Mars in the second house, Jupiter in the fourth house.

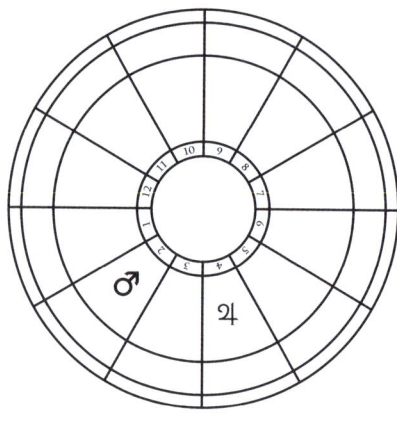

The sextile aspect between Mars and Jupiter depicted above suggests a harmonious interaction between assertive energy (Mars) and expansive opportunities (Jupiter). This sextile relationship might indicate that actions taken regarding personal resources (Mars in second) could lead to growth or opportunities in the home or family life (Jupiter in fourth).

Conversely, support from family or a stable home environment might contribute to financial growth or increased self-worth. A person might see this manifest in a surge of energy around pursuing financial opportunities that benefit the home or family, family support for personal business ventures, or just a generally optimistic and action-oriented approach to balancing work and home life.

Trine (120°, Gift)

TRINE 120°

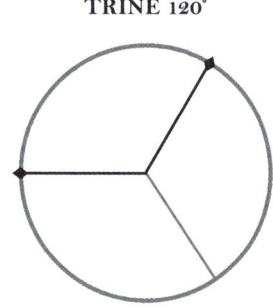

A trine is an astrological aspect that occurs when two planets

The Encyclopedia of Astrology

are approximately 120 degrees apart in the birth chart. This aspect is generally considered harmonious and beneficial, indicating a natural flow of energy between the planets involved. The planets in a trine are typically in the same element (fire, earth, air, or water), which enhances compatibility. Example: Venus in the eighth house, the Moon in the fourth house.

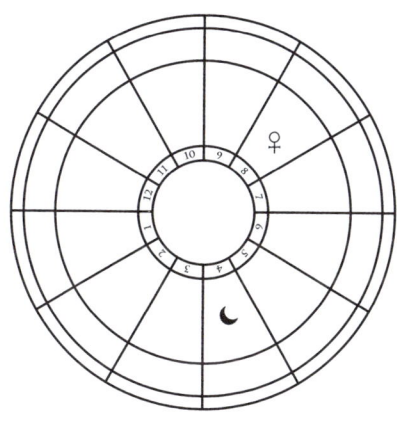

The trine aspect between the Moon and Venus shows Venus in the eighth house and the Moon in the fourth. The Moon represents emotions and intuition, while Venus represents love, beauty, and harmony. The fourth house relates to home and family, while the eighth house relates to mental health, transformation, and shared resources.

This trine suggests that while the celestial bodies are in this planetary position, intimate relationships are supporting our emotional needs and there may be another level of depth and beauty to emotional and intimate experiences.

The Challenges

Celestial bodies that are three or six signs away from each other can bring up challenges or obstacles. A square with Mars is said to be the most challenging square, and an opposition with Saturn is said to be the most challenging opposition.

Square (90°, Challenge)

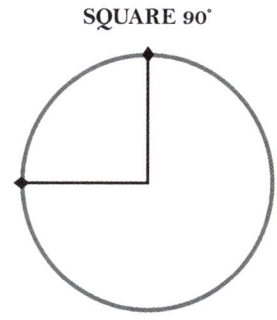

The Encyclopedia of Astrology

Planets that are three signs away from each other, or 90 degrees, are called squares. These can create additional friction or frustrations. Example: Mars in the first house, Saturn in the tenth house.

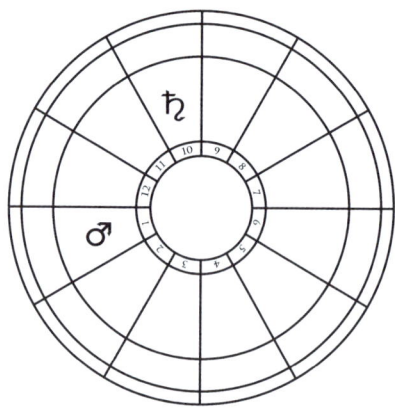

In this example of a square, Mars in the first house signifies a dynamic and assertive personality, while Saturn in the tenth house emphasizes a disciplined and ambitious approach to one's career and public image. This square creates a dynamic tension between personal assertiveness and professional responsibilities.

Opposition (180°, Challenge)

OPPOSITION 180°

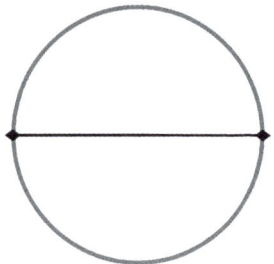

An opposition is a planetary aspect that occurs when two celestial bodies are positioned 180 degrees apart in the zodiac, placing them directly opposite each other in a natal chart. This alignment often creates a dynamic tension between the differing energies of the involved planets, leading to challenges that require balance and compromise. While oppositions can indicate areas of conflict or polarization, they also present opportunities for growth by encouraging individuals to integrate contrasting aspects of their personality or life circumstances.

Quincunx (150°, Challenge)

QUINCUNX

A quincunx, also known as an inconjunct, is a 150-degree aspect between two planets and is generally seen as a challenge. This alignment involves signs that typically share neither element nor modality, leading to a lack of common ground. Consequently, the energies of the involved planets may struggle to integrate, resulting in tension and the need for adjustment. This misalignment can manifest as internal conflicts or external situations requiring compromise and adaptation.

Dominant Aspects

Each planet has its own signature or dominant aspect in astrology, based on its symbolic energy and natural tendencies. Here are some general associations:

The Sun: Conjunction

The Sun represents identity and ego. Its energy is often focused and amplified when in conjunction with other planets, creating a blending or unity of energies.

The Moon: Sextile

Known for its nurturing and adaptive qualities, the Moon resonates with supportive and harmonious aspects, like the sextile, which encourages growth and cooperation.

Mercury: Opposition

Mercury thrives on communication, analysis, and duality. Oppositions can create a dynamic exchange of ideas, which aligns with Mercury's curious and interactive nature.

Venus: Trine
Venus is about harmony, beauty, and relationships. The trine aspect reflects the ease and natural flow Venus strives for in connections and creativity.

Mars: Square
Mars is assertive, driven, and sometimes combative. The square reflects its challenging and dynamic energy, pushing for action and resolution.

Jupiter: Trine
Jupiter's expansive and optimistic nature aligns with the trine aspect, which promotes growth, luck, and opportunity.

Saturn: Conjunction
Saturn is disciplined, structured, and focused. The conjunction represents its ability to concentrate energy and establish boundaries.

Uranus: Opposition
Uranus, the planet of innovation and disruption, thrives in oppositional dynamics, creating sudden shifts and revolutionary insights.

Neptune: Sextile
Neptune's dreamy, spiritual energy resonates with the sextile, which fosters subtle yet transformative creativity and inspiration.

Pluto: Square
Pluto's themes of transformation and power align with the intensity of the square, driving deep change and evolution through challenge.

These "signature" aspects aren't exclusive, but they reflect the planets' archetypal energies and how they might express themselves most naturally in a chart.

Chart Patterns
Chart patterns are clusters, distinct geometric shapes, or other configurations that create significant meaning. The patterns signify how the energies of the planets and celestial bodies interact and flow within a person's life, with each shape suggesting different dynamics.

Major chart patterns include:

CHART PATTERNS

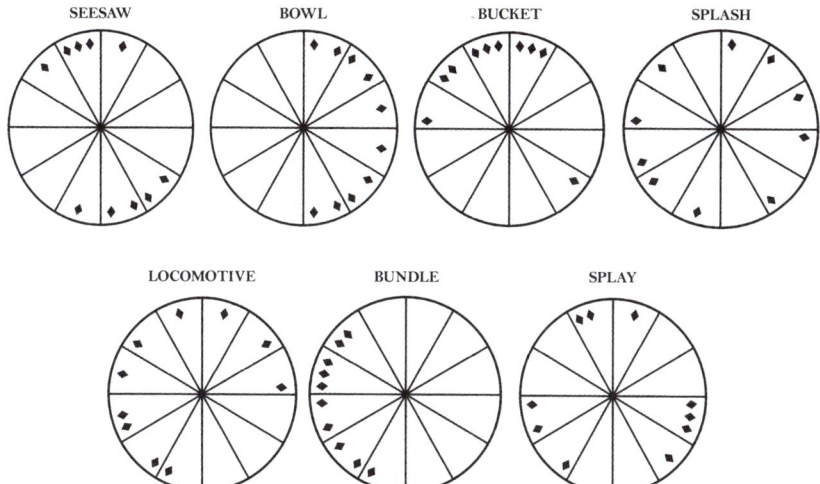

Grand Cross, or Grand Square (four planets in square aspects)

A Grand Cross, or Grand Square, is an astrological configuration where four planets form two oppositions (180-degree angles) and four squares (90-degree angles), creating a cross-like pattern in the natal chart. This alignment involves planets occupying each of the four signs within the same modality—cardinal, fixed, or mutable—resulting in a dynamic interplay of energies.

The Grand Cross is often associated with significant tension and challenges, as the involved planetary energies can be at odds, pulling the individual in multiple directions. This internal conflict may lead to feelings of indecision or being "stuck." However, navigating these challenges can foster resilience and personal growth, as the individual learns to balance and integrate the conflicting energies.

The Encyclopedia of Astrology

Grand Trine (three planets in trine aspects)

A Grand Trine is an astrological configuration where three planets form approximately 120-degree angles with each other, creating an equilateral triangle within the birth chart. This alignment occurs when each planet resides in a sign of the same element—fire, earth, air, or water—facilitating a harmonious flow of energy among them. Such a pattern often indicates that the individual possesses natural talents and strengths in areas related to the element involved, leading to ease and alignment in those aspects of life.

While a Grand Trine suggests inherent abilities and a smooth expression of energies, astrologers also warn that it can lead to complacency or a lack of motivation to pursue growth, as challenges may be less apparent.

Kite (Grand Trine with an opposition)

A kite aspect pattern in astrology is a distinctive configuration that combines a Grand Trine with an additional planet forming an opposition to one of the planets in the trine, resulting in a pattern resembling a kite. This structure includes two harmonious trine aspects (120 degrees) and two opportunistic sextile aspects (60 degrees), along with the tension of an opposition aspect (180 degrees). The Grand Trine provides a stable and harmonious flow of energy among the three planets involved, often indicating natural talents or ease in certain areas of life. The fourth planet, by opposing one of the trine planets, introduces dynamic tension that can serve as a catalyst for growth and motivation, prompting the individual to actively engage with and utilize the inherent potentials of the Grand Trine. This opposition aspect can create challenges that, when navigated effectively, lead to significant personal development and the realization of one's abilities.

Mystic Rectangle (four planets forming harmonious aspects)

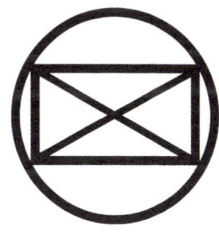

A Mystic Rectangle is an astrological aspect pattern formed when four planets are connected in a rectangular shape, consisting of two oppositions (180 degrees), two trines (120 degrees), and two sextiles (60 degrees). This configuration creates a balanced interplay between harmonious and challenging aspects, offering opportunities for growth and integration. The trines and sextiles facilitate the harmonious flow of energy, while the oppositions introduce dynamic tension that encourages the individual to address and reconcile opposing forces within their personality or life experiences. Effectively navigating a Mystic Rectangle can lead to personal development and the ability to transform challenges into strengths.

Star of David/Grand Sextile (six planets in sextile aspects)

A Star of David, also known as a Grand Sextile, is a rare and auspicious astrological configuration where six planets align to form a hexagram, consisting of two interlocking Grand Trines. This

The Encyclopedia of Astrology

pattern creates a six-pointed star within the natal chart, symbolizing harmony and balance. The Grand Sextile comprises six sextile aspects (60 degrees) and two Grand Trines (120 degrees), resulting in a harmonious flow of energy among the involved planets. This alignment often indicates a period of enhanced potential and opportunities, as the planets work synergistically to support personal growth and achievement.

The two Grand Trines typically occur in complementary elements—either fire and air or earth and water—further emphasizing the balance between different aspects of life. For instance, a Grand Sextile involving earth and water signs may enhance practical and emotional stability, while one involving fire and air signs could boost creativity and intellectual pursuits. While the Grand Sextile facilitates ease and potential, it requires conscious effort to harness its full benefits, as the harmonious energies can sometimes lead to complacency.

T-Square (three planets forming a right triangle)

A T-Square is an astrological aspect pattern involving three planets that form a configuration resembling the letter "T." This occurs when two planets are in opposition (180 degrees apart), and both are squared (90 degrees) by a third planet, known as the focal or apex planet. The signs involved in a T-Square typically share the same modality—cardinal, fixed, or mutable—intensifying the dynamic tension within the pattern. This configuration often manifests as internal or external conflicts, pushing individuals toward growth and transformation. Effectively navigating a T-Square requires conscious effort to balance the conflicting energies, turning challenges into opportunities for personal development.

Yod/Finger of God (two planets in sextile, both quincunx to a third)

A Yod, often referred to as the "Finger of God," is an astrological configuration involving three planets: two in sextile (60 degrees apart) and both quincunx (150 degrees) to a third, forming an isosceles triangle. This pattern creates a dynamic tension, highlighting areas in one's life that may require significant adjustment or transformation. The planet at the apex, receiving the quincunxes, becomes a focal point, indicating a unique challenge or mission that the individual is compelled to address. Navigating the energies of a Yod can lead to profound personal growth, as it often points to a karmic or fated path necessitating conscious effort and adaptation.

Additional Minor Patterns:
Cradle (four planets forming a bowl shape)

This pattern consists of two planets in opposition, with each end of the opposition connected by a sextile and a trine to two other planets, forming a configuration that resembles a cradle. It suggests a balance between harmony and tension, providing opportunities for growth through the integration of differing energies.

Basket (five or more planets contained within 180 degrees)

When all planets are contained within 180 degrees of the chart, it forms a bowl shape. This indicates a focused energy, with the individual seeking fulfillment in the areas of life represented by the occupied houses, while feeling a lack of motivation to develop the unoccupied areas.

Bundle (all planets contained within 120 degrees)

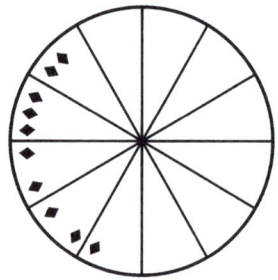

All planets clustered within a 120-degree span create a bundle pattern, signifying a concentrated focus on specific life areas, leading to intense specialization but potential neglect of other aspects.

See-Saw (planets divided into two groups)

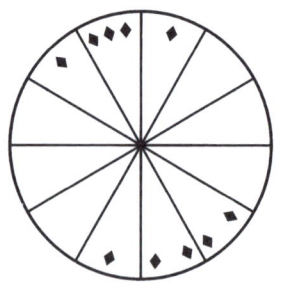

With planets divided into two opposing groups, this pattern reflects a dualistic nature, indicating a personality that oscillates between contrasting perspectives, striving for balance and integration.

Locomotive (planets spread across 240 degrees)

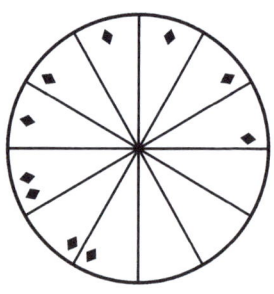

When planets occupy approximately 240 degrees of the chart, leaving a 120-degree gap, it forms a locomotive pattern. This suggests a dynamic and driven individual, propelled by the leading planet (the one just ahead of the empty space) toward goals, with the unoccupied segment representing areas of potential development.

Splash (planets evenly distributed around chart)

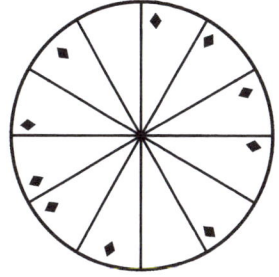

Planets evenly distributed around the chart indicate a versatile and adaptable personality, with diverse interests and the ability to engage with various life areas, though potentially lacking depth in any single focus.

Stellium (three or more planets in close conjunction)

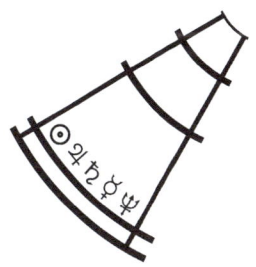

The presence of three or more planets in close conjunction within the same sign or house intensifies the energies of that area, suggesting a strong emphasis and potential for significant development in the related life themes.

Bucket (all planets on one side of the chart with one planet opposite)

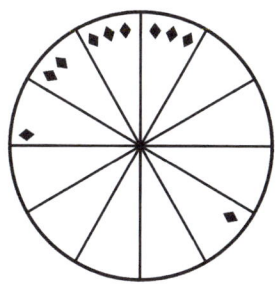

When all planets are gathered in one side of the chart it indicates a focused energy, with the individual seeking fulfillment in the areas of life represented by the occupied houses. There may be a lack of motivation to develop the unoccupied section of the chart.

Applying Aspect

An applying aspect occurs when a faster-moving celestial body, typically a planet, approaches an exact angular relationship with a slower-moving body, resulting in a decreasing angle between them. This phase is often associated with the buildup of energy or events, indicating that the influence of the aspect is intensifying as the planets move closer to exact alignment.

Aspect Tables

Aspect tables, also known as aspect grids, are tools in astrology that display the angular relationships—called aspects—between the planets in a natal chart. These tables provide a clear overview of how planetary energies interact, highlighting harmonious or challenging connections.

In an aspect table, the planets are listed along both the horizontal and vertical axes. The intersecting cells indicate the type of aspect between each pair of planets, often using specific symbols or abbreviations to represent aspects like conjunctions, squares, trines, and oppositions. This format allows astrologers to quickly assess the dynamics within a chart without analyzing each planetary position individually.

Dominants

Dominants are the most influential planets, signs, or elements in an individual's birth chart, shaping key aspects of their personality and life experiences. Identifying these dominants involves analyzing various factors, including planetary positions, aspects, house placements, and their relationships to the Sun, Moon, ascendant, and midheaven.

Dominant Planet

A dominant planet exerts significant influence over an individual's character and behavior. Determining one's dominant planet involves assessing:

Rulership: The planet ruling the ascendant (rising sign) often holds substantial sway.

Aspects: Planets forming multiple or significant aspects to others in the chart can dominate.

House Placement: Planets positioned in angular houses

The Encyclopedia of Astrology

(first, fourth, seventh, tenth) are typically more prominent.
Stelliums: A concentration of planets in a single sign or house can indicate dominance.

Dominant Signs and Elements

A dominant sign or element (fire, earth, air, water) can shape one's temperament and behaviors. This dominance is evaluated by:
Planetary Distribution: The sign or element housing the majority of planets.
Ascendant Sign: The rising sign's element contributes to overall personality traits.
Sun and Moon Signs: The elements of these luminaries add to the elemental balance.

For instance, a chart with multiple planets in water signs (Cancer, Scorpio, Pisces) suggests a dominant water element, indicating heightened sensitivity and emotional depth.

Orb

An orb refers to the allowable range of degrees by which an aspect between two planets can deviate from exactness and still be considered effective. For instance, a trine aspect is precisely 120 degrees; however, with an orb of 6 degrees, the aspect remains influential if the planets are between 114 and 126 degrees apart. The size of the orb can vary depending on the specific aspect and the planets involved. Major aspects like conjunctions and oppositions typically permit larger orbs, often up to 8 degrees, while minor aspects may have smaller allowable orbs. Aspects involving the Sun or Moon might allow for slightly wider orbs due to their prominence in the natal chart. The closer the aspect is to exactness, the stronger its influence is considered to be.

Separating Aspect

A separating aspect happens when the faster-moving planet moves away from the exact aspect, increasing the angle between them. This suggests a waning influence, as the energy or events signified by the aspect are diminishing.

The Encyclopedia of Astrology

CENTERS OF LEARNING IN WESTERN ASTROLOGY

Ancient observatories and medieval universities all shaped the development of astrological knowledge, integrating scientific, philosophical, and cultural influences. The list below encompasses some of the most significant centers of learning that influenced Western astrology.

American Federation of Astrologers (Founded in 1938)

Location: Tempe, Arizona, United States

Pioneered systematic correspondence courses and certification programs that standardized astrological education in the United States.

Astrological Association (Established in 1958)

Location: London, United Kingdom

Promotes the study and practice of astrology through conferences, publications, and research, serving as a central hub for astrologers worldwide.

Centre for Psychological Astrology (Established in 1983)

Location: London, United Kingdom

Integrates Jungian psychology with astrology, focusing on personal growth and self-awareness.

Faculty of Astrological Studies (Founded in 1948)

Location: London, United Kingdom

Educated over 10,000 students from 90 countries, offering comprehensive courses that include history, astronomy, psychology, and various astrological techniques.

House of Wisdom (8th–13th centuries)

Location: Baghdad, Iraq

Translated and preserved Greek astrological texts while developing new techniques that influenced Islamic and European astrology.

International Academy of Astrology (Operating since 1997)

Location: United States (Online)

Offers structured certificate programs through online learning, covering various astrological traditions and techniques.

Kepler College (Founded in 2000)
Location: Washington State, United States
Operated as an accredited institution until 2010 and continues to provide online courses and workshops, emphasizing the historical, philosophical, and cultural contexts of astrology.

Library of Alexandria
(c. 300 BCE–400 CE)
Location: Alexandria, Egypt
Housed early astrological texts, serving as a hub for Hellenistic astrologers who synthesized Babylonian, Egyptian, and Greek traditions, with scholars like Ptolemy creating foundational works.

Taxila University
(c. 600 BCE–500 CE)
Location: Taxila, ancient India (modern-day Pakistan)
Served as a center for Vedic astrological education, integrating astrology with disciplines like medicine and mathematics, and systematizing early astrological knowledge.

University of Bologna
(14th–16th centuries)
Location: Bologna, Italy
Maintained an official chair of astrology, where medical students studied astrology as part of their curriculum, reflecting astrology's peak integration into medieval European education.

KEY TEXTS OF WESTERN ASTROLOGY

Anthology by Vettius Valens
A comprehensive 2nd-century CE work that provides detailed insights into Hellenistic astrology, including numerous chart examples and interpretations.

The Dawn of Astrology by Nicholas Campion
A two-volume series published in 2008 and 2009, exploring the cultural history of Western

astrology from ancient times through the medieval period.

De Astronomica by Marcus Manilius
An early 1st-century poetic work that serves as one of the earliest comprehensive accounts of Roman astrology, detailing celestial phenomena and their interpretations.

The Astrologer's Guide (Anima Astrologiae) by William Lilly and Henry Coley
Published in 1676, this work translates and comments on earlier astrological writings, offering practical guidance for astrologers of the time.

Matheseos Libri VIII by Julius Firmicus Maternus
Written in the 4th century, this extensive treatise covers various aspects of astrology, including natal charts and planetary influences.

The Moment of Astrology by Geoffrey Cornelius
First published in 1994, this book challenges conventional views, proposing a divinatory approach to astrology and emphasizing the role of the astrologer's judgment.

The Real Astrology by John Frawley
Published in 2001, this text critiques modern astrological practices and advocates for a return to traditional techniques.

Tetrabiblos by Claudius Ptolemy
Written in the 2nd century CE, this foundational text systematically presents the principles of astrology, influencing both medieval and modern astrological traditions.

The Twelve Houses by Howard Sasportas
Released in 1985, this book offers an in-depth exploration of the astrological houses and their significance in personal development.

The Encyclopedia of Astrology

You Were Born for This: Astrology for Radical Self-Acceptance and Living Your Purpose by Chani Nicholas
Published in 2020, this book offers a modern approach to astrology, emphasizing self-discovery and empowerment. Nicholas guides readers in understanding their astrological charts to foster self-acceptance and align with their life's purpose.

NOTABLE FIGURES OF WESTERN ASTROLOGY

Western astrology has been shaped by brilliant thinkers across millennia. These notable figures developed the complex system we use today, adapting and innovating over time.

Adams, Evangeline (1868–1932)
Areas of influence: modern astrology, legal recognition, public education

Born in Jersey City, New Jersey, Adams came from a prominent American family and received a traditional education before studying astrology under Dr. Heber Smith. Her early interest in metaphysical subjects was strengthened by accurate predictions she made about a fire at her employer's building.

Adams became America's first prominent astrologer, successfully defending astrology in court in 1914 when charged with fortune-telling, which was illegal at the time. Laws against fortune-telling were passed to protect vulnerable people from being taken advantage of, and astrology was viewed with the same skepticism. Adams's defense included accurately reading the judge's son's horoscope, and the trial helped establish legal precedent for astrology as a skill rather than mere divination. She maintained a practice in Carnegie Hall, advised prominent figures including J.P. Morgan, and pioneered astrology's use in radio broadcasting.

Adams helped legitimize astrology in America and created a model for professional astrological practice. Her radio shows and books brought astrology to mainstream audiences, while her court victory helped establish astrology's legal status.

Major works:
- *The Bowl of Heaven* (1926)
- *Astrology: Your Place in the Sun* (1927)
- *Astrology: Your Place Among the Stars* (1930)

Bonatti, Guido (*c.* 1210–1296)
Areas of influence: medieval astrology, horary astrology, political astrology

Born in Cascia, Italy, Bonatti studied at the University of Bologna and became the leading astrologer of his time. He served as court astrologer to Emperor Frederick II and other Italian nobles, combining practical experience with scholarly expertise.

His comprehensive work *Liber Astronomiae* synthesized Arabic, Greek, and Latin sources while adding his own insights from extensive practical experience. He developed sophisticated techniques for horary astrology (a practice used to answer specific questions by analyzing the celestial positions at the moment a question is asked) and electional astrology (the practice of selecting optimal moments to initiate activities by analyzing celestial patterns), particularly for military and political applications.

Bonatti's work became a standard reference for medieval and Renaissance astrologers. His practical approach and clear writing style influenced generations of practitioners, and his *146 Considerations* remain valuable guidelines for horary astrology.

Major works:
- *Liber Astronomiae (Ten Treatises of Astronomy)*
- *146 Considerations*

Copernicus, Nicolaus (1473–1543)
Areas of influence: astronomical theory, mathematical calculations

Born in Royal Prussia (in what is now Poland), Copernicus studied

The Encyclopedia of Astrology

at the University of Kraków and later in Italy, focusing on mathematics, astronomy, and church law. His education included exposure to both astronomical calculations and astrological techniques, though he would later focus primarily on astronomical theory.

While Copernicus is best known for his heliocentric theory, proposing that the Sun, not the Earth, is at the center of the universe, his work significantly impacted astrological practice by challenging traditional geocentric calculations. Though not primarily an astrologer, his mathematical models for planetary motion eventually led to more accurate astronomical calculations that astrologers could use for chart creation.

His work initiated a revolutionary shift in understanding celestial mechanics, eventually leading to improved accuracy in astronomical calculations for astrological practice. The Copernican revolution forced astrologers to reconsider how astrological influences operate, contributing to the modernization of astrological theory.

Major works:
- *De revolutionibus orbium coelestium (On the Revolutions of the Celestial Spheres)*
- *Commentariolus* (brief overview of his heliocentric theory)

Dee, John (1527–1608)
Areas of influence: court astrology, natural philosophy, hermetic studies

Born in London to a merchant family, Dee studied at Cambridge and across Europe, developing expertise in mathematics, navigation, and astrology. His extensive library at Mortlake became one of the largest in England, containing numerous astrological and astronomical texts.

As Queen Elizabeth I's court astrologer, Dee selected her coronation date and provided astrological advice throughout her reign. He combined traditional astrology with alchemical studies and mathematical innovation, viewing these as interconnected paths to divine wisdom. His astrological work included casting horoscopes, predicting weather patterns, and advising on matters of state.

Despite later falling from royal favor under James I, Dee's influence helped establish English astrology's scholarly reputation. His detailed diaries and papers provide valuable insight into how Renaissance court astrologers combined practical observation with esoteric philosophy, setting precedents for both mathematical and spiritual approaches to astrological practice.

Major works:
- *Propaedeumata Aphoristica*
- *Monas Hieroglyphica (The Hieroglyphic Monad)*
- *General and Rare Memorials (Pertayning to the Perfect Arte of Navigation)*

Green, Jeffrey Wolf (1946–2019)
Areas of influence: evolutionary astrology, Pluto dynamics, soul purpose

Born in Hollywood, California, Green's spiritual journey began in the late 1960s. After studying with various metaphysical teachers, he went through an awakening experience that he claimed gave him direct understanding of the evolutionary journey of souls and their relationship to astrological patterns.

Green developed evolutionary astrology (a paradigm that uses the position of Pluto and its aspects to understand the soul's previous incarnations and current evolutionary intentions). His work focused on understanding karmic patterns and evolutionary lessons through the birth chart, emphasizing free will and conscious evolution rather than deterministic interpretation. He founded the School of Evolutionary Astrology in 1994 and trained thousands of students worldwide.

Green's innovations in evolutionary astrology revolutionized how many astrologers approach chart interpretation, providing a sophisticated structure for understanding soul purpose and karmic patterns. His emphasis on Pluto's significance and the nodal axis created new methods for understanding psychological and spiritual development through astrology. The School of Evolutionary Astrology continues his work through certified teachers worldwide.

Major works:
- *Pluto: The Evolutionary Journey of the Soul, Volume 1*
- *Pluto: The Soul's Evolution through Relationships, Volume 2*
- *Measuring the Night: Evolutionary Astrology and the Keys to the Soul* (with Steven Forrest, 2000)

Jung, Carl Gustav (1875–1961)

Areas of influence: psychological astrology, archetypal theory, synchronicity

Born in Kesswil, Switzerland, Jung studied medicine at the University of Basel and became a psychiatrist. His early professional years working with Sigmund Freud and studying mythology led to his development of analytical psychology, which eventually intersected with his interest in astrology.

Though not primarily an astrologer, Jung's work with astrological symbolism and his concept of synchronicity profoundly influenced modern psychological astrology. He conducted statistical studies of astrological correlations in marriage partners and developed theories about the collective unconscious that helped explain astrological archetypes.

Jung's integration of psychological concepts with astrological symbolism created the foundation for modern psychological astrology. His ideas about archetypes and the collective unconscious continue to influence how astrologers understand planetary meanings and chart interpretation.

Major works:
- *Synchronicity: An Acausal Connecting Principle*
- Letters and papers on astrological correlations

The Encyclopedia of Astrology

- Various works incorporating astrological symbolism

Kepler, Johannes (1571–1630)
Areas of influence: mathematical astrology, astronomical calculations, aspect theory

Born in Weil der Stadt, Germany, Kepler studied theology at the University of Tübingen before becoming a mathematics teacher. His role as imperial mathematician to Rudolf II allowed him to combine astronomical research with astrological practice.

While famous for his laws of planetary motion, Kepler also practiced astrology professionally, creating horoscopes for nobles and writing astrological almanacs. He attempted to reform astrology on mathematical principles, developing new theories about planetary aspects based on musical harmony and geometric ratios.

Kepler's mathematical precision improved astronomical calculations for astrological use, while his aspect theories influenced modern understanding of planetary relationships. His critical yet constructive approach to astrology helped bridge the growing divide between astronomy and astrology.

Major works:
- *De Fundamentis Astrologiae Certioribus (Concerning the More Certain Fundamentals of Astrology)*
- *Harmonices Mundi (The Harmony of the World)*
- Various astronomical-astrological almanacs

Koch, Walter (1895–1970)
Areas of influence: house systems, mathematical astrology

Born in Esslingen, Germany, Koch worked as a statistician and developed an interest in astrology through his mathematical work. His background in statistical analysis and engineering led him to approach astrological problems with mathematical precision.

In the 1960s, Koch developed his eponymous house system, which attempted to correct perceived problems with the Placidus system, particularly at extreme latitudes. He conducted extensive research on astronomical calculations and their applications to horoscope construction.

The Koch house system became widely used and remains one of the major house systems in modern astrology. His mathematical approach to astrological problems influenced the development of more precise calculation methods.

Major works:
- *The Houses of the Sun*
- Various technical papers on house division
- Astronomical-astrological calculation tables

Leo, Alan (1860–1917)
Areas of influence: modern astrology, popular education, theosophical integration

Born William Frederick Allan, in London, Leo worked as a clerk before discovering astrology through his involvement with the Theosophical Society, a school of astrological learning. He was largely self-taught in astrology, combining his studies with theosophical principles and modern psychology.

Leo revolutionized astrology by making it more accessible to the general public and shifting focus from prediction to character analysis. He founded *Modern Astrology* magazine in 1895 and established the first astrological school in modern Britain. His approach emphasized spiritual development and psychological understanding rather than fortune-telling.

Considered the father of modern astrology, Leo's psychological and character-based approach transformed astrological practice. His educational materials and organizational efforts helped establish astrology as a modern profession.

Major works:
- *Esoteric Astrology*
- *Astrology for All*
- *How to Judge a Nativity*

Lilly, William (1602–1681)
Areas of influence: horary astrology, political astrology, education

Born in Leicestershire, England to a farming family, Lilly received a classical education before apprenticing to an illiterate merchant who introduced him to astrology. He studied extensively under established astrologers and through classical texts.

As England's most prominent astrologer during the Civil War period, Lilly served both Parliamentarian and Royalist clients. His masterwork, *Christian Astrology*, was the first comprehensive astrological textbook in English, establishing systematic methods for horary and election practice.

Lilly's detailed case studies and systematic approach to horary astrology continue to influence modern practice. His *Christian Astrology* remains a foundational text for traditional astrology students.

Major works:
- *Christian Astrology*
- *Monarchy or No Monarchy in England*
- Various annual almanacs

Mirandola, Pico della (1463–1494)
Areas of influence: astrological critique, renaissance philosophy, hermetic studies

Born to Italian nobility in Mirandola, Pico received a comprehensive humanist education, studying at multiple universities and mastering Latin, Greek, Hebrew, and Arabic. His exceptional learning and wealth allowed him access to a vast range of classical and medieval astrological texts.

Though initially fascinated by astrology, Pico became one of its most influential critics, writing *Disputations Against Divinatory Astrology*. His critique focused on the logical and theological problems of deterministic astrology while maintaining interest in natural astrology (the study of celestial influences on the physical world). Despite his criticism,

The Encyclopedia of Astrology

his work helped establish a more rigorous theoretical framework for astrological practice by forcing practitioners to defend and refine their methods.

His complex relationship with astrology exemplified Renaissance intellectual tensions between classical learning, Christian theology, and empirical observation. While rejecting judicial astrology, his work preserved substantial astrological knowledge and contributed to the development of more sophisticated astrological theory during the Renaissance.

Major works:
- *Disputations Against Divinatory Astrology*
- *Oration on the Dignity of Man*
- *900 Theses* (includes astrological propositions)

Morin de Villefranche, Jean-Baptiste (1583–1656)
Areas of influence: natal astrology, determination theory

Born in Villefranche, France, Morin received a medical degree from the University of Avignon and served as an astrologer and court physician. His background in medicine and mathematics informed his systematic approach to astrology.

Morin developed a comprehensive system of natal astrology, emphasizing the importance of house determination and planetary strength. His theory of determination proposed that specific factors in a birth chart could indicate definite outcomes rather than just general tendencies.

Morin's systematic approach to natal astrology influenced modern technical astrology, particularly in France and America. His methods for determining planetary strength and house significance continue to inform traditional practice.

Major works:
- *Astrologia Gallica* (26 books)
- Various astrological and astronomical treatises

The Encyclopedia of Astrology

Nostradamus, Michel de (1503–1566)
Areas of influence: astrological prophecy, court astrology, medical astrology

Born Michel de Nostredame in Saint-Rémy-de-Provence, France, he studied medicine at the University of Montpellier and gained fame treating plague victims. His medical practice incorporated astrological timing for treatments, following the standard medical theories of his time.

As court astrologer to Catherine de Medici, he cast horoscopes for the royal children and advised on matters of state. His most famous work, *Les Prophéties*, combined astrological timing with prophetic verses inspired by celestial influences. He combined interpretations of his visions with his studies of planetary cycles to make predictions for the future.

His influence extended far beyond his lifetime, creating a model for combining astrological timing with prophetic vision. While controversial even in his own time, his work at the French court helped maintain astrology's prestige during a period when traditional practices were increasingly under scrutiny from both religious and scientific authorities.

Major works:
- *Les Prophéties*
- *Traité des Fardements et des Confitures* (medical-astrological text)

Rudhyar, Dane (1895–1985)
Areas of influence: humanistic astrology, psychological astrology

Born Daniel Chennevière, in Paris, Rudhyar was a composer and philosopher before becoming an astrologer. His broad education in Eastern and Western philosophy, psychology, and music informed his holistic approach to astrology.

Rudhyar revolutionized modern astrology by integrating it with humanistic psychology and Eastern philosophy. He reframed traditional astrological concepts

The Encyclopedia of Astrology

in psychological terms, emphasizing personal growth and transformation rather than prediction. His studies of the moon's cycles particularly influenced modern astronomical understanding.

Rudhyar's humanistic approach transformed modern astrological practice, introducing psychological and spiritual dimensions that continue to influence contemporary astrology.

Major works:
- *The Astrology of Personality*
- *The Lunation Cycle*
- *Person-Centered Astrology*

Tompkins, Sue (born 1951)
Areas of influence: modern astrology, education

Tompkins is a British astrologer and homeopath known for her contributions to modern astrology and education. After earning a degree in psychology and training in counseling, she obtained her diploma from the Faculty of Astrological Studies (FAS) in 1981. She served as FAS's Director of Schools from 1986 to 2000, receiving a fellowship in recognition of her work.

In 2000, Tompkins co-founded the London School of Astrology (LSA). She has lectured extensively across Europe, North America, Asia, and Australasia. In 2003, she received the Charles Harvey Award for exceptional service to astrology. Tompkins is the author of *Aspects in Astrology* and *The Contemporary Astrologer's Handbook*, both considered seminal works in the field. Beyond astrology, she is a registered homeopath practicing in London.

Major works:
- *Aspects in Astrology: A Guide to Understanding Planetary Relationships in the Horoscope*
- *The Contemporary Astrologer's Handbook*

ASTROLOGY AROUND THE WORLD

Astrology Around the World

The movement of the planets and celestial bodies has mesmerized and inspired people throughout history and all over the world, and even today most cultures embrace some sort of astrological wisdom and knowledge.

From the Mesopotamian astrology of the Sumerians and Babylonians to the sophisticated zodiac systems of China and India, astrology has been intertwined with the cosmological beliefs and cultural identities of societies, influencing philosophy, religion, and the sciences.

The diffusion and evolution of astrological concepts, such as the development of horoscopic astrology during the Hellenistic period and the unique astrological techniques that emerged in Egypt, Greece, Rome, and Tibet, have created a rich tapestry of astrological traditions and insights into the universal human fascination with the mysteries of the cosmos and our place within it.

While not exhaustive, the concepts and regions listed below illustrate the wide range of cultures inspired by astrology throughout history.

CHINESE ASTROLOGY

Introduction and History

The roots of Chinese astrology can be traced over 5,000 years to the Shang Dynasty (1600–1046 BCE), when early celestial observations were etched onto oracle bones. Over centuries, it evolved from basic divination practices into a refined system. This transformation reached a pivotal moment during the Han Dynasty (206 BCE–220 CE), as scholars formalized the connection between celestial events and human experiences. They estab-

The Encyclopedia of Astrology

lished the foundational principles of Chinese astrology: the 12 animal signs, five elements, and the intricate system of heavenly stems and earthly branches.

Deeply intertwined with Taoist philosophy, Chinese astrology emphasizes harmony among heaven, Earth, and humanity. The role of the Imperial Astronomer became one of the most prestigious positions in the Chinese court, offering emperors guidance through celestial analysis on vital matters like agriculture and warfare.

Chinese astrology extends its influence into various aspects of life, including traditional medicine, where a person's birth chart may influence the diagnosis of ailments and the formulation of personalized treatments. This holistic approach integrates astrological insights into healthcare, tailoring treatments to individual needs. It is also commonly used to assess compatibility in marriage and business relationships. By analyzing birth dates and zodiac signs, astrologers provide guidance on the potential harmony and success of such connections. Astrology may also be used to select auspicious dates for significant events, such as weddings, business openings, or travel. Astrologers align these events with favorable celestial patterns to promote success and balance.

As this intricate system spread across East Asia, it was embraced and adapted by Korean, Japanese, and Vietnamese cultures, each incorporating unique interpretations while preserving the core principles. Today, Chinese astrology remains a vibrant tradition, offering individuals guidance in career decisions, relationships, health, and other aspects of life. By using the Chinese zodiac and the Five Elements theory, people gain insights to navigate life's complexities and understand their destiny.

Innovations and Unique Practices
The 12 Animal Signs

Each of the 12 animals in the Chinese zodiac embodies specific traits, energies, and characteristics

The Encyclopedia of Astrology

that influence those born in their corresponding years.

The 12 animal signs emerged from an ancient story in which the Jade Emperor summoned all animals to a great race to cross the celestial river to reach the Emperor's throne—the order in which they finished determined their place in the zodiac cycle.

The Chinese lunar calendar determines these animal years, with each new year beginning on the second new moon after the winter solstice, typically falling between late January and mid-February. Unlike Western zodiac signs which change monthly, Chinese animal signs govern entire years and work in tandem with the Five Elements and yin-yang polarities to create a complex system of personality and fate calculation.

The complete zodiac cycle is called Shēngxiào (生肖) in Mandarin Chinese, which translates to "birth likeness" or "birth resemblance."

Animal Sign	Birth Years	Element and Nature
Rat	1912, 1924, 1936, 1948, 1960, 1972, 1984, 1996, 2008, 2020	Water, Yang
Ox	1913, 1925, 1937, 1949, 1961, 1973, 1985, 1997, 2009, 2021	Earth, Yin
Tiger	1914, 1926, 1938, 1950, 1962, 1974, 1986, 1998, 2010, 2022	Wood, Yang
Rabbit	1915, 1927, 1939, 1951, 1963, 1975, 1987, 1999, 2011, 2023	Wood, Yin
Dragon	1916, 1928, 1940, 1952, 1964, 1976, 1988, 2000, 2012, 2024	Earth, Yang
Snake	1917, 1929, 1941, 1953, 1965, 1977, 1989, 2001, 2013, 2025	Fire, Yin
Horse	1918, 1930, 1942, 1954, 1966, 1978, 1990, 2002, 2014, 2026	Fire, Yang
Goat	1919, 1931, 1943, 1955, 1967, 1979, 1991, 2003, 2015, 2027	Earth, Yin
Monkey	1920, 1932, 1944, 1956, 1968, 1980, 1992, 2004, 2016, 2028	Metal, Yang
Rooster	1921, 1933, 1945, 1957, 1969, 1981, 1993, 2005, 2017, 2029	Metal, Yin
Dog	1922, 1934, 1946, 1958, 1970, 1982, 1994, 2006, 2018, 2030	Earth, Yang
Pig	1923, 1935, 1947, 1959, 1971, 1983, 1995, 2007, 2019, 2031	Water, Yin

The Encyclopedia of Astrology

Rat *Shǔ* (鼠)

Personality Traits
Quick-witted, resourceful, adaptable, sharp

Lucky Elements
+ Numbers: 2, 3
+ Colors: Blue, Gold
+ Directions: North, Southeast

Unlucky Elements
- Numbers: 5, 9
- Colors: Yellow, Brown
- Direction: South

Ox *Niú* (牛)

Personality Traits
Patient, kind, stubborn, conservative

Lucky Elements
+ Numbers: 1, 4
+ Colors: White, Yellow
+ Direction: North, South

Unlucky Elements
- Numbers: 6, 7
- Colors: Blue, Red
- Direction: West

Tiger *Hǔ* (虎)

Personality Traits
Brave, confident, competitive, unpredictable

Lucky Elements
+ Numbers: 1, 3, 4
+ Colors: Blue, Gray
+ Direction: East

Unlucky Elements
- Numbers: 6, 8
- Colors: Brown
- Direction: Southwest

Rabbit *Tù* (兔)

Personality Traits
Gentle, elegant, alert, conservative

Lucky Elements
+ Numbers: 3, 4, 6
+ Colors: Red, Pink
+ Direction: East

Unlucky Elements
- Numbers: 1, 7
- Colors: Brown
- Direction: North

The Encyclopedia of Astrology

Dragon *Lóng* (龙)

Personality Traits
Confident, intelligent, enthusiastic, perfectionist

Lucky Elements
+ Numbers: 1, 6, 7
+ Colors: Gold, Silver
+ Direction: Southeast

Unlucky Elements
- Numbers: 3, 8
- Colors: Red
- Direction: Northwest

Horse *Mǎ* (马)

Personality Traits
Energetic, independent, impatient, adventurous

Lucky Elements
+ Numbers: 2, 3, 7
+ Colors: Green
+ Direction: South

Unlucky Elements
- Numbers: 1, 5
- Colors: Blue
- Direction: North

Snake *Shé* (蛇)

Personality Traits
Wise, enigmatic, graceful, materialistic

Lucky Elements
+ Numbers: 2, 8, 9
+ Colors: Red, Black
+ Direction: Southwest

Unlucky Elements
- Numbers: 1, 6
- Colors: Yellow
- Direction: Northeast

Goat *Yáng* (羊)

Personality Traits
Creative, gentle, shy, kind-hearted

Lucky Elements
+ Numbers: 2, 7
+ Colors: Brown, Red
+ Direction: Southwest

Unlucky Elements
- Numbers: 4, 9
- Colors: Blue
- Direction: Northeast

The Encyclopedia of Astrology

Monkey *Hóu* (猴)

Personality Traits
Clever, innovative, opportunistic, versatile

Lucky Elements
+ Numbers: 4, 9
+ Colors: White, Gold
+ Direction: Northwest

Unlucky Elements
- Numbers: 2, 5
- Colors: Red
- Direction: Southeast

Dog *Gǒu* (狗)

Personality Traits
Loyal, honest, responsible, anxious

Lucky Elements
+ Numbers: 3, 4, 9
+ Colors: Red, Green
+ Direction: Northwest

Unlucky Elements
- Numbers: 1, 7
- Colors: Blue
- Direction: Southeast

Rooster *Jī* (鸡)

Personality Traits
Observant, hardworking, courageous, proud

Lucky Elements
+ Numbers: 5, 7, 8
+ Colors: Gold, Brown
+ Direction: West

Unlucky Elements
- Numbers: 1, 3
- Colors: Red
- Direction: North

Pig *Zhū* (猪)

Personality Traits
Compassionate, generous, diligent, naive

Lucky Elements
+ Numbers: 2, 5, 8
+ Colors: Yellow, Gray
+ Direction: Northeast

Unlucky Elements
- Numbers: 1, 7
- Colors: Red
- Direction: South

The Encyclopedia of Astrology

Animal Sign Compatibility

Animal sign compatibility helps determine relationship dynamics, whether for business partnerships, friendships, or romantic connections.

Compatibility follows several patterns based on the four trines, or groups of three signs that share deep harmony.

The Four Trines

- First Trine: Rat, Dragon, Monkey (wisdom).
- Second Trine: Ox, Snake, Rooster (practicality).
- Third Trine: Tiger, Horse, Dog (passion).
- Fourth Trine: Rabbit, Goat, Pig (peace).

Secret Friends and Allies

- Rat and Ox support each other's goals.
- Tiger finds understanding with Pig.
- Rabbit and Dog share deep loyalty.
- Dragon and Rooster bring mutual success.
- Snake and Monkey spark creativity.
- Horse and Goat create harmony.

Conflicting Pairs

- Rat and Horse may struggle with communication.
- Ox and Goat often have opposing viewpoints.
- Tiger and Monkey approach life differently.
- Rabbit and Rooster can create tension.
- Dragon and Dog may compete for control.
- Snake and Pig have differing values.

The Five Elements add another layer to compatibility, as they can strengthen or weaken relationships between signs. For example, a Wood Dragon might find particular harmony with a Fire Snake, while potentially experiencing challenges with a Metal Tiger.

The Five Elements

The Five Elements (*Wu Xing*) form a dynamic system of relationships that governs the entire natural world, including human behavior. Rather than static elements, they represent transformative phases or energetic states—wood feeds fire, fire creates earth, earth bears metal, metal collects water, and water nourishes wood. Each element carries specific qualities, directions, seasons, colors, and spiritual resonances that influence both cosmic and earthly affairs.

Each element rules for two consecutive years before transitioning to the next. Birth years ending in 0 or 1 are metal years, 2 or 3 are water years, 4 or 5 are wood years, 6 or 7 are fire years, and 8 or 9 are earth years. For example, someone born in 1950 would be a Metal Tiger, while someone born in 1962 would be a Water Tiger.

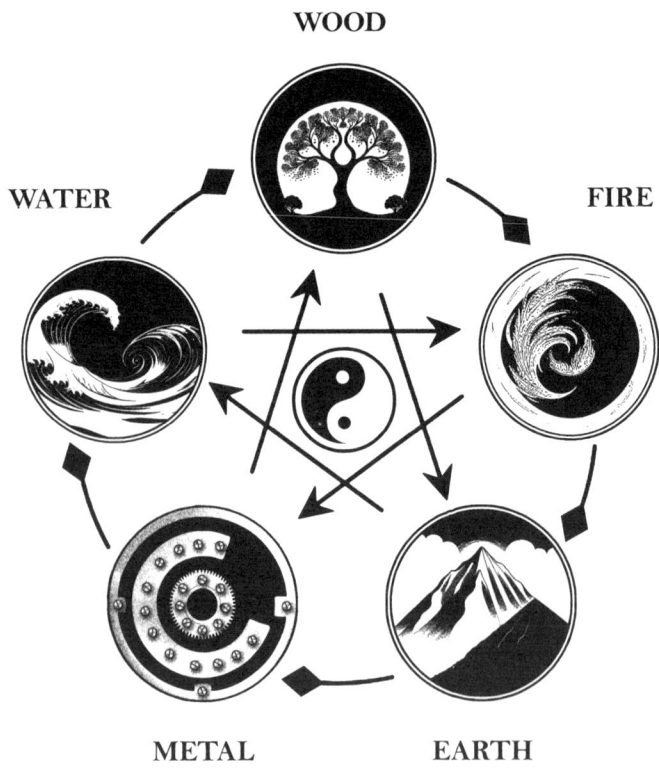

The Encyclopedia of Astrology

Wood *(Mù)*

- Direction: East
- Season: Spring
- Color: Green
- Nature: Growth, flexibility, expansion
- Personality: Idealistic, creative, visionary

Earth *(Tǔ)*

- Direction: Center
- Season: Late Summer
- Color: Yellow
- Nature: Stability, nourishment, grounding
- Personality: Practical, reliable, nurturing

Fire *(Huǒ)*

- Direction: South
- Season: Summer
- Color: Red
- Nature: Transformation, dynamism, passion
- Personality: Energetic, charismatic, adventurous

Metal *(Jīn)*

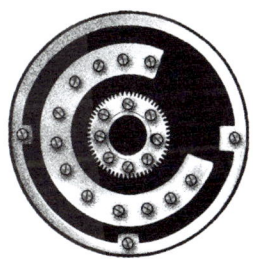

- Direction: West
- Season: Autumn
- Color: White
- Nature: Refinement, clarity, precision
- Personality: Disciplined, organized, analytical

The Encyclopedia of Astrology

Water *(Shuǐ)*

- Direction: North
- Season: Winter
- Color: Black/Blue
- Nature: Fluidity, adaptability, depth
- Personality: Intuitive, philosophical, introspective

The Five Elements interact through two primary cycles: the Generating Cycle (*Shēng*) where each element creates the next, and the Weakening Cycle (*Kè*) where each element controls another. These relationships form the foundation for understanding harmony and conflict in Chinese astrology, influencing everything from personality traits to relationship compatibility.

Additional Dynamics of the Five Elements:

Generating Cycle (*Shēng*): Like a mother nurturing her child, each element naturally produces and supports the next—water nourishes wood, wood feeds fire, fire creates earth through ash, earth bears metal in its ores, and metal collects and holds water.

Weakening Cycle (*Kè*): Each element acts as a check on another, creating necessary tension and balance—metal chops wood, wood breaks up earth, earth dams water, water extinguishes fire, and fire melts metal.

Regulating Cycle: These generative and controlling relationships work together to maintain cosmic harmony, preventing any single element from becoming too dominant while ensuring continuous transformation and renewal.

Seasonal Transitions: The Five Elements mark the progression of natural cycles, with wood representing spring's growth, fire embodying sum-

The Encyclopedia of Astrology

Element	Generates (*Shēng*)	Weakens (*Kè*)	Is Generated By	Is Weakened By
Wood	Fire (feeds flame)	Earth (breaks up soil)	Water (nourishes)	Metal (chops)
Fire	Earth (creates ash)	Metal (melts)	Wood (fuels)	Water (extinguishes)
Earth	Metal (bears ores)	Water (dams/absorbs)	Fire (creates)	Wood (breaks up)
Metal	Water (holds/carries)	Wood (splits)	Earth (produces)	Fire (melts)
Water	Wood (nourishes)	Fire (extinguishes)	Metal (contains)	Earth (dams)

mer's heat, earth ruling late summer's abundance, metal governing autumn's contraction, and water holding winter's stillness.

Healing Applications: Traditional Chinese medicine uses the Five Elements to diagnose imbalances and prescribe treatments, understanding that each element corresponds to specific organs, emotions, and physical symptoms that can be harmonized through herbs, acupuncture, and dietary adjustments.

Destiny Calculations (Four Pillars of Destiny): A person's birth elements, derived from their year, month, day, and hour of birth, reveal inherent strengths and challenges in their character while suggesting favorable directions for life decisions and relationships.

The 28 Lunar Mansions (*Xiu*)

The 28 Lunar Mansions represent equal divisions of the Moon's monthly journey through the zodiac, with each mansion marking approximately one day of the lunar cycle. Each mansion possesses unique characteristics and influences based on the fixed stars it contains and its position relative to the constellations.

Historically, the 28 Lunar Mansions were integral to various aspects of Chinese culture, including astrology, calendrical systems, and feng shui. They were used to select auspicious dates, guide agricultural activities, and make decisions about timing. The system offers a more nuanced approach to lunar cycles than the broader zodiac signs, providing 28 distinct qualities of lunar energy rather than just 12 monthly positions.

Heavenly Stems and Earthly Branches

The heavenly stems and earthly branches are a fundamental part of Chinese astrology.

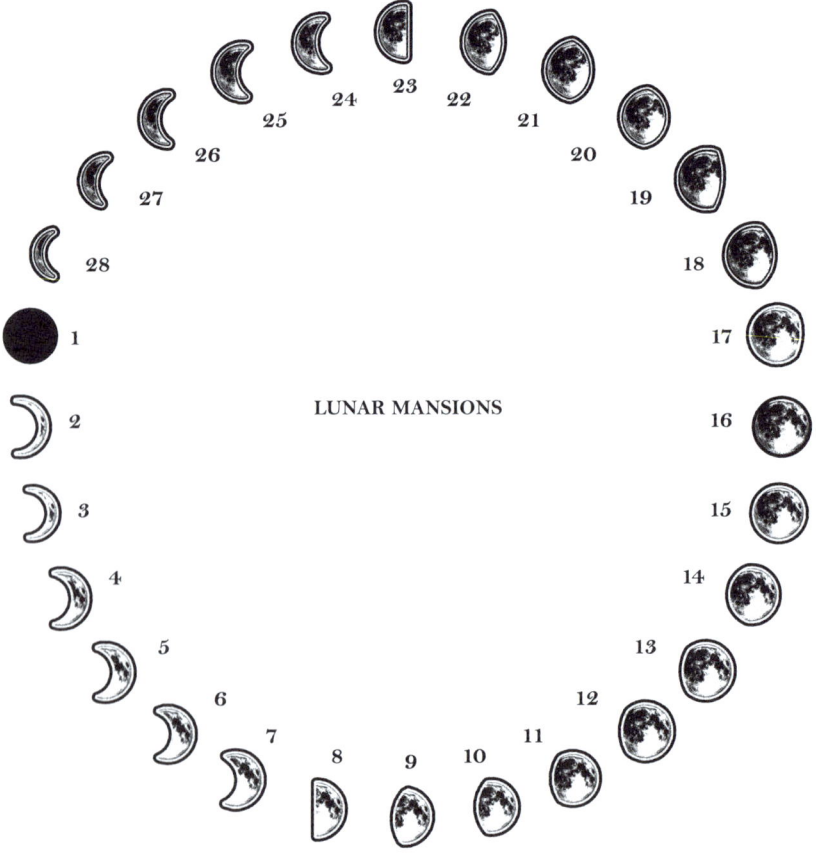

LUNAR MANSIONS

The ten heavenly stems are associated with the Five Elements and represent the cycle of yin and yang.

Jia – yang wood
Yi – yin wood
Bing – yang fire
Ding – yin fire
Wu – yang earth
Ji – yin earth
Geng – yang metal
Xin – yin metal
Ren – yang water
Gui – yin water

The earthly branches correspond to the 12-year cycle of the zodiac and are comprised of the 12 animal signs: Rat, Ox, Tiger, Rabbit, Dragon, Snake, Horse, Goat, Monkey, Rooster, Dog, Pig.

Together, the heavenly stems and earthly branches pair up in cycles to form a 60-year cycle, or sexagenary cycle, that is used to predict and interpret various aspects of an individual's life, including their personality, fortune, and compatibility with others. Each combination of a heavenly stem and an earthly branch is believed to have its own unique characteristics and influence on an individual's destiny.

By understanding the interplay between these two elements, practitioners of Chinese astrology can gain insights into an individual's strengths, weaknesses, and the potential challenges they may face throughout their life.

Four Pillars System (*Ba Zi*):

The Four Pillars system, also known as Ba Zi, is a comprehensive system of Chinese astrology that analyzes an individual's life and destiny based on the alignment of the four pillars: year, month, day, and hour of birth. Each of these pillars is represented by a combination of a

The Encyclopedia of Astrology

heavenly stem and an earthly branch, which together form a unique astrological profile for the individual.

The Four Pillars system provides a deep and detailed understanding of an individual's personality, strengths, weaknesses, and life path. By examining the interactions and balances between the elements within the four pillars, practitioners of Ba Zi can offer insights into an individual's health, relationships, career, and overall well-being. This system is widely used in Chinese culture to guide important life decisions and to help individuals navigate the challenges and opportunities that arise throughout their lives.

The Hour Pillar assigns one of the twelve zodiac animals to two-hour periods throughout the day, called the "Chinese hours" or *shi chen*. The hour of birth is considered significant in shaping a person's destiny and personality traits. For example, those born during Rat hours (11:00 p.m. to 1:00 a.m.) are believed to be resourceful and quick-witted, while Dragon hours (7:00 a.m. to 9:00 a.m.) bestow leadership qualities and vitality.

Rat (子): 11:00 p.m.–1:00 a.m.
Ox (丑): 1:00 a.m.–3:00 a.m.
Tiger (寅): 3:00 a.m.–5:00 a.m.
Rabbit (卯): 5:00 a.m.–7:00 a.m.
Dragon (辰): 7:00 a.m.–9:00 a.m.
Snake (巳): 9:00 a.m.–11:00 a.m.
Horse (午): 11:00 a.m.–1:00 p.m.
Goat (未): 1:00 p.m.–3:00 p.m.
Monkey (申): 3:00 p.m.–5:00 p.m.
Rooster (酉): 5:00 p.m.–7:00 p.m.
Dog (戌): 7:00 p.m.–9:00 p.m.
Pig (亥): 9:00 p.m.–11:00 p.m.

Eight Mansions System (*Ba Zhai*):

The Eight Mansions (*Ba Zhai*) system divides space into eight directional sectors, each associated with specific life aspects and elemental energies based on a person's birth year. These eight sectors are determined by calculating a person's Ming Gua number using their birth year, resulting in either an east or west orientation that influences their favorable and unfavorable directions.

The system provides guidance about optimal directions for activities like sleeping, working, or placing important furniture, with each person's favorable directions believed to enhance specific life aspects like health, relationships, or prosperity. People with an east orientation, for example, might be advised to face east while working to boost career success, while those with a west orientation might be encouraged to place their bed facing northwest for better sleep and health.

Life's Rise and Fall Chart (*Ming Gong*)

A Life's Rise and Fall Chart, also known as a Ming Gong chart, is a tool used in Chinese astrology to understand an individual's life journey and potential. The chart maps the peaks and valleys of a person's potential life journey through the Chinese zodiac signs.

It divides life into 12 phases, each influenced by a specific animal sign's energy and characteristics. This traditional forecasting tool examines how these energies affect career, relationships, health, and spiritual development during different life periods.

To create a Life's Rise and Fall Chart, an astrologer needs the person's birth date, time, and location. This information is used to determine the individual's birth zodiac sign and the placement of the other zodiac signs in the chart.

Rather than predicting fixed outcomes, the Ming Gong chart reveals natural cycles of opportunity and challenge. The 12 phases build upon each other progressively, with earlier phases laying groundwork for later developments. Each stage has its own focus—early phases often deal with education and foundation-building, middle phases with career and relationships, and later phases with wisdom and spiritual matters.

Nine Star Ki

Nine Star Ki combines elements of Chinese astronomy and numerology, assigning each person one of nine numbers based on their birth year, with each number corresponding to a direction, element, and color. The system derives from the magic square of three (*Lo Shu*) and the movement patterns of the Big Dipper constellation, where each number represents different energetic qualities—for instance, 1 represents water and wisdom, while 9 symbolizes fire and illumination.

The nine stars (Ki) move in yearly cycles, creating a predictive system that helps determine favorable directions, career paths, and relationship dynamics. Each number's position shifts annually in a specific pattern, believed to influence both personal fortunes and global events according to traditional Chinese cosmology.

Purple Star Astrology (*Zi Wei Dou Shu*)

Purple Star Astrology originated in China during the Tang Dynasty as Zi Wei Dou Shu, combining elements of traditional Chinese astrology with the Emperor's privileged astronomical knowledge previously reserved for royal divination. The system relies on birth hour calculations to identify a person's "Purple Star," representing their core destiny, along with auxiliary stars that influence different aspects of life.

This method is distinct from both Western astrology and traditional Chinese zodiac systems, using complex mathematical formulas to plot positions in a chart divided into 12 palaces that correspond to different life areas. Each palace contains varying numbers of stars—both beneficial and challenging—whose positions and relationships create a detailed narrative of an individual's life path.

The name "Purple Star" refers to the North Star (Polaris) and its surrounding stars, which

ancient Chinese astronomers called the Purple Forbidden Enclosure because of its imperial associations. This celestial pattern was considered particularly significant as it appeared motionless while other stars rotated around it, symbolizing the Emperor's fixed position at the center of earthly affairs.

The system evaluates the influence of up to 109 stars, with the main Purple Star being the most significant, similar to how the Sun functions in Western natal astrology. The interpretation focuses heavily on timing, with each palace activated during specific periods of life, allowing practitioners to forecast favorable and challenging times for various activities.

Yin-Yang Polarity
The concept of yin and yang represents the fundamental duality that exists in all things. yin embodies the feminine, receptive, dark, and cool qualities, while yang represents the masculine, active, light, and warm aspects—neither force is superior, and both are necessary for wholeness. This polarity concept extends beyond just gender and is applied to things like day/night, hot/cold, activity/rest, etc.

In Chinese astrology, this polarity appears in multiple layers: each animal sign is either yin or yang, with signs alternating in the zodiac cycle; each element expresses both yin and yang qualities; and even hours of the day are divided into yin and yang periods. This interplay helps determine personality traits, relationship dynamics, and the most auspicious timing for important activities.

Chinese Festivals that Celebrate the Zodiac
Spring Festival (Lunar New Year, late January to early February)
The Spring Festival celebrates the lunar new year and the

The Encyclopedia of Astrology

transition to a new zodiac animal, bringing unique customs and decorations specific to the incoming sign. Red paper cuttings, lanterns, and other ornaments feature the year's animal, while traditional foods are carefully chosen and prepared to honor its qualities. Some dishes might be specifically avoided during celebrations if they're considered unlucky for that particular zodiac animal, as the festival emphasizes harmony with the new year's celestial energies.

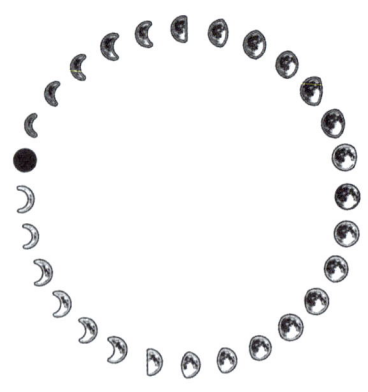

Lantern Festival (15th Day of First Lunar Month)

The Lantern Festival (*Yuánxiāo Jié*) marks the final day of traditional lunar new year celebrations on the 15th day of the first lunar month. Colorful lanterns adorned with zodiac animals illuminate the night, while special glutinous rice balls called tangyuan are often arranged in patterns representing the zodiac. The festivities include solving traditional riddles with zodiac themes and watching dance performances that highlight the current year's animal sign.

Mid-autumn Festival (15th Day of 8th Lunar Month)

The Mid-autumn Festival (*Zhōngqiū Jié*), celebrated on the 15th day of the eighth lunar month, features mooncakes intricately decorated with zodiac symbols and designs. Family gatherings are sometimes arranged with consideration for zodiac compatibility, creating harmonious celebrations enhanced by zodiac-themed lanterns and decorations. The festival's traditional moon-viewing customs often incorporate specific timing based on zodiac influences, connecting celestial observation with astrological significance.

The Encyclopedia of Astrology

Centers of Learning

The Directorate of Astronomy (Qintian Jian)

Established during the Han Dynasty and continuing through the Qing period, this official bureau oversaw all imperial astronomical and astrological matters. The group employed hundreds of astronomers, astrologers, and mathematicians who maintained calendars, tracked celestial phenomena, and provided divination services for the court. The bureau's extensive records provide valuable insights into the development of Chinese astrological practices.

The Imperial Observatory (Guanxiang Tai)

The Beijing Ancient Observatory was constructed in 1442 during the Ming Dynasty and served as China's primary center for astronomical and astrological studies for over 500 years. Court astrologers used sophisticated bronze instruments to track celestial movements and make predictions for the empire.

The Purple Mountain Observatory (Zijin Shan)

Founded in 1934, this modern institution continues ancient traditions while incorporating contemporary astronomical research. Though primarily focused on astronomy, it maintains archives of historical astrological texts and techniques. The observatory's collection of ancient instruments and texts provides important resources for understanding the development of Chinese astrology.

The White Cloud Temple (Baiyun Guan)

Founded in the Tang Dynasty, this temple in Beijing became a major center for astrological studies and divination practices, and focuses on Taoist principles. The temple housed an extensive collection of texts on astrology and maintained traditions of both practical divination and theoretical study. Masters at the temple developed sophisticated systems combining astrology with Taoist philosophy and meditation practices.

 Key Texts

The Dunhuang Manuscripts

The Dunhuang Manuscripts, discovered in the Mogao Caves, date from approximately the 4th to the 11th centuries CE. They encompass a vast array of documents, including religious, secular, and scientific texts. Among these are astrological treatises and divination manuals that shed light on early Chinese astrological techniques, such as the Dunhuang Star Chart, which is considered the oldest known star atlas.

Treatise on Astrology of the Kaiyuan Period (Kaiyuan Zhanjing)

Compiled between 714 and 724 CE during the Tang Dynasty by Gautama Siddha, this encyclopedic work comprises 120 volumes with approximately 600,000 words. It integrates Chinese and Indian astrological traditions, including translations of Indian astronomical tables, such as Aryabhata's sine table.

The I Ching

The I Ching (Book of Changes) originated as a divination manual during the Western Zhou period (1046–771 BCE). Its current form was consolidated during the late Warring States period (475–221 BCE) into the early Han Dynasty (206 BCE–220 CE). The text's 64 hexagrams, composed of broken and unbroken lines, represent various cosmic principles and their interactions. Its correlative thinking has profoundly influenced Chinese metaphysics, including astrology.

Notable Figures
Guo Pu (276–324 CE)

Areas of influence: Chinese astrology, divination systems, geographical feng shui

Guo Pu is renowned as a Taoist mystic, geomancer, and commentator on ancient texts. He is often referred to as the "father of feng shui" due to his seminal work, *The Book of Burial* (*Zangshu*), which is considered the first authoritative source on feng shui principles, the system that governs spatial arrangement and orientation in relation to the flow of energy (qi).

Major works:
- *The Book of Burial*
- *Explanations of Divination*
- *Commentaries on the Classic of Mountains and Seas*

Li Chunfeng (602–670 CE)

Areas of influence: mathematical astrology, calendar reform, astronomical calculations

Li Chunfeng was a prominent mathematician, astronomer, and historian during the Tang Dynasty. He played a significant role in calendar reform and is credited with designing the Linde calendar. Additionally, he contributed to the development of the armillary sphere by adding a ring to represent the lunar path, enhancing the instrument's accuracy in astronomical observations.

Major works:
- *The Linde Calendar*
- *Commentary on Mathematical Classic of the Zhou Dynasty*
- *Treatise on Astrology and Mathematics*

Liu Xin (46 BCE–23 CE)

Areas of influence: Chinese astronomy, calendar systems, astrological theory

Liu Xin was a distinguished astronomer, mathematician, and bibliographer during the Western Han Dynasty. He is known for his work on the *Triple Concordance Calendar System* and his efforts in cataloging and preserving ancient Chinese texts.

Major works:
- *Triple Concordance Calendar System*
- *Discussions of the Stars*
- *Commentary on the Five Classics*

The Encyclopedia of Astrology

Ma Danyang (1123–1183)
Areas of influence: Taoist astrology, Ba Zi system, spiritual cultivation

Ma Danyang, also known as Ma Yu, was a prominent Taoist master and one of the Seven True Daoists of the North during the Jin Dynasty. He was a disciple of Wang Chongyang, the founder of the Quanzhen School of Taoism. Ma Danyang is known for his contributions to Taoist internal alchemy and spiritual cultivation practices.

Major works:
- *Treatise on the Four Pillars*
- *Methods of Spiritual Timing*
- *The Inner Path of Destiny*

Zheng Xiaoyun (1949–present)
Areas of influence: Zi Wei Dou Shu, *modern Chinese astrology, educational methods*

Zheng Xiaoyun is a contemporary scholar and practitioner of Chinese metaphysics, specializing in *Zi Wei Dou Shu* (Purple Star Astrology). He has developed systematic methods for teaching this complex system to modern students, bridging traditional accuracy with contemporary applications.

Major works:
- *Essential Principles of Purple Star Astrology*
- *Modern Applications of Zi Wei Dou Shu*
- *Traditional Methods for Contemporary Practice*

Myths and Legends
Chang Flies to the Moon

Chang'e, wife of the divine archer Hou Yi, swallowed an immortality elixir meant for her husband and floated to the Moon, where she lives eternally. Her ascension explains the

The Encyclopedia of Astrology

Moon's phases—when the Moon is full, Chang'e is said to be at her most beautiful, and when it wanes, she turns away in loneliness. This tale became central to the Mid-autumn Festival, where people honor Chang'e while celebrating the harvest moon.

The immortal jade rabbit keeps Chang'e company on the Moon, eternally grinding herbs for elixirs in its mortar and pestle. Some versions say the rabbit was a gift from Hou Yi to ease his wife's solitude, while others claim it was already there, having earned its place through an act of self-sacrifice for the Jade Emperor. Their story connects to Chinese medical astrology, as the Moon's phases are believed to influence the potency of herbal medicines.

Chang'e's legend also relates to the lunar mansions (*xiu*) used in Chinese astrology. Her flight path to the Moon supposedly traced these divisions in the night sky, and astrologers still consider these mansions when timing important events, particularly those relating to love and separation—themes central to Chang'e's tale.

The Jade Emperor's Race

The Jade Emperor announced a great race to determine the order of the zodiac animals, declaring that the first 12 to cross the celestial river would earn their place in the cosmic cycle. The clever Rat convinced the strong but slow Ox to carry him across the river, then jumped off at the last moment to claim first place. This established not only the order of the zodiac but also the complementary relationships between certain animals.

The Cat, originally friends with the Rat, was supposed to compete but overslept when the Rat failed to wake them as promised. This betrayal explains why cats now chase rats, and why there is no cat in the Chinese zodiac. Each animal's performance in the race reflects their zodiac characteristics—the Dragon stopped to help others despite its ability to fly, showing its noble nature, while the Pig's late arrival due to stopping for food and naps represents its relaxed attitude.

The river crossing itself symbolizes the celestial river (Milky Way) in Chinese astronomy, and the positions the animals took during the race correspond to their traditional positions in the sky. This cosmic arrangement influences how Chinese astrologers interpret the compatibility between different zodiac signs, with animals that helped each other during the race generally being considered more harmonious matches.

Pan Gu Creates Heaven and Earth
In the beginning, the universe was a swirling chaos, contained within a great cosmic egg. Inside this egg, Pan Gu, the first being, grew for 18,000 years until one day he awoke and shattered it with an axe. The lighter elements of the egg rose to form the heavens, while the heavier elements sank to create the earth.

To prevent the sky and earth from collapsing back together, Pan Gu stood between them, pushing them apart. Each day he grew taller, the heavens rising higher, and the earth growing thicker. This continued for another 18,000 years, during which Pan Gu's breath became the wind, his voice the thunder, and his eyes the Sun and Moon.

When Pan Gu's work was complete, he laid down to rest and transformed into the natural world. His bones became mountains, his blood rivers, and his hair the stars in the night sky. The stars, arranged in constellations, served as guides for measuring time and space. These constellations later formed the basis for the Chinese lunar calendar, which astrologers use to interpret the rhythms of the cosmos and their influence on human life.

Pan Gu's sacrifice established the order of the universe, a harmony that remains central to Chinese thought. His story reminds us that the heavens and earth are interconnected, with the stars above shaping the destinies of those below. This belief forms the foundation of Chinese astrology, where celestial patterns reflect the natural order Pan Gu created.

CULTURAL VARIATIONS IN ASIA

Chinese astrology provided the foundation that different Asian cultures adapted and modified to align with their own beliefs and traditions. Each region developed unique interpretations and practices while maintaining core connections to the original system, creating rich variations that reflect their distinct cultural histories and spiritual beliefs.

JAPANESE ASTROLOGY (*ONMYŌDŌ*)

As Chinese astrology found its way into Japan through cultural exchanges, it blended with native Shinto beliefs and practices, giving rise to the distinct tradition of *Onmyōdō*, a system deeply rooted in Japan's spiritual heritage.

Introduction and History

Building on the foundational principles of yin-yang and the Five Elements from Chinese astrology, Japanese Onmyōdō developed into a unique tradition with its own practices and innovations. The Chinese concepts, encompassing astronomy, calendar-making, and divination, were initially transmitted by Buddhist monks and scholars from mainland Asia. Recognizing their value, the Japanese Imperial Court institutionalized these practices. The Taihō Code of 701 CE established the Bureau of Onmyō (Onmyōryō) within the Imperial government.

During the Heian period (794–1185), Onmyōdō evolved by incorporating Shinto rituals and Buddhist elements, reflecting Japan's syncretic religious landscape. This period saw the development of unique practices such as *katatagae* (ritual avoidance of certain directions) and *monoimi* (abstinence to avoid impurity), which became integral to court ceremonies and daily life.

The Encyclopedia of Astrology

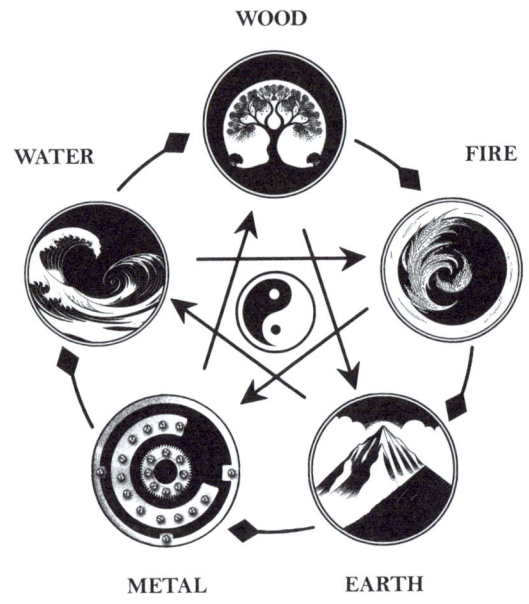

Despite its official prohibition in 1870 during the Meiji Restoration, Onmyōdō's influence persists in modern Japan. Practices such as determining auspicious days for events and rituals to avert misfortune remain prevalent. Recently, Onmyōdō has experienced a cultural resurgence, inspiring literature, films, and popular media, thereby continuing to shape Japan's spiritual and cultural identity.

Innovations and Unique Practices
Onmyōdō introduced several distinctive practices that became integral to Japanese culture:

Urban Geomancy
Like feng shui in China, Onmyōdō included an assessment of land and environmental energies that guided the placement of structures and the planning of cities, aiming to harmonize human activities with natural forces.

The Encyclopedia of Astrology

Exorcisms and Purification Rituals

Onmyōji, or practitioners of Onmyōdō, conducted ceremonies to ward off malevolent spirits and impurities, ensuring spiritual and communal well-being. Onmyōji also practiced divination and astrology to predict future events and advise on auspicious timings for various activities, such as planting crops or launching military campaigns.

Key Texts

Senji Ryakketsu

Attributed to Abe no Seimei, this text is considered one of the oldest extant books on Onmyōdō from the Heian period. It comprises 36 chapters detailing various fortune-telling techniques, totaling approximately 9,000 Chinese characters. The divinations cover aspects of daily life, such as determining the gender of an unborn child, locating lost objects, and offering personal life advice. The divination techniques often involve interpreting celestial patterns and understanding the influences of yin and yang, as well as the Five Elements (wood, fire, earth, metal, and water), so its methodologies are inherently connected to the astrology.

Kin'ugyokuto-shū

Also known as *The Book of the Golden Crow and the Jade Rabbit*, this text is regarded as one of the most important works in Onmyōdō. It delves into cosmological theories and rituals central to the practice, reflecting its syncretic nature by incorporating elements from Taoist and Buddhist traditions.

Notable Figures

Two prominent families, the Kamo and Abe clans, played pivotal roles in the development and transmission of Onmyōdō practices.

Abe no Seimei (921–1005 CE)

Perhaps the most renowned onmyōji, Seimei was celebrated for his profound knowledge of divination, astronomy, and spir-

The Encyclopedia of Astrology

itual matters. His abilities became legendary, and he was later deified, with numerous shrines, such as the Seimei Shrine in Kyoto, dedicated to him.

Kamo no Yasunori (917–977 CE)

A prominent onmyōji and court astrologer, Yasunori served the imperial court with distinction. He was instrumental in preserving and formulizing Onmyōdō practices, and his lineage continued through his son, Kamo no Mitsuyoshi, who later taught Abe no Seimei, another notable Japanese astrologer.

Myths and Legends
The Amaterasu Cave

The Amaterasu Cave myth explains the celestial phenomenon of a solar eclipse and the importance of cosmic balance. In the myth, Amaterasu's brother, Susanoo, wreaked havoc in her heavenly kingdom—destroying her rice fields and throwing a flayed horse into her weaving hall. The goddess retreated into a cave, taking all light with her. The world plunged into darkness, allowing evil spirits to roam freely.

The gods gathered to devise a plan to lure her out. Ame-no-Uzume, the goddess of mirth, performed a bawdy dance that caused all the gods to laugh uproariously. Curious about the commotion, Amaterasu peeked out of the cave, catching her reflection in a mirror the gods had hung. While distracted, the god of strength pulled her from the cave, and other deities sealed it with a sacred rope. This tale explains not only solar eclipses but also the sacred mirrors found in Shinto shrines and the relationship between cosmic and earthly harmony.

Orihime and Hikoboshi

The Tanabata legend speaks of Orihime, the weaver star princess (Vega), and Hikoboshi, the celestial herder (Altair). Orihime's father, the Sky King, arranged their marriage, but their love was so intense that they neglected their duties—Orihime stopped weaving the cosmic fabric and Hikoboshi's cows wandered across heaven.

THE MILKY WAY
galaxy

Angered, the Sky King separated them with the Celestial River (Milky Way), allowing them to meet only once a year on the seventh day of the seventh month. If it rains on Tanabata, the magpies cannot form their bridge, and the lovers must wait another year—explaining why clear skies on this date are considered auspicious for romance and creativity.

KOREAN ASTROLOGY (*SAJU PALJA*)

Saju Palja (사주팔자), meaning "Four Pillars of Destiny," represents Korea's system of celestial divination that combines Chinese principles with distinctive Korean cultural elements such as Mudang and Korean shamanic traditions.

The Four Pillars of Destiny is an astrological practice that came from Chinese astrology, with a person's horoscope originating from their year, month, day, and hour of birth.

Introduction and History

Korean astrology emerged during the Three Kingdoms period (57 BCE–935 CE), primarily through exchanges with China, but developed its unique characteristics

The Encyclopedia of Astrology

during the Goryeo (918–1392) and Joseon (1392–1910) dynasties. The Royal Bureau of Astronomy (Gwansanggam) institutionalized astrological practices, maintaining detailed astronomical records, creating star maps and calendars, and performing divination for the royal court. These court astrologers played crucial roles in determining auspicious dates for state rituals and providing guidance on governmental affairs.

The Joseon Dynasty particularly emphasized the importance of Saju, integrating it with Neo-Confucian philosophy and establishing it as a respected academic discipline. Scholar-officials studied and documented celestial phenomena, creating comprehensive astrological texts that combined mathematical precision with philosophical insight. Saju also intersected with Korean shamanic practices, offering spiritual guidance and insights into personal destiny.

Saju remains deeply embedded in Korean culture. Today, it continues to guide personal and professional decisions, both through traditional consultations and modern digital platforms, showcasing its enduring relevance in both Korea and the global diaspora.

Innovations and Unique Practices

Korean astrology developed several distinctive features that set it apart from other East Asian systems.

Gunghap

Gunghap assesses the compatibility between individuals, particularly in the context of marriage. It analyzes the harmony between two people's Saju (also known as "Four Pillars of Destiny") to predict the success and harmony of their relationship. Traditionally, families consulted fortune-tellers to evaluate Gunghap before approving marriages, believing that compatible Saju would lead to a prosperous and harmonious marriage.

Taeun

Taeun refers to the "Great Luck" or "Major Fortune" cycles in a person's life, as determined by their Saju. These cycles, typically spanning ten years each, are influenced by the interactions of the Five Elements (wood, fire, earth, metal, water) and yin-yang energies present in an individual's birth chart. By analyzing Taeun, astrologers provide insights into how different life aspects—such as career, relationships, health, and personal development—may be affected during each cycle.

Key Texts

Cheonmun Ryucho
A comprehensive astronomical and astrological text compiled during the Joseon Dynasty, documenting celestial observations and their divinatory interpretations.

Cheonsang Yeolcha Bunyajido
A 14th-century Korean star map commissioned by King Taejo in 1395. It accurately charts 1,467 stars and 264 constellations visible from Korea, reflecting the celestial sphere as observed from the Korean peninsula.

Nam Sago's Prophecies
Attributed to Nam Sago, a 16th-century scholar proficient in mechanics, geomancy, astrology, divination, and physiognomy.

Saju Gilui
A foundational text explaining the principles of Four Pillars astrology and its practical applications in Korean context.

Notable Figures

Lee Sun-ji 1406–1465
A prominent court astronomer who authored several influential works on astronomy and calendrical calculations, contributing to the systematic development of Korean astrological practices.

Jang Yeong-sil c. 1390–after 1442
A renowned scientist and inventor during the Joseon Dynasty, Jang Yeong-sil was born into a low-status family but rose to prominence under King Sejong's patronage. He developed vari-

The Encyclopedia of Astrology

ous astronomical instruments, including the water clock (*Jagyeokru*) and the celestial globe (*Honcheonui*), significantly advancing Korean astronomical observation and timekeeping.

Yi Hwang 1501–1570

Also known as Toegye, Yi Hwang was a prominent Confucian scholar whose philosophical writings often intersected with cosmology and the metaphysical aspects of astrology. His interpretations influenced the integration of Confucian thought with astrological concepts in Korea.

Myths and Legends
The Legend of Prince Jumong

The Legend of Prince Jumong begins with Lady Yuhwa, who was bathing when a beam of sunlight touched her, leading to her miraculous pregnancy. After growing up in the kingdom of Buyeo, Jumong demonstrated supernatural abilities, including perfect archery skills that were said to be granted by the celestial powers that heralded his birth. The myth connects Korean royal authority directly to celestial forces, establishing a framework where astronomical events were seen as divine messages about leadership and power—a belief that would influence Korean court astrology for centuries.

The Seven Star Spirit (Chilseong)

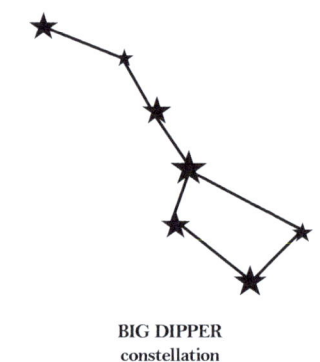

BIG DIPPER
constellation

When a kind-hearted fisherman was swept away by a terrible storm, his seven sons vowed to find him. They journeyed across mountains and rivers, braving countless dangers. After weeks of searching, the brothers climbed a sacred mountain and prayed fervently to the heavens

The Encyclopedia of Astrology

for help. Their love and piety moved the gods, who transformed the brothers into the seven stars of the Big Dipper, or Chilseong, granting them a place in the sky to guide sailors and protect humanity.

From that moment, the Big Dipper became a symbol of devotion and familial love, shining brightly in the night sky as a reminder of the sacred bond between parent and child. The constellation continues to inspire those who look to the heavens, embodying the values of love, sacrifice, and guidance.

MONGOLIAN ASTROLOGY (*ZURKHAI*)

Zurkhai, meaning "calculation of time" in Mongolian, represents a synthesis of Chinese astrological principles, Tibetan Buddhist cosmology, and Mongolia's indigenous shamanic traditions. This system is deeply attuned to natural rhythms and celestial patterns, reflecting the Mongolian people's profound connection to their environment. It combines astronomical observations with practical knowledge of weather, animal behavior, and seasonal changes, forming a comprehensive framework for understanding and navigating life.

Introduction and History

Mongolian astrology traces its roots to pre-Imperial shamanic traditions, gaining a formal structure during the Yuan Dynasty (1271–1368), when Mongolian rulers facilitated cultural exchanges with Tibet and China. The 16th-century establishment of Buddhist monasteries further enriched Zurkhai by incorporating Tibetan Buddhist astronomical calculations and philosophical principles. Astrologer-shamans historically advised tribal leaders and later khans, influencing migration patterns, military strategies, and ceremonial life.

During the Soviet era, Zurkhai faced suppression but survived in rural communities and private practice. Its revival in the 1990s reflects a broader resurgence of traditional Mongolian culture. Today, Zurkhai continues to guide rural and urban practitioners in selecting auspicious dates for rituals, agricultural cycles, and even personal milestones, demonstrating its enduring relevance.

Innovations and Unique Practices

Mongolian astrology developed distinctive features reflecting its nomadic heritage:

Seasonal Divination (Улирлын зурхай)

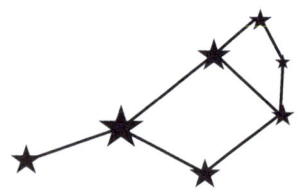

PLEIADES
constellation

A sophisticated system for predicting weather patterns and determining optimal times for seasonal migration, incorporating both celestial observations and traditional ecological knowledge. This practice often involves consulting lunar and solar calendars for guidance on migration, hunting, and harvest times. In this practice, specific stars or constellations, such as the Pleiades or Ursa Major, are particularly significant in seasonal planning.

Animal Cycle Interpretation

A unique approach to the 12-year animal cycle that emphasizes the relationship between cosmic forces and livestock welfare, crucial for pastoral communities. Mongolian interpretations sometimes emphasize compatibility not just with individuals but between herds and their caretakers, often guiding breeding or grazing decisions.

Tenger (Sky) Observations

Traditional Mongolian shamans often interpreted signs in the sky, such as the alignment of stars and weather phenomena, as messages from the Tenger (sky spirits).

The Encyclopedia of Astrology

 ## Key Texts

Mongol Odon Zurkhai *(Created sometime between 1890s and 1920s)*
This text provides a description of traditional Mongolian astrology, highlighting its development as a distinct branch of knowledge in medieval Mongolia. It underscores the enduring belief in and adherence to these practices, with various types of astrological calendars issued annually before the Lunar New Year.

Tegus Buyantu Zurkhai, *1747*
Created by the monk Ishbaljir (1704–1788), this system forms the basis of the traditional Mongolian lunisolar calendar. It integrates Buddhist astronomical calculations with indigenous timing methods.

Notable Figures
Ishbaljir (1704–1788)
The Mongolian monk and scholar Ishbaljir developed the Tegus Buyantu astrology system in 1747, which forms the basis of the traditional Mongolian lunisolar calendar. This system integrates Buddhist astronomical calculations with indigenous timing methods.

Zanabazar (1635–1723)
Zanabazar played a foundational role in integrating Tibetan Buddhist practices, including astronomical and astrological elements, into Mongolian culture. While not directly known for authoring astrological texts, his era marked significant cultural synthesis that shaped Mongolian astrology. His work in art, philosophy, and Buddhism laid the groundwork for the broader acceptance of Buddhist-derived astrological practices in Mongolia.

Myths and Legends
Erkhii Mergen and the Seven Suns
In ancient times, the world was scorched by the relentless heat of seven suns, making life unbearable for all living beings. Erkhii Mergen, a legendary archer renowned for his unparalleled

skill, vowed to alleviate this suffering. With unwavering determination, he shot down six of the seven suns, each arrow extinguishing a blazing orb.

As he aimed for the seventh, a swallow flew before his arrow, causing it to miss; this spared the final sun, ensuring the world retained light and warmth. The swallow's tail was split by the arrow, which is why swallows have forked tails today. Honoring his promise, Erkhii Mergen then transformed into a marmot, symbolizing his humility and sacrifice.

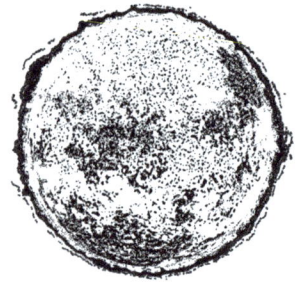

Börte Chino, the Blue Wolf

Börte Chino, the Blue Wolf, stands at the heart of Mongolian mythology as the revered progenitor of the Mongol people. According to legend, Börte Chino was sent from the heavens, a creature of celestial origin marked by its radiant blue hue—a color sacred in Mongolian culture, symbolizing the eternal sky. Together with Gua Maral, the beautiful white doe, Börte Chino journeyed across vast landscapes, embodying the union of strength and grace, sky and earth. From their union sprang the ancestors of the Mongol tribes, establishing a divine lineage that linked the Mongols to the heavens themselves. Börte Chino's presence in folklore symbolizes resilience, leadership, and a guiding spirit born of celestial favor. To this day, Börte Chino serves as a spiritual archetype for resilience and unity, a reminder that the heavens guide and protect those who honor their origins and seek balance with the universe.

TIBETAN ASTROLOGY (*JUNG TSI*)

Jung Tsi represents a fusion of Indian and Chinese astrological traditions, integrated with Buddhist cosmology and indigenous Tibetan practices. This system's distinctive approach combines the mathematical precision of Indian sources with Chinese origins, interpreted through the lens of Buddhist philosophy and enriched by local shamanic wisdom.

Introduction and History

Tibetan astrology formally emerged during the 7th–8th centuries CE under the reign of King Songtsen Gampo, who facilitated the translation of pivotal Chinese and Indian astrological texts. This period marked a cultural renaissance, laying the groundwork for Tibet's unique adaptation of astrological knowledge. During the Second Diffusion of Buddhism (10th–12th centuries), the establishment of major monasteries further systematized these practices. Specialized departments known as Tsi Khang became hubs of astronomical calculation, calendar-making, and ritual astrology.

Despite political upheavals and external influences, Tibetan astrology has remained a vital tradition. Monastic institutions have ensured its preservation, with astrologer-monks combining ancient methods with modern computational tools to meet contemporary needs.

In the modern era, Jung Tsi continues to thrive, addressing both spiritual and practical concerns. Practitioners guide religious ceremonies, determine auspicious dates for events, and support Tibetan medicine through calendar-based treatments. This integration of multiple traditions highlights Tibet's role as a cultural crossroads, reflecting the timeless relevance and adaptability of this ancient science.

Innovations and Unique Practices

Tibetan astrology developed several distinctive features:

Life-Force Calculations (Srog)

Determines the vitality or "life force" for a specific year. Practitioners evaluate the alignment of elements and planets to fore-

The Encyclopedia of Astrology

cast an individual's health and overall energy levels. This emphasizes the interconnectedness of physical and spiritual well-being. A strong Srog is not just about physical vitality; it also reflects harmony between the individual's spiritual path and the cosmic order.

Medical Astrology (Men-Tsi)

Tibetan astrologers often work in conjunction with Tibetan doctors to recommend the best times for harvesting medicinal plants and preparing remedies. These calculations consider celestial movements, lunar phases, and planetary alignments. Astrological charts are sometimes used to determine the elemental imbalances in a patient, which guides treatments like dietary adjustments, herbal formulas, and spiritual interventions.

Obstacle Year Calculations (Keg-Tsi)

A unique method for identifying and mitigating potentially challenging periods in an individual's life based on their birth year's relationship to the current year. This is a well-recognized aspect of Tibetan astrology. The concept involves analyzing one's Lha, Lungta, and other life forces to predict periods of vulnerability or obstacles. Remedies such as rituals (*pujas*), protective amulets, or specific mantras are often prescribed to mitigate challenges.

Key Texts

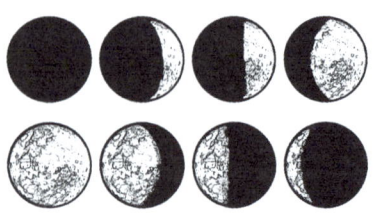

The White Beryl (Baidurya Karpo)

Authored by Desi Sangye Gyatso (1653–1705), the regent to the Fifth Dalai Lama, this 17th-century treatise is a comprehensive work that systematizes Tibetan astrological traditions. It integrates various astrological systems, including Indian,

Chinese, and indigenous Tibetan practices, into a cohesive framework. The text is renowned for its detailed explanations and is accompanied by illuminated manuscripts that depict astrological and divinatory charts.

Other related Tibetan texts include *The Blue Beryl*, *The Black Beryl*, and *The Red Beryl*.

Notable Figures
Desi Sangye Gyatso (1653–1705)
Desi Sangye Gyatso was the regent of the Fifth Dalai Lama and a pivotal figure in Tibetan history. He authored comprehensive works on both medicine and astrology, notably the *Blue Beryl* and *White Beryl* treatises, which systematized Tibetan medical and astrological knowledge. In 1694, he founded the Chagpori Medical College (Men-Tsee-Khang) in Lhasa, establishing standard practices that continue to influence Tibetan medicine and astrology today.

Phugpa Lhundup Gyatso (1851–1930)
Phugpa Lhundrub Gyatso was a renowned 15th-century astrologer who composed an astrological treatise called *The Oral Teachings of Pundarika* (*Pad dkar zhal lung*). His work founded the Phugpa calendar, which became the main calendar system of Tibet. This lunisolar calendar has been modified over the centuries and remains in use today.

Myths and Legends
The Origin of the Kalachakra: The Wheel of Time
Long ago, in the mythical kingdom of Shambhala, a sacred teaching known as the Kalachakra, or the "Wheel of Time," was revealed to a chosen king by the Buddha himself. The Buddha appeared in his radiant form to King Suchandra, who had traveled to India seeking enlightenment. Understanding the interconnectedness of the cosmos and human life, the Buddha imparted knowledge of time

cycles, celestial movements, and their influence on earthly events.

The Kalachakra teachings described the intricate dance of the planets, the influence of lunar cycles, and the hidden power of eclipses. These celestial truths were not only a guide for understanding destiny but also a path toward spiritual awakening. The king brought this wisdom back to Shambhala, where it flourished as the heart of Tibetan astrology, weaving together the cycles of the heavens with the journey of the soul. Over centuries, the Kalachakra teachings became a cornerstone of Tibetan astrology, guiding kings, monks, and ordinary people alike in their pursuit of harmony with the universe.

The Cosmic Dance of Rahu and Ketu: Guardians of Eclipses

RAHU

The myth of Rahu and Ketu explains the power of eclipses in Tibetan astrology, and is a tale that's deeply influenced by Vedic astrology. Long ago, the celestial nectar of immortality was churned from the cosmic ocean. Rahu, a cunning demon, disguised himself as a god to steal a sip of the sacred elixir. As he drank, the Sun and Moon gods exposed his deception to Vishnu, who beheaded him before the nectar reached his body. However, having consumed the nectar, Rahu's head and Ketu's body became immortal and ascended to the skies.

From that day, Rahu and Ketu vowed vengeance, chasing the

Sun and Moon across the heavens. Whenever they catch them, an eclipse occurs, symbolizing their eternal cosmic pursuit. In Tibetan astrology, these shadow planets are considered powerful forces influencing karmic events, spiritual growth, and the cycles of fortune and misfortune. Their story reminds humanity of the delicate balance between light and shadow, both in the cosmos and within ourselves.

KETU

VIETNAMESE ASTROLOGY (*TỬ VI*)

Tử vi, or Vietnamese astrology, represents Vietnam's adaptation of Chinese astrological principles, enriched by unique cultural and mythological influences. While retaining core concepts, Tử vi integrates elements that reflect Vietnamese traditions, such as ancestral veneration and connections to local spirits, particularly those linked to rivers and coastal regions.

Introduction and History

Vietnamese astrology evolved during the centuries of Chinese cultural influence (111 BCE–939 CE), but it developed distinctive characteristics as Vietnam established its independence. Under the Lý and Trần Dynasties (11th–14th centuries), astrology flourished within the royal court. Official astrologers combined the mathematical precision of Chinese systems, such as the sexagesimal cycle and Purple Star Astrology (*Tử Vi Đẩu Số*), with local spiritual beliefs. This blend underscored the significance of natural elements and ancestral heritage in Vietnamese culture.

Vietnam's adaptation of the zodiac (*Mười hai con giáp*) is also notable, featuring a 12-year cycle associated with animal signs matching the Chinese system but with a unique inclusion—the Cat replaces the

The Encyclopedia of Astrology

Rabbit. The zodiac influences personality assessments, compatibility readings, and decisions about auspicious dates for events like weddings, business openings, and house building.

Innovations and Unique Practices
The Cat and the Water Buffalo

One of the most distinctive features of the Vietnamese zodiac is the inclusion of the Cat in place of the Rabbit, which is found in the Chinese zodiac. The Cat symbolizes qualities such as intelligence, grace, and agility, traits that resonate with Vietnamese values and the animal's revered status in local folklore. People born in the Year of the Cat are often thought to be calm, charming, and adaptable, making them well-suited for harmonious relationships and a balanced approach to life.

The Water Buffalo holds the second position in the Vietnamese zodiac, symbolizing diligence, strength, and patience. Deeply rooted in Vietnam's agrarian culture, the water buffalo represents the enduring connection between people and the land. As a steadfast companion in rice cultivation, it embodies perseverance and humility, qualities celebrated in Vietnamese society. Those born in the Year of the Buffalo are believed to be hard-working, dependable, and resilient, reflecting the spirit of this iconic animal.

Key Texts

Tử Vi Đẩu Số Toàn Thư
Translated to *The Complete Book of Purple Star Astrology*, this comprehensive work delves into the principles and applications of Tử Vi Đẩu Số, a system of destiny analysis based on the positions of stars at the time of one's birth.

The Encyclopedia of Astrology

Tử Vi Hàm Số (The Functions of Tử Vi)

This text delves into the mathematical and functional aspects of Tử Vi calculations, providing practitioners with tools to interpret astrological charts accurately.

Tử Vi Chỉ Nam (Guide to Tử Vi)

Serving as a practical handbook, this guide offers step-by-step instructions for casting and interpreting Tử Vi charts, making it valuable for both beginners and seasoned astrologers.

Notable Figures

Lương Đắc Bằng (1470–1540)

A distinguished scholar and mentor to Nguyễn Bỉnh Khiêm, Lương Đắc Bằng was known for his expertise in Confucianism and astrology. He authored several works on divination and played a pivotal role in transmitting astrological knowledge to his disciples.

Trần Đoàn (circa 870–989)

Also known as Hi Di tiên sinh, Trần Đoàn was a Chinese Taoist scholar whose works on astrology and numerology, particularly the *Tử Vi Đẩu Số*, greatly influenced Vietnamese astrological practices. His teachings were integrated into Vietnamese culture, shaping the development of local astrological systems.

Myths and Legends

Lạc Long Quân and the Descendants of the Fairy and Dragon

The Vietnamese Dragon, or *rồng*, holds a distinct role in mythology, symbolizing power, protection, and the spirit of Vietnam itself. It is deeply tied to the legend of Lạc Long Quân, the Dragon Lord, and Âu Cơ, the fairy who gave birth to the Vietnamese people.

According to legend, Lạc Long Quân descended from the sea to protect the land and its people, bringing with him the rains and taming the wild rivers. He fell in love with Âu Cơ, a mountain fairy, and together they had a hundred children—50 of whom followed their father to the seas and 50 of whom stayed with their mother in the mountains, symbolizing the unity of Vietnam's diverse regions.

The Encyclopedia of Astrology

In Vietnamese astrology, the dragon embodies the qualities of strength, leadership, and harmony. Its presence reminds the people of their divine ancestry and the balance needed between land and water, tradition and progress, to thrive.

EGYPTIAN ASTROLOGY
Introduction and History

Egyptian astrology developed alongside the flourishing civilization of the Nile, deeply intertwined with the religious beliefs and practical needs of the time. Because of their shared roots, Egyptian astrology is inexorably tied to Hellenistic astrology, with a shared intellectual heritage that developed during the Ptolemaic period (305–30 BCE) and flourished into the Roman Empire era. During this time, Egypt was under the control of the Ptolemaic Dynasty, a Greek ruling class that facilitated vibrant cultural and intellectual exchanges between the Greek and Egyptian worlds. This is the dynasty that built the Great Library of Alexandria, with rulers positioning themselves both as Greek kings and Egyptian pharaohs.

Egyptian astrology linked celestial bodies with gods and cosmic order. For example, the Sun, represented by Ra, was believed to travel across the sky daily, battling chaos in the underworld at night. The Moon was associated with Thoth, the god of wisdom and writing, who played a role in maintaining balance and measuring time. The Egyptians also revered the constellation Orion, whom they connected with Osiris, the god of the afterlife, and believed that the stars could influence a person's fate both in life and after death.

ORION
constellation

The Encyclopedia of Astrology

Astrology in ancient Egypt had both spiritual and practical applications. Farmers relied on the alignment of stars, particularly Sirius, to determine planting and harvesting seasons. Priests and astrologers used planetary movements to set the dates for religious festivals and rituals. Human life was directly connected to celestial happenings.

Observations of the stars and celestial cycles were integral to their understanding of the cosmos and their calendar. The Egyptians identified 36 star groups, known as *decans*, which rose sequentially every ten days, marking time throughout the year. The star Sirius (Sothis) held special significance, as its heliacal rising coincided with the annual flooding of the Nile, a critical event for agriculture.

Astrology also played a critical role in legitimizing pharaonic power. The alignment of pyramids and temples often corresponded with significant celestial events, symbolizing the connection between the king and the gods.

Egyptian astrology has had a lasting cultural and historical impact. Its influence can be seen in Hellenistic and Roman astrology, particularly in the emphasis on lunar and solar cycles. The rediscovery of Egyptian star charts and inscriptions in the 19th century, such as those at the temples of Dendera and Edfu, provided insight into ancient Egyptians' advanced understanding of the cosmos. Egyptian astrology is celebrated for its spiritual depth, its connection to the rhythms of nature, and its enduring contributions to the development of celestial studies.

Innovation and Unique Practices
Dendera Zodiac

Unlike Mesopotamian astrology, early Egyptian astrology did not initially include a zodiac. However, during the Hellenistic period, Egyptian and Babylonian traditions merged, leading to the adoption of the zodiac system in Egyptian practices.

The Dendera Zodiac—an astronomical ceiling relief discovered in the Temple of Hathor

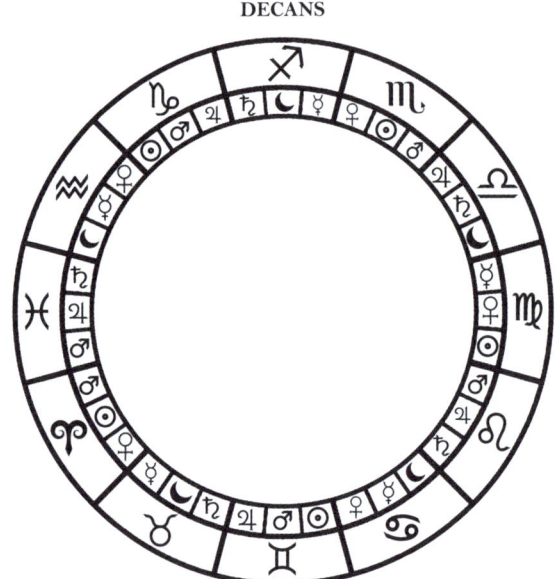

at Dendera—depicts 12 zodiac signs alongside traditional Egyptian motifs. While it includes many of the zodiac symbols familiar today, it is more of a star map rather than a birth chart or astrological chart. The image features all five planets known to the ancient Egyptians (those visible to the naked eye—Mercury, Venus, Mars, Jupiter, Saturn), depicted in an alignment that occurs only once every thousand years, along with illustrations of both a solar and lunar eclipse. Astrophysicists have used the planetary alignment to date the depicted sky to a period between June 15 and August 15, 50 BCE.

Decans

The 36 decans were integral to ancient Egyptian astronomy and timekeeping, dividing the 360-degree ecliptic into 36 segments, each spanning 10 degrees. Each decan corresponded to a specific star or constellation, rising heliacally (appearing on the eastern horizon just before dawn) every ten days. This system informed the Egyptian calendar, dividing the night into "hours" and the year into ten-day periods.

The decans were not only astronomical markers but also held religious significance, each linked to specific deities and used in rituals. Their heliacal risings were crucial for determining the timing of religious festivals and agricultural activities, embedding them deeply in the cultural and spiritual life of ancient Egypt. The sequence of these star patterns began with Sopdet (Sirius), and each decanal star was associated with a specific god.

Sirius, the Dog Star

SIRIUS
constellation

Sirius held great importance for Egyptian culture. Personified in early Egyptian texts as the goddess Sopdet ("skilled woman"), the star's heliacal rising was associated with the flooding of the Nile, a critical event for agriculture.

Astrologically, Sirius was believed to influence both the earthly realm and the divine. Its prominence in the sky was thought to guide the deceased through the afterlife, acting as a celestial beacon. Priests and astrologers likely observed the star to time rituals, agricultural cycles, and religious festivals, embedding Sirius deeply in both practical and spiritual life.

Star Clocks

Examples of Egyptian star clocks were charts or pictures found on coffin lids and tombs depicting detailed records of the night sky. These artifacts demonstrate a sophisticated knowledge of planetary movements as far back as 3,000 years ago.

The star clocks are also thought to have served as guides

for the deceased in the afterlife. Inscriptions often included instructions on navigating the night sky, emphasizing the decans' role in maintaining cosmic order and linking the living to the divine.

One of the most detailed sources for Egyptian star clocks is the *Book of Nut*, an ancient astronomical text that outlines the movements of the stars, including the decans, across the sky. This text shows how the Egyptians conceptualized the heavens as a reflection of their mythological and cosmological beliefs. The decans were not merely timekeeping tools; they symbolized the eternal cycle of life, death, and rebirth.

Centers of Learning
The Library of Alexandria
Established in the 3rd century BCE, this renowned center of learning housed numerous astrological texts. Scholars such as Claudius Ptolemy likely studied and taught here, significantly shaping Hellenistic astrology. The library was believed to house hundreds of thousands of scrolls and texts from across the ancient world, collected through royal decrees and contributions from visiting scholars, making it a repository of unparalleled knowledge and a hub for intellectual exchange.

Mouseion
Founded alongside the Library of Alexandria in approximately 300 BCE, the Mouseion was a premier research institution where scholars studied sciences like astronomy and astrology. Its golden years were in the 3rd–2nd centuries BCE. In addition to being a research institution, the Mouseion functioned as a scholarly community where resident researchers were supported by the state, providing them with resources to pursue studies in astronomy, medicine, philosophy, and other sciences in a collaborative environment.

The Temple of Karnak
The Temple of Karnak in Egypt (*c.* 2000–30 BCE) functioned as an ancient observatory and religious

center aligned with solstices, where celestial movements were studied in relation to earthly events, as reflected in the Dendera complex's astronomical ceiling. Beyond its religious functions, Karnak was a dynamic cultural and ceremonial site where priests observed celestial events, such as the solstices, from specific architectural alignments that reinforced the temple's connection to divine cosmic order.

Key Texts

The Astronomical Ceiling of Senenmut's Tomb

The tomb of Senenmut, a high-ranking official under Queen Hatshepsut, features one of the earliest examples of an astronomical ceiling. This beautifully decorated surface includes depictions of the northern and southern star constellations, lunar cycles, and decans, reflecting the Egyptians' precise celestial knowledge. The ceiling serves as both a funerary text and a celestial map, guiding Senenmut's soul to the afterlife while demonstrating the connection between astronomy and Egyptian spiritual practices.

The Book of Nut

The Book of Nut is an ancient Egyptian cosmological text that provides insights into the Egyptian understanding of the heavens. Named after Nut, the sky goddess, this text describes the movements of the Sun, Moon, stars, and planets, as well as the decans—36 star groups used for timekeeping and astrological purposes. It was often inscribed on temple walls and ceilings, particularly in tombs, to guide the deceased through the afterlife by aligning their journey with celestial order. The text exemplifies the fusion of mythology and practical astronomy that characterized Egyptian astrology.

The Cairo Calendar (Ramesseum Papyrus IV)

The Cairo Calendar, a papyrus from the Middle Kingdom

(*c.* 1800 BCE), is one of the first examples of a day-by-day astrological almanac, detailing celestial influence on daily life. The calendar details lucky and unlucky days and astrological predictions. Each day of the year was connected to the movements of stars and planets, making this an essential artifact for understanding the intersection of astrology and daily life in ancient Egypt.

The Dendera Zodiac

The Dendera Zodiac, found in the Temple of Hathor, at Dendera in Egypt, is one of the most famous examples of ancient Egyptian astronomy and astrology. Created during the late Ptolemaic period (*c.* 50 BCE), it blends traditional Egyptian symbols with the Hellenistic zodiac introduced after Alexander the Great's conquest. The circular relief depicts the 12 zodiac signs, including familiar figures like Aries, Taurus, and Gemini, alongside Egyptian constellations, such as the sky goddess Nut and representations of decans (star groups used to divide the night).

The *Zodiac* not only illustrates the merging of Greek and Egyptian astronomical traditions but also highlights the Egyptians' sophisticated understanding of celestial cycles. Today, it is considered a significant artifact of cultural and astronomical history, offering insight into how ancient civilizations integrated their spiritual beliefs with astronomical observation.

Notable Figures
*Imhotep (*c. *27th century* BCE*)*

Imhotep is a well-documented polymath, known for his role as an architect, physician, and high priest under Pharaoh Djoser. While his contributions to medicine and architecture, including designing the Step Pyramid at Saqqara, are more prominent, his position as high priest of Ra suggests he was involved in celestial observations and rituals that likely informed early Egyptian astrology.

Claudius Ptolemy (c. 100–170 CE)
Although not Egyptian by origin, Ptolemy lived and worked in Alexandria, Egypt, during the Roman period. His work *Tetrabiblos* synthesized Greek, Egyptian, and Babylonian astrological traditions and had a lasting impact on astrology.

See more in **Hellenistic Astrology**.

Senenmut
A high-ranking official under Queen Hatshepsut, who ruled c. 1479–1458 BCE, Senenmut oversaw the construction of his tomb featuring one of the earliest astronomical ceilings. This indicates his role in celestial observation and its integration into Egyptian spiritual practices.

The High Priests of Heliopolis
The temple complex at Heliopolis is thought to have housed one of the earliest observatories, dating back to the Old Kingdom (c. 2686–2181 BCE). Here, priests tracked the movements of the Sun, stars, and planets to create lunisolar calendars. The priests here developed systems of star-based rituals and calendars that influenced astrological thinking.

Myths and Legends
The Love of Isis and Osiris
Osiris, god of the afterlife, and Isis, goddess of magic, shared a love so profound that it echoed through the cosmos. Osiris was beloved by the people for bringing order and civilization while Set, his brother, brought chaos and barren desert. Set was jealous and bitter and created a trap for Osiris, tricking him, then killing and dismembering him and scattering the remains so that he could not be resurrected.

Isis, who was both Osiris's wife and sister, was heartbroken. She embarked on a quest to gather his pieces and resurrect him. Guided by the stars and aided by the falcon-headed god Thoth, Isis used her magical knowledge to bring Osiris back to life long enough to conceive their son, Horus. Together, their union reminded Egyptians that celestial alignments influenced earthly regeneration, prosperity, and the soul's immortality.

Even today, Isis is associated with Sirius, the primary star that the Egyptians used to track cycles and time, and Osiris is associated with the constellation Orion. Features of the cosmos were seen as manifestations of divine forces and the continuation of life beyond death.

Ra's Journey Through the Zodiac

Every night, the sun god Ra embarked on a perilous journey through the underworld aboard his solar barque. As he traveled, he passed through 12 gates, each representing a zodiac sign and an hour of the night. At each gate, Ra faced trials, including monstrous serpents and shadowy spirits, testing his strength and resolve.

One of his greatest battles was against Apep, the serpent of chaos, who tried to swallow the Sun and plunge the world into darkness. With the help the cat-headed goddess Bastet and the hawk-headed god Horus, Ra defeated Apep, ensuring the dawn would rise again. This legend ties the sunrise to Ra's nightly triumphs, illustrating how each hour of the night and each decan carried its own meaning and influence over human endeavors.

The Birth of the Sacred Days

In the myth of Nut, the sky goddess, and Geb, the earth god, their love was so great that they remained in an eternal embrace, obsessed with each other to the point that they weren't doing their duties and their negligence was preventing life from flourishing.

Ra, the sun god, commanded them to separate, and Shu, the god of air, forced them apart. Heartbroken, Nut turned to Thoth, the god of wisdom and time, for a solution. Thoth gambled with the Moon and won five extra days to add to the calendar year, allowing Nut to give birth to her children: Osiris, Isis, Set, Nephthys, and Horus the Elder. These five days became sacred markers in the Egyptian calendar.

GREEK ASTROLOGY
Introduction and History

Greek astrology emerged during the Hellenistic period (*c.* 4th century CE), heavily influenced by Mesopotamian and Egyptian practices and traditions. Early Greek innovations focused on harmonizing astrology with the rational, mathematical approach popularized by philosophers such as Plato and Pythagoras.

The Greeks expanded on earlier systems by introducing the concept of an individual horoscope or birth chart which represented the positions of celestial bodies at the time of an individual's birth. This innovation enabled astrology to move beyond omens for rulers and nations, making it a tool for personal insight. Claudius Ptolemy, an astronomer and astrologer of the 2nd century CE, codified Greek astrological practices in his influential text, the *Tetrabiblos*. This work synthesized Babylonian observations, Egyptian star lore, and Greek philosophical ideas, and has provided a systematic foundation for Western astrology.

Greek astrology was deeply intertwined with the idea of cosmic harmony. The seven classical planets (the Sun, Moon, Mercury, Venus, Mars, Jupiter, and Saturn) were believed to influence life on Earth. Each planet was associated with a deity and attributed with specific qualities. The Greeks adhered to the principle of "as above, so below," believing that celestial movements mirrored and influenced earthly events, aligning with their philosophical explo-

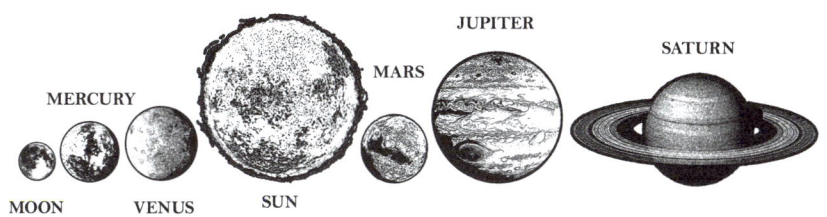

The Encyclopedia of Astrology

rations of fate, free will, and the soul's connection to the cosmos.

The Greeks adopted the Mesopotamian model of dividing the zodiac into 12 equal signs, each linked to one of the four elements (fire, earth, air, water) and three modalities (cardinal, fixed, mutable). These divisions provided a framework for interpreting individual character traits and life events. Astrologers also used houses, segments of the horoscope that represented different aspects of life, such as wealth, relationships, and health. The precision of Greek mathematical tools, including their advancements in geometry, allowed for accurate calculations of planetary positions, which became central to astrological predictions.

Astrology became widely popular in Greek society, serving both philosophical and practical purposes. It influenced decisions in politics, warfare, and personal matters. Leaders consulted astrologers for guidance and the practice was also deeply integrated into medicine, with the positions of celestial bodies thought to affect physical and mental health, guiding treatments.

Innovations and Unique Practices

Aspects

The Greek astrologers refined and systematized the concept of aspects. They used geometrical principles to define angular relationships—e.g., conjunction (0°), sextile (60°), square (90°), trine (120°), opposition (180°). Certain aspects were associated with harmony (e.g., trines) and others with tension (e.g., squares), reflecting Greek philosophical ideas about balance and conflict. These relationships were understood as energetic interactions between planets. The roots of aspects can be traced to Pythagorean ideas about harmony and numerical relationships, connecting astrology to music and geometry.

Integration of Planetary Rulership

Greeks introduced the concept of planetary rulership, assigning each planet to a zodiac sign based on its qualities and perceived relationships. For example, Mars rules Aries, and Venus rules Taurus. This innovation created a more cohesive relationship between celestial bodies and astrological interpretation.

Planetary rulerships were tied to the Chaldean Order of planetary spheres and reflected the idea of cosmic hierarchy. The Greeks also introduced the domicile system, where each planet rules one daytime and one nighttime sign, as well as the concept of exaltation and detriment.

The Four Humors

Greek astrology integrated with medicine and agriculture, linking planetary movements to health, seasonal cycles, and body parts. The practice of melothesia assigned each zodiac sign to a specific part of the human body, influencing medical diagnoses and treatments.

The humors were integral to Greek astrology because they linked the physical body to celestial influences. Each humor was associated with certain planets.

Blood: Associated with spring, air, and sanguine temperament. Ruled by Jupiter.
Yellow Bile: Associated with summer, fire, and choleric temperament. Ruled by Mars.
Black Bile: Associated with fall, earth, and melancholic temperament. Ruled by Saturn.
Phlegm: Associated with winter, water, and phlegmatic temperament. Ruled by the Moon.

Centers of Learning
Delphi

Known as the site of the famous Oracle of Apollo, Delphi was a spiritual and intellectual hub where debates about fate, divine will, and the cosmos flourished. These discussions influenced early Greek cosmology and provided philosophical foundations that later intersected with astrology's exploration of celestial influence and human destiny.

The Encyclopedia of Astrology

Library of Alexandria

The Library of Alexandria was a Greek-led institution during the Hellenistic period. It housed critical texts on astrology, including translations of Babylonian and Egyptian works into Greek, enabling the synthesis of astrological traditions.

See more under **Egyptian Astrology**.

Platonic Academy in Athens

Originally founded by Plato, the Platonic Academy thrived again during the Hellenistic period. While the academy was not explicitly focused on astrology, its discussions on fate, determinism, and the cosmos laid the groundwork and philosophy that was later adopted by Hellenistic astrologers.

The Astronomical Center of Rhodes

The island of Rhodes became a key intellectual hub for astronomical studies in the 3rd century BCE, providing foundational calculations that advanced astrological precision.

Key Texts

Anthology by Vettius Valens (2nd century CE)

Anthology by Vettius Valens is a practical manual filled with real-life examples of astrological charts and predictions. Written by a working astrologer, it provides detailed techniques for interpreting natal charts and forecasting events, making it an invaluable resource for understanding ancient astrology in practice.

Carmen Astrologicum by Dorotheus of Sidon (1st century CE)

Dorotheus of Sidon's *Carmen Astrologicum* is a didactic poem that offers one of the earliest systematic guides to astrology. It covers natal astrology, predictive techniques, and planetary significations. Though it was originally composed in Greek, much of the work survives only in an Arabic translation (by Umar al-Tabari) and a subsequent Latin version.

Tetrabiblos by Claudius Ptolemy (2nd century CE)
The *Tetrabiblos* is one of the most influential texts in Western astrology, offering a systematic synthesis of Greek astrological thought. It discusses the principles of natal and mundane astrology, along with planetary influences and aspects.

See more in **Hellenistic Astrology**.

Notable Figures
Eudoxus of Knidos (c. 390–340 BCE)
Eudoxus of Knidos was a pioneering Greek astronomer and mathematician who developed the first known geometric model of the universe using concentric spheres to explain planetary motion. While not explicitly astrological, his work influenced the Greek understanding of celestial harmony, which became foundational for astrological studies. His emphasis on the ordered, mathematical structure of the cosmos deeply influenced Plato and later thinkers, bridging early Greek cosmology with the systematic study of celestial influences.

Hipparchus (c. 190–120 BCE)
Born in Nicaea (modern-day Turkey), Hipparchus conducted most of his work on the island of Rhodes. While primarily remembered as an astronomer, Hipparchus made significant contributions to both astronomical measurement and astrological practice. He is credited with inventing the astrolabe, a sophisticated tool that allowed precise measurement of celestial positions and became essential for both astronomical observation and astrological chart calculation. His discovery of the precession of the equinoxes—the gradual shift of the equinoctial points through the zodiac—fundamentally impacted how later astrologers understood long-term celestial cycles.

The Encyclopedia of Astrology

Myths and Legends
The Myth of Orion: The Hunter Turned Constellation

ORION
constellation

Orion was a mighty hunter, a giant, said to be so skilled that no beast could escape his aim. He boasted of his prowess, claiming he could rid the Earth of all wild creatures. This boast angered Gaia, the earth goddess, who sent a giant scorpion to stop him. A fierce battle ensued, and though Orion fought valiantly, he was ultimately stung and succumbed to the scorpion's poison.

Moved by his bravery and hunting skill, Zeus placed Orion in the heavens as a constellation, where he shines as a symbol of courage and human ambition. The constellation Scorpius, representing the scorpion, was also placed in the sky, forever chasing Orion. When one rises in the sky, the other sets, ensuring their rivalry continues for eternity.

The Tale of Callisto and the Bear Constellations

Callisto was a beautiful nymph and a devoted follower of Artemis, the virgin huntress. Despite her vow of chastity, Zeus, enchanted by her beauty, disguised himself and tricked her into an affair. Callisto bore a son, Arcas, but when Hera discovered the betrayal, she transformed Callisto into a bear out of jealousy.

Years later, Arcas, now grown, unknowingly encountered his mother in her bear form while hunting. As he raised his spear to strike, Zeus intervened, preventing a tragic mistake. To honor them both, he placed Callisto and Arcas in the sky as the constellations Ursa Major and Ursa Minor, the Great Bear and the Little Bear. Their position near the celestial pole ensures they never dip below the horizon, a

The Encyclopedia of Astrology

reminder of love enduring even through transformation.

The Story of Andromeda and Perseus

Andromeda was the daughter of Cepheus and Cassiopeia, rulers of Ethiopia. Cassiopeia, known for her vanity, boasted that her beauty surpassed even that of the sea nymphs, the Nereids. Offended, the god Poseidon sent a sea monster to ravage the kingdom as punishment. To appease the god, the king and queen chained their daughter to a rock as a sacrifice.

Just as the beast approached, the hero Perseus appeared, fresh from slaying the Gorgon Medusa. Wielding Medusa's head and its magical powers, Perseus turned the monster to stone and saved Andromeda. They married, and their love became legendary. Zeus immortalized their story in the night sky, placing the constellations of Andromeda, Perseus, Cassiopeia, and Cepheus among the stars, forever intertwining their fates.

HELLENISTIC ASTROLOGY
Introduction and History

Hellenistic astrology, flourishing from the 3rd century BCE to the 6th century CE, represents one of the most pivotal developments in the history of astrology. Rather than being tied to one particular location and culture, Hellenistic astrology encompasses the rich synthesis of Mesopotamian, Egyptian, and Greek astronomical traditions. This period saw the blending of diverse intellectual frameworks, producing a system that would become the foundation of modern Western astrology. Central to this fusion was the melding of practical celestial observation with philosophical concepts of fate, free will, and the cosmos' relationship to human life.

The core contributions of Hellenistic astrology include innovations still integral to astrological practice today. The doctrine of the 12 houses, which ties planetary positions to specific life areas, first emerged in this period. The development of aspects—angular relationships

The Encyclopedia of Astrology

between planets that describe their dynamic interactions—was another critical advancement. Additionally, the emphasis on the ascendant, or the zodiac sign rising at the moment of birth, became a defining feature of the Hellenistic system.

Key texts from this era established a lasting intellectual framework for astrology. Dorotheus of Sidon's *Carmen Astrologicum* provided one of the earliest systematic guides to natal and electional astrology, blending Mesopotamian techniques with Greek interpretive methods. Claudius Ptolemy's *Tetrabiblos* synthesized astronomical data with philosophical underpinnings, articulating a model of astrology deeply grounded in Aristotelian cosmology. Ptolemy's work introduced principles such as planetary dignity and debility, which evaluate a planet's ability to express its nature based on its position in the zodiac. These principles remain central to astrological analysis.

The city of Alexandria, as a crossroads of Greek, Egyptian, and Babylonian scholarship, became the epicenter of Hellenistic astrological development. Birth charts from this region offer insight into the sophistication of Hellenistic astrology. Surviving examples reveal a meticulous approach, integrating planetary placements by zodiac sign, house, and aspect to craft nuanced interpretations of individual character, fate, and potential. The emphasis on predictive techniques underscored astrology's role as both a philosophical and practical tool for understanding life's cycles.

Philosophically, Hellenistic astrology reflected the Greek worldview's deep engagement with the concepts of fate and the divine. The Stoic notion of cosmic determinism—wherein the universe operates as a rational, interconnected whole—found resonance in astrological practice. Simultaneously, the Platonic and Aristotelian emphasis on the soul's journey and the interplay of divine order and human agency enriched astrological interpretations, adding layers of moral and spiritual significance. Hellenistic astrology also introduced the concept of *katharsis*, or purification, through understanding one's astrological chart. This perspective framed astrology not merely as a tool for prediction, but as a guide to self-awareness and alignment with cosmic rhythms.

Hellenistic astrology occupies a unique position in the history of astrological thought. It served as a bridge between earlier Babylonian and Egyptian practices and the later developments of medieval Islamic astrology, which further refined its techniques and expanded its scope. Many of its core principles and methodologies remain foundational to Western astrology, underscoring its enduring influence and central role in the evolution of the astrological tradition.

Innovations and Unique Practices

Aristotelian Cosmology

A geocentric model of the universe developed by Aristotle, describing Earth as the stationary center of concentric celestial spheres. It emphasizes the purposeful motion of heavenly bodies, the distinction between the earthly elements and the celestial substance *aether* (later adapted in Englsh to *ether*), and the interconnection of the cosmos, forming the philosophical basis for many ancient astrological systems.

Ascendant

Hellenistic astrologers developed the ascendant and midheaven as vital chart points, along with a sophisticated house system. The ascendant, also known as the rising sign, refers to the zodiac sign that was rising on the eastern horizon at the exact time of a person's birth. It represents the lens through which one experiences and interacts with the world. The ascendant sign colors one's per-

ARISTOTELIAN COSMOLOGY

sonality, physical appearance, and initial reactions. It is considered one of the most important placements in an astrological birth chart, as it shapes the overall tone and flavor of an individual's life and character.

Aspects

Hellenistic astrologers refined the concept of aspects, identifying degree-based relationships that are foundational today. Astrological aspects refer to the angular relationships between the positions of celestial bodies in a birth chart or horoscope. The main aspects include conjunction, when two or more planets are in the same sign and degree, strengthening and complementing their energies; opposition, when two planets are directly across from each other, creating tension and a need for balance; square, when planets are at right angles, creating challenges and obstacles to overcome; trine, when planets are in harmony, allowing for ease and flow between their energies; and sextile, when planets are in a supportive, cooperative relationship.

The Encyclopedia of Astrology

Cosmic Determinism

Stoic philosophy particularly emphasized cosmic determinism in Hellenistic astrology (also known as astrological determinism). This is belief that the positions and movements of celestial bodies at the time of people's births shape their personality, guide their life events, and predetermine their future. It stands in contrast to the concept of free will, as it suggests that external, impersonal cosmic forces rather than individual agency are the primary drivers of human experience and destiny. This philosophical debate over the existence and degree of free will versus astrological predetermination remains an ongoing area of disagreement and discussion within the fields of astrology, philosophy, and psychology.

Midheaven

The midheaven, also known as the Medium Coeli (MC), refers to the highest point in a birth chart or horoscope. During the Hellenistic era, it was defined as the zenith of the chart, marking the cusp of the 10th house. The midheaven symbolizes one's public persona, career path, life purpose, and reputation. It indicates the area of life where an individual is most likely to achieve success, recognition, and fulfillment.

The sign and degree placement of the midheaven provides

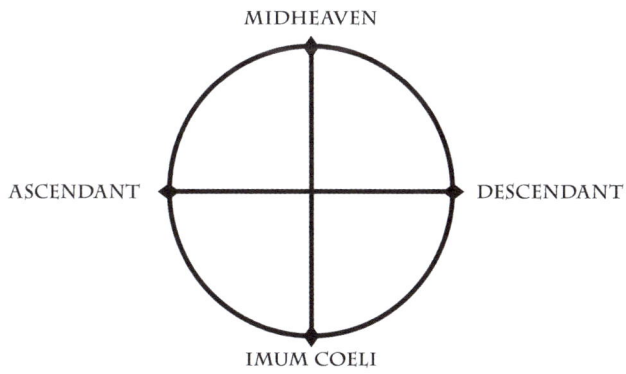

The Encyclopedia of Astrology

insights into an individual's vocational inclinations, leadership potential, and how they are perceived by others in a professional context. As one of the key angular points in an astrological chart, the midheaven is considered crucial for understanding an individual's life trajectory and worldly ambitions.

Planetary Dignity

Planetary dignity in astrology refers to the varying degrees of influence and power that different planets are believed to have in a horoscope or birth chart. The concept is based on the idea that some planets are more "at home" in certain zodiac signs, and therefore exert a stronger, more beneficial effect when placed in those signs.

The main types of planetary dignity include rulership, when a planet is in the sign it rules; exaltation, when a planet is thought to be strengthened in a specific sign; detriment, when a planet is placed in the sign opposite the one it rules; and fall, when a planet is in the sign opposite its exaltation. Astrologers use the principle of planetary dignity to determine the relative power and influence of the planets in an individual's birth chart, as planets in strong dignity are believed to have a more prominent and positive impact.

Centers of Learning

Antioch Academies (Antioch, Syria)

Established in 300 BCE by Seleucus I Nicator, Antioch served as a bridge between Greek and Eastern traditions. Its golden years spanned the 3rd century BCE–1st century CE, during which it played a key role in disseminating Hellenistic astrology.

Library of Pergamon (Pergamon, Asia Minor, in modern-day Turkey)

The Library of Pergamon was founded around 197 BCE under King Eumenes II. It reached its peak in the 2nd–1st centuries BCE, fostering studies in astrology and other sciences. According to historical accounts, the library housed approximately 200,000 volumes, though exact numbers are subject to speculation. This great library was second only to the Library at Alexandria during this era.

Key Texts

Matheseos Libri VIII by Firmicus Maternus (4th century CE)

Firmicus Maternus authored *Matheseos Libri VIII (Eight Books of Astrology*, a comprehensive Latin treatise on astrology aimed at making Hellenistic astrological practices accessible to Roman audiences. This is a significant work that bridges Hellenistic and Roman astrological traditions, providing insight into the adaptation of Greek astrological concepts within Roman society. The work delves into natal charts, planetary influences, and predictive techniques, blending astrological knowledge with Roman culture and society.

Tetrabiblos by Claudius Ptolemy (2nd century CE)

The *Tetrabiblos* is the cornerstone of Hellenistic astrology, written by the renowned scholar Claudius Ptolemy. It aimed to systematize astrology as a scientific discipline, integrating it with astronomy and philosophical reasoning. Covering the zodiac, planets, aspects, and houses, it provided a rational framework that heavily influenced later Western astrology.

On Inceptions by Hephaistio of Thebes (4th century CE)

Hephaistio of Thebes's *On Inceptions* is a comprehensive summary of earlier Hellenistic astrological works, focusing on electional astrology (katarchic astrology). It provides detailed guidance on choosing auspicious times for events and interpreting planetary configurations.

Notable Figures

Dorotheus of Sidon (1st century CE)

Born in Sidon (in modern-day Lebanon), Dorotheus worked within the thriving Hellenistic astrological tradition. While details of his education are limited, his writings demonstrate extensive knowledge of both

Babylonian and Egyptian astrological practices.

His masterwork, *Carmen Astrologicum*, written in verse form, provided comprehensive instructions for electional and horary astrology. He developed sophisticated techniques for determining favorable times for various activities and established many of the traditional rules for answering horary questions.

Hephaistio of Thebes
(c. 380–415 CE)

Hephaistio, a Hellenized Egyptian astrologer from Thebes, was active during late antiquity. While specific details of his education remain scarce, his extensive work reflects a deep engagement with earlier astrological traditions, particularly those of Dorotheus of Sidon and Claudius Ptolemy.

His principal work, the *Apotelesmatics* (also known as *Apotelesmatika*), is a comprehensive three-book treatise that endeavors to synthesize and reconcile the methodologies of his predecessors. In this compilation, Hephaistio preserved substantial excerpts from earlier authorities, some of which might have been lost without his efforts. The first two books focus on general and natal astrology, drawing heavily from Ptolemaic principles, while the third book addresses katarchic astrology, aligning more with the approaches of Dorotheus.

Maternus, Firmicus
(c. 300–350 CE)

Firmicus Maternus's major work, *Matheseos Libri VIII*, written before his conversion to Christianity, represents the most complete surviving text of Roman astrology. He detailed techniques for natal, electional, and mundane astrology (or the study of astrology as it impacts nations, cities, and large groups of people), preserving many Hellenistic methods that might otherwise have been lost.

His work serves as a crucial bridge between ancient and medieval astrology, preserving detailed technical information about classical astrological practice. His writings influenced medieval European astrologers and continue to provide valuable insights into ancient techniques.

Nechepso and Petosiris

Nechepso and Petosiris are legendary figures central to the development of Hellenistic astrology, often credited as co-authors of foundational astrological texts. Nechepso, traditionally depicted as an Egyptian pharaoh, and Petosiris, a high priest of Thoth, symbolize the union of political authority and divine wisdom.

Their writings, likely composed under the pseudonyms in the 2nd or 1st century BCE, synthesized Egyptian religious cosmology, Babylonian star lore, and Greek philosophical ideas. The influence of these writings shaped medieval and even Renaissance astrological traditions. They exemplify the syncretic spirit of Hellenistic intellectual culture, blending Greek, Egyptian, and Mesopotamian elements into a cohesive esoteric framework.

Their legacy is emblematic of the Hellenistic fascination with Egypt as a source of mystical wisdom, cementing their place in the canon of astrological and occult literature. While their historical reality remains uncertain, their symbolic and intellectual contributions endure as touchstones in the history of astrology.

Ptolemy, Claudius (c. 100–170 CE)

Born in Egypt during Roman rule, Ptolemy lived and worked primarily in Alexandria, then a major center of learning. His masterwork *Tetrabiblos* established the fundamental principles of Western astrology, systematically connecting celestial phenomena to earthly events through natural philosophical principles. As an astronomer and mathematician, he developed sophisticated models for planetary motion that remained influential for over a millennium, though his geocentric model was eventually superseded by heliocentric understanding.

The *Tetrabiblos* remains one of the most influential astrological texts ever written, establishing many techniques still used today. His systematic approach to astrological interpretation and emphasis on natural causation helped legitimize astrology as a field of study.

Myths and Legends

Because Hellenistic astrology is a blend of Egyptian, Mesopotamian, and Roman astrology, the myths and legends also blend the lore and origin stories of each culture.

The Myth of Heracles and the Zodiac

Heracles, the greatest of Greek heroes, was tasked with completing 12 labors as penance for his actions under the spell of Hera's wrath. These labors, from slaying the Nemean Lion to capturing Cerberus, symbolized the trials and triumphs of human existence. Each labor was monumental, testing Heracles' strength, courage, and resilience, and upon his success, Zeus immortalized his son's journey in the heavens.

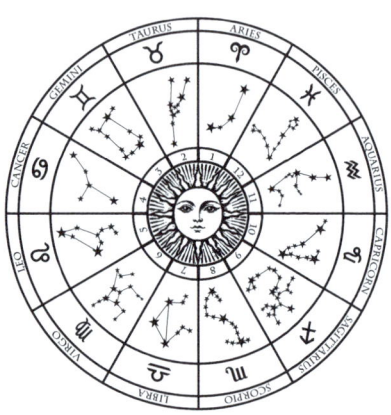

The 12 constellations of the zodiac were born from these labors, with each sign reflecting the qualities and challenges Heracles faced. Aries represents the boldness of the Golden Ram, while Leo embodies the might of the Nemean Lion. Through these celestial symbols, the myth of Heracles ties the zodiac to the cycles of life, offering a cosmic reminder of humanity's ability to overcome adversity and grow through perseverance.

The Titanomachy, or Battle of the Titans

Before the gods reigned supreme, the Titans ruled the cosmos under the leadership of Kronos,

The Encyclopedia of Astrology

the Titan of time. However, Kronos's tyranny was destined to end, as foretold by prophecy, and his son Zeus rose against him in a cataclysmic battle known as the Titanomachy. The war between the Titans and the Olympians raged for ten years, with the heavens trembling under the clash of celestial forces. In the end, Zeus and his siblings triumphed, casting the Titans into Tartarus and establishing a new divine order.

This myth resonates deeply with astrology through the symbolism of Saturn (Kronos) and Jupiter (Zeus), representing cycles of time and the shifting dynamics of power. Saturn, the planet of structure and limitation, reflects Kronos's rigid rule and the inevitability of decline, while Jupiter embodies Zeus' expansive energy, growth, and the promise of renewal. The Titanomachy serves as a reminder of the cosmic cycles that govern all things, from the rise and fall of civilizations to the ebbs and flows of individual lives. Astrologers see these planetary archetypes as guides, helping humanity navigate periods of challenge and transformation, just as Zeus forged a new era from the chaos of war.

ISLAMIC ASTROLOGY
Introduction and History

The Islamic Golden Age (8th–14th centuries CE) marked a transformative period in astrological history, when scholars preserved and expanded upon Hellenistic knowledge while developing sophisticated new techniques. Centers of learning such as the House of Wisdom in

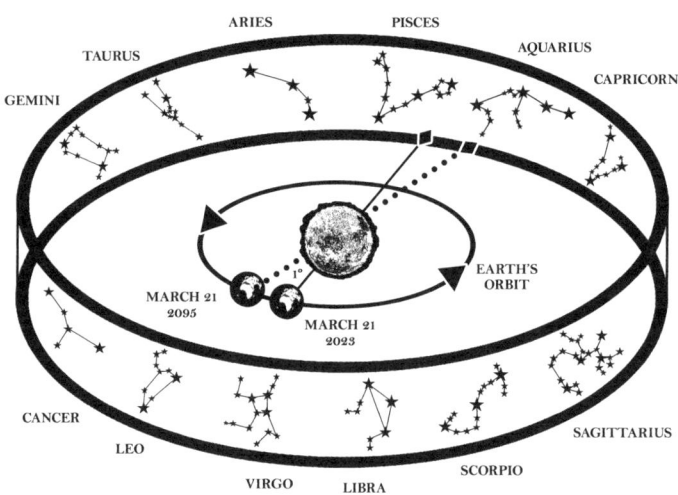

ASTRONOMICAL PRECESSION

Baghdad became nexus points where Greek texts were translated into Arabic and enhanced with Persian and Indian astronomical insights. Islamic astrologers refined mathematical methods for calculating planetary positions, developed new timing techniques, and created detailed systems for analyzing planetary strengths and dignities.

Islamic astrologers made several crucial innovations that influenced later Western practice. They developed sophisticated methods for determining planetary strength, including the system of essential dignities that's still used today. The concept of progressions—a predictive technique that advances the birth chart—was significantly refined during this period. They also created new mathematical tools for precise astronomical calculations, including trigonometric tables and advanced computational methods.

Beyond technical innovations, Islamic astrologers integrated astrology with natural philosophy and medicine, including the development of sophisticated theories about how celestial influences affected the physical world, such as detailed correla-

The Encyclopedia of Astrology

tions between planets and bodily health. Medical astrology flourished, with physicians using astrological timing to guide treatments and surgeries. This holistic approach influenced European medicine well into the Renaissance.

The sophisticated observatories built during this period, like the Observatory at Maragheh, in modern-day Iran, provided more accurate data for both astronomical and astrological work. These improved observational techniques led to more precise ephemerides and astronomical tables.

The influence of Islamic astrology spread through various routes into medieval Europe. The ancient trade networks of the Spice Road facilitated not just the exchange of goods but also the transmission of astrological knowledge, with merchant caravans carrying manuscripts and astronomical instruments between major Islamic centers and Western Europe. Additionally, the translation movement centered in Toledo, Spain, during the 12th century made Arabic astrological texts available in Latin. These translations introduced European scholars to both ancient Greek works preserved by Islamic scholars and the new techniques developed during the Islamic Golden Age. This transmission profoundly shaped Western astrological practice, establishing methods and concepts that remain influential today.

Medical Astrology and Healthcare
Islamic physicians integrated astrology into medicine, creating a detailed system linking celestial movements to health and treatment timing. They expanded humoral theory by associating planets and zodiac signs with specific organs and ailments—such as the Sun with the heart or Aries with the head. Physicians used astronomical tables to determine the best times for treatments, often aligning bloodletting, surgeries, or medication with lunar phases or planetary alignments.

Astrological medicine included the following:

Critical Days: Predicting disease outcomes based on lunar phases.
Planetary Correlations: Connecting celestial bodies with diseases and body parts.
Timed Interventions: Scheduling treatments using planetary hours.
Preventive Measures: Advising seasonal and dietary adjustments aligned with celestial cycles.

Bimaristans (Islamic hospitals) employed astrologers alongside physicians, ensuring treatments were optimized for celestial conditions. This integration marked a holistic approach, combining science, philosophy, and astrology to improve patient care.

The Ninth Sphere and Cosmology
The Ninth Sphere, or Primum Mobile, was central to Islamic cosmology, symbolizing the universe's outermost boundary and the force driving the celestial spheres. Completing a daily rotation, it governed the heavens' motion and linked the physical world with the divine. Astrologers viewed it as a crucial interface for understanding how celestial mechanics influenced earthly events, blending metaphysics with astrology in a uniquely Islamic worldview.

Sufi Astrology
Sufi mystics, practitioners of Islam who tend to focus on inward work rather than outward ritual, see the heavens as a mirror of the soul's journey toward unity with Allah, with each star and celestial movement symbolizing a stage of spiritual transformation. The stars, in this view, are guides to understanding divine order and aligning one's life with it. By contemplating the stars through this mystical lens, Sufis turn astrology into a devotional practice, a path to recognizing the interconnectedness of the cosmos and the divine.

Talismanic Magic

Islamic talismanic magic harmonized celestial science, spirituality, and craftsmanship. Practitioners created talismans using precise astrological timings, inscribed symbols, and carefully selected materials to harness planetary and stellar energies. These objects aimed to attract protection, health, or prosperity, reflecting the interconnectedness of the cosmos and human life.

Grimoires (magic textbooks) such as *Picatrix* and *Shams al-Ma'arif* codified this tradition, blending astrology, mysticism, and philosophy into practical guides for creating talismans. This practice highlighted the Islamic world's intellectual sophistication and its belief in aligning human intention with the divine order of the heavens.

The Translation Movement

The translation movement of the Islamic Golden Age ensured the survival and enhancement of ancient astrological knowledge. Greek texts, such as Ptolemy's *Tetrabiblos*, were translated into Arabic and enriched with Persian and Indian insights. These advancements, transmitted via centers like Toledo, Spain, shaped European astrology, ensuring its continued evolution and integration into Western thought.

Zijes

Detailed astronomical tables, or *zijes*, were an innovation from Persia—they provided precise planetary positions and later informed Islamic astrological practices. This legacy continued under Islamic rule, where scholars expanded on these foundations, developing advanced predictive techniques and philosophical frameworks for astrology.

The Encyclopedia of Astrology

Centers of Learning

Persian astrology centered around major learning institutions that combined astronomical observation with astrological interpretation. The Academy of Gondishapur, founded in the 3rd century CE, became particularly renowned for translating Greek texts while developing new astrological techniques.

The Academy of Gondishapur

The Academy of Gondishapur, established during the Sassanid Empire (224–651 CE), was one of the most renowned intellectual centers of the ancient world. Located in present-day Iran, Gondishapur was a hub of learning where scholars from diverse cultural backgrounds—including Greek, Indian, and Persian traditions—gathered to exchange knowledge.

Al-Andalus (Islamic Spain)

During Islamic rule in Spain, centers of learning flourished, particularly in cities such as Córdoba and Toledo. These institutions became conduits for the transmission of astrological knowledge from the Islamic world to Europe. Scholars translated Arabic texts into Latin, facilitating the integration of astrological concepts into Western thought. The region's intellectual environment fostered advancements in various sciences, including astrology.

Harran University

Established in 717 CE by Umayyad Caliph Umar II in Harran (modern-day southeastern Turkey), Harran University was among the earliest Islamic institutions of higher learning. It became renowned for its liberal intellectual environment, attracting scholars who studied mathematics, philosophy, medicine, astrology, astronomy, and natural sciences. Notable figures such as Al-Battani and Thābit ibn Qurra were associated with this institution. The university also played a pivotal role in translating Greek and Syriac texts into Arabic, thereby preserving and transmitting classical knowledge.

The Encyclopedia of Astrology

The House of Wisdom in Baghdad

The House of Wisdom (Bayt al-Hikma) in Baghdad served as a monumental intellectual center during the Islamic Golden Age, operating from roughly 800–1258 CE. It functioned as a combination of library, translation bureau, research institute, and observatory where scholars of diverse backgrounds studied both astronomy and astrology alongside other sciences.

The institution played a crucial role in preserving and advancing astrological knowledge by translating ancient Greek, Persian, and Indian texts into Arabic. Scholars there developed sophisticated techniques for calculating planetary positions and refined methods for birth chart interpretation, with notable figures like Al-Khwarizmi and Abu Ma'shar making significant contributions to both mathematical astronomy and astrological theory.

Observatory at Maragheh

The Maragheh Observatory, established in 1259 under the patronage of Hulagu Khan and directed by Persian polymath Nasir al-Din al-Tusi, was a pivotal institution in the advancement of Islamic astronomy. Located in present-day Iran, it attracted prominent scholars and fostered significant developments in observational techniques and astronomical instruments.

The observatory's scholars produced the zijes, comprehensive astronomical tables that refined planetary motion models and corrected Ptolemaic parameters. The innovative work at Maragheh influenced subsequent observatories, including Ulugh Beg's in Samarkand, and contributed to the evolution of astronomical thought, impacting both Islamic and later European astronomy.

The Observatory at Ray (Modern Tehran)

The Observatory at Ray, located in what is now modern Tehran, Iran, emerged as a significant center of scientific and astrological study during the Islamic

Golden Age (8th–13th centuries CE). Ray was home to prominent scholars who contributed to advancements in astronomy, mathematics, and astrology.

Key Texts

The Book of Thousands by Al-Balkhi (10th century)

This is a classic text in Islamic astrology, focusing on detailed timing techniques and mundane predictions. While the full manuscript has not survived intact, references and fragments in later works provide insight into its content and its influence on Persian and medieval European astrology.

Elements of Astrology by Al-Biruni

Al-Biruni's *Elements of Astrology* is a meticulously structured manual that combines rigorous scientific methodology with astrological theory. Written for both beginners and experts, the book covers essential concepts such as planetary positions, houses, aspects, and calculations. Al-Biruni also incorporated insights from mathematics, astronomy, and geography, demonstrating his commitment to a rational approach. His text remains a key reference for understanding the technical and theoretical foundations of Islamic astrology.

The Great Introduction by Abu Ma'shar

Abu Ma'shar, one of the most influential Islamic astrologers, authored *The Great Introduction*, a foundational text that integrates Hellenistic, Indian, and Persian astrological traditions into a cohesive framework. This work systematically outlines the principles of astrology, including planetary influences, celestial mechanics, and the interplay between astrology and philosophy. It served as a bridge between earlier astrological systems and later medieval European astrology, profoundly shaping the discipline's development.

Introduction to Astrology by Al-Qabisi

Al-Qabisi's *Introduction to Astrology* is a concise yet comprehensive guide that focuses on the practical application of astrological principles. The work emphasizes the importance of ethical considerations in astrological practice and provides detailed explanations of natal chart interpretation, planetary dignities, and predictive techniques. Al-Qabisi's accessible style made this text a popular resource for students of astrology in both the Islamic world and medieval Europe.

Zij-i Ilkhani

The *Zij-i Ilkhani* is a specific zij, or set of astronomical tables, compiled under the patronage of the Ilkhanid ruler Hülegü Khan in the 13th century. It was produced by the renowned Persian astronomer Nasir al-Din al-Tusi at the Maragha Observatory and was one of the most advanced and accurate zijes of its time.

Notable Figures

al-Biruni, Abu Rayhan (973–1048)

Al-Biruni demonstrated extraordinary intellectual capabilities from an early age. He received extensive education in mathematics, astronomy, and multiple languages, allowing him to study various cultural and scientific traditions. His approach to astrology was uniquely empirical and cross-cultural. While serving in the courts of various rulers, he traveled extensively throughout India, learning Sanskrit and studying Indian astronomical traditions. He developed sophisticated mathematical techniques for calculating planetary positions and determining astrological aspects, while maintaining a skeptical approach that questioned and tested traditional assumptions.

al-Qabisi, Abd al-Aziz (c. 935–967)

Born in what is now northern Iraq, Al-Qabisi (Latinized as Alcabitius) studied both astronomy and astrology in Baghdad

The Encyclopedia of Astrology

under leading scholars of his time. His education encompassed traditional Arabic astrology while incorporating elements from Persian and Indian traditions, reflecting the cosmopolitan nature of medieval Islamic scholarship.

His most influential work, *Introduction to the Art of Astrology*, became a standard textbook in medieval Europe through Latin translations. Al-Qabisi's influence extended well beyond the Islamic world, with his works being required reading in European universities until the 17th century. His house system remained popular throughout medieval Europe, and his methods for determining planetary dignity continue to influence traditional astrology.

Masha'allah (c. 740–815)

Born in Basra (modern-day Iraq), Masha'allah ibn Athari was a Jewish astrologer and scholar who flourished during the early Abbasid period. Initially trained in theology and philosophy, he later became one of the pioneering figures of Islamic astrology, contributing to the integration of Persian, Hellenistic, and Indian astrological traditions into the Islamic intellectual framework.

Masha'allah played a key role in the Abbasid court and his systematic methods and detailed commentaries made his texts essential resources for both Islamic and European astrologers. His writings were widely translated into Latin, ensuring their lasting impact on medieval European astrology.

Ma'shar, Abu (787–886)

Born in Balkh (modern-day Afghanistan), Abu Ma'shar initially studied Islamic traditions before discovering astrology later in life. His education expanded to include Greek philosophy and mathematics under the guidance of al-Kindi, leading him to develop a sophisticated understanding of both theoretical and practical astrology.

Ma'shar synthesized Aristotelian natural philosophy with Hellenistic astrology, creating comprehensive systems for prediction and interpretation. His mathematical models for planetary movements became foundational texts for both Islamic and European astrologers, and his work on planetary cycles influenced astrological thinking for centuries.

Myths and Legends

Islamic teachings tend to emphasize theological principles and historical narratives over mythology, so traditional Islamic culture does not feature myths in the same way as other traditions. Different teachings of the Qur'an and Sufism both embrace and warn against astrology.

Harut and Marut

The story of the angels Harut and Marut is included in the Qur'an. These angels were sent to test humanity and taught people mystical arts, including astrology, under strict conditions. This tale highlights the dual nature of such knowledge: it can guide and enlighten but also mislead when misused.

The Legend of King Jamshid

King Jamshid, a key figure in Persian mythology, was a visionary king and a spiritual luminary believed to have been endowed with extraordinary wisdom directly by Ahura Mazda, the supreme deity of Zoroastrianism. This divine knowledge included mastery over the stars, granting him unparalleled insight into the workings of the cosmos and the fates of humanity.

Jamshid's celestial understanding allowed him to construct a grand calendar that synchronized the movements of the heavenly bodies with earthly cycles. Through this, he established the Nowruz festival, marking the Persian New Year and the spring equinox. This event was not only a celebration of renewal and abundance but also a reflection of Jamshid's ability to bridge the divine and earthly realms through astrology. The alignment of Nowruz with the vernal equinox reinforced its significance, embodying harmony between cosmic order and terrestrial life.

Under his reign, astrology became a means of connecting with the divine and interpreting human destiny. Jamshid's knowledge was seen as both a gift and a responsibility, enabling him to guide his people through predictions and celestial signs. His legacy in Persian astrology exemplifies the ancient belief in the stars as divine guides, capable of shaping societies and spiritual practices.

JYOTISH ASTROLOGY (INDIAN)

Introduction and History

Jyotish, meaning "science of light" in Sanskrit, represents the comprehensive traditional system of astrology in India and throughout South Asia. Often referred to as "Vedic astrology" in the West, this term emerged in the 20th century to align the system with the ancient Vedic scriptures. However, Jyotish as a tradition has developed over thousands of years with its roots in the Vedic period (*c.* 1500–*c.* 500 BCE).

During the Vedic age, astrology was integral to daily life and political decision-making, with its principles encoded in early texts like the Rigveda and later codified in classical works such as the Brihat Parashara Hora Shastra and Brihat Samhita. By this time, Jyotish had evolved into distinct branches, including Ganita (astronomy) and Phalita (astrology).

This tradition includes 12 zodiac signs (Rashis), 27 lunar mansions (Nakshatras), 16 types of divisional charts (Shodashvarga), and several planetary periods (Dashas). Unlike Western astrology, which uses the tropical zodiac based on the seasons, Jyotish relies on the sidereal zodiac, which tracks the actual positions of constellations relative to fixed stars.

The system of Jyotish incorporates the 27 Nakshatras, which divide the ecliptic into equal segments, reflecting the Moon's monthly journey through the fixed stars. Jyotish astrologers also use Varga charts, detailed divisional charts, to analyze spe-

The Encyclopedia of Astrology

cific aspects of life. Additionally, the system emphasizes planetary periods known as dashas, which predict when karmic patterns are likely to manifest.

Innovations and Unique Practices

Bhavas (Houses)

The Jyotish natal chart is divided into twelve Bhavas, or houses, each representing specific areas of life, such as career, relationships, health, and wealth. This is similar to the house system of Western astrology. Bhavas can vary in significance depending on the house system used.

Dashas

Dashas, in Jyotish astrology, refer to planetary periods that provide a framework for understanding the timing of events in an individual's life. They are based on the position of the Moon in a person's natal chart and describe how different planets influence specific periods of time.

The most widely used house system is the Vimshottari Dasha,

The Encyclopedia of Astrology

which divides a 120-year cycle into planetary periods ruled by the nine grahas, or planets: Sun, Moon, Mars, Mercury, Jupiter, Venus, Saturn, Rahu (North Node), and Ketu (South Node). Each planet has a set duration, which represents the type of influence it exerts during its period:

Ketu: 7 years
Venus: 20 years
Sun: 6 years
Moon: 10 years
Mars: 7 years
Rahu: 18 years
Jupiter: 16 years
Saturn: 19 years
Mercury: 17 years

Each major period, or mahadasha, is further subdivided into smaller periods called antardashas, which are also governed by planets. This subdivision allows for a more precise prediction of events.

The effects of a dasha depend on the planet's placement, dignity, and relationship with other planets in the natal chart. Dashas help astrologers predict the timing of life events like career changes, marriage, financial growth, or challenges, offering a timeline of when specific karmic influences will unfold.

Karma and Karmic Patterns

Karma in Jyotish represents the accumulated actions, choices, and deeds of a person, which leave imprints on the soul. These imprints determine the circumstances and experiences one encounters in this lifetime.

Karma is categorized into three types:

Sanchita Karma: The sum total of all accumulated karma from past lives, stored in a "cosmic bank account."

Prarabdha Karma: A portion of Sanchita Karma allocated to be experienced in this lifetime. It manifests as the fixed circumstances of one's life, such as family, health, or inherent talents.

Kriyaman Karma: The actions performed in the current life, which create new karma and influence the future.

Jyotish astrology identifies the specific karmic imprints shaping one's current life through the positions and interactions of planets in the natal chart.

Karmic Patterns

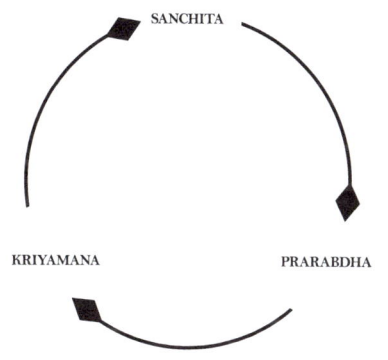

Karmic patterns are recurring themes or tendencies in a person's life that arise from karmic imprints. These patterns may manifest in areas such as relationships, career, health, or spiritual growth. In Jyotish, karmic patterns are often identified through:

Planets like Saturn and the lunar nodes (Rahu and Ketu) are strongly linked to karma and karmic lessons. For example, Saturn represents discipline and accountability for past actions, while Rahu and Ketu highlight unresolved desires and past-life influences.

Specific houses, such as the sixth, eighth, and twelfth, relate to challenges, transformations, and spiritual liberation, often connected to karmic themes. Additionally, planetary periods can activate karmic patterns, bringing them to the forefront for resolution or further development. Interactions between planets in the chart indicate karmic debts, obligations, or opportunities for growth.

Nakshatras, or Lunar Mansions

Nakshatras are the 27 lunar mansions or constellations that form a fundamental part of Jyotish astrology. They represent specific segments of the celestial sphere, each spanning 13 degrees and 20 minutes of the zodiac. The Moon's position in a nakshatra at the time of birth holds significant importance, as it reflects the deeper qualities of an individual's personality, life path, and karmic influences.

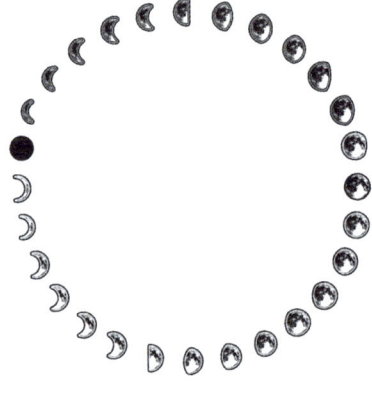

The entire zodiac of 360 degrees is divided into 27 equal parts, corresponding to the nakshatras. A 28th nakshatra, Abhijit, is sometimes included for specific calculations.

Each nakshatra is further divided into four quarters, each spanning 3 degrees and 20 minutes. These padas link the nakshatras to the 12 zodiac signs and provide detailed insights into a person's character and destiny.

Rashi Chart

A Rashi chart (also known as a Lagna chart) is the foundational chart that maps the positions of the planets in the twelve zodiac signs, or Rashis, at the exact time, date, and place of an individual's birth. It serves as the primary reference point for analyzing a person's life, character, and destiny.

The framework of the Rashi chart are the 12 signs of the zodiac, starting with Aries (Mesha) and ending with Pisces (Meena). Each Rashi spans 30 degrees of the 360-degree zodiac. The Lagna, or ascendant, determines the starting point of the chart and influences the individual's physical appearance, personality, and overall life approach. The Rashis are closely aligned with the Hellenistic and Western astrological zodiac.

Rashis (Signs)

Mesha (Aries)
Symbol: Ram
Element: Fire
Ruling Planet: Mars (Mangal)
Key Traits: Energetic, bold, pioneering, and sometimes impulsive.

Mithuna (Gemini)
Symbol: Twins
Element: Air
Ruling Planet: Mercury (Budha)
Key Traits: Curious, communicative, versatile, and sometimes restless.

Vrishabha (Taurus)
Symbol: Bull
Element: Earth
Ruling Planet: Venus (Shukra)
Key Traits: Practical, reliable, sensual, and sometimes stubborn.

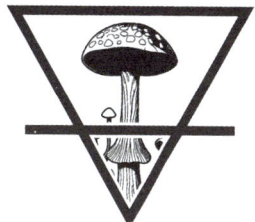

Karka (Cancer)
Symbol: Crab
Element: Water
Ruling Planet: Moon (Chandra)
Key Traits: Emotional, nurturing, intuitive, and sometimes moody.

The Encyclopedia of Astrology

Simha (Leo)

Symbol: Lion
Element: Fire
Ruling Planet: Sun (Surya)
Key Traits: Confident, ambitious, regal, and sometimes dominant.

Tula (Libra)

Symbol: Scales
Element: Air
Ruling Planet: Venus (Shukra)
Key Traits: Balanced, diplomatic, artistic, and sometimes indecisive.

Kanya (Virgo)

Symbol: Maiden
Element: Earth
Ruling Planet: Mercury (Budha)
Key Traits: Analytical, detail-oriented, modest, and sometimes critical.

Vrishchika (Scorpio)

Symbol: Scorpion
Element: Water
Ruling Planet: Mars (Mangal) and Ketu (South Node, co-ruler)
Key Traits: Intense, passionate, transformative, and sometimes secretive.

The Encyclopedia of Astrology

Dhanu (Sagittarius)
Symbol: Archer
Element: Fire
Ruling Planet: Jupiter (Guru)
Key Traits: Optimistic, adventurous, philosophical, and sometimes reckless.

Kumbha (Aquarius)
Symbol: Water Bearer
Element: Air
Ruling Planet: Saturn (Shani) and Rahu (North Node, co-ruler)
Key Traits: Innovative, humanitarian, independent, and sometimes eccentric.

Makara (Capricorn)
Symbol: Crocodile (or Sea Goat)
Element: Earth
Ruling Planet: Saturn (Shani)
Key Traits: Disciplined, practical, ambitious, and sometimes reserved.

Meena (Pisces)
Symbol: Fish
Element: Water
Ruling Planet: Jupiter (Guru)
Key Traits: Compassionate, imaginative, spiritual, and sometimes escapist.

The Encyclopedia of Astrology

Grahas (Planets)

The nine grahas, or planets/celestial bodies (Sun, Moon, Mars, Mercury, Jupiter, Venus, Saturn, Rahu, and Ketu) are plotted within the chart based on their positions in the zodiac at the time of birth. Their placement in signs and houses reveals their influence on various aspects of life.

Ketu and Rahu are lunar nodes. Together, Rahu and Ketu form the shadow planets or Chhaya Grahas, as they don't have a physical presence in the sky like other planets. Ketu represents the South Node of the Moon, which is the point where the Moon's orbit crosses the ecliptic plane while descending.

Sidereal

Sidereal refers to a system of astrology or astronomy that measures celestial positions relative to the fixed stars rather than the shifting positions of the Earth's equinoxes. This approach contrasts with the tropical system, which bases its calculations on the Sun's position relative to the Earth's equinoxes and the seasons.

In Jyotish, the sidereal zodiac is used to calculate the positions of planets, houses, and signs. Jyotish emphasizes the fixed

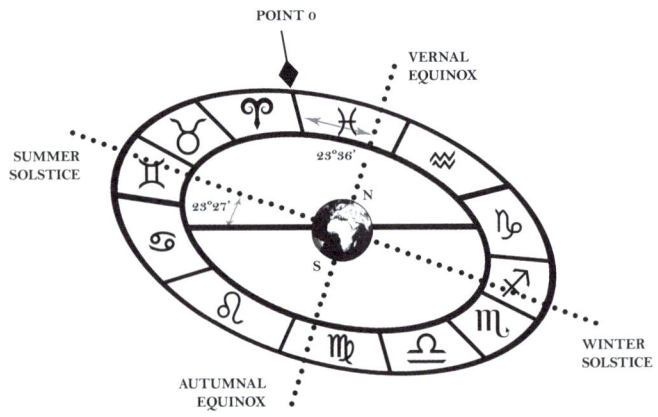

SIDEREAL ZODIAC

The Encyclopedia of Astrology

star background and assigns great importance to the actual constellations in the sky. The sidereal zodiac aligns closely with the observable night sky, offering a more astronomically anchored approach compared to the tropical zodiac.

The difference between the tropical and sidereal zodiacs is known as the *ayanamsha*, which accounts for the precession of the equinoxes (the gradual shift of Earth's axis over time). The sidereal system adjusts for this shift, keeping the zodiac aligned with the constellations as they appear in the sky, whereas the tropical system does not.

Jyotish uses this sidereal framework to analyze birth charts by mapping the positions of planets in their corresponding signs at the exact time of birth, predict dashas (planetary periods) and transits for timing events and understanding karmic influences.

The framework also emphasizes the nakshatras (lunar mansions), which are unique to the sidereal system and provide an additional layer of detail in readings. This sidereal alignment is integral to the philosophy of Jyotish, as it connects the individual's life and destiny to the cosmic patterns observable in the heavens.

Varga Chart

A Varga refers to the divisional charts derived from the main natal chart to provide deeper insights into specific areas of life. These charts are created by dividing each sign of the zodiac into multiple parts, assigning a specific planet or sign to each division, and then recalculating the planetary positions within those divisions.

Each Varga chart serves a distinct purpose, focusing on particular aspects of life, such as relationships, career, wealth, or spiritual growth. The study of Vargas allows astrologers to fine-tune their interpretations and predictions.

Some of the most commonly used Varga charts include:

Navamsa (D9): Marriage, partnerships, and spiritual dharma.
Dashamsa (D10): Career, profession, and public image.
Shodashamsa (D16): Vehicles and comforts.
Chaturvimshamsha (D24): Education and learning.
Shashtiamsha (D60): Past life karma and overall fate.

Vargas are used to confirm and deepen interpretations of the main Rashi chart. A planet's strength and placement in its relevant Varga chart enhance or reduce its ability to deliver favorable results in its area of influence. By integrating the Varga charts with the main Rashi chart, Jyotish offers a highly detailed and precise framework for understanding a person's life journey.

The Vedas

Some of the most significant texts in the Hindu religion are known as the Vedas. Coming from the Sanskrit word for knowledge (*Veda*), they are a compilation of four incredibly influential texts. They have been passed down in an oral tradition first appearing around the second millennium BCE, and many of the mantras are still recited out loud to this day. While there are a few different interpretations, most sects of Hinduism recognize the Vedas as a sacred text.

There are four texts in particular: The Rigveda, Yajurveda, Samaveda, and Atharvaveda. Each of these is broken down into four more subdivisions. First, there are the Samhitas, the mantras, and benedictions that are offered. Next comes the Aranyakas, the rituals and ceremonies that go into the religion.

Also included in the Vedas are the Brahmanas—commentaries upon the aforementioned rituals and the Upanishads, the texts that discuss knowledge, meditations, philosophy, and more.

Yogas

There are the yogas—the predefined combinations of planets to understand one's life. There are so many different topics that come into play here, and you will need to have a solid understanding of them all if you hope to begin implementing Vedic astrology.

Centers of Learning
Kashi (Varanasi)
Varanasi, also known as Kashi, has been a revered center of learning and spirituality in India, running continuously since ancient times. Here, Jyotish was closely linked to Vedic studies and rituals. Scholars in Varanasi have contributed significantly to astrological treatises, ensuring the preservation and transmission of Jyotish principles across generations.

Kerala (c. 7th–18th centuries CE)
Kerala became a notable center for Jyotish and astronomy during the medieval period, with a tradition of scholarly excellence in mathematical astrology. The Kerala School of Astronomy and Mathematics significantly enhanced computational techniques, improving the precision of Jyotish calculations.

Nalanda University (c. 5th–12th centuries CE)
Located in present-day Bihar, India, Nalanda was one of the world's first great residential universities and a key center for the study of various disciplines, including astronomy and astrology. Jyotish was taught here as part of a broader curriculum that integrated mathematics, philosophy, and astronomy, fostering advancements in predictive techniques and planetary calculations.

Taxila University (c. 600 BCE–500 CE)
Taxila was a major center for Vedic astrological education, where Jyotish was studied alongside disciplines like mathematics and medicine. It played a crucial role in systematizing and preserving early astrological knowledge that is foundational to Jyotish.

Ujjain (c. 4th century BCE–18th century CE)
An ancient city in central India, Ujjain was home to the legendary

The Encyclopedia of Astrology

astronomer-astrologer Varahamihira and the seat of the Ujjain School of Astronomy. Renowned as a hub for astronomical studies, Ujjain helped refine the mathematical and observational aspects of Jyotish, particularly in the development of panchangas (almanacs).

Key Texts

Brihat Parashara Hora Shastra (c. 1st millennium CE)
Attributed to Sage Parashara, this is one of the most authoritative and comprehensive texts on Jyotish. It covers a wide range of topics, including planetary influences, divisional charts, and predictive techniques, forming the foundation of modern Vedic astrology.

Brihat Jataka (c. 6th century CE)
Written by Varahamihira, this text is a seminal work on predictive astrology. It is known for its clarity and practical approach to interpreting horoscopes, covering topics like planetary combinations (yogas) and their effects.

Surya Siddhanta (c. 4th–5th century CE)
An ancient astronomical text that underpins Jyotish calculations. It provides mathematical frameworks for planetary motions, eclipses, and timekeeping, essential for constructing accurate charts.

Phaladeepika (c. 13th century CE)
Written by Mantreswara, this text focuses on the predictive aspects of Jyotish, including the effects of planetary placements, dasa (planetary periods), and remedies. It is known for its practical approach to horoscope analysis.

Notable Figures

Sage Parashara (c. 1st millennium BCE)
The author of the foundational *Brihat Parashara Hora Shastra*, Parashara is regarded as the father of Jyotish astrology. His work laid the framework for

astrological principles and predictive methods still in use today.

Varahamihira (c. 6th century CE)
A brilliant mathematician, astronomer, and astrologer, Varahamihira authored *Brihat Jataka*, one of the most influential texts on horoscopy. His encyclopedic knowledge and explanation of earlier traditions established him as a key figure in Jyotish.

Mantreswara (c. 13th century CE)
Author of *Phaladeepika*, Mantreswara excelled in systematizing predictive astrology, focusing on practical techniques and remedies for interpreting horoscopes.

K.N. Rao (b. 1931)
A prominent contemporary astrologer, K.N. Rao is known for his research-oriented approach and the introduction of new predictive methods. He has contributed to training and institutionalizing Jyotish in India.

Myths and Legends
The Legend of Rahu and Ketu
In ancient times, during the churning of the cosmic ocean by the gods (devas) and demons (asuras) to obtain the nectar of immortality (Amrita), a demon named Svarbhanu disguised himself as a god to partake in the nectar. The Sun (Surya) and Moon (Chandra) noticed this deception and alerted Lord Vishnu, who swiftly severed Svarbhanu's head with his discus. However, having consumed the nectar, both the head and the body became immortal.

The Encyclopedia of Astrology

The head came to be known as Rahu and the body as Ketu. In Jyotish astrology, Rahu and Ketu are considered shadow planets, representing the north and south lunar nodes, respectively. They are believed to influence eclipses and are associated with karmic forces that affect human lives. Rahu symbolizes material desire and obsession, while Ketu signifies spiritual detachment and liberation.

The Myth of Shani

Shani (Saturn) is one of the most feared and revered planetary deities in Jyotish astrology. His influence is associated with discipline, karmic justice, and spiritual growth. According to Hindu mythology, Shani is the son of Surya (the Sun) and Chhaya, a shadow of Surya's consort, Sandhya. His dark complexion and solemn nature were attributed to his mother's penance and devotion during pregnancy.

Despite being Surya's son, Shani was often at odds with his father. One famous myth explains why Shani's gaze is believed to bring hardship. When Shani was born, his gaze accidentally fell on Surya, causing his father's chariot to halt and his brilliance to dim. Surya, angered, cursed Shani to be associated with delay and obstruction.

Later, recognizing Shani's power and devotion, Lord Shiva made him a powerful planetary deity, granting him dominion over karma and justice. Shani's role in Jyotish astrology is to teach discipline, humility, and patience, often through challenges and trials. His transit (Sade Sati, the seven-and-a-half-year period of Saturn's influence) is considered a time of intense personal growth and transformation.

MESOAMERICAN ASTROLOGY

Introduction and History

The Aztec and Mayan civilizations, central to the Mesoamerican cultural region in Mexico and Central America, shared a profound connection to the cosmos that permeated their social, agricultural, and spiritual lives. These civilizations developed advanced astronomical systems and intricate calendars that served as essential tools for understanding the dynamic interplay of celestial and terrestrial cycles. For both cultures, the heavens were active participants in the rhythms of daily life. Celestial phenomena were interpreted as signals from divine forces, dictating the timing of human activities and tying in the movements of the stars and planets to society.

The Mayan civilization, flourishing from around 2000 BCE–1500 CE, was concentrated in the Yucatan Peninsula and the modern territories of Guatemala, Belize, and parts of Mexico and Honduras. Renowned for their monumental architecture and mathematical precision, the Mayans developed the Long Count calendar to track vast cosmic cycles. Complementing this were the Haab (a 365-day solar calendar) and the Tzolk'in (a 260-day ritual calendar), used to harmonize daily life and religious practices with celestial phenomena.

The Aztecs rose to prominence centuries later, peaking during the 14th–16th centuries CE. Centered in the Valley of Mexico, they built their capital, Tenochtitlan, on an island in Lake Texcoco. Their calendrical systems, including the Tonalpohualli (a sacred 260-day calendar) and the Xiuhpohualli (a 365-day solar calendar), reflect an intricate understanding of celestial patterns. These systems shaped agricultural cycles, religious festivals, and even the timing of warfare.

Despite the temporal and geographic separation, both civilizations viewed the heavens as dynamic forces that shaped daily life and connected the divine to humanity. The Sun, Moon, and Venus were particularly significant, often associated with powerful deities. For example, Venus was linked to Quetzalcoatl in Aztec culture and played a central role in Mayan astronomical codices (illustrated manuscripts). Observatories like the Mayan Temple of Kukulkán and the Aztec Templo Mayor demonstrate both cultures' emphasis on aligning architecture and ritual practices with cosmic order. From agricultural festivals to human sacrifices timed with eclipses and equinoxes, these rituals were performed to maintain harmony between the heavens and the Earth.

By connecting daily life with celestial events, these civilizations not only interpreted the stars but also created a legacy of astronomical knowledge that continues to fascinate scholars today.

Innovations and Unique Practices
260-Day Ritual Calendar

The 260-day ritual calendar (Tzolk'in for the Mayans and Tonalpohualli for the Aztecs) paired 20 day signs with 13 numbers to create a unique cycle of days. It served as a guide for

The Encyclopedia of Astrology

divination, personal destinies, and ritual timing. While the Mayans emphasized its role in linking spiritual and cosmic cycles, the Aztecs incorporated the calendar into statecraft, aligning it with political events and sacrificial rites.

365-Day Solar Calendar

The 365-day solar calendar (Haab for the Mayans and Xiuhpohualli for the Aztecs) organized time into 18 months of 20 days, with five "nameless" days, which were considered unlucky. Both calendars tracked agricultural and ceremonial timing, but the Mayans used the Haab in conjunction with the Long Count for cosmic cycles, while the Aztecs emphasized practical applications in governance and ritual.

20 Day Signs

Twenty day signs, each with symbolic meanings, formed the foundation of both systems. These signs were tied to deities, cardinal directions, and colors, reflecting the integration of cosmology and daily life.

Crocodile

Beginnings, creativity, and protection.
  Color: Red
  Direction: East

Wind

Communication, movement, and change.
  Color: White
  Direction: North

House

Stability, home, and introspection.
  Color: Black
  Direction: West

Lizard

Adaptability and survival. Symbolizes renewal and resourcefulness.
  Color: Yellow
  Direction: South

Snake

Transformation, fertility, and duality.
  Color: Red
  Direction: East

MAYAN/AZTEC SOLAR CALENDAR

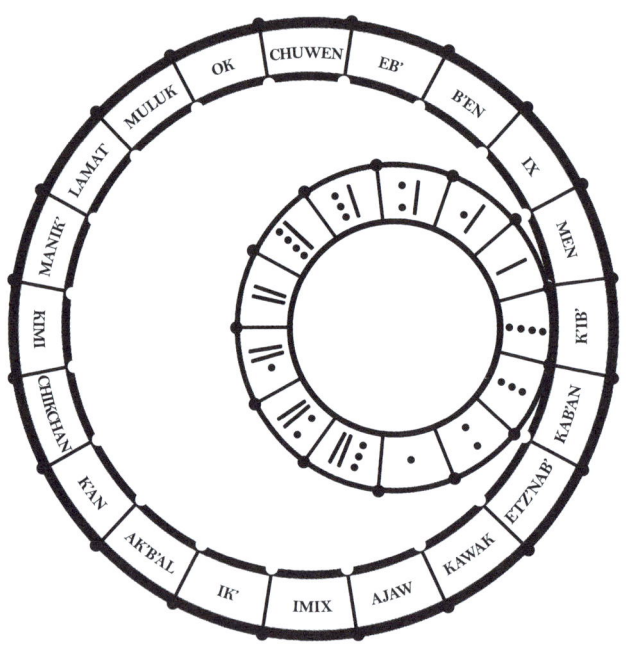

Death
Endings, transformation, and introspection.
   Color: White
   Direction: North

Deer
Harmony, gentleness, and strength.
   Color: Black
   Direction: West

Rabbit
Fertility, creativity, and joy.
   Color: Yellow
   Direction: South

Water
Emotion, purification, and intuition.
   Color: Red
   Direction: East

Dog
Loyalty, guidance, and protection.
   Color: White
   Direction: North

The Encyclopedia of Astrology

Monkey
Playfulness, artistry, and wit.
Color: Black
Direction: West

Grass
Resilience, humility, and healing.
Color: Yellow
Direction: South

Reed
Balance, strength, and connection. Tied to the god Tezcatlipoca, the Smoking Mirror.
Color: Red
Direction: East

Jaguar
Strength, courage, and secrecy.
Color: White
Direction: North

Eagle
Vision, independence, and freedom.
Color: Black
Direction: West

Owl/Vulture
Renewal, purification, and knowledge.
Color: Yellow
Direction: South

Movement
Change, dynamism, and transformation.
Color: Red
Direction: East

Flint
Clarity, precision, and sacrifice.
Color: White
Direction: North

Storm/Rain
Fertility, abundance, and blessings.
Color: Black
Direction: West

Flower
Beauty, creativity, and joy.
Color: Yellow
Direction: South

The 4 Colors
Red
Red symbolizes the beginning, the guiding path, and the life-giving force of the Sun. It represents blood, fire, and

The Encyclopedia of Astrology

energy—the red corn. Anthropologically, when we rise in the morning, our instinct is to face the east, gazing toward the sunrise, drawn to its life-affirming warmth and illumination.

Black

Black is likened to the black corn and represents the mysteries of the night, darkness, and death. It signifies rest and renewal, offering a chance to recover energy depleted during the day. In this sense, it also symbolizes hope, as the night promises the opportunity to complete unfinished tasks the following day, creating a sense of continuity.

In our bodies, black manifests in moles, the black of our eyes, and our hair. A black candle burns out faster than others, a natural phenomenon attributed to its absorption of heat—an apt metaphor for the intensity and transience of life.

White

White is compared to white corn and signifies purity, life, and the essence of creation. It embodies the color of semen, egg whites, seeds, air, the breath of life, bones, and the whites of our eyes. White reflects the sustaining and generative forces that give life its vitality.

Yellow

Yellow is associated with the cosmic life force Q'anil, which encompasses fertility, abundance, seeds, and the cycle of life. Yellow represents maturity, the essence of the seed, wealth, and potential. It also symbolizes sterility or illness when the seed fails to germinate, reminding us of the need to honor and give thanks to Q'anil for fertility and growth. Yellow is seen in the skin and muscles, embodying the physical manifestation of life.

Green

Green is the color of nature—the environment, plants, and the living world. It reflects the interconnectedness of all life and the need to seek permission for our actions in the natural world. The loss of these values has led to many of the challenges we face today, reminding us of the importance of harmony with nature.

Blue

Blue represents the vastness of the atmosphere, the water, and the air. It is the color of the elements that sustain and connect all living things, encompassing the flow and cycle of life.

13 Numbers

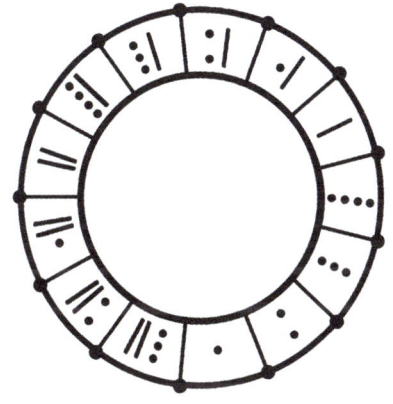

Both Mayan and Aztec systems incorporated a cycle of 13 numbers. In the Mayan calendar, these numbers interacted with the 20 day signs to produce the 260 unique days of the Tzolk'in. The Aztec Tonalpohualli also combined 13 numbers with 20 day signs to form its 260-day cycle.

Unity (1): Beginnings, creation, and initiation. Represents potential and the spark of life.
Duality (2): Polarity, relationships, and balance between opposites.
Movement (3): Action, dynamism, and the integration of opposites.
Stability (4): Foundation, order, and structure.
Empowerment (5): Creativity, freedom, and empowerment.
Flow (6): Harmony, equilibrium, and the ability to move with balance.
Reflection (7): Introspection, analysis, and connection to spiritual insight.
Justice (8): Manifestation, fairness, and material balance.
Patience (9): Completion, cycles, and the energy of eternity.
Manifestation (10): Achievement, realization, and leadership.
Release (11): Transition, change, and letting go.
Understanding (12): Collaboration, cooperation, and collective wisdom.

The Encyclopedia of Astrology

Ascension (13): Transformation, spiritual awakening, and transcendence.

4 Year Bearers

Both cultures assigned specific day signs as Year Bearers, marking the commencement of their solar years. In the Mayan Haab calendar, Year Bearers were the Tzolk'in day names that coincided with the first day of the Haab year.

The Aztecs had a similar practice, with certain day signs designated as Year Bearers in their 365-day calendar.

4 Cardinal Directions

Both the Mayan and Aztec systems associated day signs and deities with the four cardinal directions, integrating cosmology and geography into their calendars. In Mayan tradition, each direction was linked to specific colors and deities, influencing various aspects of life and ritual. The Aztecs similarly connected day signs and gods to the cardinal directions, which played a crucial role in their cosmology and ceremonial practices.

The four cardinal directions each represent a "house" or realm of influence, each tied to specific day signs, elements, gods, and themes in daily life.

Day Lords

In Mesoamerican astrology, each day in the ritual 260-day calendar (Tzolk'in for the Maya and Tonalpohualli for the Aztecs) was governed by a specific deity, often referred to as a Day Lord.

These deities influenced the character of the day and the fate of individuals born under it, providing spiritual guidance for personal and societal decisions. While the Maya also assigned divine forces to the days, the Aztecs uniquely emphasized the role of Day Lords in governance, aligning imperial events such as coronations and military campaigns with the divine character of specific days. This shared practice reflects the broader Mesoamerican belief in the interconnectedness of cosmic and human cycles, though with distinct cultural interpretations.

AZTEC ASTROLOGY
Introduction and History

The Aztec civilization reached its zenith between the 14th and 16th centuries CE. For the Aztecs, celestial movements held a profound connection to earthly existence. The stars, planets, and their cycles were integral to the Aztec cultural and spiritual identity, influencing daily life, religious practices, and governance. Through their intricate calendars, such as the Tonalpohualli (260-day ritual calendar) and the Xiuhpohualli (365-day solar calendar), the Aztecs aligned human activities with the rhythms of the cosmos.

The impact of Aztec astrology is still felt in daily life in Mexico. The Aztec Sun Stone (Piedra del Sol), a massive carved representation of the Aztec cosmos and the myth of the Five Suns, remains one of Mexico's most iconic artifacts. It is prominently displayed in the Museo Nacional de Antropología in Mexico City and features on Mexican pesos and other national symbols. Additionally, Aztec symbols, including those derived from their astrological signs, continue to inspire art, jewelry, fashion, and cultural identity in modern Mexico.

Innovations and Unique Practices
Codices

The Aztecs created codices (illustrated manuscripts) that depicted astrological signs, deities, and rituals. These codices, such as the *Codex Borbonicus*, were used not only for reference but also as tools for divination.

Five Suns Creation Myth

An Aztec creation myth describes the successive eras of the world, each governed by a "sun," or cosmic age, and shaped by the interactions of gods and celestial forces. According to this myth, the current world, the Fifth Sun, exists after the previous four were destroyed by elemental forces like wind, fire, water, and earthquakes. This understanding of the universe is deeply tied to Aztec astrology, including the calendar systems,

The Encyclopedia of Astrology

and reflects the cyclical nature of time as demonstrated by the movement of celestial bodies.

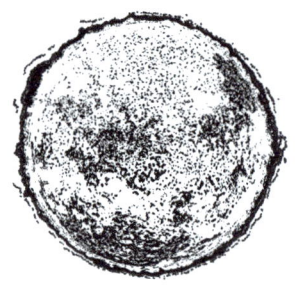

Omen Readings
Aztec astrologers, or *tonalpouhqui*, used the *Tonalpohualli* to read omens for warfare, coronations, agricultural cycles, and other significant political events. This practical application for statecraft and warfare was far more pronounced in Aztec astrology than in Mayan practices.

Tonalamatl
At birth, individuals were assigned a Tonalamatl, a personalized chart based on the Tonalpohualli calendar. This determined their fate, character, and life path, shaping decisions about career, marriage, and societal roles. Sources vary on how much the Aztec Tonalamatl impacted daily decisions of ordinary citizens.

Tonalpohualli
The Tonalpohualli, central to Aztec astrology, is a 260-day ritual calendar used to determine the fate and character of days, as well as the destinies of individuals born under them. It consists of 20 day signs, each paired sequentially with one of 13 numbers, creating a unique combination for every day. Governed by specific deities, or *Tonaltecuhtli*, the calendar served as a tool for divination, aligning human activities with cosmic rhythms and guiding rituals, agricultural practices, and political decisions. Its integration with Aztec mythology and statecraft made it a cornerstone of their spiritual and societal systems.

Centers of Learning
The Calmecac (Priestly Schools)
The Calmecac were schools for the Aztec elite, designed to prepare young nobles for roles as

priests, scholars, and leaders. Instruction included decoding astrological symbols and codices, ensuring that students gained a profound understanding of the cosmos and its influence on human affairs, along with a broader context of Aztec governance and ritual, which were inseparable from astrology. Graduates of the Calmecac became the primary astrologers and diviners of the Aztec Empire, advising rulers, overseeing public rituals, and determining the timing of important ceremonies based on celestial alignments.

Templo Mayor (Great Temple)

Located in the heart of Tenochtitlán (modern-day Mexico City), the Templo Mayor was the most important religious and ceremonial site for the Aztecs. The building was aligned with the stars—designed at its foundation to view and honor solstices and equinoxes. Priests at the temple studied the movements of the Sun, Moon, Venus, and other celestial bodies to guide their calendars.

The dual pyramids of the Templo Mayor were dedicated to Huitzilopochtli (god of the Sun and war) and Tlaloc (god of rain and agriculture), reflecting the integration of astrology with the cycles of life, death, and rebirth.

Tlillan Tlapallan (House of Darkness and Light)

It may be a stretch to include this in the "Centers of Learning," but in Aztec cosmology, Tlillan Tlapallan, often translated as the "Land of Darkness and Light," represented a conceptual, metaphysical realm embodying the duality of existence. It was a place where the forces of creation and destruction, order and chaos, coexisted in a delicate balance.

The journey to Tlillan Tlapallan was associated with spiritual enlightenment and the attainment of esoteric knowledge, tying it to the broader Mesoamerican emphasis on understanding the universe's interconnected forces. This dualistic concept influenced Aztec rituals, governance, and their intricate calendrical systems, emphasizing the harmony required to sustain both life and the cosmos.

Key Texts

Codex Borgia

A pre-Columbian Mesoamerican manuscript, the *Codex Borgia* is one of the most detailed sources of Aztec astrology. It includes depictions of the Tonalpohualli calendar, day signs, deities, and rituals tied to celestial movements. The codex reveals how astrological cycles governed ceremonies, warfare, and agricultural activities. It is currently housed in the Apostolic Library of the Vatican.

Codex Borbonicus

Likely written by Aztec priests shortly after the Spanish conquest, the *Codex Borbonicus* focuses on the Tonalpohualli and contains detailed illustrations of the 20 day signs and their associated deities. The codex was likely used for divination and teaching astrology. It is currently held in the Bibliothèque de l'Assemblée nationale in Paris.

Codex Mendoza

While primarily a tribute record for the Spanish crown, the *Codex Mendoza* contains sections detailing Aztec calendrical and astrological systems, as well as their role in governance and military campaigns. It's currently housed in the Bodleian Library at Oxford University.

Codex Fejérváry-Mayer

A richly illustrated Mesoamerican manuscript, this codex includes an intricate representation of the Tonalpohualli and the cardinal directions, integrating astrology with cosmology and ritual practice. This document is held in the World Museum in Liverpool.

Notable Figures

Tlacaelel (1398–1487)

As the principal architect of Aztec state ideology, the ruler Tlacaelel elevated the worship of Huitzilopochtli (the sun god) and strengthened the role of astrological rituals in unifying the empire. Tlacaelel emphasized the connection between celestial cycles and the empire's legitimacy, instituting ceremonies tied to the Sun's movements, such as the New Fire Ceremony, which marked the end of a 52-year calendar cycle.

Tlacaelel's reforms ensured that astrology became integral to Aztec political and religious life, influencing decisions at the highest levels of leadership.

Moctezuma II (1466–1520)

The last emperor of the Aztec Empire, Moctezuma II, was deeply engaged with astrology and divination. He relied heavily on astrologers and omens to guide decisions during his reign, especially as he faced the arrival of the Spanish. His belief in astrological predictions shaped his responses to external threats, which ultimately put the entire civilization at risk.

Nezahualcóyotl (1402–1472)

Ruler of Texcoco and a contemporary of Tlacaelel, Nezahualcóyotl was renowned for his intellectual and cultural contributions. He promoted the study of astronomy and astrology within his kingdom, encouraging the construction of observatories and the preservation of astrological texts.

Nezahualcóyotl's architectural projects included temples aligned with celestial events, such as the solstices and equinoxes. His poetry reflects an awareness of the cosmos and its cycles, demonstrating the spiritual importance of astrology in Aztec thought. As both a scholar and a leader, Nezahualcóyotl bridged the scientific and spiritual aspects of Aztec astrology, fostering a tradition of intellectual inquiry that influenced surrounding regions.

Myths and Legends
The Creation of the Fifth Sun

In the Aztec cosmos, the world had been destroyed and re-created four times, each era ending in catastrophe—floods, winds, fires, and jaguars. The current era, the Fifth Sun, began with an act of cosmic sacrifice. After the previous Sun was extinguished, the gods convened at the sacred city of Teotihuacán to decide who would become the new Sun. Two deities stepped forward: Tecciztecatl, proud and adorned with wealth, and Nanahuatzin, humble and blemished by illness. The gods decreed that the one who leapt first into the sacrificial fire would claim the monumental role of illuminating the world.

As the moment of decision arrived, Tecciztecatl hesitated, his pride giving way to fear. It was Nanahuatzin, unassuming yet courageous, who cast himself into the flames without hesitation, transforming into the radiant Sun. Tecciztecatl, shamed by his cowardice, followed, but the gods punished his reluctance by making him the dim Moon.

To set the Sun in motion, ensuring the cycles of day and night, the gods sacrificed themselves, spilling their divine essence to empower the cosmos. This ultimate act of selflessness established the Aztec principle of reciprocity, where human sacrifices were offered to maintain cosmic balance and the movement of the Sun.

The Birth of Venus as the Morning Star

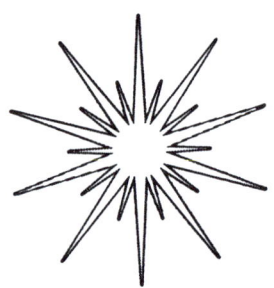

THE MORNING STAR

In Aztec mythology, Venus, embodied by the god Tlahuizcalpantecuhtli, served as both a symbol of beauty and a harbinger of conflict. Ambitious and determined, Tlahuizcalpantecuhtli sought to challenge the Sun's

The Encyclopedia of Astrology

supremacy and claim the heavens for himself. Armed with celestial darts, he hurled them at the Sun in an act of defiance. However, his aim faltered, and the Sun retaliated with overwhelming force, casting Tlahuizcalpantecuhtli down from the heavens.

Fallen but transformed, Tlahuizcalpantecuhtli became Venus, the Morning Star, tasked with heralding the Sun's arrival each day. Forever bound to his celestial rival, he retained his dual nature: a bringer of light and a harbinger of war. This myth reflects Venus's erratic and cyclical movements in the sky, as well as its association with both beauty and strife.

In Aztec astrology, Venus's cycles were meticulously tracked and incorporated into the Tonalpohualli calendar. The planet's appearances marked significant periods for warfare and rituals, demonstrating its profound influence on both the spiritual and practical aspects of Aztec life. The story of Tlahuizcalpantecuhtli exemplifies the cosmic tension between light and darkness, order and chaos, central to Aztec cosmology.

MAYAN ASTROLOGY
Introduction and History

Mayan astrology was rooted in the calendrical systems of the ancient Maya civilization that developed in the Yucatan Peninsula and Guatemala. Flourishing in Mesoamerica between 2000 BCE and 1600 CE, Mayan astrology was characterized by its focus on cycles, sacred time, and the interplay between celestial and terrestrial realms.

Mayan astrology placed a strong emphasis on celestial alignment and events, integrating their knowledge of and fascination with equinoxes, solstices, and planetary movements into their beliefs, as well as their ceremonial practices and architectural designs. Structures such as the Pyramid of Kukulkan at Chichen Itza were built to align with astronomical events and demonstrate this integration.

One concept central to Mayan astrological beliefs was the

PYRAMID OF KUKULKAN AT CHICHEN ITZA

world tree (Wacah Chan), which connected the underworld, the Earth and nature, and the planet and constellations, highlighting the interconnectedness between realms. Mayan astrology, with its profound integration of celestial cycles and sacred time, remains a testament to the Maya's sophisticated understanding of the planets and stars and their brilliant innovations.

Innovations and Unique Practices

Haab Calendar

The Haab, a 365-day solar calendar, structured into 18 months of 20 days each and a final short month of five "nameless" days, guided the Maya's agricultural and civil activities, bridging celestial cycles with earthly life.

Long Count Calendar

The Long Count calendar, a sophisticated system for tracking vast spans of time, enabled the Maya to record historical events and align them with cosmic cycles, reflecting their unparalleled understanding of chronology and the universe.

Maya Cross

In Mayan astrology, a personalized birth chart is known as a Maya Cross. It is created using the Tzolk'in calendar, which is a 260-day sacred calendar. This chart incorporates the individual's Day Sign, their primary sign, as well as other influences derived from their birth date. The Maya Cross is used to gain insight into a person's life purpose, spiritual path, and cosmic connections.

Tzolk'in

The Tzolk'in calendar, or the Sacred Round, is a cornerstone of Mayan astrology. Like the Aztec astrological system, this calendar consists of 260 days, divided into 20 day signs and 13 numbers. This calendar represents a spiritual cycle, mapping out energies and influences for each day. The interplay between the 20 day signs and the 13 numbers creates a total of 260 unique combinations, each with its own personality and meaning.

World Tree

The World Tree, or Ceiba tree, is a central symbol in Mayan cosmology and astrology. It represents the *axis mundi*, or the connection between the heavens, Earth, and the underworld. In Mayan thought, the World Tree is a metaphorical guide, mapping the universe and aligning human life with cosmic order.

In Mayan astrology, the World Tree embodies the cardinal directions—north, south, east, and west—each associated with a color and energy:

East (Red): Birth, renewal, and new beginnings.
West (Black): Death, transformation, and introspection.
North (White): Wisdom, clarity, and intellect.
South (Yellow): Growth, warmth, and vitality.

At the center of the World Tree is the axis itself, representing balance and the connection between spiritual and earthly realms. This concept underpins the Mayan practice of seeking alignment between personal energies and cosmic forces.

Centers of Learning
Copan (Honduras)

A renowned center for astronomical and astrological studies, Copan features stelae and altars with detailed celestial inscriptions, demonstrating the integration of astrological knowledge into religious and political life.

El Caracol at Chichen Itza (Mexico)

Known as "The Snail," this ancient observatory features architectural alignments with important celestial events, such as the solstices and the movements of Venus, which were critical to Mayan astrological and calendrical systems.

Temple of the Sun at Palenque (Mexico)

This temple is associated with solar worship and astrological practices, reflecting the Maya's intricate understanding of solar cycles. The Temple of the Sun has several archaeological elements that allow the light to pass in specific ways on the summer solstice, winter solstice, and equinoxes. When the Sun is directly overhead on May 7 and August 5, certain areas in the temple are illuminated. These dates represent the beginning of planting and harvesting season respectively.

Observatory at Uxmal (Mexico)

This site includes structures aligned with astronomical phenomena, emphasizing the Mayans' advanced knowledge of celestial movements. Uxmal features structures with precise alignments to astronomical phenomena, underscoring the Maya's advanced knowledge of celestial movements. The Governor's Palace, for instance, is oriented towards the setting Sun at the summer solstice.

Key Texts

The Dresden Codex

One of the most significant surviving pre-Columbian Mayan texts, containing detailed information on Mayan astrology, including calculations related to the Tzolk'in (the 260-day ceremonial calendar) and the Haab (the 365-day solar calendar). The codex includes tables that

The Encyclopedia of Astrology

record the movements of the planets, particularly Venus, and offers insight into the astrological significance of various days and cycles.

The Madrid Codex
This codex includes important astronomical and astrological content and features tables of the Tzolk'in and Haab' calendars, as well as information on the eclipses and planetary movements, with Venus playing a key role in Mayan astrology.

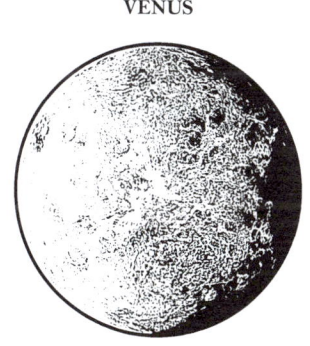

VENUS

Popol Vuh
While not strictly a manual of astrology, the *Popol Vuh* is the sacred text of the K'iche' Maya. It includes mythological stories that interweave celestial events, particularly the movements of the Sun, Moon, and Venus, with the creation and destiny of the world. This text is crucial for understanding how Mayan cosmology, including astrology, was reflected in their religious myths.

Notable Figures
Ah Xook (c. 8th century CE)
Ah Xook, often associated with the royal court of Copan, was a scribe and astrologer whose name is found on inscriptions detailing astrological cycles and celestial events. He is credited with interpreting the movements of Venus and its significance in warfare and ritual. His detailed records of Venus's phases are considered foundational to Mayan astrology's emphasis on planetary cycles.

K'inich Janaab Pakal (603–683 CE)
The ruler of Palenque, K'inich Janaab Pakal, also known as Pakal the Great, is renowned for integrating astrological sym-

bolism into dynastic narratives. His tomb, the Temple of the Inscriptions, aligns with celestial events, illustrating his belief in astrology's power to legitimize kingship. His reign saw the codification of solar and lunar cycles as essential elements of political and spiritual authority.

Lady Six Sky (682–741 CE)

A prominent queen and regent of Naranjo, Lady Six Sky employed astrology to reinforce her divine authority. Her inscriptions frequently referenced celestial alignments, particularly lunar and Venus cycles, to time political ceremonies. Her influence extended the role of astrology in legitimizing female leadership in Mayan society.

Myths and Legends
The Hero Twins and the Ballgame of the Underworld

The story of the Hero Twins, Hunahpu and Xbalanque, features prominently in the Popol Vuh. The twins defeat the lords of Xibalba, the Mayan underworld, by outwitting them in a ritual ballgame. Their victory symbolizes the triumph of light over darkness and order over chaos. In Mayan astrology, the twins are associated with celestial cycles, particularly the movements of the Sun and Moon, which reflect their duality and coordination.

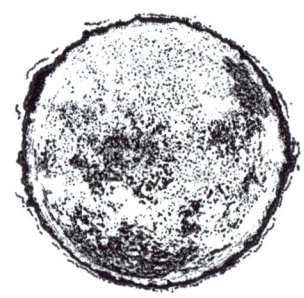

The Hero Twins' journey mirrors the interplay of the day-night cycle and the transitions of celestial bodies across the heavens. The ballcourt itself

The Encyclopedia of Astrology

was seen as a symbolic gateway between Earth and the cosmos, with the ballgame representing celestial dynamics, such as the movements of the Sun, Moon, and planets.

The Creation of the World and the Three Hearthstones

In Mayan cosmology, the creation of the world is symbolized by the placement of three hearthstones, marking the alignment of celestial bodies during significant moments in time. These hearthstones are said to correspond to specific stars in the constellation Orion, which the Maya saw as central to their understanding of the cosmos.

The myth describes the gods setting these hearthstones in place to establish the cosmic order, tying them to Mayan astrological systems that emphasized the alignment of stars and planets. Ritual hearths on Earth mirrored these celestial formations, symbolizing the connection between human and divine actions and the importance of astrological timing in rituals.

The Descent and Ascent of Venus

The Maya tracked Venus's phases with extraordinary precision, associating the planet's visibility and invisibility with cycles of death, rebirth, and divine action. The myth of Kukulkan (the feathered serpent deity) descending to the underworld and later re-emerging mirrors Venus's disappearance and reappearance in the sky.

This myth underpinned Mayan astrology's use of Venus cycles in warfare and religious ceremonies. The reappearance of Venus as the Morning Star was considered an auspicious time to begin battles or conduct rituals, symbolizing victory and renewal. The descent of Kukulkan also tied Venus to agricultural cycles, with the planet's phases influencing planting and harvesting times.

MESOPOTAMIAN ASTROLOGY (BABYLONIAN)
Introduction and History

The Sumerians were among the first to record observations of celestial bodies, focusing on identifying recurring patterns in the heavens rather than practicing formal astrology. They associated celestial bodies with deities such as the Moon (Nanna/Sin), the Sun (Utu/Shamash), and Venus (Inanna). These early observations were deeply intertwined with religious and agricultural practices, guiding planting and harvesting cycles through a lunar calendar that divided the year into months based on the Moon's phases.

While the Sumerians did not develop astrology as a formal system, their celestial observations laid the groundwork for later astrological traditions. Their meticulous recording of heavenly movements became a foundation for the advanced systems that followed.

Mesopotamian astrology, often referred to as Babylonian astrology, emerged in the cradle of civilization, Mesopotamia (a region covering modern-day Iraq and parts of Syria, Kuwait, Turkey, and Iran). The Babylonians expanded upon Sumerian practices, creating a systematic form of astrology. Around the 5th century BCE, they introduced the concept of the zodiac, dividing the ecliptic into 12 equal parts. This innovation marked a shift from general celestial observations to the detailed use of astrology for divination, personal horoscopes, and predicting events such as eclipses or planetary movements. They also compiled extensive records of celestial omens, most notably in the *Enuma Anu Enlil*, a collection of over 7,000 interpretations of astronomical phenomena.

The terms "Mesopotamian astrology" and "Babylonian astrology" are often used interchangeably, but there is a distinction. Mesopotamian astrology encompasses the broader geographical and temporal scope of the Sumerians, Babylonians, and Assyrians, while Babylonian astrology specifically refers to the practices that flourished during the Babylonian period (approximately 1894–539 BCE). Assyrian scholars also played a significant role in preserving and expanding Babylonian astrological texts during the first millennium BCE. Since the Babylonians made the most significant and well-documented contributions to early astrological development, their name has become closely associated with the entire tradition of ancient Mesopotamian celestial divination.

The *Enuma Anu Enlil* is a testament to the sophistication of Mesopotamian astrology. This compilation includes interpretations of celestial events and their potential effects on the earthly realm. For example, the planet Venus, associated with the goddess Inanna (later Ishtar), symbolized love and war. Its movements were thought to predict success or calamity in these domains. Similarly, the *Venus Tablet of Ammisaduqa* meticulously documented the planet's appearances and disappearances, emphasizing its importance in Babylonian thought.

While Mesopotamian astrology itself faded with the decline of Babylonian civilization, its influence persists. The zodiac, originally a Babylonian invention, remains central to modern astrology. Although the division of the sky into 12 houses was formalized in Hellenistic astrology, it drew heavily on earlier Babylonian concepts. Modern astrologers also continue to use the seven classical planets—a concept derived from Babylonian planetary worship. Additionally, the Babylonians' sexagesimal (base-60) numeral system underpins the 360-degree division of circles, a fundamental element of contemporary astronomical and astrological calculations, and the 60-second and 60-minute division of time.

Mesopotamian astrology laid the groundwork for Greek, Indian, and Islamic astrological systems, influencing cultures across millennia. By bridging the divine and the mundane through their meticulous recordings of the night sky, Mesopotamian astrologers not only shaped spiritual practices but also contributed to the development of science, timekeeping, and astronomy.

The Encyclopedia of Astrology

Innovations and Unique Practices

Mesopotamian astrology was founded on the belief that the heavens and Earth were interconnected, with celestial patterns reflecting divine will. This principle, known as "as above, so below," guided both spiritual and practical aspects of life.

Babylonian Zodiac System
Created the first known division of the ecliptic into 12 30-degree segments, laying the groundwork for modern zodiac signs.

Planetary Periods
Developed mathematical methods for tracking and predicting planetary cycles, including synodic periods (time between similar positions of a planet, e.g., conjunctions).

Eclipse Tracking
Designed sophisticated systems for forecasting lunar and solar eclipses, employing patterns such as the Saros cycle (approximately 18 years, 11 days).

Horoscopic Astrology
Pioneered the creation of personal birth charts (horoscopes) based on the exact time of birth, marking the earliest form of individualized astrology.

Mathematical Astronomy
Invented the sexagesimal (base-60) numeral system, enabling precise astronomical calculations and timekeeping still reflected in our use of 60 minutes in an hour and 360 degrees in a circle.

Planetary Week
Established the concept of a seven-day week, with each day associated with a planetary ruler (e.g., Saturn for Saturday), forming the basis of our modern calendar week.

Aspect Theory
Introduced early ideas of planetary relationships (aspects) and their astrological influences, such as conjunctions and oppositions.

Mundane Astrology
Developed systems for using celestial observations to predict political and economic events, an early form of political astrology.

Astronomical Diaries
Maintained meticulous records of celestial events and their earthly correlations, providing a database for interpreting the influence of heavenly movements over time.

Centers of Learning
Temple of Esagila in Babylon (modern-day Iraq)
The Temple of Esagila served as the primary center of Mesopotamian astrological learning. It housed a prestigious school of astrologer-priests who maintained astronomical records spanning centuries on clay tablets. The archives included the *Enuma Anu Enlil* scribal tradition, a cornerstone of celestial omen interpretation, and the temple served as a training ground for court astrologers advising kings and nobles.

Eanna Temple in Uruk (modern-day Iraq)
The Eanna Temple in Uruk specialized in mathematical astronomy, advancing sophisticated techniques for predicting planetary movements. The temple maintained detailed observational records and trained astronomers to integrate these calculations into religious and practical frameworks.

Temple of Ekur in Nippur (modern-day Iraq)
The Ekur Temple, dedicated to the god Enlil, emphasized celestial divination techniques. It functioned as both a repository for extensive omen collections and a center for training priests in interpretative methods. This made Nippur a spiritual and intellectual hub for Mesopotamian astrology.

Temple Observatory at Borsippa (modern-day Iraq)

The Ezida Temple in Borsippa, dedicated to the god Nabu, was renowned for its specialized planetary observations and eclipse predictions. Operating as a sister site to Babylon's Esagila, it played a vital role in the collaborative efforts of Mesopotamian astrological research. Together, these temples upheld their influence as centers of astronomical and astrological learning until the decline of Babylonian civilization around the 1st century BCE. Their knowledge endured through Greek and Persian translations, leaving a lasting legacy.

Key Texts

Enuma Anu Enlil

A collection of approximately 68 to 70 tablets containing celestial omens, astronomical observations, and weather predictions. Compiled over several centuries, with significant contributions during the Old Babylonian period (c. 1900–1600 BCE) and later during the Kassite period (c. 1595–1155 BCE). The text comprises around 6,500 to 7,000 omens and established foundational principles for Mesopotamian astrological practices.

The Venus Tablet of Ammisaduqa

Dating from the First Babylonian Dynasty (c. 1700–1600 BCE), this text records detailed observations of Venus's appearances and disappearances over a 21-year period. It demonstrates a sophisticated understanding of planetary cycles and their significance for divination, providing some of the earliest known systematic planetary observations.

MUL.APIN

Compiled around 1000 BCE, this two-tablet series presents a systematic overview of Babylonian astronomical and astrological knowledge. It contains star catalogs, methods for tracking celestial movements, and

The Encyclopedia of Astrology

instructions for correlating astronomical phenomena with terrestrial events.

The Astronomical Diaries

A series of clay tablets recording daily celestial observations from the 8th to the 1st century BCE. These diaries represent one of the longest continuous scientific records from the ancient world. The systematic observations of planetary movements, weather patterns, and significant events formed the basis for astrological predictions and advancements in mathematical astronomy.

Notable Figures
Berossus (c. 350–270 BCE)
A priest of Marduk in Babylon, Berossus established the first known school of astrology on the Greek island of Kos, serving as a crucial bridge between Babylonian and Hellenistic traditions. As court astrologer to Antiochus I, he wrote the *Babyloniaca*, a comprehensive history of Babylonian civilization that included detailed accounts of their astronomical and astrological practices. His influence can be traced through numerous classical authors who referenced his work, establishing him as a key figure in the transmission of Babylonian astrological knowledge to the Greek world.

Enheduanna (c. 2285–2250 BCE)
Enheduanna, the high priestess of the moon god Nanna in ancient Mesopotamia, held a role deeply intertwined with celestial observation and religious practices.

Her responsibilities included maintaining the lunar calendar essential for scheduling religious festivals and agricultural activities. In her collection of

The Encyclopedia of Astrology

Temple Hymns, one of the earliest preserved works from Mesopotamia, she wrote, "She measures the heavens above and stretches the measuring cord on the Earth."

Kidinnu (c. 400–350 BCE)

Based in Sippar, Kidinnu made groundbreaking discoveries in mathematical astronomy, particularly in understanding lunar motion and velocity. His calculations of the lunar month's length were remarkably accurate, differing from modern measurements by only a few seconds.

His system for tracking the Moon's complex motion remained the most accurate until the Renaissance, earning him recognition from later Greek astronomers. His work profoundly influenced both astronomical calculation and astrological practice, establishing mathematical methods that would be used for centuries in both fields.

Nabu-rimanni (c. 560–480 BCE)

Born in Babylon, Nabu-rimanni served as chief astronomer under several rulers. His rigorous mathematical approach to celestial observations established new standards for astronomical calculation and prediction. His influence shaped both technical astronomy and its practical applications in astrology, particularly through his refined mathematical tables that improved the accuracy of horoscopic astrology and timing predictions.

*Sudines (*fl. c. *240 BCE)*

A Babylonian astrologer who worked at the court of Attalus I of Pergamon, Sudines helped introduce Mesopotamian astrological techniques to the Hellenistic world. His influence persisted through later Greek and Roman authors who cited his authority on matters of astrology and gemology, marking him as an important figure in the development of Hellenistic astrological practice.

Myths and Legends
The Tale of Inanna's Celestial Journey

Inanna, the radiant Queen of Heaven, looked upon her city of Uruk and yearned for more than its earthly splendor. Her heart was set on the *me*, the sacred powers of the gods, hidden in the distant city of Eridu, where the wise god Enki reigned. Determined, she journeyed to his kingdom, her beauty and wit shining as bright as the morning star. Enki welcomed her warmly, offering a feast of beer and song. As they celebrated, Enki, overcome by joy and drink, granted her the me—divine decrees that governed the arts of civilization and the secrets of the heavens.

At dawn, Inanna gathered the shimmering treasures and loaded them onto the Boat of Heaven to return to Uruk. But Enki, sobered by morning's light, regretted his generosity and unleashed the forces of chaos—sea monsters and demons—to reclaim what he had lost. Inanna read the stars and whispered their secrets, commanding the heavens to calm the storm. One by one, the monsters fell away, and Inanna sailed back to Uruk triumphantly.

Safely back in Uruk, the people gathered in awe as Inanna revealed the gifts she had brought. From that day forward, her priestesses and astrologer-priests carried the knowledge of Venus, her celestial star, as a divine legacy. Inanna's triumph became a tale of wonder, her light forever guiding the heavens and the hearts of her people.

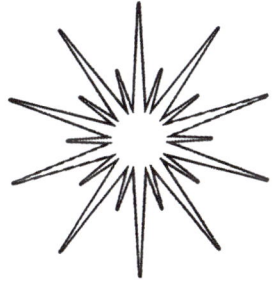

The Creation of the Celestial Tablets

In the time of chaos, before the world was formed, the great god Marduk rose to power. After defeating the primordial serpent Tiamat, he split her body to create the heavens and the Earth.

The Encyclopedia of Astrology

From her eyes flowed the rivers, and from her body, he shaped the cosmos. To mark his victory and establish law in the universe, Marduk placed the stars in the sky, arranging them into constellations that would guide the passage of time. He set the paths of the planets and decreed their movements, crafting a celestial map.

Marduk assigned the Moon to measure the months and seasons and ordered the Sun to regulate the days and years. The heavens became a living document, where the gods inscribed their messages for humanity in the movements of celestial bodies. To ensure this divine order was understood, Marduk gave the knowledge of reading the skies to humanity. He taught priests and scribes how to interpret the stars, record their observations, and seek meaning from what they saw. Over time, this sacred knowledge was compiled into texts such as the *Enuma Anu Enlil*, forming the foundation of Mesopotamian astrology.

NORTH AMERICAN INDIGENOUS ASTROLOGY
Introduction and History

Native American and First Nation peoples in North America represent diverse cultures with distinct spiritual and astronomical traditions. While some groups developed systems for connecting celestial movements to individual destiny, most Indigenous groups from this region focus on aligning community rhythms, ceremonial timing, and cultural storytelling with the cosmos. The stars and planets guide not only agricultural cycles but also spiritual practices.

The study of Indigenous star wisdom is probably more accurately considered ethnoastrology rather than conventional astrology. Ethnoastrology is the study of how societies integrate celestial knowledge into daily life—and ethnocosmology is how cultures explain their place in the cosmos through myths and practical observation. These frameworks help define how Native American and First

The Encyclopedia of Astrology

Nation peoples developed sophisticated systems for living in harmony with cosmic rhythms without necessarily creating predictive astrological models.

One innovation from this region is the 13-moon calendar observed by several Indigenous nations, including the Anishinaabe, Haudenosaunee, and Cree. This lunar calendar consists of 13 moons, each reflecting changes in the environment and guiding seasonal activities. The Anishinaabe, for instance, name each moon to correspond with local seasonal influences, such as the "Spirit Moon" in January and the "Bear Moon" in February. Similarly, the Haudenosaunee have 13 ceremonies throughout the year, each representing one of the 13 moons and following seasonal changes on the land. This system emphasizes the interconnectedness of natural events and cultural practices, fostering a harmonious relationship between the community and the cosmos.

The Cherokee offer a notable exception, employing a Venus-

The Encyclopedia of Astrology

based calendar system similar to Mesoamerican traditions. Their practices more closely align with what we typically recognize as astrology, linking celestial positions to personal characteristics and life paths, and are further described in this section.

Tribal Myths and Legends

Following are a collection of retellings of just a few Native American myths and legends that showcase different knowledge of, and appreciation for, the cosmos and celestial bodies. There are many powerful nations in the history of Indigenous people of the Americas and many different retellings of the myths—this is a small selection.

Apache—The Path of Spirits

Apache mythology describes the Milky Way as the "Path of Spirits," a celestial road that bridges the earthly world and the afterlife. This shimmering ribbon of stars is thought to guide the souls of the departed on their journey to the spirit world. Each soul, upon leaving its earthly vessel, embarks on this luminous path, following the gentle glow of the stars to its final resting place. The Milky Way thus serves as both a beacon and a sacred trail, symbolizing the unbroken connection between the living and those who have passed on.

THE MILKY WAY
galaxy

This belief reflects the Apache's deep spiritual connection to the natural world and their understanding of life as a journey intertwined with the cosmos. The stars that make up the Milky Way are seen not merely as celestial bodies but as the footprints of countless spirits who have walked the path before. It is said that the light of the stars offers comfort to those grieving, a reminder that their loved ones are never truly gone but have joined the eternal dance of the universe. Through the "Path of Spirits," the Apache honor the enduring cycle of life, death, and the boundless realms beyond.

Anishinaabe (Ojibwe) Nation— The Fisher and the Wintermaker

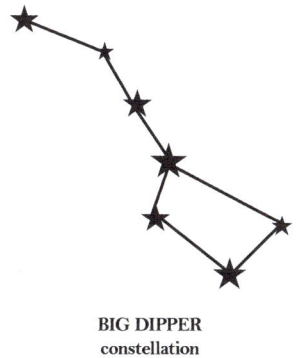

BIG DIPPER
constellation

In Anishinaabe (Ojibwe) tradition, the myths of Ojiig Anang (the Fisher Star) and Biboonikeonini (the Wintermaker) are interconnected through their association with seasonal changes and their positions in the night sky. The Fisher's journey to bring warmth to the Earth, resulting in his placement as the Big Dipper constellation, symbolizes the transition from winter to summer. Conversely, the Wintermaker, identified with the constellation Orion, heralds the arrival of winter with his outstretched arms spanning the sky. Together, these constellations serve as celestial markers for the changing seasons, guiding the Anishinaabe in their preparation for seasonal activities and ceremonies.

Blackfoot or Siksika Nation—Star Boy, or Scarface, and the Sun Dance

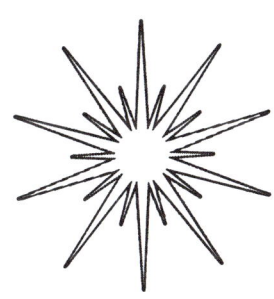

THE MORNING STAR

Star Boy is the son of Feather Woman, a mortal who was taken to the sky by Morning Star, the son of the Sun and Moon. Despite the divine lineage, Star

The Encyclopedia of Astrology

Boy was born with a scar, leading to his earthly name, Scarface.

Seeking to remove his scar and gain acceptance, he embarked on a challenging journey to the celestial realm. With the assistance of his grandfather, the Sun, he was healed and returned to his people, bringing with him the sacred Sun Dance ceremony, which holds profound spiritual significance in Blackfoot culture. The Sun Dance timing traditionally coincides with the summer solstice, a period marked by the longest daylight hours, symbolizing renewal and the peak of life. The ceremony typically spans several days and serves as a time for communal gathering, spiritual renewal, and the reaffirmation of cultural values.

Cree Nation—Great Bear and the Seven Birds

In Cree cosmology, the constellation known in Western astronomy as the Big Dipper is perceived as "Mista Muskwa," the Great Bear. According to Cree legend, Mista Muskwa was a formidable bear whose actions caused turmoil among the animals. To restore harmony, seven birds, referred to as "Tepakoop Pinesisuk" (the Seven Birds), embarked on a quest to chase the bear away. Their pursuit was so relentless that both the bear and the birds ascended into the sky, where they were immortalized as constellations.

CORONA BOREALIS
constellation

The Big Dipper represents Mista Muskwa, while the nearby Corona Borealis constellation symbolizes the Seven Birds. This story not only explains the origin of these star formations but also serves as a celestial reminder of the importance of balance and respect within the natural world.

The Encyclopedia of Astrology

Iroquois, also known as the Haudenosaunee Confederacy—The Sky Woman

Long ago, in the luminous Sky World above the clouds, lived Sky Woman, a being of wisdom and grace. One day, while tending the sacred tree that gave light and life to her realm, the tree was uprooted, leaving a great hole in the sky. Drawn by the mystery below, Sky Woman leaned too far and fell, clutching seeds from the tree in her hands. Below her, only a vast watery expanse stretched out, and the beings of the water saw her descent. Birds flew up to catch her, softening her fall, while the Great Turtle rose from the depths, offering his broad, strong shell as a resting place. The animals, led by the brave muskrat, dove deep to retrieve mud from the sea floor. Though it cost muskrat his strength, he surfaced with mud, which the animals spread across Turtle's back, creating the land we now call Turtle Island (or North America).

As Sky Woman walked upon the land, planting the seeds she had carried, life began to flourish—trees stretched skyward, rivers carved their paths, and plants grew in harmony. At night, Sky Woman looked up and saw the Great Turtle reflected in the heavens as a constellation, its shell mirroring the stars that marked the seasons. This sacred image reminded her people of the connection between the Earth and the cosmos, each guiding the other in balance. The Turtle's celestial form still guides the Iroquois people, marking the rhythms of planting, harvest, and the cycles of life. Sky Woman's fall was no accident; it was a gift that brought life, bridging the heavens and the Earth in eternal unity.

Lakota—Wi and Hanwi—the Sun and the Moon

In Lakota tradition, Wi (the Sun) and Hanwi (the Moon) were once inseparable, journeying together across the sky and sharing their light with both the spirit world and the earthly realm. Their harmonious union was disrupted by a trickster's scheme involving Ite, a beautiful woman from the Buffalo Nation. Ite's ambition, fueled by the trickster's deceit, led her to usurp Hanwi's place beside Wi during a sacred feast. Hanwi, upon discovering this betrayal, felt profound shame and concealed her face.

As a consequence of this disruption, the chief spirit, Skan, decreed that Wi and Hanwi would be separated, assigning them dominion over day and night, respectively. Hanwi was condemned to traverse the night sky alone, revealing her face fully only when farthest from Wi, symbolized by the full moon. As she approaches Wi, she veils her face, leading to the new moon. This celestial arrangement not only explains the lunar phases but also signifies the creation of time periods, with Hanwi governing the month and night, and Wi overseeing the day.

Navajo—the Thunderbirds

The Pleiades constellation is known as Dilyéhé, or the Flint Boys, a group of seven star-children tied to the sacred order of the cosmos. The story begins when the Earth and sky were separated, and Black God (Haashch'ééshzhiní), a deity central to Navajo creation stories, was tasked with arranging the stars.

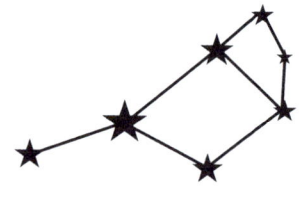

PLEIADES
constellation

Among his most precious placements were the Flint Boys, a cluster of seven stars he carried on his ankle. As Black God moved, stamping his foot in rhythmic beats, the stars ascended higher and higher—from his ankle to his knee, then to his hip, shoulder, and finally to his forehead, where they found their eternal home. This act symbolized Black God's power and connection to the universe, and the Flint Boys became a marker of time and seasons.

Pueblo—The Coyote and the Fourth World

The Pueblo people's reverence for the cosmos is still visible today, reflected in their architectural achievements. For instance, the Sun Temple in Mesa Verde National Park, Colorado, is believed to have been constructed with astronomical alignments in mind. Its D-shaped structure is oriented to capture solar and lunar cycles, indicating an advanced understanding of astronomy among the Ancestral Puebloans.

Similarly, Chaco Canyon in New Mexico houses several structures aligned with cardinal directions and celestial events. The Sun Dagger petroglyph on Fajada Butte is a notable example, where light patterns mark solar and lunar cycles, suggesting that it was used as an ancient calendar.

In the Santa Ana Pueblo creation story of the Coyote and the Fourth World, the world was once shrouded in darkness, with all living beings residing in the Third World. The animals' spirit leader, seeking to bring light to the new Fourth World, wove yucca mats and combined them with hot coals to craft the Sun, Moon, and stars. He selected certain animals, including Squirrel, Rabbit, and Badger, to ascend to the Fourth World, each carrying a piece of this radiant creation to illuminate the cosmos.

Coyote, known for his mischievous nature and past transgressions, was forbidden from joining this sacred journey. Defiant, he hid and later followed the other animals to the Fourth World. When Coyote was discovered, the spirit leader was summoned to address his disobedience. This tale serves as a lesson on the consequences of defying communal decisions and the importance of adhering to guidance within the Pueblo culture.

Modern Native American Astrology—The Medicine Wheel

While some cultures can trace astrological practices back to images or writing from as far back as 5000 BCE, a written guide

The Encyclopedia of Astrology

to Native American astrology is a more recent addition to global traditions. According to a 1980 publication called *The Medicine Wheel*, authors Sun Bear and Wabun have defined a new astrological system to link the stars to people's daily life and their overall journey. As a member of the Obijiwa tribe, Sun Bear has said he created this system to "help all people relate better to our Earth Mother … and find a kinship with the universe."

In this new tradition, each of the four seasons is divided into three sections. The moon phase at the time of your birth determines your initial position on the Medicine Wheel, with the first moon of the year beginning at the winter solstice. Your primary totem reveals your unique strengths, talents, and responsibilities. While Western astrology offers a fixed sign, in the system of the Medicine Wheel personal growth requires moving beyond a single totem over your lifetime. It is encouraged for individuals to journey through the zodiac wheel, exploring the various moons, totems, plants, and elements that shape their path, gaining deeper wisdom and connection along the way.

Spirit Animals and Birth Totems
Snow Goose
December 22–January 19
Traits: Honorable, ethical, traditional, sensitive, powerful, inflexible
Corresponds with: Earth Renewal Moon
Plant: Birch tree
Mineral: Crystal quartz
Color: White
Clan: Turtle Clan
Element: Earth
Spirit Keeper: Waboose (North)
Complementary Totem: Flicker (June 21–July 22)

Otter
January 20–February 18
Traits: Joyful and playful, talkative, trustworthy, skeptical
Corresponds with: The Rest and Cleansing Moon
Plant: Quaking Aspen

Mineral: Silver
Color: Silver
Clan: Butterfly Clan
Element: Air
Spirit Keeper: Waboose (North)
Complementary Totem: Sturgeon (July 23–August 22)

Cougar

February 19–March 20
Traits: Mysterious, calm and deliberate, deep and psychic, moody
Corresponds with: The Big Winds Moon
Plant: Plantain
Mineral: Turquoise
Color: Blue/green
Clan: Frog Clan
Element: Water
Spirit Keeper: Waboose (North)
Complementary Totem: Brown Bear (August 23–September 22)

Falcon (Hawk)

March 21–April 19
Traits: Dynamic, optimistic, adventurous, innovative, energetic, clear-sighted, feisty
Corresponds with: The Budding Trees Moon
Plant: Dandelion
Mineral: Fire opal
Color: Yellow
Clan: Thunderbird Clan
Element: Fire
Spirit Keeper: Wabun (East)
Complementary Totem: Raven (September 23–October 23)

Beaver

April 20–May 20
Traits: Grounded, hard-working, strong, stable, independent, stubborn
Corresponds with: Frogs Return Moon
Plant: Blue camus
Mineral: Chyrsocolla
Color: Blue
Clan: Turtle Clan
Element: Earth
Spirit Keeper: Wabun (East)
Complementary Totem: Snake (October 24–November 21)

The Encyclopedia of Astrology

Deer
May 21–June 20
Traits: Graceful, intuitive, resourceful, adaptable, creative
Corresponds with: Budding Trees Moon
Plant: Yarrow
Mineral: Agate
Color: White and green
Clan: Butterfly Clan
Element: Air
Spirit Keeper: Wabun (East)
Complementary Totem: Elk (November 22–December 21)

Flicker (Woodpecker)
June 21–July 21
Traits: Warm, loving, sensitive, nurturing, intense, vulnerable
Corresponds with: Strong Sun Moon
Plant: Wild rose
Mineral: Carnelian agate
Color: Pink
Clan: Frog Clan
Element: Water
Spirit Keeper: Shawnodese (South)
Complementary Totem: Snow Goose (December 22–January 19)

Sturgeon (Salmon)
July 22–August 21
Traits: Charismatic, big hearted, strong-willed, courageous, brash
Corresponds with: Ripe Berries Moon
Plant: Raspberry
Mineral: Garnet and iron
Color: Red
Clan: Thunderbird Clan
Element: Fire
Spirit Keeper: Shawnodese (South)
Complementary Totem: Otter (January 20–February 18)

Brown Bear
August 22–September 21
Traits: Wise, confident, fair, practical, perfectionistic
Corresponds with: Harvest Moon
Plant: Violet
Mineral: Amethyst
Color: Purple
Clan: Turtle Clan
Element: Earth
Spirit Keeper: Shawnodese (South)

Complementary Totem: Cougar (February 19–March 20)

Raven

September 22–October 22
Traits: Adaptable, balanced, intelligent, charming, communicative
Corresponds with: Ducks Fly Moon
Plant: Mullein
Mineral: Bloodstone jasper
Color: Brown
Clan: Butterfly Clan
Element: Air
Spirit Keeper: Mudjekeewis (West)
Complementary Totem: Falcon (March 21–April 19)

Snake

October 23–November 21
Traits: Intuitive, mystical, vibrant, active, transformative, wary
Corresponds with: Freeze Up Moon
Plant: Thistle
Mineral: Copper and malachite
Color: Orange
Clan: Frog Clan
Element: Water
Spirit Keeper: Mudjekeewis (West)
Complementary Totem: Beaver (April 20–May 20)

Elk

November 22–December 21
Traits: Humanitarian, insightful, reflective, independent, fearless, competitive
Corresponds with: Long Snows Moon
Plant: Black spruce
Mineral: Obsidian
Color: Black
Clan: Thunderbird Clan
Element: Fire
Spirit Keeper: Mudjekeewis (West)
Complementary Totem: Deer (May 21–June 20)

The Medicine Wheel serves as a guide for this transformative journey, offering a structured path for individuals to explore various aspects of their being and the natural world. By moving through the different cycles and directions of the wheel, one can achieve a harmonious balance and a deeper understanding of one's place within the greater cosmic order.

The journey through the totems is propelled by one's commitment to self-discovery and the pursuit of balance within the interconnected cycles of life. By engaging with the lessons and energies associated with each direction and totem on the wheel, individuals can gain deeper insights into themselves and their relationship with the universe.

Key Texts

The Medicine Wheel: Earth Astrology by Sun Bear and Wabun Wind, first published in 1980, is a foundational text that blends Native American spiritual wisdom with astrological concepts. The book offers readers a structured system for understanding their place in the world through the Medicine Wheel, incorporating the cycles of nature, personal growth, and the interconnectedness of all life.

CHEROKEE ASTROLOGY
Introduction and History

The Cherokee Nation originally inhabited the southeastern United States—including present-day Georgia, Tennessee, and North Carolina, but were forced to relocate to Oklahoma in 1838. Their forced migration was especially brutal and violent, and the path of their journey is now referred to as the Trail of Tears.

Cherokee astrology, deeply embedded in the cultural fabric of the Cherokee Nation, reflects their belief in the interconnectedness of the stars, the Earth, nature, and all living beings. Traditional Cherokee astrologers view the stars not as distant entities but as vital reflections of earthly existence, where every element of life on Earth mirrors celestial patterns.

Their astrological framework shares similarities with the Mesoamerican systems. This system combines 20 day signs and 13 numerical markers in a cyclic interplay that governs ceremonial timings, agricultural practices, and personal destinies.

The Encyclopedia of Astrology

Innovations and Unique Practices

Assignment of Day and Number Signs to Newborns

Newborns were assigned a day sign, which provided insights into their personality and potential, strengths and weaknesses, while their corresponding number sign outlined their role within the larger community.

Cherokee Moon Calendar

The Cherokee also followed a lunar calendar comprising 13 moon cycles, each with distinct names and associated ceremonies. This lunar system played a vital role in agricultural practices, ceremonial events, and daily life, reflecting the Cherokees' deep connection to lunar phases.

Daykeeper

Central to Cherokee astrological practice was the Daykeeper, a revered figure responsible for aligning the calendar with solar and lunar cycles. By determining the most auspicious days for specific ceremonies and activities, the Daykeeper maintained harmony between human actions and cosmic rhythms.

Kituwah Mound

Kituwah, in modern-day North Carolina, often referred to as the "Mother Town" of the Cherokee, holds significant cultural and spiritual importance. It was a central site for ceremonies and cultural activities. While specific documentation linking Kituwah directly to the preservation and transmission of astrological teachings is limited, its role as a ceremonial hub suggests it was integral to various aspects of Cherokee spiritual life.

Key Texts

Myths of the Cherokee by James Mooney (1900)

This foundational work documents Cherokee myths, legends, and cosmology, collected during the late 19th century. While it primarily focuses on stories, it includes references to the Cherokee understanding of celestial bodies, the Four Directions, and the interconnectedness of the cosmos with daily life.

The Sacred Formulas of the Cherokees by James Mooney (1891)

This collection includes prayers, songs, and rituals, many of which are tied to the cycles of nature and celestial events. The sacred formulas reflect the Cherokee view of time and the cosmos, offering glimpses into how celestial rhythms influenced ceremonies and healing practices.

Myths and Legends
Star Woman

In Cherokee lore, Star Woman is believed to guide farmers, her light signaling the times for planting and harvesting. Her presence symbolizes the deep relationship between the celestial and earthly realms, where the cycles of the stars align with the rhythms of life on Earth. For the Cherokee, this connection reinforces the importance of living in harmony with the natural world.

Star Woman is also seen as a spiritual messenger, bridging the celestial and earthly realms. During ceremonies, Cherokee elders call upon her to bless the land and provide wisdom. Her story reminds the Cherokee people that the stars are more than distant lights; they are kin, deeply intertwined with their history, culture, and daily lives. Through the guidance of Star Woman, the Cherokee find balance, nourishment, and a profound connection to the cosmos.

The Lord of the Dance

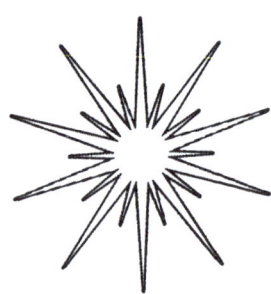

The Lord of the Dance is a revered figure in Cherokee mythology, identified with the North Star, or Polaris. This sacred star serves as the eternal anchor point in the night sky, around which the heavens revolve in a ceaseless celestial dance. These dances symbolize the harmony and order of the universe, with each participant reflecting the purposeful motion of celestial bodies. In this way, the North Star serves as the central figure in a grand celestial choreography, reminding the Cherokee people of their place in the larger cosmos and the importance of living in balance with the natural world.

The Long Man

The Cherokee name for the Milky Way is the "Long Man," a celestial river that flows eternally through the sky. This river is seen as a spiritual path that guides souls to the afterlife. In Cherokee belief, the Long Man connects the earthly rivers to the celestial ones, symbolizing the unity of the physical and spiritual worlds.

According to legend, the Long Man was created by divine beings to provide direction and wisdom to both the living and the departed. The stars within the Milky Way are thought to represent the footsteps of ancestors, lighting the way for those who come after them. The Cherokee use the Long Man to orient themselves spiritually, reflecting their belief that the cosmos is an ongoing story of life, death, and renewal.

NORSE ASTROLOGY
Introduction and History

Norse traditions, while lacking a structured zodiac system like those found in Babylonian or Hellenistic astrology, were deeply intertwined with the stars. The ancient Norse people observed the movements of the Sun, Moon, and planets for practical purposes like navigation and seasonal planning and imbued them with rich spiritual significance. The Vikings, renowned for their seafaring prowess, relied on celestial markers such as the Big Dipper and used innovative tools like sunstones to find their way even on cloudy days.

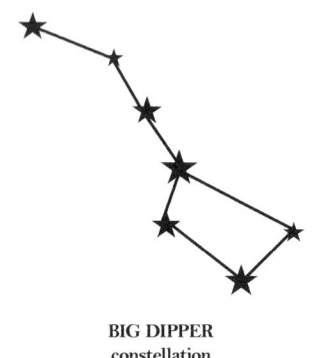
BIG DIPPER
constellation

Norse cosmology revolved around Yggdrasil, the great World Tree that connected the nine realms of existence: Asgard, Midgard, Helheim, and others. These realms symbolized different aspects of life and were believed to align with cosmic forces. The concept of wyrd, or destiny, played a central role in their worldview, with the Norns—mystical weavers of fate—shaping the paths of gods and mortals alike. Though the Norse did not assign celestial bodies to individuals' lives as modern astrology does, they viewed the stars as a living force that influenced their world through cycles, seasons, and omens.

Astronomy was also central to the Norse calendar and rituals. Archaeological evidence, such as stone circles and burial site alignments, suggests the Norse tracked solar events such as solstices and equinoxes, using these celestial markers to structure their agricultural and religious festivals. Mythologically, celestial bodies like the Sun (Sól) and Moon (Máni) were personified and linked to grand cosmic dramas, such as their eternal chase by the wolves Sköll and Hati, which would culminate in Ragnarök. These stories intertwined cosmic patterns with the Norse understanding of life's cycles, death, and rebirth.

Modern interest in Norse astrology has emerged alongside the revival of Norse paganism (Ásatrú), blending historical traditions with contemporary interpretations. Contemporary systems often incorporate rune magic, cosmology, and astronomical observations to reconstruct practices that align with the symbolic and mythological framework of the Norse.

The Encyclopedia of Astrology

Innovations and Unique Practices

Nine Worlds System

The Nine Worlds formed the foundation of Norse cosmology, interconnected by the great World Tree, Yggdrasil. Each realm represented a distinct aspect of existence and was home to different beings, from gods to giants to humans. While there is no historical evidence tying these realms to specific stars or constellations, celestial imagery was an important part of Norse mythology and storytelling.

Asgard

The realm of the Aesir gods, including Odin, Thor, and Frigg. Asgard was considered a celestial domain and the seat of divine power, connected to Midgard (the human world) by the Bifröst, a rainbow bridge.

Alfheim

The luminous realm of the Light Elves, often associated with beauty, creativity, and magic. It was described as a place of radiance and peace, under the protection of the Vanir god Freyr.

Nidavellir

The underground realm of the dwarves, master craftsmen known for forging legendary items such as Thor's hammer, Mjölnir. This realm was depicted as dark and rich with resources.

Midgard

The world of humans, positioned at the center of Yggdrasil's branches. Midgard was surrounded by an impassable ocean and protected by the gods from the chaos of the outer worlds.

Jotunheim

The wild and untamed homeland of the Jotnar (giants). This realm was often described as a place of wilderness and danger, symbolizing the chaotic forces that opposed the gods.

Vanaheim

The home of the Vanir gods, associated with fertility, prosperity, and nature. Though less is recorded about this realm, it was

considered equally powerful to Asgard.

Niflheim
A primordial realm of ice, cold, and mist. Niflheim played a role in Norse cosmogony as the source of icy rivers that mingled with the fire of Muspelheim to create the first being, Ymir.

Muspelheim
The realm of fire and heat, inhabited by fire giants like Surtr. Muspelheim was integral to the Norse creation story and prophesied to play a role in Ragnarök, the end of the world.

Helheim
The underworld ruled by Hel, daughter of Loki. Helheim was the destination for those who died of illness or old age, in contrast to the heroic dead who went to Valhalla or Folkvangr.

Runes
The 24 runes of the Elder Futhark were associated with celestial patterns and used to interpret the will of the gods,

with specific runes linked to different realms of Yggdrasil.

There are some sources online that discuss a zodiac based on Norse runes. This is a modern innovation and has little historical basis.

Sunstone Navigation

Vikings used crystals of Iceland spar (calcite) to locate the Sun's position even on cloudy days, enabling precise navigation. Recent experiments have confirmed this technique's effectiveness by tracking polarized light patterns.

Yggdrasil, or the World Tree

Yggdrasil, the cosmic World Tree in Norse mythology, symbolizes the axis connecting the nine worlds, with its roots and branches reaching realms like Asgard, Midgard, and Hel. While interpretations sometimes link Yggdrasil to the North Star (Polaris) as the celestial axis, these connections are largely symbolic.

In mythology, Yggdrasil's three roots reach significant wells: Urðarbrunnr (Well of Fate), Mímisbrunnr (Well of Wisdom), and Hvergelmir (Bubbling Spring). Norse cosmology reflects an intricate worldview where celestial movements and mythological narratives are deeply intertwined.

Centers of Learning

Goseck Circle in Germany (c. 4900 BCE)

The Goseck Circle, located in Saxony-Anhalt, Germany, is one of Europe's oldest known solar observatories, dating back to approximately 4900 BCE. This Neolithic structure features entrances aligned with the sunrise and sunset during the winter solstice, indicating its use in astronomical observations.

Ale's Stones (Ales Stenar) in Sweden

Ale's Stones is a megalithic monument in southern Sweden, comprising 59 large boulders arranged in the shape of a ship. Research suggests that the monument is aligned with the sunset during the summer solstice, indicating its potential use in tracking solar positions.

 Key Texts

The Poetic Edda (compiled *c.* 13th century)
A collection of Old Norse poems compiled from earlier traditional sources, providing key insights into Norse cosmology and the relationship between celestial bodies and the nine worlds. Though primarily mythological, these verses contain references to astronomical observations and their influence on daily life and religious practices.

The Galdrabók (*c.* 1600)
An Icelandic grimoire containing magical spells and rituals, some of which reference celestial timing and lunar phases. This text preserves some elements of earlier Norse astronomical practices and their application in magical operations.

Notable Figures
Snorri Sturluson (1179–1241)
An Icelandic historian, poet, and politician who recorded much of what we know about Norse cosmology and astronomical traditions. His systematic documentation of Norse mythology in the *Prose Edda* provides crucial information about how the Norse understood celestial movements and their relationship to the nine worlds and the Yggdrasil.

Oddi Helgason (c. 1125–1200)
Known as "Star-Oddi," he created sophisticated calculations for determining the positions of the Sun and stars, particularly for navigation purposes. Made in Iceland, his observations were recorded in the manuscript *Odda-tala* (*Oddi's Tale*), which contains detailed information about solar positions throughout the year. His calculations were so accurate that modern astronomers have verified their precision.

The Encyclopedia of Astrology

Myths and Legend
The Wolves: Sköll and Hati

In Norse mythology, the wolves Sköll and Hati hold a pivotal role in the cosmic cycle, particularly in relation to the Sun and Moon. Sköll, whose name means "Mockery," chases the Sun, while Hati, meaning "Hate," pursues the Moon. This eternal chase symbolizes the passage of time and the natural rhythms of day and night, creating a celestial dance observed from the mortal realm.

According to the myth, Sköll and Hati are descendants of the giant wolf Fenrir, and their pursuit is tied to the apocalyptic events of Ragnarök. During this time of cosmic upheaval, it is prophesied that the wolves will finally catch their prey, devouring the Sun and Moon and plunging the world into darkness. This act serves as a precursor to the end of the gods and the rebirth of the world, emphasizing themes of destruction and renewal inherent in Norse cosmology.

In Norse astrology, Sköll and Hati are sometimes seen as forces influencing the cycles of light and shadow in human life. Their mythological chase reminds us of the relentless passage of time and the duality of creation and destruction. These wolves serve as powerful symbols of transformation, urging us to find balance amid the cycles of chaos and order that define existence.

ROMAN ASTROLOGY
Introduction and History

Roman astrology emerged primarily as an adaptation of Greek astrological practices between 100 BCE and 200 CE, according to most sources. The Romans adopted the Greek zodiac, their use of horoscopes, and the seven classical planets, integrating these elements into their own cultural and religious frameworks and giving them the names Western astrologers use today. Greek texts, particularly Ptolemy's *Tetrabiblos*, served as foundational references for Roman astrologers, who often studied under Greek teachers or read translated works.

One of the main innovations that Roman astrologers brought to the Greek and Roman zodiac system was pragmatism. While Greek astrology often incorporated philosophical concepts, such as cosmic harmony and the soul's relationship to the stars, Romans emphasized astrology's practical applications, particularly in politics, warfare, and daily life.

Astrology was used in ancient Rome to divine the favor of gods and ensure proper religious rituals. Romans also placed greater emphasis on omens derived from eclipses, comets, and planetary alignments, blending astrology with traditional Roman divination.

Roman astrology became deeply tied to imperial power. Emperors such as Augustus used astrology to legitimize their rule, claiming their birth aligned with favorable celestial events. The Roman Senate occasionally banned astrology for the general populace, fearing its potential to incite rebellion or undermine authority. Roman astrology was widely used to predict the outcomes of military campaigns, political decisions, and natural disasters. For instance, the astrologer Nigidius Figulus reportedly predicted Julius Caesar's rise to power. Astrology also found its way into everyday Roman life, with individuals consulting astrologers for guidance on marriage, health, and business.

Innovations and Unique Practices
Integration with Daily Life and Religion

Beyond elite circles, astrology permeated everyday Roman life, with individuals seeking guidance

The Encyclopedia of Astrology

on personal matters such as marriage, health, and business. Also, Roman astrology was deeply intertwined with state religion and politics, influencing decisions and legitimizing authority.

Lot Astrology

Lot astrology was a technique specialized in Roman astrology that focused on deriving symbolic points, called lots, within a natal chart to provide deeper insights into a person's life. These points were calculated mathematically using the positions of specific planets and other chart factors, such as the ascendant.

The most well-known of these is the Lot of Fortune (*Pars Fortunae*), which represented material well-being, physical health, and circumstances of fate. It was calculated based on the distance between the Sun and Moon and then projected from the ascendant. Other lots, such as the Lot of Spirit and Lot of Eros, were used to explore different aspects of life, including career, relationships, and spiritual purpose.

Roman astrologers valued lot astrology because it offered a mathematical approach to fate and free will, blending philosophical ideas of destiny with practical interpretations of planetary influence. The system underscored the belief that specific life events or conditions could be traced to mathematical and cosmic harmony, aligning with broader Hellenistic thought on astrology's role in understanding the cosmos.

Lot of Children

Formula: Derived from Jupiter and the Moon.
Focus: Fertility, offspring, and parenting.

Lot of Eros (Love and Desire)

Formula: Ascendant + (Venus–Lot of Fortune)
Focus: Relationships, passion, and romantic connections.

Lot of Fortune

Formula: Ascendant + (Moon–Sun)

The Encyclopedia of Astrology

Focus: Material success, physical health, and overall fortune.

Lot of Marriage
Formula: Often varies, but commonly derived from Venus, the Moon, or the 7th house.
Focus: Partnerships, relationships, and marriage.

Lot of Sickness
Formula: Based on Saturn and the ascendant.
Focus: Health issues, challenges, and physical vulnerabilities.

Lot of Spirit (Daimon)
Formula: Ascendant + (Sun–Moon)
Focus: Mental and spiritual pursuits, personal drive, and aspirations.

Lot of Victory
Formula: Derived from Jupiter and the Lot of Spirit.
Focus: Success in endeavors, overcoming obstacles.

Lot of Wealth
Formula: Often involves the Sun, Jupiter, and the Lot of Fortune.
Focus: Financial prosperity and resources.

The Oculus of the Pantheon

The Pantheon, built around 126 CE under Emperor Hadrian, embodies astrological symbolism through its precise architectural design. The oculus—a 27-foot circular opening in the dome—acts as a solar marker, with sunlight moving in a circular path across the interior throughout the day, while the dome itself represents the celestial sphere with its five rings, thought to correspond to planetary orbits. The building's proportions follow sacred geometry, with the height equaling the diameter (142 feet), creating a perfect sphere that could fit within a cube—a design that reflects the Roman understanding of the cosmos.

The Encyclopedia of Astrology

Centers of Learning

Rome did not establish formal centers of astrological learning like the philosophical schools of Greece, though astrologers often served as private tutors or advisors within elite Roman households, imparting astrological knowledge to their patrons. Also, astrological ideas were discussed and propagated through literary works and intellectual gatherings, contributing to the spread of astrological concepts among the educated classes.

Key Texts

Astrological Treatises by Paulus Alexandrinus (4th century CE)

The *Astrological Treatises* by Paulus Alexandrinus is a concise handbook for interpreting natal charts, focusing on planetary rulerships, aspects, and the lots (such as the Lot of Fortune). It was widely referenced by Byzantine astrologers for its clarity and practicality.

Astronomica by Marcus Manilius (*fl.* 1st century CE)

A didactic poem in five books that explores the cosmos's structure, the zodiac's significance, and the influence of celestial bodies on human destiny. The work delves into various astrological concepts, including the zodiac signs, aspects, and houses, providing a comprehensive guide to the astrological knowledge of the time.

Notable Figures

Figulus, Nigidius (c. 98–45 BCE)

Born around 98 BCE, Publius Nigidius Figulus was a distinguished Roman scholar and politician. He served as praetor (one of Rome's two magistrates) in 58 BCE and was a contemporary and ally of Cicero. Historical accounts attribute to Nigidius prophetic abilities, such as foretelling the future greatness of Octavian (the future Emperor Augustus) on the day of his birth.

*Manilius, Marcus (*fl. *1st century CE)*

Scholars suggest Marcus Manilius was active during the reigns

The Encyclopedia of Astrology

of Emperors Augustus and Tiberius, placing his work in the early 1st century CE. Manilius is best known for his unfinished poem *Astronomica*, an extensive didactic work that blends astronomical knowledge with astrological theory. Composed in hexameter verse, the poem reflects the influence of earlier poets such as Lucretius, Virgil, and Ovid, and emphasizes the providential order of the universe and the role of divine reason.

Porphyry of Tyre (c. 234–305 CE)
Born in Tyre (modern-day Lebanon), Porphyry studied in Athens under Longinus before becoming a student of Plotinus in Rome. His extensive education in Neoplatonic philosophy and mathematics informed his approach to astrology, which sought to integrate philosophical principles with practical techniques. His house system remains in use today, particularly valued for its simplicity and effectiveness. Though primarily a philosopher, his contributions to astrological technique demonstrate how ancient thinkers viewed astrology as part of a comprehensive approach to understanding reality, worthy of serious mathematical and philosophical consideration.

Thrasyllus of Mendes (died 36 CE)
Thrasyllus of Mendes, also known as Thrasyllus of Alexandria, was a Greek-Egyptian scholar active during the late 1st century BCE and early 1st century CE. Thrasyllus's unique position as a Greek scholar and astrologer within the Roman imperial court exemplifies the cultural and intellectual exchanges between Greek and Roman traditions during this period.

Myths and Legends
Romulus and the Founding of Rome Under the Stars
The myth of Romulus and Remus, the twin founders of Rome, has celestial undertones that tie it to Roman astrology. According to legend, when the twins were deciding where to build their city, they turned to the heavens for guidance. Romulus

The Encyclopedia of Astrology

chose the Palatine Hill, while Remus favored the Aventine Hill. To settle the dispute, they looked for a sign.

ARIES

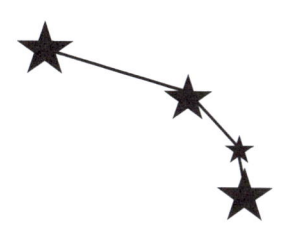

Remus saw six vultures flying over Aventine Hill. The birds were seen as messengers of Mars, the god of war and the twins' divine father. But over Palatine Hill, Romulus saw 12, which was a divine number. Romulus took this as a sign that he had the gods' blessing to rule. In his zeal, Romulus began building the city walls, and when Remus mocked and leaped over them, Romulus struck him down, solidifying his destiny as the first king of Rome. Roman astrologers later connected this myth to the constellation Aries, representing Mars and the Roman virtues of strength and conquest.

The Sibylline Books and Astrological Prophecy

The story of the Sibylline Books intertwines the celestial with the prophetic. According to Roman legend, an oracle approached King Tarquin the Proud with nine sacred books. These volumes were said to contain astrological secrets and divine knowledge about Rome's future. When Tarquin refused her high price, the oracle burned three of the books and offered the remaining ones at the same price. After repeating this twice more, Tarquin relented and purchased the final three books, recognizing their profound value.

These books were later stored in the Temple of Jupiter and consulted during crises to guide Rome's fate. Astrologically, the books were believed to hold cryptic guidance tied to the movements of the planets and stars. The Sibyl herself was seen as a channel for cosmic wisdom, embodying the Roman belief in the heavens' power to influence earthly events.

The Encyclopedia of Astrology

PLANETS & CELESTIAL BODIES

Planets and Celestial Bodies

The planets and celestial bodies—from the life-giving Sun to the mysterious outer planets—form the core elements of astrological interpretation. Each celestial body carries its own energy and symbolism, influencing different aspects of life as it moves through the zodiac signs and houses of a birth chart.

The core energies and qualities of planets remain remarkably consistent across different astrological traditions, though their interpretations and applications can vary. Mercury, for instance, has an association with communication, intellect, and movement whether viewed through Western, Vedic, or Chinese systems—though Vedic astrology may place greater emphasis on Mercury's role in mathematics and analytical ability, while Western traditions might focus more on its qualities of adaptability and exchange.

These common threads likely emerged because ancient cultures observed similar apparent behaviors and cycles of the visible planets, though each tradition developed its own sophisticated frameworks for working with these energies.

SATURN

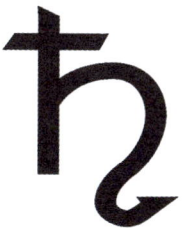

Structure, discipline, limits, time, responsibility

Basic Information
Rules: Capricorn and Aquarius (traditional)
Day: Saturday (from Saturn's Day)
Symbol: ♄ (represents Saturn's sickle or scythe)

Celestial Body
Saturn is the sixth planet from the Sun, famous for its distinctive ring system. It takes approxi-

The Encyclopedia of Astrology

mately 29.4 years to orbit the Sun, spending about 2.5 years in each zodiac sign. The planet appears pale yellow-gold and is the most distant of the classical planets visible to the naked eye. Saturn's direct energy supports the cultivation of discipline, the structured pursuit of goals, and the establishment of boundaries.

Saturn goes retrograde annually for about 4.5 months. During this phase, Saturn's influence shifts inward, prompting reflection on responsibilities, boundaries, and long-term goals. It is often a time to revisit and strengthen foundational structures in life.

Mythology

Saturn (Kronos in Greek mythology) was the father of Jupiter and ruler of the Golden Age. Though he devoured his children to prevent a prophecy of being overthrown, he's also associated with agriculture, time, and cycles. His mythological duality reflects both restriction and wisdom gained through experience.

In Roman culture, Saturn was celebrated during the midwinter festival of Saturnalia, a time of revelry, role reversal, and gift-giving, reflecting his association with cycles and the Golden Age.

Practical Applications

Saturn in Birth Charts

Saturn's placement in a birth chart reveals where we face our greatest challenges and where we're asked to develop discipline and maturity. Often called the Great Teacher, Saturn brings lasting rewards only after sustained effort and learning important life lessons.

In astrological birth charts, the ascendant marks the cusp of the first house. The houses are then numbered sequentially in a counterclockwise direction around the chart. Each house corresponds to different areas of life, and their positioning is influenced by the chosen house system.

Saturn in the Houses

First House: Self-image, appearance, and first impression. Saturn in the first house of a birth chart brings a serious demeanor and strong sense of personal responsibility. May indicate early life challenges that build character and self-discipline.

Second House: Personal finances, possessions, and values. Saturn in the second house indicates careful money management and delayed financial rewards. Strong focus on building secure material foundation through hard work.

Third House: Communication and siblings. Saturn in the third house creates structured communication patterns and serious study habits. May restrict or cause issues in relationships with siblings.

Fourth House: Home, family, and roots. Suggests karmic family patterns and perhaps challenging early home life. Brings structured approach to home and family matters.

Fifth House: Creativity, romance, and children. Indicates careful approach to creativity and selective romantic choices.

Sixth House: Health, daily routines, and service. Brings strong work ethic and methodical approach to daily tasks. Health matters require attention and disciplined routines.

Seventh House: Partnerships, marriage, and contracts. Suggests mature partnerships possibly starting later in life. Partners may be older or bring important life lessons.

Eighth House: Transformation, shared resources, and intimacy. Indicates careful handling of shared resources and deep research abilities. An inheritance may come with significant responsibilities.

Ninth House: Higher education, travel, and philosophy. Creates scholarly approach to higher learning. Travel and philosophical understanding come through careful study and experience.

Tenth House: Career, public image, and achievements. Natural placement bringing career success through persistent effort. Strong ambition and administrative abilities.

Eleventh House: Friendships, groups, and aspirations. Builds long-lasting friendships and structured approach to group work. May feel isolated from peers in younger years.

Twelfth House: Subconscious, spirituality, and hidden matters. Indicates private struggles that build wisdom. Requires working through karmic patterns and hidden fears.

Saturn in the Signs

When a planet is seen from Earth at the time of birth to be in the section of the sky where the constellation is located, the planet's influences are filtered through the characteristics associated with that sign.

Aries: Brings cautious approach to leadership. Learning to balance initiative with patience.

Taurus: Creates slow but secure material growth. Building lasting value through persistent effort.

Gemini: Results in methodical learning and careful communication. May restrict or structure mental activities.

Cancer: Manifests as emotional reserve and strong foundation-building.

Leo: Shows as disciplined creative expression. Learning to balance authority with responsibility.

Virgo: Expresses through perfectionism and masterful attention to detail. Excellence through practice.

Libra: Results in serious approach to relationships. Learning balance through overcoming obstacles.

Scorpio: Creates profound transformation through discipline. Mastering control of deep emotions.

Sagittarius: Shows as structured philosophical

understanding. Learning wisdom through limitation.

Capricorn: Natural placement bringing executive ability and ambition. Achievement through persistence.

Aquarius: Traditional ruler bringing innovative yet practical solutions. Structured approach to progress.

Pisces: Brings structure to spiritual life. Learning to balance material and spiritual responsibilities.

JUPITER

♃

Growth, luck, wisdom, abundance, expansion

Basic Information

Jupiter Rules the Signs: Sagittarius and Pisces

Jupiter's Day: Thursday (from Thor's Day, Thor being associated with Jupiter in Roman mythology)

Jupiter's Symbol: ♃ (traditionally interpreted as a crescent rising above a cross)

Celestial Body

Jupiter is the largest planet in our solar system, a gas giant with distinctive bands of swirling clouds and a famous Great Red Spot. It completes its orbit around the Sun in approximately 12 years, spending about one year in each zodiac sign. Jupiter's direct motion expands opportunities, fosters optimism, and inspires personal and philosophical growth.

During its annual retrograde period, lasting approximately four months, its forward progression appears to reverse. Astrologically, Jupiter retrograde encourages introspection about growth, opportunities, and philosophical beliefs, offering a chance to reassess how expansion aligns with deeper personal values.

The Encyclopedia of Astrology

Mythology

Jupiter (Zeus in Greek mythology) was the king of the gods, associated with abundance, wisdom, and good fortune. He overthrew his father Saturn to rule Mount Olympus, wielding thunderbolts and dispensing justice while being known for his expansive, generous, and sometimes excessive nature.

Practical Applications

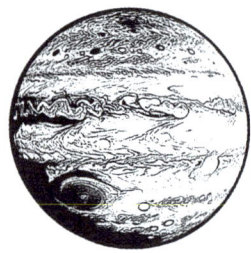

Jupiter in Birth Charts

Jupiter represents growth and wisdom and is thought to bring good fortune. The house and sign in which Jupiter appears in a person's unique birth chart can influence how and where these qualities appear in a person's life.

In astrological birth charts, the ascendant marks the cusp of the first house. The houses are then numbered sequentially in a counterclockwise direction around the chart. Each house corresponds to different areas of life, and their positioning is influenced by the chosen house system.

Jupiter in the Houses

First House: Self-image, appearance, and first impressions. Brings natural optimism, physical expansion, and a fortunate personal presence. People may appear jovial and wise, with opportunities seemingly falling into their lap.

Second House: Personal finances, possessions, and values. Indicates potential financial abundance and material good fortune. Can bring multiple income streams but also tendencies toward extravagant spending.

Third House: Communication and siblings. Bestows gift for teaching, writing, and communication. Brings opportunities through siblings and neighbors, with potential for successful short journeys.

Fourth House: Home, family, and roots. Creates an expansive, welcoming home environment. Indicates good fortune through real estate and family inheritance.

Fifth House: Creativity, romance, and children. Brings luck in creative ventures, romance, and speculation. Children may bring special blessings or opportunities.

Sixth House: Health, daily routines, and service. Indicates success through service to others, potential healing abilities. Good health generally, though watch for excess.

Seventh House: Partnerships, marriage, and contracts. Attracts beneficial partnerships and successful marriages. Partners may be teachers or people from foreign nations.

Eighth House: Transformation, shared resources, and intimacy. Brings benefits through shared resources, inheritance, or partner's wealth. Spiritual transformation through deep studies.

Ninth House: Higher education, travel, and philosophy. Jupiter in its natural house brings exceptional luck with higher education, travel, and spiritual pursuits. Strong philosophic insight.

Tenth House: Career, public image, and achievements. Indicates career success, especially in teaching, law, or religion. Natural leadership abilities and good reputation.

Eleventh House: Friendships, groups, and aspirations. Brings beneficial friendships and group associations. Success through networking and humanitarian pursuits.

Twelfth House: Subconscious, spirituality, and hidden matters. Offers spiritual protection and hidden benefits. Can indicate work in institutions or behind-the-scenes success.

Jupiter in the Signs

When a planet is seen from Earth at the time of birth to be in the section of the sky where the constellation is located, the planet's influences are filtered through the characteristics associated with that sign.

Aries: Brings bold, enthusiastic expansion and leadership opportunities. May rush into growth experiences headfirst.

Taurus: Steady, practical growth and material wealth. Patient effort may pay off financially and abundance shows up in the home.

Gemini: Expands intellectual horizons and communication abilities. Many interests but may spread energy too thin.

Cancer: Emotional growth and nurturing wisdom. Family expansion and domestic happiness highlighted.

Leo: Creative expansion and dramatic good fortune. Natural teachers and generous leaders.

Virgo: Growth through service and skill refinement. Success through attention to detail and practical wisdom.

Libra: Expansion through partnerships and diplomacy. Artistic growth and social success.

Scorpio: Deep psychological and spiritual transformation. Hidden resources bring opportunities.

Sagittarius: Jupiter in its home sign brings natural good fortune and wisdom. Success through higher education and travel.

Capricorn: Practical achievement and structured growth. Success through discipline and authority.

Aquarius: Innovation and humanitarian expansion. Success through community and progressive ideas.

Pisces: Jupiter in its traditional home brings spiritual wisdom and artistic inspiration. Success through compassion and intuition.

MARS

Action, drive, passion, courage, aggression

Basic Information

Rules: Aries (and traditionally Scorpio)
Day: Tuesday (from "Tyr's Day," after the Norse god of war, associated with Mars)
Symbol: ♂ (represents a shield and spear)

Celestial Body

Known as the Red Planet, Mars is the fourth planet from the Sun. It takes about 687 days to orbit the Sun, spending about 6-7 weeks in each zodiac sign. Mars's forward energy drives decisive action, unwavering determination, and the pursuit of desires.

Mars's retrograde cycle, occurring roughly every two years and lasting for about 60-80 days, alters this pattern. During retrograde, Mars appears to move backward through the zodiac, extending its stay in one or more signs. These periods are seen as opportunities to reassess motivations, energy levels, and long-term goals, as forward momentum often slows during this time.

Mythology

Mars (Ares in Greek mythology) was the god of war, representing aggressive energy, courage, and action. Though often portrayed as violent and impulsive, he was also associated with protection, assertiveness, and the warrior spirit. As the lover of Venus, he represented the passionate side of love.

Practical Applications

Mars in Birth Charts

Mars's placement shows how we assert ourselves, pursue our desires, and express our drive and ambition. It reveals our fighting style, how we take action, and where we direct our energy most naturally.

In astrological birth charts, the ascendant marks the cusp of the first house. The houses are then numbered sequentially in a counterclockwise direction around the chart. Each house corresponds to different areas of life, and their positioning is influenced by the chosen house system.

Mars in the Houses

First House: Self-image, appearance, and first impressions. Direct, forceful approach to life. Strong physical energy and competitive drive.
Second House: Personal finances, possessions, and values. Energy directed toward acquiring resources. Strong drive for financial security.
Third House: Communication and siblings. Mental assertiveness and quick communication. Strong drive to learn and share ideas.
Fourth House: Home, family, and roots. Energy focused on home and family matters. Strong drive for emotional security.
Fifth House: Creativity, romance, and children. Passionate creativity and romantic pursuit. Strong competitive spirit in sports and games.
Sixth House: Health, daily routines, and service. Energy directed toward work and health. Strong drive for self-improvement.
Seventh House: Partnerships, marriage, and contracts. Energy expressed through partnerships. Strong confrontational or cooperative tendencies.
Eighth House: Transformation, shared resources, and intimacy. Powerful transformative energy. Strong drive for intimacy and investigating mysteries.
Ninth House: Higher education, travel, and philosophy. Energy directed toward exploration and learning. Strong drive for adventure.
Tenth House: Career, public image, and achievements.

Ambitious drive for achievement. Strong career motivation and leadership.
Eleventh House: Friendships, groups, and aspirations. Energy directed toward group activities. Strong drive for social reform.
Twelfth House: Subconscious, spirituality, and hidden matters. Hidden or internalized energy. Strong behind-the-scenes action.

Mars in the Signs

When a planet is seen from Earth at the time of birth to be in the section of the sky where the constellation is located, the planet's influences are filtered through the characteristics associated with that sign.

Aries: Natural placement bringing pure warrior energy. Direct and pioneering action.
Taurus: Steady, persistent action. Strong determination and physical stamina.
Gemini: Quick, versatile energy. Strong mental drive and diverse interests.
Cancer: Indirect action driven by feelings. Strong emotional defense mechanisms.
Leo: Dramatic, creative action. Strong leadership drive and showmanship.
Virgo: Precise, methodical action. Strong drive for perfection and analysis.
Libra: Action through diplomacy. Strong drive for fairness and partnership.
Scorpio: Traditional ruler bringing intense, strategic action. Strong regenerative power.
Sagittarius: Adventurous, expansive action. Strong drive for freedom and truth.
Capricorn: Disciplined, ambitious action. Strong drive for status and achievement.
Aquarius: Independent, innovative action. Strong drive for reform and rebellion.
Pisces: Subtle, intuitive action. Strong spiritual or artistic drive.

SUN

Vitality, ego, purpose, will, leadership

Basic Information
Rules: Leo
Day: Sunday (from "Sun's Day")
Symbol: ☉ (ancient shield with center point, symbol of divine protection)

Celestial Body
The Sun is our star, the center of our solar system and source of life-giving energy. Its direct energy radiates vitality, clarity, and the drive to express one's core self. From Earth's perspective, it appears to move through one zodiac sign each month, completing its cycle in a year. It's approximately 109 times wider than Earth and accounts for 99.86% of the solar system's mass.

Mythology
In different cultures, the Sun was often the supreme deity— Ra in Egypt, Helios/Apollo in Greece, Sol in Rome. These gods typically represented life force, divine authority, and the principle of consciousness. They rode chariots across the sky, bringing light and order to the world.

Practical Applications

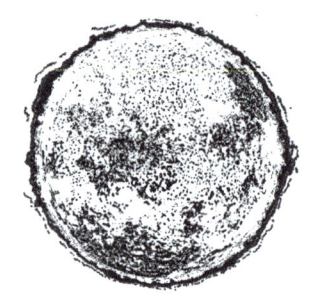

The Sun in Birth Charts
The Sun's placement in a birth chart represents one's core identity, basic personality, and life purpose. Often called the "Central Light" of the chart, its position

The Encyclopedia of Astrology

reveals how you express your essential self and where you naturally shine brightest.

In astrological birth charts, the ascendant marks the cusp of the first house. The houses are then numbered sequentially in a counterclockwise direction around the chart. Each house corresponds to different areas of life, and their positioning is influenced by the chosen house system.

The Sun in the Houses

First House: Self-image, appearance, and first impressions. Creates strong personality and natural leadership. Self-expression comes easily and presence is noticed.

Second House: Personal finances, possessions, and values. Identity develops through material resources and values. Strong drive to build security and worth.

Third House: Communication and siblings. Self-expression through communication and learning. Natural teacher or writer.

Fourth House: Home, family, and roots. Core identity tied to home and family. Strong need for emotional security and private life.

Fifth House: Creativity, romance, and children. Natural placement bringing creative self-expression. Strong drive for recognition and romance.

Sixth House: Health, daily routines, and service. Identity expressed through service and skill. Focus on health and daily routines.

Seventh House: Partnerships, marriage, and contracts. Self discovery through relationships. Strong need for partnership and cooperation.

Eighth House: Transformation, shared resources, and intimacy. Identity transforms through deep experiences. Power to regenerate and influence others.

Ninth House: Higher education, travel, and philosophy. Self-expression through higher learning and travel. Natural philosopher or teacher.

The Encyclopedia of Astrology

Tenth House: Career, public image, and achievements. Identity tied to career and public role. Strong drive for achievement and recognition.
Eleventh House: Friendships, groups, and aspirations. Self-expression through groups and humanitarian causes. Strong ideals and friendship bonds.
Twelfth House: Subconscious, spirituality, and hidden matters. Identity develops through spiritual or hidden matters. Need for retreat and self-reflection.

The Sun in the Signs

When the Sun is seen from Earth at the time of birth to be in the section of the sky where the constellation is located, the planet's influences are filtered through the characteristics associated with that sign.

Aries: Direct, pioneering self-expression. Natural leadership and independent spirit.
Taurus: Steady, practical approach. Strong connection to physical world and sensory experiences.
Gemini: Versatile, curious nature. Strong communication skills and adaptability.
Cancer: Nurturing, emotional expression. Strong connection to home and family.
Leo: Natural placement bringing dramatic self-expression. Strong creative and leadership abilities.
Virgo: Analytical, service-oriented approach. Strong attention to detail and practical skills.
Libra: Diplomatic, partnership oriented. Strong sense of fairness and aesthetic appreciation.
Scorpio: Intense, transformative expression. Strong emotional depth and investigative nature.
Sagittarius: Adventurous, philosophical approach. Strong drive for expansion and meaning.
Capricorn: Ambitious, structured expression. Strong sense of responsibility and authority.

The Encyclopedia of Astrology

Aquarius: Original, humanitarian approach. Strong drive for innovation and social progress.

Pisces: Intuitive, compassionate expression. Strong spiritual connection and artistic sensitivity.

VENUS

Love, beauty, pleasure, harmony, attraction

Basic Information

Rules: Taurus and Libra
Day: Friday (from "Freya's Day," Freya being the Norse goddess associated with Venus)
Symbol: ♀ (traditionally representing the mirror of Venus)

Celestial Body

Often called Earth's sister planet, Venus is the second planet from the Sun and the brightest natural object in Earth's night sky after the Moon. Venus's natural motion inspires the effortless flow of love, harmony, and the appreciation of beauty and pleasure. It takes 225 days to orbit the Sun and typically spends about 4-5 weeks in each zodiac sign, but this changes during its retrograde phase, which occurs approximately every 18 months and lasts for about 40-43 days.

During retrograde, Venus appears to reverse its motion from Earth's perspective, causing it to remain in one zodiac sign for an extended period. Astrologically, Venus retrogrades are significant times for reevaluating relationships, finances, and personal values, as these areas often come into sharper focus.

Mythology

Venus (Aphrodite in Greek mythology) was the goddess of love, beauty, pleasure, and fertility.

The Encyclopedia of Astrology

Born from sea foam, she was considered the most beautiful of the goddesses. Her influence extended beyond romantic love to include diplomacy, art, and the cultivation of beauty in all forms.

Practical Applications

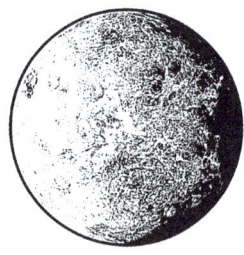

Venus in Birth Charts

Venus's placement reveals how we give and receive love, what we find beautiful, and our approach to pleasure and our values. As the planet of attraction, it shows what we're drawn to and how we create harmony in our lives.

In astrological birth charts, the ascendant marks the cusp of the first house. The houses are then numbered sequentially in a counterclockwise direction around the chart. Each house corresponds to different areas of life, and their positioning is influenced by the chosen house system.

Venus in the Houses

First House: Self-image, appearance, and first impressions. Natural charm and attractive presence. Strong focus on personal appearance and grace.

Second House: Personal finances, possessions, and values. Natural placement bringing appreciation for luxury and comfort. Strong financial instincts.

Third House: Communication and siblings. Charming communication style and artistic writing ability. Strong social connections locally.

Fourth House: Home, family, and roots. Creates beautiful home environments. Strong desire for domestic harmony and comfort.

Fifth House: Creativity, romance, and children. Romantic nature and artistic talents. Strong creative expression and joy in pleasure.

Sixth House: Health, daily routines, and service. Finding beauty in service and daily routines. Strong attention to health and wellness.

Seventh House: Partnerships, marriage, and contracts. Natural placement bringing diplomatic skills and partnership focus. Strong relationship needs.

Eighth House: Transformation, shared resources, and intimacy. Deep attraction to mysteries and transformation. Strong magnetic appeal and intimate bonds.

Ninth House: Higher education, travel, and philosophy. Finding beauty in knowledge and foreign cultures. Strong artistic or philosophical values.

Tenth House: Career, public image, and achievements. Charming public presence and artistic career potential. Strong professional relationships.

Eleventh House: Friendships, groups, and aspirations. Attractive social presence and diplomatic group skills. Strong platonic connections.

Twelfth House: Subconscious, spirituality, and hidden matters. Secret romances or artistic inspiration from solitude. Strong spiritual approach to beauty.

Venus in the Signs

When the Sun is seen from Earth at the time of birth to be in the section of the sky where the constellation is located, the planet's influences are filtered through the characteristics associated with that sign.

Aries: Direct approach to love and passionate artistic expression. Values initiative and excitement.

Taurus: Natural placement bringing strong appreciation for sensual pleasures. Values stability and comfort.

Gemini: Flirtatious, intellectual approach to love. Values mental connection and variety.

Cancer: Nurturing, emotional approach to love. Values security and emotional bonds.

Leo: Dramatic, romantic approach to love. Values grand gestures and creative expression.
Virgo: Practical, service-oriented approach to love. Values improvement and attention to detail.
Libra: Natural placement bringing diplomatic charm. Values harmony and balanced relationships.
Scorpio: Intense, transformative approach to love. Values deep emotional connections.
Sagittarius: Adventurous approach to love and beauty. Values freedom and cultural experiences.
Capricorn: Traditional approach to love and commitment. Values status and long-term security.
Aquarius: Unconventional approach to love and friendship. Values independence and uniqueness.
Pisces: Romantic, dreamy approach to love. Values spiritual connection and artistic expression.

MERCURY

Communication, thought, learning, movement, connections

Basic Information

Rules: Gemini and Virgo
Day: Wednesday (from "Woden's Day," Woden being the Norse god that shares characteristics with Mercury)
Symbol: ☿ (represents the caduceus—a staff with intertwined snakes)

Celestial Body

The smallest planet and closest to the Sun, Mercury orbits the Sun in just 88 days, spending about 3-4 weeks in each zodiac sign. Mercury's direct energy facilitates clear communication, efficient learning, and the seamless exchange of ideas.

The Encyclopedia of Astrology

Mercury's retrograde phases occur three to four times a year and last for about three weeks. These periods are marked by an apparent backward motion of Mercury in the sky, often associated with disruptions in communication, travel, and technology. Retrogrades are also considered valuable times for reflection, revisiting past ideas, and resolving unfinished matters.

Mythology

Mercury (Hermes in Greek mythology) was the messenger of the gods, patron of travelers, merchants, and thieves. Known for his wit, speed, and intelligence, he guided souls to the underworld and carried messages between realms. His winged sandals and caduceus symbolized swift communication and commerce.

Practical Applications

Mercury in Birth Charts

Mercury's placement reveals our communication style, learning patterns, and how we process information. As the planet of the mind, it shows how we think, speak, and connect ideas.

In astrological birth charts, the ascendant marks the cusp of the first house. The houses are then numbered sequentially in a counterclockwise direction around the chart. Each house corresponds to different areas of life, and their positioning is influenced by the chosen house system.

The Encyclopedia of Astrology

Mercury in the Houses

First House: Self-image, appearance, and first impressions. Quick mind and strong verbal presence. Natural ability to express personal thoughts.

Second House: Personal finances, possessions, and values. Practical thinking and financial aptitude. Communication focused on resources and values.

Third House: Communication and siblings. Natural placement bringing strong communication skills. Excellence in writing and learning.

Fourth House: Home, family, and roots. Deep thinker about home and family. Strong emotional memory and intuitive communication.

Fifth House: Creativity, romance, and children. Creative communication and playful mind. Strong ability to teach and entertain.

Sixth House: Health, daily routines, and service. Natural placement bringing analytical thinking. Strong attention to detail and practical solutions.

Seventh House: Partnerships, marriage, and contracts. Diplomatic communication style. Strong ability to see multiple perspectives.

Eighth House: Transformation, shared resources, and intimacy. Deep, investigative mind. Strong ability to uncover hidden information.

Ninth House: Higher education, travel, and philosophy. Philosophical thinking and broad learning. Strong interest in higher education and travel.

Tenth House: Career, public image, and achievements. Strategic mind and professional communication. Strong ability to convey authority.

Eleventh House: Friendships, groups, and aspirations. Innovative thinking and group communication. Strong networking abilities.

Twelfth House: Subconscious, spirituality, and hidden matters. Intuitive mind and subtle communication. Strong connection to unconscious knowledge.

Mercury in the Signs

When the Sun is seen from Earth at the time of birth to be in the section of the sky where the constellation is located, the planet's influences are filtered through the characteristics associated with that sign.

Aries: Quick, direct communication style. Thinks and speaks with urgency.

Taurus: Methodical, practical thinking. Communicates with deliberation and stability.

Gemini: Natural placement bringing versatile communication. Quick, curious mind.

Cancer: Emotional thinking patterns. Communicates with sensitivity and care.

Leo: Dramatic, expressive communication. Thinks with creativity and confidence.

Virgo: Natural placement bringing precise analysis. Detailed, systematic thinking.

Libra: Diplomatic, balanced thinking. Communicates with charm and fairness.

Scorpio: Deep, penetrating mind. Communicates with intensity and strategy.

Sagittarius: Broad, philosophical thinking. Communicates with optimism and wisdom.

Capricorn: Structured, practical mind. Communicates with authority and purpose.

Aquarius: Original, innovative thinking. Communicates with uniqueness and insight.

Pisces: Intuitive, imaginative mind. Communicates with empathy and creativity.

MOON

Emotions, intuition, nurturing, cycles, memory

Basic Information

Rules: Cancer
Day: Monday (from "Moon's Day")
Symbol: ☽ (represents the crescent moon)

The Encyclopedia of Astrology

Celestial Body

Earth's only natural satellite, the Moon completes its orbit in approximately 29.5 days. The Moon rises between 30 and 70 minutes earlier each day so it moves quickly through the zodiac during each cycle, spending about 2.5 days in each sign. The Moon's gravitational pull affects Earth's tides, and it's the only celestial body where humans have set foot. The Moon's motion reflects the continuous rhythm of emotional cycles and the nurturing connection to life's phases.

Mythology

The Moon has been personified across cultures as feminine deities —Selene/Artemis in Greece, Luna in Rome, Chang'e in China. These goddesses typically represented intuition, cycles, emotions, and nurturing energy. Many cultures saw the Moon as keeper of mysteries and guardian of the night.

Practical Applications

The Moon in Birth Charts

The Moon's placement reveals our emotional nature, instinctive reactions, and what we need to feel secure. As the fastest-moving celestial body in astrology, it represents our moods, habits, and unconscious patterns inherited from early life experiences.

In astrological birth charts, the ascendant marks the cusp of the first house. The houses are then numbered sequentially in a counterclockwise direction around the chart. Each house corresponds to different areas of life, and their positioning is influenced by the chosen house system.

The Moon in the Houses

First House: Self-image, appearance, and first impressions. Strong emotional

The Encyclopedia of Astrology

sensitivity and intuitive responses. Moods clearly visible to others.
Second House: Personal finances, possessions, and values. Security needs tied to material resources. Emotional comfort through tangible possessions.
Third House: Communication and siblings. Emotional expression through communication. Strong need to share feelings and learn.
Fourth House: Home, family, and roots. Natural placement bringing deep emotional roots. Strong connection to home and family.
Fifth House: Creativity, romance, and children. Emotional fulfillment through creativity and play. Strong need for romance and self-expression.
Sixth House: Health, daily routines, and service. Emotional satisfaction through service and routines. Strong connection between moods and health.
Seventh House: Partnerships, marriage, and contracts. Emotional needs met through relationships. Strong desire for partnership and harmony.
Eighth House: Transformation, shared resources, and intimacy. Deep emotional intensity and transformative feelings. Strong intuitive understanding of others.
Ninth House: Higher education, travel, and philosophy. Emotional growth through exploration and learning. Strong need for meaningful experiences.
Tenth House: Career, public image, and achievements. Emotions influenced by public life and career. Strong need for recognition and achievement.
Eleventh House: Friendships, groups, and aspirations. Emotional fulfillment through friendships and groups. Strong humanitarian instincts.
Twelfth House: Subconscious, spirituality, and hidden matters. Deep subconscious emotional patterns. Strong need for spiritual connection and solitude.

The Encyclopedia of Astrology

The Moon in the Signs

When the Sun is seen from Earth at the time of birth to be in the section of the sky where the constellation is located, the planet's influences are filtered through the characteristics associated with that sign.

Aries: Quick emotional reactions and independent needs. Instinctive leadership qualities.
Taurus: Steady emotional nature and need for comfort. Strong connection to physical security.
Gemini: Changeable emotions and need for mental stimulation. Strong communication needs.
Cancer: Natural placement bringing deep feelings and nurturing instincts. Strong emotional memory.
Leo: Dramatic emotional expression and need for recognition. Strong creative instincts.
Virgo: Practical emotional approach and need for order. Strong analytical response to feelings.
Libra: Harmonious emotional nature and need for partnership. Strong desire for balance.
Scorpio: Intense emotional depth and need for intimacy. Strong emotional resilience.
Sagittarius: Adventurous emotional nature and need for freedom. Strong philosophical instincts.
Capricorn: Reserved emotional expression and need for achievement. Strong sense of emotional responsibility.
Aquarius: Unique emotional patterns and need for independence. Strong humanitarian instincts.
Pisces: Sensitive emotional nature and need for spiritual connection. Strong empathic abilities.

URANUS

Revolutionary, unconventional, innovative, electrifying, liberating

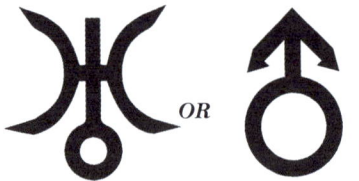

The Encyclopedia of Astrology

Basic Information
Rules: Aquarius (modern rulership)
Day: No traditional day association (discovered in 1781)
Symbol: ♅ (represents Herschel's symbol for his discovery, combined with the Mars symbol's spear)

Celestial Body
The first planet discovered by telescope, Uranus is the seventh planet from the Sun and tilts uniquely on its side. A blue-green gas giant, it was mistaken for both a comet and a star. Uranus's forward motion drives innovation, sudden breakthroughs, and the push toward freedom and individuality.

It takes about 84 years to circle the Sun, and spends about seven years in each zodiac sign, and its retrograde phase occurs annually for roughly five months. When retrograde, Uranus emphasizes internal breakthroughs, urging individuals to reflect on personal freedom, innovation, and the need for meaningful change.

Mythology
Uranus (Ouranos in Greek mythology) was the primordial sky god and first ruler of the universe, father of the Titans. He represents the heavens themselves and was considered the embodiment of creative force, innovation, and cosmic order. Cast down by his son Saturn, his story represents breakthrough and radical change.

In modern astrology, Uranus symbolizes innovation, rebellion, and sudden change, embodying the sky god's disruptive yet creative influence.

Practical Applications

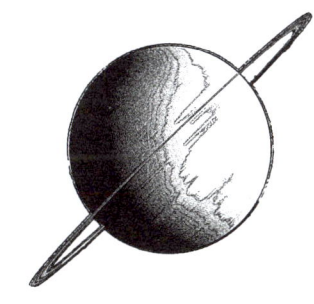

Uranus in Birth Charts
Uranus's placement shows where we experience sudden changes, breakthroughs, and the urge for

The Encyclopedia of Astrology

freedom. As the planet of revolution and innovation, it reveals where we're most unconventional and where we might experience unexpected developments.

In astrological birth charts, the ascendant marks the cusp of the first house. The houses are then numbered sequentially in a counterclockwise direction around the chart. Each house corresponds to different areas of life, and their positioning is influenced by the chosen house system.

Uranus in the Houses

First House: Self-image, appearance, and first impressions. Unique personal style and unpredictable behavior. Strong need for personal freedom.

Second House: Personal finances, possessions, and values. Unconventional approach to money and values.

Third House: Communication and siblings. Innovative thinking and unusual communication style. May have flashes of brilliant ideas.

Fourth House: Home, family, and roots. Unconventional home life or family structure. Could experience sudden changes in living situation.

Fifth House: Creativity, romance, and children. Original creativity and unusual romantic attractions.

Sixth House: Health, daily routines, and service. Innovative work methods and unusual health approaches. Sudden changes in daily routine.

Seventh House: Partnerships, marriage, and contracts. Unconventional relationships and partnerships. Unexpected encounters with others.

Eighth House: Transformation, shared resources, and intimacy. Sudden transformations and unusual spiritual insights. Unexpected shared resources may reveal themselves.

Ninth House: Higher education, travel, and philosophy. Revolutionary philosophies and sudden travels. Breakthrough spiritual insights.

Tenth House: Career, public image, and achievements. Unconventional career path and unusual public image. Sudden professional changes.
Eleventh House: Friendships, groups, and aspirations. Natural placement bringing humanitarian vision. Revolutionary group activities.
Twelfth House: Subconscious, spirituality, and hidden matters. Hidden rebellions and unconscious insights. Unexpected spiritual awakening.

Uranus in the Signs

When the Sun is seen from Earth at the time of birth to be in the section of the sky where the constellation is located, the planet's influences are filtered through the characteristics associated with that sign.

Aries: Revolutionary personal initiative. Sudden breakthroughs in identity.
Taurus: Radical changes in values and resources. Revolutionary approach to stability.
Gemini: Innovative communication methods. Sudden intellectual breakthroughs.
Cancer: Unconventional emotional expression. Revolutionary approach to home.
Leo: Original creative expression. Sudden romantic developments.
Virgo: Innovative work methods. Revolutionary approach to health and service.
Libra: Unconventional relationships. Sudden changes in partnerships.
Scorpio: Revolutionary transformation. Sudden deep insights.
Sagittarius: Breakthrough philosophies. Sudden long-distance travels.
Capricorn: Revolutionary structures. Sudden changes in authority.
Aquarius: Natural placement bringing humanitarian innovation. Revolutionary social change.
Pisces: Spiritual breakthroughs. Sudden mystical experiences.

The Encyclopedia of Astrology

NEPTUNE

Dreams, mysticism, illusion, spirituality, transcendence

Basic Information
Rules: Pisces (modern rulership)
Day: No traditional day association (discovered in 1846)
Symbol: Ψ (represents Neptune's trident)

Celestial Body
The eighth planet from the Sun, Neptune is a blue ice giant known for its strong winds and dark storms. It takes about 165 years to orbit the Sun, spending approximately 14 years in each zodiac sign. Named for its blue color resembling the sea, it's the fourth-largest planet by diameter and can't be seen without a telescope. Neptune's natural flow inspires dreams, spiritual connection, and a heightened sense of compassion and creativity.

Neptune's retrograde period occurs annually for about five months. Retrograde Neptune softens its usual dreamy and outwardly inspirational influence, directing its energy inward. This period often enhances intuitive insights, encourages spiritual exploration, and brings hidden illusions into awareness.

Neptune's influence is generational due to its long orbit, shaping the collective ideals, spirituality, and artistic movements of entire age groups.

Mythology
Neptune (Poseidon in Greek mythology) was god of the seas, earthquakes, and horses. Brother to Jupiter and Pluto, he ruled the oceans with his trident, controlling waters and sea creatures. Associated with both creation and destruction, he represented the mysterious depths of emotion and intuition, as well as the power to both calm and stir the waters.

The Encyclopedia of Astrology

Practical Applications

Neptune in Birth Charts

Neptune's placement shows where we experience dissolution of boundaries, spiritual connection, and our highest ideals. As the planet of dreams and illusion, it reveals where we might encounter both inspiration and confusion, and where we access our mystical nature.

Since Neptune is one of the outer planets, its influence tends to be more generational (affecting larger groups born during its long stay in each sign) while its house placement shows where we personally experience its mystical and sometimes confusing energy.

In astrological birth charts, the ascendant marks the cusp of the first house. The houses are then numbered sequentially in a counterclockwise direction around the chart. Each house corresponds to different areas of life, and their positioning is influenced by the chosen house system.

Neptune in the Houses

First House: Self-image, appearance, and first impressions. Chameleon-like personality and strong intuition. Difficulty defining personal boundaries.

Second House: Personal finances, possessions, and values. Unclear boundaries with resources. Spiritual approach to material matters.

Third House: Communication and siblings. Imaginative communication style. Learning through intuition and dreams.

Fourth House: Home, family, and roots. Mystical connection to home and family. Unclear family boundaries or history.

Fifth House: Creativity, romance, and children. Artistic creativity and romantic idealization. Spiritual approach to pleasure.

The Encyclopedia of Astrology

Sixth House: Health, daily routines, and service. Sensitivity to work environment. Healing abilities and psychosomatic conditions.

Seventh House: Partnerships, marriage, and contracts. Idealization of partners. Spiritual connections in relationships.

Eighth House: Transformation, shared resources, and intimacy. Deep psychic abilities. Mystical transformation experiences.

Ninth House: Higher education, travel, and philosophy. Spiritual visions and philosophical inspiration. Dream-like travels.

Tenth House: Career, public image, and achievements. Career involving inspiration or service. Unclear professional direction.

Eleventh House: Friendships, groups, and aspirations. Idealistic hopes and humanitarian dreams. Spiritual connection to groups.

Twelfth House: Subconscious, spirituality, and hidden matters. Natural placement bringing profound spiritual awareness. Deep unconscious connection.

Neptune in the Signs

When the Sun is seen from Earth at the time of birth to be in the section of the sky where the constellation is located, the planet's influences are filtered through the characteristics associated with that sign.

Aries: Idealistic personal initiative. Spiritual approach to identity.

Taurus: Mystical connection to nature. Dissolving material attachments.

Gemini: Imaginative communication. Intuitive learning style.

Cancer: Emotional sensitivity and psychic receptivity. Dissolving family patterns.

Leo: Spiritual creativity. Romantic idealization.

Virgo: Service through compassion. Dissolving perfectionism.

Libra: Romantic idealism. Spiritual partnerships.

Scorpio: Deep psychological insight. Mystical transformation.

The Encyclopedia of Astrology

Sagittarius: Spiritual philosophy. Dissolving belief limitations.
Capricorn: Practical mysticism. Dissolving structural boundaries.
Aquarius: Humanitarian ideals. Spiritual revolution.
Pisces: Natural placement bringing pure spiritual connection. Ultimate dissolution of ego.

PLUTO

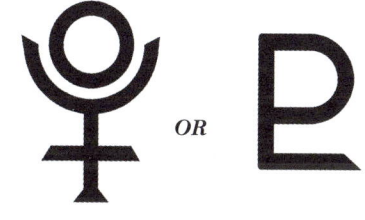

Transformation, power, depth, rebirth, intensity

Basic Information

Rules: Scorpio (modern rulership)
Day: No traditional day association (discovered in 1930)
Symbol: ♇ (combines the letters P and L)

Celestial Body

Now classified as a dwarf planet, Pluto is the most notable object in the Kuiper Belt, a vast region of icy objects beyond Neptune's orbit. It takes 248 years to orbit the Sun. Despite its reclassification, it remains one of the most potent forces in astrology. Pluto's direct energy initiates profound transformation, the uncovering of hidden truths, and the regeneration of personal and collective power.

Pluto spends anywhere from 12 to 31 years in a zodiac sign, with retrogrades occurring annually for about 5–6 months. Retrograde Pluto intensifies its transformative energy, urging deep introspection and the opportunity to confront fears, let go of outdated patterns, and embrace regeneration at a personal or collective level.

Mythology

Pluto (Hades in Greek mythology) was god of the underworld, ruler of death and rebirth. Brother to Jupiter and Neptune, he possessed a helmet of invisi-

The Encyclopedia of Astrology

bility and controlled all the Earth's mineral wealth. Though often feared, he represented not just death but transformation and regeneration, governing both endings and powerful new beginnings.

Practical Applications

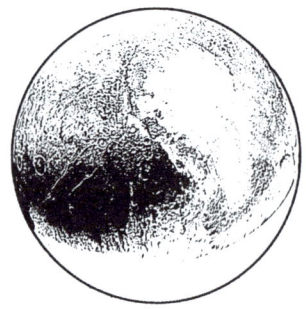

Pluto in Birth Charts

Pluto's placement reveals where we experience profound transformation, power dynamics, and regeneration. As the planet of death and rebirth, it shows where we face our deepest fears and experience the most intense personal evolution.

Like Neptune, Pluto's slow movement makes its sign placement more generational, while its house position shows where we personally experience its transformative power. Pluto's influence, though sometimes feared, ultimately leads to necessary evolution and empowerment through releasing what no longer serves us.

In astrological birth charts, the ascendant marks the cusp of the first house. The houses are then numbered sequentially in a counterclockwise direction around the chart. Each house corresponds to different areas of life, and their positioning is influenced by the chosen house system.

Pluto in the Houses

First House: Self-image, appearance, and first impressions. Intense personal presence and transformation of identity. Powerful self-expression.

Second House: Personal finances, possessions, and values. Deep transformation of values and resources. Power through personal possessions.

Third House: Communication and siblings. Profound

communication abilities. Transformation through learning and sharing.
Fourth House: Home, family, and roots. Deep family patterns and emotional transformation. Power struggles at home.
Fifth House: Creativity, romance, and children. Intense creative power and dramatic self-expression. Transformation through romance.
Sixth House: Health, daily routines, and service. Profound transformation through work and health. Power through service.
Seventh House: Partnerships, marriage, and contracts. Intense relationships and partnership transformations. Power dynamics with others.
Eighth House: Transformation, shared resources, and intimacy. Natural placement bringing deep psychological insight. Powerful regenerative abilities.
Ninth House: Higher education, travel, and philosophy. Transformation through higher learning and travel. Power through knowledge.
Tenth House: Career, public image, and achievements. Powerful career impact and public transformation. Authority issues.
Eleventh House: Friendships, groups, and aspirations. Transformation through groups. Power in collective movements.
Twelfth House: Subconscious, spirituality, and hidden matters. Deep unconscious transformation. Hidden power and spiritual regeneration.

Pluto in the Signs

When the Sun is seen from Earth at the time of birth to be in the section of the sky where the constellation is located, the planet's influences are filtered through the characteristics associated with that sign.

Aries: Transformation of personal identity. Power through initiative.
Taurus: Transformation of values and resources. Power through stability.

The Encyclopedia of Astrology

Gemini: Transformation of thought patterns. Power through communication.
Cancer: Transformation of emotional patterns. Power through nurturing.
Leo: Transformation of creative expression. Power through authenticity.
Virgo: Transformation through analysis and service. Power through improvement.
Libra: Transformation of relationships. Power through partnership.
Scorpio: Natural placement bringing intense transformation. Pure regenerative power.
Sagittarius: Transformation of beliefs. Power through wisdom.
Capricorn: Transformation of structures. Power through authority.
Aquarius: Transformation of society. Power through revolution.
Pisces: Transformation of spiritual connection. Power through surrender.

BLACK MOON LILITH

Independence, shadows, sexuality, wildness, truth

Unlike planets, Black Moon Lilith's motion appears to move backwards at times due to the Moon's orbital patterns. It spends about 9–10 months in each zodiac sign and takes about 8 years, 10 months to complete a full cycle through the zodiac.

BASIC INFORMATION

Not a physical body, but rather a mathematical point
Symbol: ⚸ (a stylized crescent moon atop a cross)
Takes approximately 9 years to complete its orbit

The Encyclopedia of Astrology

Celestial Point

Black Moon Lilith (also called the mean lunar apogee) represents the furthest point of the Moon's orbit from Earth. It's not a physical body but a calculated point marking where the Moon's orbit creates its greatest distance from Earth, showing where the Moon's gravitational pull is weakest. Black Moon Lilith's direct motion symbolizes the unrestrained flow of primal power, fierce independence, and the reclamation of suppressed truths.

Black Moon Lilith's motion appears retrograde at times due to the Moon's orbital dynamics. During these phases, its symbolic influence of raw independence, primal power, and repressed truths may make people feel more introspective, prompting a deep confrontation with shadow aspects of the self.

Mythology

Lilith appears in ancient Mesopotamian texts and Jewish folklore as Adam's first wife who refused to be subservient. She represents the divine feminine in her wild, untamed form, associated with independence, sexuality, and rejection of patriarchal authority. Some traditions cast her as a demon, others as a powerful goddess figure.

Practical Applications

Black Moon Lilith in Birth Charts

Lilith's placement reveals where we encounter our raw, uncontrolled power and where we might face rejection or exile for being our authentic selves. It shows areas where we refuse to submit to social expectations and where we access our primal wisdom.

In astrological birth charts, the ascendant marks the cusp of the first house. The houses are then numbered sequentially in a counterclockwise direction around the chart. Each house corresponds to different areas of life, and their positioning is influenced by the chosen house system.

Lilith in the Houses

First House: Self-image, appearance, and first impressions. Strong, untamed self-expression. Magnetic

The Encyclopedia of Astrology

but sometimes intimidating presence.
Second House: Personal finances, possessions, and values. Unconventional relationship with resources. Raw power through self-worth.
Third House: Communication and siblings. Taboo communications. Speaking unspeakable truths.
Fourth House: Home, family, and roots. Deep ancestral wisdom. Challenging family dynamics or home situation.
Fifth House: Creativity, romance, and children. Wild creative expression. Intense romantic or sexual energy.
Sixth House: Health, daily routines, and service. Alternative healing abilities. Rejection of conventional health or work structures.
Seventh House: Partnerships, marriage, and contracts. Intense relationship dynamics. Partnership patterns involving power struggles.
Eighth House: Transformation, shared resources, and intimacy. Natural placement bringing occult powers. Deep connection to shadow work.
Ninth House: Higher education, travel, and philosophy. Forbidden knowledge or beliefs. Exile from traditional spiritual systems.
Tenth House: Career, public image, and achievements. Challenging authority through authenticity. Unconventional public image.
Eleventh House: Friendships, groups, and aspirations. Radical social positions. Rejection from or of groups.
Twelfth House: Subconscious, spirituality, and hidden matters. Hidden power and unconscious wild nature. Deep spiritual mysteries.

Lilith in the Signs
When the Sun is seen from Earth at the time of birth to be in the section of the sky where the constellation is located, the planet's influences are filtered through the characteristics associated with that sign.

Aries: Raw independence and fierce self-assertion. Refuses to be controlled.

Taurus: Primal connection to body and earth. Unconventional material values.
Gemini: Speaking dangerous truths. Challenging conventional thought.
Cancer: Deep emotional wisdom. Rejection of traditional nurturing roles.
Leo: Wild creative force. Refuses to dim personal power.
Virgo: Sacred sexuality. Rejection of purity standards.
Libra: Raw relationship power. Challenging partnership conventions.
Scorpio: Intense transformative energy. Deep connection to taboo.
Sagittarius: Wild spiritual truth. Rejection of religious dogma.
Capricorn: Primal authority. Challenging societal structures.
Aquarius: Radical liberation. Rejection of social norms.
Pisces: Mystical wisdom. Connection to forbidden spirituality.

CHIRON

Wounds, healing, teaching, bridges, wisdom

Basic Information

Not a traditional planet, but a comet-like body between Saturn and Uranus
Symbol: ⚷ (represents a key)
Discovered in 1977

Celestial Body

Chiron is a small celestial body classified as both an asteroid and a comet, and because of this dual nature often called a "centaur." It takes approximately 50 years to complete its journey around the Sun. Its unusual orbit crosses paths with multiple planets, symbolizing its role as a bridge between different realms. Chiron's forward movement bridges the realms of wounding and healing, facilitating growth

The Encyclopedia of Astrology

through wisdom and the integration of life's deepest lessons.

Chiron's orbit between Saturn and Uranus causes it to retrograde annually for about five months. During this period, the "wounded healer" archetype turns inward, encouraging reflection on personal wounds and offering insights into how they can become sources of wisdom and healing for others.

Mythology

Chiron was an immortal centaur in Greek mythology, different from the typically wild centaurs. Known as the "wounded healer," he was a wise teacher of medicine, music, and prophecy. Despite his ability to heal others, he couldn't heal his own eternal wound from a poisoned arrow. He eventually gave up his immortality to free Prometheus.

Practical Applications
Chiron in Birth Charts

Chiron's placement reveals our deepest wounds and how they become our greatest gifts for helping others. Often called the "wounded healer," it shows where we've experienced pain but also where we develop unique wisdom and healing abilities.

In astrological birth charts, the ascendant marks the cusp of the first house. The houses are then numbered sequentially in a counterclockwise direction around the chart. Each house corresponds to different areas of life, and their positioning is influenced by the chosen house system.

Chiron in the Houses

First House: Self-image, appearance, and first impressions. Wounds around identity and self-expression. Teaching others self-acceptance.

Second House: Personal finances, possessions, and values. Wounds around self-worth and resources. Teaching others about true value.

Third House: Communication and siblings. Wounds around communication and learning. Teaching others to express themselves.

Fourth House: Home, family, and roots. Wounds around family and emotional security. Teaching others about belonging.

Fifth House: Creativity, romance, and children. Wounds around creativity and self-expression. Teaching others to embrace joy.

Sixth House: Health, daily routines, and service. Wounds around health and service. Teaching others about holistic healing.

Seventh House: Partnerships, marriage, and contracts. Wounds around relationships. Teaching others about healthy partnerships.

Eighth House: Transformation, shared resources, and intimacy. Wounds around intimacy and transformation. Teaching others about deep healing.

Ninth House: Higher education, travel, and philosophy. Wounds around belief and meaning. Teaching others to find their truth.

Tenth House: Career, public image, and achievements. Wounds around achievement and authority. Teaching others about authentic success.

Eleventh House: Friendships, groups, and aspirations. Wounds around belonging to groups. Teaching others about community.

Twelfth House: Subconscious, spirituality, and hidden matters. Wounds around spirituality and surrender. Teaching others about transcendence.

Chiron in the Signs

When the Sun is seen from Earth at the time of birth to be in the section of the sky where the constellation is located, the planet's influences are filtered through the characteristics associated with that sign.

Aries: Wounds around identity and courage. Healing through self-initiative.

Taurus: Wounds around security and worth. Healing through self-value.

The Encyclopedia of Astrology

Gemini: Wounds around communication. Healing through expression.
Cancer: Wounds around nurturing and safety. Healing through emotional connection.
Leo: Wounds around creativity and recognition. Healing through authentic self-expression.
Virgo: Wounds around perfection and service. Healing through acceptance.
Libra: Wounds around relationships and harmony. Healing through balance.
Scorpio: Wounds around power and intimacy. Healing through transformation.
Sagittarius: Wounds around faith and meaning. Healing through wisdom.
Capricorn: Wounds around authority and achievement. Healing through responsibility.
Aquarius: Wounds around belonging and uniqueness. Healing through innovation.
Pisces: Wounds around boundaries and spirituality. Healing through compassion.

OTHER CELESTIAL BODIES

As astronomers discover new celestial bodies, or learn more about what they are, astrologers begin to track their meaning and influence. For example, the dwarf planets beyond Pluto have gained attention in modern evolutionary astrology, particularly Eris, which symbolizes discord and feminine warrior energy. Meanwhile, traditional fixed stars continue to hold significance in both ancient and modern astrological practices.

Many celestial bodies discovered in modern times, such as Ceres, Eris, and Sedna, also experience retrograde motion annually for varying durations. Retrograde phases for these bodies invite introspection on their unique themes.

Following is a list of stars and other bodies with astronomical and astrological importance.

Aldebaran: A royal fixed star in Taurus known as "The Watcher of the East" and associated with military honors, war, and courage.

The Encyclopedia of Astrology

Castor: One of the twin stars in Gemini, associated with writers, storytellers, and those who work with their hands.

Ceres: As both a dwarf planet and asteroid, represents nourishment, mothering, agriculture, and cycles of loss and return. Orbits in the asteroid belt between Mars and Jupiter.

Eris: Dwarf planet discovered in 2003, associated with feminine warrior energy, discord, and forcing hidden truths to surface.

Gonggong: Dwarf planet discovered in 2007, sometimes associated with chaos and flooding.

Haumea: Dwarf planet discovered in 2003–4, associated with rebirth, fertility, and a goddess in Hawaiian mythology.

Makemake: Dwarf planet discovered in 2005, associated with environmental activism and connection to nature.

Orcus: Dwarf planet discovered in 2004, associated with oath-keeping and punishment of oath-breakers.

Pleiades: Star cluster in Taurus associated with grief, sorrow, and spiritual initiation.

Pollux: The second twin star in Gemini, associated with athletics, boxing, and martial pursuits.

Quaoar: Dwarf planet discovered in 2002, associated with Native American creation mythology and new beginnings.

Regulus: Major fixed star in Leo known as "Heart of the Lion," associated with royalty, success, and potential downfall through revenge.

Sedna: Dwarf planet discovered in 2003, associated with marine life, climate change, and victim-perpetrator healing.

Spica: Bright fixed star in Virgo associated with artistic and scientific talents, success, and wealth through skilled work.

The Encyclopedia of Astrology

CELESTIAL EVENTS

BLUE MOONS

When two full moons occur in the same calendar month or the third full moon in an astronomical season with four full moons, the term "Blue Moon" applies. While not visibly blue, these events happen roughly every 2.5 years and are considered potent times for the Moon's energy, especially for intentions that seemed impossible or "once in a blue moon" opportunities. This makes these events special for both astronomers and astrologers.

CONJUNCTIONS

When two or more planets align at the same zodiac degree, their energies merge and intensify. Notable conjunctions, such as Jupiter-Saturn's "Great Conjunction" every 20 years, have been interpreted as omens signaling societal shifts and new cycles. For example, the 2020 Great Conjunction in Aquarius marked the dawn of a 200-year era of Air sign conjunctions, reflecting technological and intellectual advancements. In astrology, conjunctions amplify planetary themes, making them powerful for focus and initiation.

CONJUNCTION

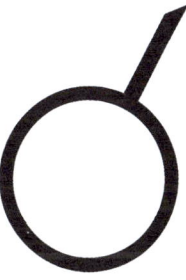

ECLIPSE
Annular solar eclipse

During a solar eclipse the Moon passes in front of the Sun. If a solar eclipse occurs when the Moon is at apogee, it will have a slightly smaller diameter than the Sun, so rather than blocking out all of the Sun's light to produce totality, you instead get a

The Encyclopedia of Astrology

ring of light visible around the Moon. This is an annular eclipse and it is sometimes referred to as a "ring of fire."

Lunar Eclipse

Lunar eclipses occur when Earth casts its shadow on the full moon, intensifying the emotional and transformational aspects of the lunar cycle. These events often bring hidden truths to light and mark pivotal endings or karmic completions. They can also bring closure and emotional healing. Historically seen as omens, they are potent times for rituals of release, healing, and profound change.

Penumbral Lunar Eclipse

During a lunar eclipse the Moon passes through Earth's shadow. There are two components of the shadow, the darker umbra and the lighter penumbra. During a penumbral lunar eclipse, Earth only passes through the penumbral shadow and it causes only a hint of darkening along the edge of the Moon.

Solar Eclipse

A solar eclipse occurs when the new moon aligns with the Sun and blocks its light. This creates a powerful portal for new beginnings and change, disrupting existing patterns to enable quantum leaps in specific life areas. Ancient cultures often regarded solar eclipses as times of divine intervention or significant omens.

The Encyclopedia of Astrology

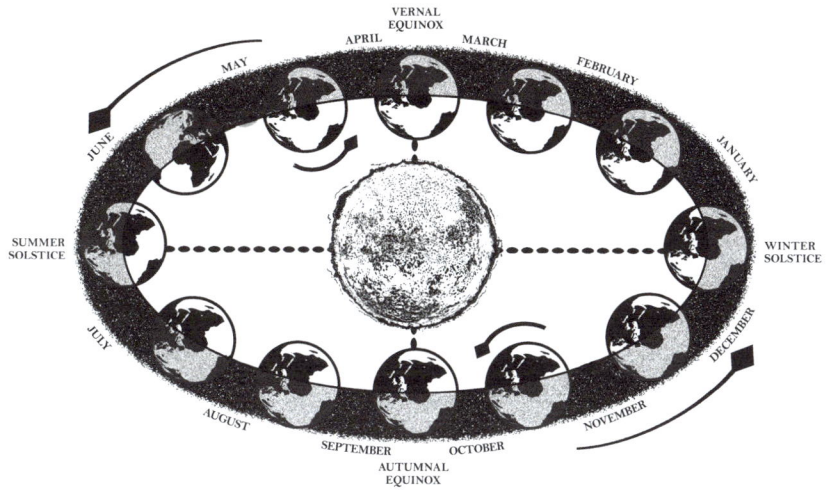

SOLSTICE AND EQUINOX DIAGRAM

EQUINOXES

Equinoxes occur when the Sun crosses the celestial equator, creating equal day and night due to Earth's axial tilt. The spring (vernal) equinox, marking the Sun's entry into Aries, begins the astrological new year and symbolizes renewal and growth. The autumn equinox, when the Sun enters Libra, emphasizes balance and reflection as the harvest season begins. Cultures worldwide celebrate these points of equilibrium.

FULL MOON

The full moon, with the Sun and Moon in opposite zodiac signs, represents a peak in energy and illumination. This phase highlights the need for balance and compromise across opposing areas of life. Full moons are linked to culminations, revelations, and the blossoming of intentions set during the new moon. Specific zodiac alignments, such as a Libra full moon, underscore themes like partnership and fairness. Rituals during this phase often focus on gratitude, release, or celebration.

The Encyclopedia of Astrology

METEOR SHOWERS

Meteor showers result from Earth passing through streams of comet debris, creating radiant displays of light as particles burn up in the atmosphere. Each shower is tied to a source constellation, like the Perseids from Perseus, and carries unique energetic significance. Spiritually, meteor showers symbolize wishes, inspiration, and transformative insight, making them excellent times for meditation and intention setting.

NEW MOON

The new moon marks the monthly reset point when the Sun and Moon align in the same zodiac sign, offering fertile ground for fresh starts and intentions. This phase represents the void of potential before manifestation. Each zodiac sign imbues the new moon with distinct energy—for example, a Capricorn new moon supports goal-setting and discipline, while a Cancer new moon fosters emotional connection and care. Reflective journaling and vision boards are popular practices during this phase.

RETROGRADES, PLANETARY RETROGRADES

When planets appear to move backward from Earth's perspective, they invite introspection and reassessment. Mercury retrograde is known for its impact on communication and technology; Mars retrograde revisits energy and drive; Venus retrograde examines relationships and values.

Each retrograde period's effects are influenced by the zodiac sign and astrological house it occurs in. For instance, Mercury retrograde in Gemini might amplify misunderstandings but also offer clarity upon review.

The Encyclopedia of Astrology

SPRING EQUINOX

The spring equinox marks the Sun's crossing of the celestial equator, creating equal day and night while heralding the start of Aries season and the astrological new year. This powerful point of balance launches the Sun's northward journey and longer days in the northern hemisphere. Many cultures mark this turning point with renewal festivals including Easter, Holi, Songkran, and Passover.

SOLSTICES

The solstices mark the Sun's extremes in the sky due to Earth's axial tilt. The summer solstice brings the longest day, celebrating abundance, growth, and light's triumph, while the winter solstice holds the longest night, symbolizing introspection, renewal, and the Sun's rebirth. Celebrations like Yule and Midsummer honor these turning points as times of profound spiritual connection.

STATIONS, PLANETARY STATIONS

Planetary stations occur when a planet appears to pause before changing direction (stationing direct or retrograde). These still points amplify the planet's energy, creating moments of intense focus and transformation. For instance, when Saturn stations, themes of discipline, responsibility, and long-term planning often come to the forefront. These potent periods are ideal for meditating on the planet's influence and adjusting goals or strategies accordingly.

SUPERMOONS

A supermoon happens when a full or new moon coincides with the Moon's closest approach to Earth (perigee). These events amplify the Moon's visible size and gravitational effects, often coinciding with heightened emotional intensity and significant events. While tidal forces are slightly stronger during supermoons, their effects on weather remain minimal. Super-

The Encyclopedia of Astrology

moons are seen as ideal times for manifesting intentions, as the energy feels especially potent and expansive.

WANING MOON PHASES

The waning moon phases represent the Moon's decreasing light as it moves from full to new, supporting closure, release, and introspection.

Waning Gibbous: Encourages sharing wisdom and reflecting on lessons learned from the cycle's culmination.

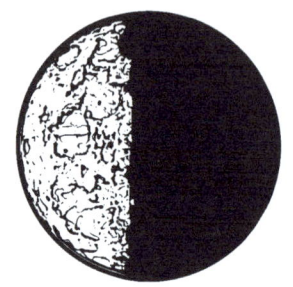

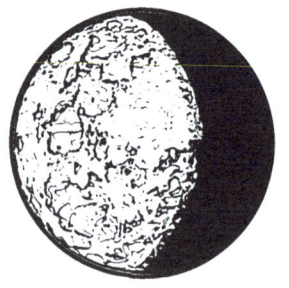

Waning Crescent: Represents surrender and preparation for renewal. This phase is excellent for clearing clutter, detoxing, and letting go of the past.

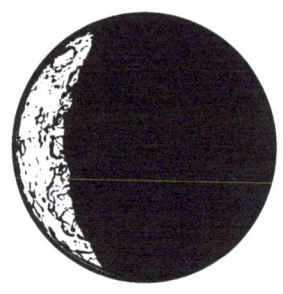

Waning Quarter: Challenges us to release habits, relationships, or beliefs that no longer serve us.

Traditionally, these phases are associated with banishing rituals, emotional processing, and preparing for the next cycle of growth.

The Encyclopedia of Astrology

WAXING MOON PHASES

The waxing moon phases symbolize increasing light and energy, representing growth, momentum, and creation as the Moon moves from new to full.

Waxing Crescent: Encourages setting intentions and planting the seeds of new goals or projects.

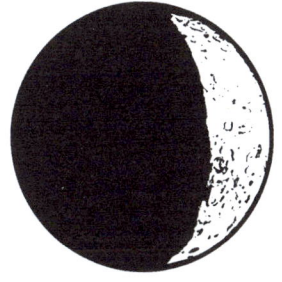

Waxing Quarter: Marks a time for taking action and overcoming initial obstacles. It symbolizes courage and commitment to the path ahead.

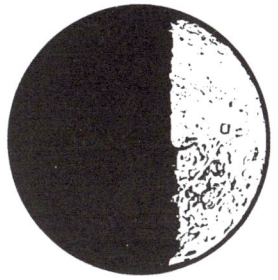

Waxing Gibbous: Focuses on refining efforts, making adjustments, and building toward the full moon's peak energy.

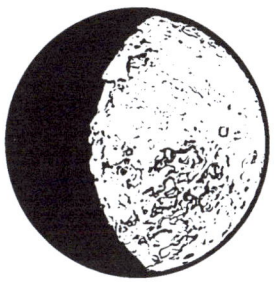

These phases traditionally support spellwork for increase, growth, and attraction.

The Encyclopedia of Astrology

ALMANAC OF UPCOMING CELESTIAL EVENTS

Five-year Almanac

2026

Take a peek into the future. This five-year almanac presents the astronomical positions of celestial bodies alongside astrological interpretations through the lens of the tropical zodiac. These dates were provided by an astronomer consultant and viewed for accuracy using the Stellium software.

While the tropical zodiac—the most commonly used Western system—maintains fixed dates for each sun sign (Aries beginning around March 21, Taurus around April 20, and so on), astronomical reality shows that the Sun actually enters these constellations on significantly different dates. This contrast offers an opportunity to explore astrology from both a symbolic and observational perspective.

January 10: Jupiter reaches opposition in Gemini. Jupiter's opposition in Gemini brings a powerful surge of communicative energy and intellectual curiosity that may manifest as unexpected opportunities in education, travel, or publishing. This alignment creates fertile ground for networking and information exchange, with Jupiter's expansive qualities amplified when viewed from Earth, potentially bringing significant breakthroughs in how we process and share knowledge.

January 20: Sun moves from Sagittarius to Capricornus. As the Sun transitions from free-spirited Sagittarius to disciplined Capricornus, there's a collective shift from philosophical exploration to practical

The Encyclopedia of Astrology

ambition and structured planning. This celestial movement marks a time when dreams begin to crystallize into tangible goals, calling for increased responsibility and patience while working toward long-term success.

February 4: Uranus ends retrograde motion in Taurus. Uranus stationing direct in Taurus signals an awakening in financial systems and values-based structures that have been under internal review during the retrograde period. This planetary shift forward enables revolutionary ideas around resources, sustainability, and security to gain momentum, potentially triggering sudden breakthroughs in stagnant material situations.

February 16: Sun moves from Capricornus to Aquarius. The Sun's ingress into Aquarius from Capricornus marks a transition from conventional hierarchical thinking to innovative, community-oriented perspectives that value equality and humanitarian progress. This solar shift illuminates the collective consciousness with progressive ideals and technological inspiration, encouraging us to break free from outdated structures in favor of future-focused collaboration.

February 17: Lunar New Year, the Year of the Fire Horse. The Fire Horse gallops in with vibrant energy, bringing swift movement, passion, and a spirit of freedom. Fire intensifies the Horse's natural boldness, making this a dynamic year for ambition, risk-taking, and adventure. Independence and innovation thrive under this influence, though its fiery nature demands balance to prevent impulsive actions. This period encourages courage in pursuing goals and embracing change.

February 17: Annular solar eclipse, visible from southern parts of Africa and South America, Pacific, Atlantic, Indian Ocean and Antarctica. This annular solar eclipse creates a powerful reset point in the collective consciousness, particularly affecting global issues connected to the regions within its path. The "ring of fire" formed during this eclipse symbolizes the burning away of outdated paradigms while seeding new beginnings that will gradually unfold over the following six months.

February 26: Mercury in retrograde until March 30 in Pisces and Aquarius. Mercury retrograde moving between dreamy Pisces and analytical Aquarius creates a period of communication confusion where logical thinking may be clouded by emotion, requiring careful attention to details in contracts, travel plans, and technology. This retrograde journey invites us to revisit visionary ideas and innovative concepts from a more intuitive perspective, potentially revealing overlooked connections between spiritual insights and intellectual frameworks.

March 2 to 3: Total lunar eclipse, visible in eastern parts of Europe, Asia, Australia, North America, South America, Pacific, Atlantic, Indian Ocean, Arctic and Antarctica. This total lunar eclipse creates a powerful emotional culmination point where hidden feelings surface dramatically, demanding acknowledgment and integration into our conscious awareness. The global visibility of this eclipse suggests a collective emotional revelation that transcends cultural boundaries, potentially triggering significant shifts in how we relate to security needs and emotional attachments on both personal and societal levels.

March 11: Sun moves from Aquarius to Pisces. As the Sun glides from innovative Aquarius into mystical Pisces, our collective focus shifts from intellectual revolution to spiritual dissolution of boundaries and heightened compassion. This transition invites a month-long immersion in imagination, intuition, and empathic connection, where logical certainties give way to fluid possibilities and the boundaries

The Encyclopedia of Astrology

between self and other become increasingly permeable.

March 12: Jupiter ends retrograde motion in Gemini. Jupiter stationing direct in Gemini signals an acceleration of intellectual expansion and communication opportunities that have been internally developing during the retrograde phase. The forward movement of this benefic planet in the sign of duality and information exchange promises renewed optimism in learning environments, media ventures, and cross-cultural dialogues, with previously delayed projects now gaining momentum and public recognition.

March 20: Northern hemisphere vernal/spring equinox, southern hemisphere autumn equinox. The equinox marks a point of perfect balance between day and night, symbolizing harmony between opposing forces. Astrologically, this represents a powerful time for setting intentions related to balance. For the northern hemisphere, the spring equinox marks the astrological new year as the Sun enters Aries, bringing fresh energy and new beginnings. For the southern hemisphere, the autumn equinox brings the energy of harvest and preparation.

April 18: Sun moves from Pisces to Aries. The Sun's ingress into Aries from Pisces ignites a fiery surge of initiative and self-assertion after a period of spiritual reflection, marking the true astrological new year with renewed vitality and courage. This solar shift encourages bold action, leadership, and pioneering spirit, though its impulsive energy requires channeling to avoid unnecessary conflicts while maximizing its potential for fresh starts and dynamic breakthroughs.

May 8: Pluto begins retrograde motion in Capricornus. Pluto turning retrograde in Capricornus initiates a profound inward journey of examining power structures and entrenched systems that may be reaching obsolescence in our personal and collective lives. This transformative period invites deep internal restructuring of ambitions and authority relationships, temporarily slowing external manifestations of change while intensifying subconscious processing of what must ultimately be released or regenerated.

May 13: Sun moves from Aries to Taurus. As the Sun transitions from impulsive Aries to steadfast Taurus, the collective energy shifts from initiation to consolidation, bringing a more grounded and sensory-oriented approach to our pursuits. This solar ingress encourages stabilization of resources, practical implementation of previously launched ideas, and heightened appreciation for physical comforts and natural beauty, though resistance to change may increase as security needs take precedence.

May 31: Blue moon (second full moon in a month). This rare blue moon intensifies the emotional illumination typically associated with full moons, creating an amplified cycle of revelation and culmination that may feel like emotional experiences are occurring in concentrated succession. The unusual doubling of lunar fullness in one calendar month suggests an opportunity for accelerated emotional processing and heightened intuitive downloads, potentially bringing rapid closure to situations that would normally take longer to resolve.

June 21: Sun moves from Taurus to Gemini. As the Sun shifts from steadfast Taurus to versatile Gemini, our collective focus transforms from material security to intellectual curiosity and social connection. This solar ingress activates a month of heightened communication, information exchange, and mental agility, encouraging us to explore diverse perspectives and adapt quickly to changing circumstances while potentially creating some restlessness as stability gives way to variability.

The Encyclopedia of Astrology

June 21: Northern hemisphere summer solstice, southern hemisphere winter solstice. This powerful solstice point marks the longest day in the north and longest night in the south, creating a peak moment of solar energy that highlights the extremes of light and darkness in our yearly cycle. This cosmic threshold represents maximum creative potential in the northern hemisphere and deepest introspection in the southern hemisphere, offering a profound opportunity to honor the cyclical nature of existence and align with the Earth's natural rhythms.

June 29: Mercury in retrograde until July 24 in Gemini. Mercury retrograding in its home sign of Gemini creates a particularly potent period of communication recalibration, potentially causing significant misunderstandings and technical glitches in areas related to information exchange, travel, and learning. This retrograde invites a thorough review of our thinking patterns and communication styles, offering valuable insights if we slow down to reconsider our assumptions, though patience will be essential as the messenger planet appears to move backward through its most comfortable territory.

July 8: Neptune begins retrograde motion in Pisces. Neptune turning retrograde in its home waters of Pisces initiates a dreamlike period of inner spiritual exploration and dissolution of illusions that have clouded our perception of reality. This introspective phase encourages reconnection with intuition and compassion while potentially revealing deceptions or self-delusions that have been operating beneath conscious awareness, creating opportunities for greater authenticity if we're willing to face uncomfortable truths about our ideals and fantasies.

July 20: Sun moves from Gemini to Cancer. The Sun's transition from intellectual

Gemini to nurturing Cancer shifts our collective focus from mental stimulation to emotional security and familial connections. This solar ingress illuminates themes of home, heritage, and emotional needs, potentially triggering protective instincts and nostalgic feelings while offering an opportunity to strengthen foundations and care for ourselves and loved ones with greater tenderness and intuitive understanding.

July 26: Saturn begins retrograde in Pisces. Saturn turning retrograde in mystical Pisces creates a period of serious reassessment regarding spiritual disciplines, boundaries around compassion, and structures within creative or healing endeavors. This reflective phase may temporarily slow external progress in these areas while deepening internal commitment to spiritual maturity, potentially revealing where we've been either too rigid or too permeable in our approach to transcendent experiences and emotional boundaries.

July 27: Pluto reaches opposition in Capricornus. Pluto's opposition in Capricornus brings hidden power dynamics and systemic corruption to the surface, creating a peak moment of intensity in the ongoing transformation of governmental, corporate, and authoritative structures. This powerful alignment illuminates shadow aspects of ambition and control, potentially triggering significant revelations about leadership and accountability while offering an opportunity to consciously engage with profound questions about how power is wielded in both personal and collective spheres.

August 10: Sun moves from Cancer to Leo. The Sun's transition from nurturing Cancer to expressive Leo shifts our collective focus from emotional security to creative self-expression and passionate leadership. This solar ingress ignites a month of heightened dramatic energy, pride, and courage, encouraging authentic self-presentation and grand gestures while potentially amplifying ego-driven conflicts if we fail to balance self-confidence with genuine appreciation for others.

August 12: Total solar eclipse, visible from Europe, northern parts of Asia, North/West Africa, much of North America, Pacific, Atlantic and Arctic. This powerful total solar eclipse represents a profound reset in matters of identity, creativity, and leadership, with its widespread visibility suggesting global implications for power structures and self-expression. The temporary darkening of the royal Sun creates a cosmic portal for planting seeds of authentic leadership and heart-centered purpose that will unfold over the coming months, potentially triggering significant shifts in how we perceive authority figures and our own creative potential.

August 27 to 28: Partial lunar eclipse, visible from Europe, western parts of Asia, Africa, North America, South America, Pacific, Atlantic, Indian Ocean and Antarctica. This partial lunar eclipse illuminates unresolved emotional patterns and relationship dynamics that have been operating beneath conscious awareness, particularly in areas related to service, health, and daily routines. The global visibility of this eclipse suggests a collective emotional revelation about the connection between wellness and emotional fulfillment, potentially triggering significant insights about how our unconscious emotional needs affect our productivity and physical well-being.

September 11: Uranus begins retrograde motion in Taurus. Uranus turning retrograde in stable Taurus initiates a period of internal revolution regarding resources, values, and security needs that may temporarily appear dormant on the surface while intensifying beneath. This five-month retrograde invites innovative reconsideration of financial systems and material attachments, potentially revealing where we've been resistant to necessary changes in how we interact with the Earth and its resources.

September 16: Sun moves from Leo to Virgo. As the Sun shifts from dramatic Leo to analytical Virgo, our collective focus transforms from creative self-expression to practical improvement and detailed assessment. This solar ingress activates a month of heightened discernment, service orientation, and systematic problem-solving, encouraging us to refine our methods and attend to the specifics that create efficiency while potentially increasing tendencies toward criticism if perfectionism goes unchecked.

September 23: Northern hemisphere autumn equinox, southern hemisphere vernal/spring equinox. This equinox creates perfect balance between light and darkness, marking a pivotal turning point in the wheel of the year that energetically resets collective consciousness toward either harvest or planting depending on hemisphere. This powerful moment of equilibrium between opposing forces offers an opportunity to assess relationships and partnerships with greater objectivity, as the cosmic scales temporarily achieve perfect balance before tipping toward the next phase of natural progression.

September 26: Neptune reaches opposition in Pisces. Neptune's opposition in its home sign of Pisces brings spiritual insights, creative inspiration, and collective dreams to their fullest illumination, potentially dissolving boundaries between dimensions. This mystical alignment heightens intuitive capacities and artistic vision while potentially creating confusion around practical matters, offering a cosmic opportunity to bridge the gap between imagination and reality if we can maintain discernment while embracing expanded consciousness.

The Encyclopedia of Astrology

October 3: Venus in retrograde until November 12 in Virgo. Venus retrograding in perfectionistic Virgo creates a challenging period for relationships, finances, and self-worth as the planet of love appears to move backward through a sign that emphasizes flaws and improvements. This retrograde invites a reevaluation of our standards in love and aesthetics, potentially revealing where critical tendencies have undermined appreciation and where service has replaced authentic connection, offering valuable insights if we approach the process with compassion rather than judgment.

October 16: Pluto ends retrograde motion in Capricornus. Pluto stationing direct in ambitious Capricornus signals an acceleration of external transformation in power structures, corporations, and governmental systems after months of internal processing and hidden developments. This powerful shift forward enables deeply transformative changes that have been brewing beneath the surface to manifest more visibly, potentially triggering significant restructuring of hierarchies and authority systems as evolutionary pressures demand accountability.

October 30: Sun moves from Virgo to Libra. The Sun's transition from analytical Virgo to harmonious Libra shifts our collective focus from practical problem-solving to relationship dynamics and the pursuit of balance and beauty. This solar ingress illuminates themes of partnership, justice, and diplomatic negotiation, encouraging elegant solutions to conflicts while potentially creating indecision as multiple perspectives are given equal consideration in the pursuit of fairness.

November 23: Sun moves from Libra to Scorpius. As the Sun plunges from balanced Libra into intense Scorpius, our collective energy transforms from diplomatic harmony-seeking to

The Encyclopedia of Astrology

profound psychological exploration and power dynamics. This solar shift activates a month of heightened emotional depth, transformative encounters, and access to hidden truths, encouraging courageous confrontation with shadow material while potentially intensifying jealousy, obsession, or manipulation if unconscious fears remain unaddressed.

November 25: Uranus reaches opposition in Taurus. Uranus's opposition in steadfast Taurus brings revolutionary developments regarding financial systems, resources, and security needs to a dramatic culmination point that can no longer be ignored. This powerful alignment illuminates the tension between stability and change, potentially triggering unexpected breakthroughs or breakdowns in material structures while offering an opportunity to consciously integrate innovative approaches to earthly concerns with practical considerations.

December 12: Jupiter begins retrograde motion in Leo. Jupiter turning retrograde in dramatic Leo initiates a period of internal expansion regarding creative expression, leadership, and heart-centered ambitions that may temporarily slow external growth while deepening authentic connection to purpose. This reflective phase invites reconsideration of where we've been excessive in self-promotion or overly optimistic about recognition, potentially revealing more sustainable approaches to sharing our unique gifts with the world.

December 13: Neptune ends retrograde motion in Pisces. Neptune stationing direct in its home waters of Pisces signals an acceleration of spiritual awareness, creative inspiration, and collective healing after months of internal dream-work and intuitive processing. This mystical shift forward enables visionary ideals and compassionate initiatives to gain momentum in the outer world, potentially dissolving artificial boundaries between people as shared humanity becomes more apparent through artistic expression and spiritual connection.

December 21: Northern hemisphere winter solstice, southern hemisphere summer solstice. This powerful solstice point marks the longest night in the north and longest day in the south, creating a profound threshold moment that initiates a new seasonal cycle with important energetic implications. This cosmic turning point represents the rebirth of light in the northern hemisphere and its fullest expression in the southern hemisphere, offering a sacred opportunity to honor natural cycles while setting intentions aligned with the profound energy of culmination and renewal.

December 24: Supermoon in Cancer. A Cancer supermoon typically emphasizes the need for emotional sanctuary, connecting with loved ones, honoring ancestral ties, and attending to domestic matters. It often brings deeply intuitive insights and can trigger significant emotional revelations related to our sense of belonging and security. This lunar event encourages protective instincts toward those we consider family (whether by blood or choice) and may bring subconscious patterns around caregiving and receiving care into clearer awareness.

2027

January 12: Mars begins retrograde in Leo. This retrograde period encourages introspection regarding personal power and creative expression. Ambitions may feel temporarily stalled, prompting a collective reevaluation of assertiveness and

leadership dynamics. This phase offers an opportunity to refine approaches to self-expression and initiative, favoring patience over impulsive action.

January 20: Sun moves from Sagittarius to Capricornus. This transit shifts collective energy toward practicality and ambition. Career aspirations and long-term planning receive cosmic support.

January 22: Leo supermoon. This Leo supermoon amplifies emotions tied to self-expression, creativity, and recognition. There may be a heightened collective desire for acknowledgment and appreciation of individual talents. The intensified lunar energy in Leo presents an opportunity to release blocks related to authenticity or fears of standing out. This period highlights the balance between healthy confidence and ego-driven validation, encouraging a shift from seeking external approval to embracing intrinsic self-worth.

February 6: Annular solar eclipse, visible from much of Africa, South America, Pacific, Atlantic and Antarctica. This eclipse marks a significant turning point, bringing new beginnings related to authority and long-term aspirations. Opportunities may arise that align with a deeper sense of purpose, revealing pathways toward greater authenticity and leadership. This celestial event underscores the importance of embracing personal evolution and stepping into roles that reflect one's true ambitions.

February 6: Lunar new year, the Year of the Fire Goat. The Fire Goat infuses creativity, warmth, and idealism into the year's energy. While the Goat is known for its gentle and artistic nature, fire enhances confidence and the drive for self-expression. This combination supports strong emotional connections, artistic pursuits, and visionary leadership. It is a year that values both beauty and social harmony, with a heightened passion for personal and collective growth.

February 8: Uranus ends retrograde motion in Taurus. Innovative financial solutions and practical breakthroughs gain momentum. Revolutionary approaches to security and resources move forward after a period of internal recalibration.

February 9: Mercury in retrograde until March 3 in Aquarius and Capricornus. Communication misunderstandings and technology glitches require extra patience and clarity. Review and revise plans rather than initiating new projects.

February 11: Jupiter reaches opposition in Leo. Opportunities for recognition and creative expansion reach a climactic point. Balancing self-expression with collaboration creates the most favorable outcomes.

February 16: Sun moves from Capricornus to Aquarius. Collective consciousness shifts toward innovation and humanitarian concerns. Explore ways to make unique contributions to group endeavors.

February 19: Mars at opposition in Leo. Passionate energy and competitive drives reach peak intensity. Channeling this forceful energy constructively prevents conflicts while fueling creative achievements.

February 20 to 21: Penumbral lunar eclipse, visible from Europe, Asia, North/West Australia, Africa, much of North America, South America, Pacific, Atlantic, Indian Ocean, Arctic and Antarctica. Subtle emotional revelations bring clarity to relationship patterns and unconscious behaviors. This gentle eclipse supports releasing outdated emotional attachments.

March 11: Sun moves from Aquarius to Pisces. This transit brings heightened intuition and emotional sensitivity to the collective consciousness. Artistic inspiration flows more freely, making this an excellent period for creative and spiritual pursuits.

March 20: Northern hemisphere vernal/spring equinox, southern hemisphere autumn equinox. The equinox marks a point of perfect balance between day and night, symbolizing harmony between opposing forces. Astrologically, this represents a powerful time for setting intentions related to balance. For the northern hemisphere, the spring equinox marks the astrological new year as the Sun enters Aries, bringing fresh energy and new beginnings. For the southern hemisphere, the autumn equinox brings energy of harvest and preparation.

April 1: Mars ends retrograde motion in Leo. Forward momentum returns to creative projects and matters requiring assertiveness and courage. Energy and motivation increase, allowing confident strides toward goals that may have stalled during the retrograde period.

April 13: Jupiter ends retrograde motion in Cancer. Expansion in domestic, emotional, and nurturing areas of life accelerates after a period of internal growth. Family matters, home projects, and emotional healing receive a beneficial boost of optimistic energy.

April 18: Sun moves from Pisces to Aries. The collective energy shifts toward initiative, courage, and new beginnings. This transit favors bold action and decisive movement, encouraging confidence in pursuing new ventures. After the reflective and intuitive Pisces season, Aries brings a surge of motivation and a readiness to take charge.

May 10: Pluto begins retrograde motion in Capricornus. Deep internal transformation related to authority, career structures, and ambition intensifies. This period invites examination of unconscious power dynamics and releasing control mechanisms that no longer serve.

The Encyclopedia of Astrology

May 13: Sun moves from Aries to Taurus. Stability, sensuality, and practical resource management become energetic focal points. This grounding influence helps manifest concrete results from the initiatives begun during Aries season.

May 20: Seasonal blue moon in Scorpio (third full moon in an astronomical season containing four full moons). This Scorpio blue moon intensifies emotional depth and transformative energies, making it a powerful time for profound personal revelations. The rare blue moon amplifies Scorpio's natural investigative qualities, bringing hidden truths to the surface and creating opportunities for emotional detoxification and psychological healing.

June 11: Mercury in retrograde until July 5 in Gemini, Orion and Taurus. This retrograde brings communication challenges and requires careful attention to details, especially regarding information exchange and travel plans. Use this period to revise thinking patterns and reconnect with siblings or neighbors.

June 21: Sun moves from Taurus to Gemini. This transit energizes intellectual curiosity and social connections in the collective consciousness. Versatility and communication skills become highlighted, making this an excellent period for learning and sharing ideas.

June 21: Northern hemisphere summer solstice, southern hemisphere winter solstice. This powerful point of maximum light (northern hemisphere) or darkness (southern hemisphere) marks a significant energetic shift in the annual cycle. The solstice invites celebration of achievements while setting intentions aligned with the changing seasonal energies.

July 11: Neptune begins retrograde motion in Pisces. Neptune's retrograde in its home sign of Pisces invites a

The Encyclopedia of Astrology

reassessment of illusions, ideals, and intuitive perceptions. During this period, unconscious beliefs and fantasies may surface for evaluation, bringing both clarity and disillusionment. While spiritual insight deepens, there is a need for discernment to separate inspiration from deception. This transit supports inner exploration, making it a powerful time for meditation, dreamwork, and creative refinement.

July 20: Sun moves from Gemini to Cancer. Collective focus shifts toward home, family, and emotional security. Nurturing impulses and protective instincts strengthen during this transit.

July 29: Pluto reaches opposition in Capricornus. Power dynamics and deep structural transformations reach a climactic point of visibility. Hidden control mechanisms within institutions and authority structures become exposed, prompting necessary evolution.

August 2: Total solar eclipse, visible from Europe, South/West Asia, Africa, eastern parts of North America, Atlantic and Indian Ocean. This powerful eclipse initiates profound new beginnings related to identity and life purpose. Significant opportunities for personal reinvention emerge that align with authentic self-expression.

August 7: Saturn begins retrograde motion in Pisces. The structures supporting spiritual growth and emotional boundaries require reassessment and reinforcement. Internal discipline around setting limits becomes essential as Saturn's inward turn highlights where compassion has become unhealthy sacrifice.

August 10: Sun moves from Cancer to Leo. Creative self-expression and leadership qualities take center stage during this heart-centered solar transit. This shift encourages the recognition and celebration of

The Encyclopedia of Astrology

individuality, emphasizing confidence, passion, and personal authenticity. The energy of Leo supports bold pursuits, inspiring a greater willingness to share talents and embrace opportunities for creative and personal growth.

August 16 to 17: Penumbral lunar eclipse, visible from western parts of Europe, northern parts of Asia, much of Australia, North/West Africa, North America, South America, Pacific, Atlantic and Antarctica. Subtle emotional revelations illuminate relationship patterns and unconscious reactions. This gentle eclipse supports releasing emotional attachments that limit growth while highlighting where genuine connection thrives.

September 15: Uranus begins retrograde motion in Taurus. Unexpected shifts in financial matters and value systems turn inward for reassessment. This period invites innovative thinking about resources and security while revealing resistance to necessary changes.

September 16: Sun moves from Leo to Virgo. Collective energy shifts toward analysis, improvement, and practical service. This transit supports new systems of organization and focusing on health routines with renewed attention to detail.

September 23: Northern hemisphere autumn equinox, southern hemisphere vernal/spring equinox. This balanced point between light and darkness brings harmony to opposing forces and energies. The shifting seasons support releasing what's complete while preparing for the more introspective months ahead.

September 28: Neptune reaches opposition in Pisces. Spiritual insights and creative inspiration reach peak intensity and visibility. The veil between worlds thins, making this an exceptionally potent time for meditation, artistic expression, and compassionate connection.

The Encyclopedia of Astrology

October 8: Mercury in retrograde until October 28 in Virgo. Communication around work, health, and daily routines requires extra clarity and patience. This retrograde particularly affects analytical thinking, prompting a review of systems and procedures that may need refinement.

October 18: Saturn reaches opposition in Pisces, Pluto ends retrograde motion in Capricornus. With Saturn reaching opposition in Pisces, responsibilities related to spiritual growth and emotional boundaries reach a culmination point. Limitations around compassion and sacrifice become clearly visible, creating opportunities to establish healthier structures. As Pluto ends its retrograde motion, transformative energies related to authority, career, and societal structures move forward with renewed intensity. Power dynamics that have been internally processing now manifest externally with evolutionary force.

October 30: Sun moves from Virgo to Libra. Collective focus shifts toward relationships, harmony, and fair negotiations. Balance between self and others becomes the central theme during this partnership-oriented transit.

November 23: Sun moves from Libra to Scorpius. This transit deepens collective energy toward transformation, intimacy, and psychological exploration. Power dynamics become more intense, creating opportunities for profound healing and regeneration.

November 30: Uranus reaches opposition in Taurus. Revolutionary changes regarding resources, values, and financial systems reach a climactic point of visibility. Unexpected breakthroughs and epiphanies about material security illuminate new possibilities that challenge conventional approaches.

December 16: Neptune ends retrograde motion in Pisces.

Spiritual insights, creative inspiration, and compassionate initiatives gain momentum after a period of internal development. Dreams and intuitive messages become clearer guides as Neptune's forward motion helps manifest higher visions in tangible ways.

December 17: Sun moves into Sagittarius. Collective consciousness expands toward optimism, adventure, and philosophical exploration. This transit supports broadening horizons and connecting with larger truths that give meaning to daily experience.

December 22: Northern hemisphere winter solstice, southern hemisphere summer solstice. This powerful turning point marks the darkest day (northern hemisphere) or brightest day (southern hemisphere) of the year, signaling a significant shift in energetic cycles. The solstice invites inner reflection or outer celebration while honoring the eternal rhythm between light and darkness.

December 26: Saturn ends retrograde motion in Pisces. Structures supporting spiritual growth and emotional boundaries move forward with renewed clarity. Hard-earned wisdom about setting compassionate limits begins to manifest tangible results after a period of internal recalibration.

2028

January 11 to 12: Partial lunar eclipse, visible from Europe, North/West Asia, Africa, North America, South America, Pacific, Atlantic, Indian Ocean, Arctic. This eclipse occurring across multiple continents suggests a period of emotional culmination and release. With this eclipse visible across so many regions, it may indicate collective emotional revelations or significant endings that affect many people. This eclipse could bring closure to situations that began six months earlier.

January 14: Jupiter begins retrograde in Virgo. Jupiter represents expansion, growth, and good fortune. When retrograde in analytical Virgo, this suggests a time to reconsider how we approach details, health, and service to others.

January 20: Sun moves from Sagittarius to Capricornus. Brings a collective focus on structure, responsibility, and long-term goals. The energy shifts from Sagittarius's exploratory nature to Capricorn's disciplined approach. This is traditionally a time to set practical goals and create solid foundations for the year ahead.

January 24: Mercury in retrograde until February 14 in Aquarius and Capricornus. This retrograde spanning two signs suggests communication challenges affecting both innovative thinking (Aquarius) and organizational structures (Capricornus). Expect delays in technology, miscommunications in groups, and the need to revise plans related to career and social connections.

January 26: Annular solar eclipse, visible from South/West Europe, North/West Africa, southern and eastern parts of North America, South America, Pacific and Atlantic. This solar eclipse represents powerful new beginnings related to community, technology, and humanitarian efforts. Solar eclipses often signify significant fresh starts. With its wide visibility, this eclipse could trigger collective shifts.

January 26: Lunar new year, the Year of the Earth Monkey. The Earth Monkey brings a blend of resourcefulness, intelligence, and grounded practicality. While the Monkey is naturally

The Encyclopedia of Astrology

clever and playful, the Earth element stabilizes its quick-thinking tendencies, fostering strategic action rather than impulsive decisions. This year favors innovative problem-solving, steady progress, and long-term planning, making it an excellent time for laying solid foundations in both personal and professional endeavors.

February 10: Leo supermoon. This full moon in Leo amplifies emotions and creative energies, bringing dramatic culminations to personal projects and relationships. Its powerful lunar energy heightens confidence and self-expression, perfect for celebrating achievements or releasing what no longer serves.

February 13: Uranus ends retrograde motion in Taurus. As Uranus stations direct in Taurus, expect sudden breakthroughs or shifts in financial matters, personal values, and physical resources. This planetary movement activates dormant innovations related to sustainability and practical resources, potentially triggering unexpected but necessary changes to established systems.

February 16: Sun moves from Capricornus to Aquarius. This shift brings collective energy from structured Capricorn discipline to innovative Aquarian thinking, emphasizing community, humanitarian concerns, and unconventional approaches. Expect a growing desire for freedom, originality, and social connection as the focus moves from career ambitions to group dynamics and future-oriented thinking.

March 11: Sun moves from Aquarius to Pisces. The Sun entering Pisces shifts collective energy from intellectual innovation to emotional intuition and spiritual connection. This transition brings increased sensitivity, compassion, and artistic inspiration while encouraging boundary dissolution and surrender to universal themes.

The Encyclopedia of Astrology

March 11: Virgo supermoon. This full moon in Virgo illuminates matters of health, service, and practical organization with heightened emotional intensity. Its amplified energy creates perfect conditions for releasing perfectionism and celebrating the details while finding balance between critical thinking and compassionate acceptance.

March 12: Jupiter reaches opposition in Leo. Jupiter's opposition in Leo creates a dramatic expansion of self-expression, creativity, and leadership potential at its peak visibility from Earth. This alignment offers magnificent opportunities for recognition and growth in areas related to performance, romance, and children while challenging us to balance personal glory with receptivity to others.

March 20: Northern hemisphere vernal/spring equinox, southern hemisphere autumn equinox. The equinox marks a point of perfect balance between day and night, symbolizing harmony between opposing forces. Astrologically, this represents a powerful time for setting intentions related to balance. For the northern hemisphere, the spring equinox marks the astrological new year as the Sun enters Aries, bringing fresh energy and new beginnings. For the southern hemisphere, the autumn equinox brings energy of harvest and preparation.

April 18: Sun moves from Pisces to Aries. This transition marks the true astrological new year as the Sun leaves dreamy Pisces and ignites pioneering Aries energy, bringing a surge of initiative, courage, and self-assertion. Expect a collective shift from spiritual surrender to decisive action as the cosmic energy supports new beginnings, leadership, and the confidence to pursue personal desires.

May 11: Venus in retrograde until June 22 in Taurus, Pluto begins retrograde motion in Capricornus. Venus retrograding

The Encyclopedia of Astrology

in its home sign of Taurus prompts a deep reevaluation of personal values, finances, and relationships, especially concerning security and material comfort. Simultaneously, Pluto's retrograde in Capricornus intensifies internal power dynamics and structural transformations, creating a potent period for confronting shadow aspects within established systems and personal ambitions.

May 13: Sun moves from Aries to Taurus. The Sun entering Taurus shifts collective energy from impulsive action to steady manifestation, emphasizing patience, sensuality, and practical resource-building. This transition grounds fiery Aries initiatives into tangible form, bringing persistence to projects and a heightened appreciation for physical comforts and natural beauty.

May 15: Jupiter ends retrograde motion in Leo. Jupiter stationing direct in Leo releases a flood of creative expansion, magnifying opportunities for self-expression, romance, and joyful leadership after months of internal reflection. This forward motion reinvigorates confidence and generosity, accelerating growth in areas related to performance, recognition, and heart-centered endeavors.

May 22: Mercury in retrograde until June 14 in Taurus. Mercury retrograde in Taurus challenges communication around material matters, creating potential delays in financial transactions and misunderstandings about values and resources. This period calls for reviewing budgets, reconsidering purchases, and reassessing what truly provides security while exercising patience with slowed practical progress.

June 20: Northern hemisphere summer solstice, southern hemisphere winter solstice. This powerful turning point marks maximum light in the north and maximum darkness in the south, creating a global polarity of energies that highlights themes of fullness versus reflection. The solstice amplifies the Cancer–Capricorn axis of nurturing versus achievement, encouraging balance between emotional security and worldly responsibility across hemispheres.

June 21: Sun moves from Taurus to Gemini. The Sun entering Gemini shifts collective focus from material stability to intellectual curiosity, communication, and social connection. This transition lightens the atmosphere, accelerating the pace of interactions and bringing versatility to approaches after the fixed determination of Taurus season.

July 6 to 7: Partial lunar eclipse, visible from Europe, Asia, Australia, Africa, southern and eastern parts of South America, Pacific, Atlantic, Indian Ocean and Antarctica. This partial lunar eclipse in Capricorn brings emotional culminations related to career, authority, and long-term structures across multiple continents. Its wide visibility suggests collective revelations about responsibility and achievement, potentially exposing hidden power dynamics within established systems.

July 20: Sun moves from Gemini to Cancer. The Sun entering Cancer shifts collective energy from intellectual curiosity to emotional nurturing, emphasizing home, family, and security needs. This transition deepens feelings and intuition while highlighting the importance of creating safe spaces and honoring personal roots and traditions.

July 22: Total solar eclipse, visible from southern parts of Asia, Australia, Pacific, Indian Ocean and Antarctica. This powerful total solar eclipse in Cancer represents a profound new beginning related to emotional foundations, family structures, and intuitive knowing. Its transformative energy creates opportunities for significant emotional resets and new approaches to nurturing, particularly affecting the southern hemisphere with intensified themes of home, heritage, and emotional security.

July 30: Pluto reaches opposition in Capricornus. Pluto's opposition in Capricornus brings hidden power dynamics within societal structures into stark visibility, particularly involving government, corporations, and authority figures. This alignment intensifies transformational energies at their peak, forcing confrontation with shadow aspects of ambition and control while offering potential for profound regeneration of systems.

August 10: Sun moves from Cancer to Leo. The Sun entering Leo shifts collective focus from emotional security to creative self-expression, leadership, and personal recognition. This transition brightens the atmosphere with confidence and generosity, encouraging heart-centered action and the courage to shine authentically after the protective phase of Cancer season.

August 24: Saturn begins retrograde motion in Aries. Saturn retrograde in Aries creates tension between forward momentum and necessary restraint, prompting a revision of boundaries, responsibilities, and leadership structures. This retrograde challenges impulsive action with disciplined reflection, forcing a reconsideration of how personal willpower aligns with long-term commitments and obligations.

September 16: Sun moves from Leo to Virgo. The Sun entering Virgo shifts collective energy from creative self-expression to practical analysis and improvement. This transition brings increased attention to detail, service, and health matters after Leo's dramatic displays, encouraging refinement of methods and helpful contributions.

The Encyclopedia of Astrology

September 19: Uranus begins retrograde motion in Taurus. Uranus retrograde in Taurus turns revolutionary energies inward, triggering internal shifts in values, financial approaches, and relationship to physical resources. This retrograde phase prompts questioning of material security systems and personal attachments, potentially revealing innovative solutions to resource challenges through introspection rather than external disruption.

September 20: Mercury in retrograde motion until October 11 in Virgo. Mercury retrograde in its home sign of Virgo creates pronounced communication challenges around details, health matters, and service-oriented tasks. This retrograde demands extraordinary precision while simultaneously making it difficult to achieve, perfect for revising methods, refining skills, and reorganizing systems rather than implementing new procedures.

September 22: Northern hemisphere autumn equinox, southern hemisphere vernal/spring equinox. This balanced moment of equal light and darkness emphasizes the Libra–Aries axis, highlighting themes of relationship versus individuality across hemispheres. The equinox creates a powerful energy portal for harmonizing opposites, with northern regions turning toward connection and compromise while southern areas experience renewal and initiative.

October 20: Pluto ends retrograde motion in Capricornus. Pluto stationing direct in Capricornus releases transformative energies that have been building internally, pushing power dynamics and structural changes into external manifestation. Could trigger significant shifts in government, business, and established hierarchies.

October 30: Sun moves from Virgo to Libra. The Sun entering Libra shifts collective focus from analytical improvement to harmonious connection, emphasizing relationships, justice, and balanced decision-making. This transition brings diplomatic energy after Virgo's meticulous scrutiny, encouraging cooperation, aesthetic appreciation, and the consideration of multiple perspectives.

October 30: Saturn reaches opposition in Aries. Saturn's opposition in Aries creates maximum tension between individual ambition and structural limitation, bringing conflicts between authority and autonomy to a critical culmination point. This alignment forces a reckoning with responsibility and leadership challenges, highlighting where impulsive action meets necessary boundaries and where personal will must integrate with collective obligations.

November 23: Sun moves from Libra to Scorpius. The Sun entering Scorpius deepens the collective energy from surface harmony to psychological intensity, bringing focus to shared resources, transformation, and hidden truths. This transition moves from Libra's balanced deliberation into profound emotional territory, encouraging deep investigation, passionate commitment, and the courage to confront what lies beneath appearances.

December 3: Uranus reaches opposition in Taurus. Uranus at opposition in Taurus brings revolutionary energies around material security, values, and resources to their peak visibility and impact. This alignment creates maximum tension between stability and disruption, potentially triggering sudden breakthroughs or breakdowns in financial systems, environmental approaches, and personal relationship to physical comfort.

December 17: Neptune ends retrograde motion in Pisces. Neptune stationing direct in its home sign of Pisces releases a flood of spiritual insight, creative inspiration, and collective compassion after months of internal dream-weaving. This forward motion clarifies spiritual vision and artistic direction, potentially dissolving illusions that have been reconsidered during the retrograde while activating renewed connection to universal themes.

December 21: Northern hemisphere winter solstice, southern hemisphere summer solstice. This powerful pivot point marks maximum darkness in the north and maximum light in the south, emphasizing the Capricorn–Cancer axis of worldly achievement versus emotional nurturing. The solstice creates a profound energy portal for honoring cycles of manifestation and release, with northern regions turning toward structured ambition and southern areas experiencing fullness and creative abundance.

December 31 to January 1: Monthly blue moon (second full moon in a month) and total lunar eclipse, visible from Europe, Asia, Australia, Africa, northern and western parts of North America, Pacific, Atlantic, Indian Ocean and Arctic. This rare combination of blue moon and total lunar eclipse in Cancer creates an extraordinarily potent emotional culmination bridging years, bringing dramatic revelations about security, family, and emotional foundations. Its timing at the calendar year transition amplifies themes of release and renewal, suggesting powerful collective transformation around nurturing, protection, and intuitive knowing that affects much of the world.

2029

January 7: Saturn ends retrograde motion in Aries. Saturn's direct motion in Aries will accelerate projects related to leadership and initiative after months of review and restructuring. This planetary shift signals a time when restrictive forces begin to lift, allowing for more straightforward progress in areas where Saturnian discipline and Aries energy intersect.

January 7: Mercury in retrograde until January 28 in Capricornus and Sagittarius. This Mercury retrograde period will cause communication delays and misunderstandings particularly affecting business planning and long-distance communications. As Mercury backtracks from structured Capricornus into philosophical Sagittarius, expect to revisit and revise plans, with technological issues and travel disruptions being especially pronounced.

January 14: Partial solar eclipse, visible from North America, Pacific and Atlantic. This partial solar eclipse will temporarily dim sunlight across North America and portions of the Pacific and Atlantic, creating observable changes in ambient light and possibly affecting animal behavior. The eclipse represents a significant celestial alignment that will impact solar energy collection systems and provide valuable scientific observation opportunities.

January 20: Sun moves from Sagittarius to Capricornus. The Sun's transition into Capricornus shifts the solar energetic focus from expansion and exploration to structure and discipline. This regular zodiacal progres-

The Encyclopedia of Astrology

sion marks a time when the Sun's illumination highlights practical concerns and responsibilities rather than philosophical pursuits.

February 11: Jupiter begins retrograde in Virgo. Jupiter's retrograde in Virgo will slow down expansion in areas related to health, service, and analytical processes for several months. This apparent backward motion of the planet of growth will prompt reassessment of systems and methodologies, with particular focus on refining rather than expanding.

February 13: Lunar new year, the Year of the Earth Rooster, Uranus ends retrograde motion in Taurus. The Earth Rooster ushers in a disciplined, detail-oriented, and pragmatic energy. Roosters are known for their precision and strong work ethic, and the Earth element reinforces these qualities, emphasizing reliability and methodical progress. This is a year where patience and persistence yield significant rewards. Organizational skills and strategic thinking take center stage, favoring career advancements and well-structured goals.

February 15: Mars begins retrograde in Virgo. Mars retrograde in Virgo will redirect energies inward, potentially causing frustration but providing opportunity for refined action and methodology. This relatively rare Mars retrograde will particularly affect projects requiring precision and detail, with progress slowing to allow for necessary corrections and improvements.

February 16: Sun moves from Capricornus to Aquarius. The Sun's ingress into Aquarius shifts solar energy from hierarchical structures toward community and innovation. This transition illuminates collective concerns and innovative solutions, marking a period where the spotlight moves from traditional authority to distributed networks and humanitarian ideals.

The Encyclopedia of Astrology

March 11: Sun moves from Aquarius to Pisces. The Sun entering Pisces dissolves boundaries between practical reality and spiritual idealism, enhancing collective empathy and artistic inspiration. This transit increases sensitivity to subtle energies and compassionate understanding, though it may also bring confusion around clear definitions and structured approaches.

March 20: Northern hemisphere vernal/spring equinox, southern hemisphere autumn equinox. The equinox marks a point of perfect balance between day and night, symbolizing harmony between opposing forces. Astrologically, this represents a powerful time for setting intentions related to balance. For the northern hemisphere, the spring equinox marks the astrological new year as the Sun enters Aries, bringing fresh energy and new beginnings. For the southern hemisphere, the autumn equinox brings energy of harvest and preparation.

March 25: Mars reaches opposition in Virgo. Mars opposition intensifies critical analysis and perfectionist tendencies, potentially manifesting as conflicts around methodologies and service approaches. This alignment heightens awareness of flaws in systems while providing energy to implement precise corrections, though patience may be tested in the process.

March 30: Libra supermoon. This Libra supermoon dramatically illuminates relationship dynamics and partnership imbalances with heightened emotional intensity. The amplified lunar energy brings relationship issues to culmination points, with opportunities for significant rebalancing of give-and-take dynamics in all forms of collaboration.

April 12: Jupiter reaches opposition in Virgo. Jupiter's opposition expands awareness around health matters, work methodologies, and service opportunities with heightened clarity. This alignment magnifies both the benefits and excesses of systematic approaches, offering perspective on where refinement serves growth and where perfectionism hinders progress.

April 18: Sun moves from Pisces to Aries. The Sun entering Aries marks the astrological new year, injecting fresh courage and initiative after the dreamy Piscean waters. This fiery transition supports bold new beginnings and self-directed action, though it may also trigger impulsiveness and competitive energies that require channeling.

April 28: Scorpio supermoon. This full moon intensifies emotional depths, bringing powerful revelations and transformative encounters around shared resources and intimate connections. The heightened lunar energy illuminates secrets and power dynamics, creating potential for profound healing or intensified conflict depending on how this energy is channeled.

May 2: Mercury in retrograde until May 25 in Taurus and Aries. Mercury retrograde in Taurus and Aries creates communication challenges around financial matters and personal initiatives, requiring careful review of resources and impulsive decisions. This retrograde period invites reassessment of values and self-assertion, with opportunities to correct misunderstandings about material security before moving forward with renewed clarity.

May 5: Mars ends retrograde motion in Virgo. Mars turning direct in Virgo releases pent-up energy around work projects and health initiatives after months of internal refinement and revision. This shift allows for more effective implementation of precisely calibrated actions, particularly in service-oriented activities and analytical processes that benefit from the retrospective period.

May 13: Sun moves from Aries to Taurus, Pluto begins retrograde motion in Capricornus.

The Sun entering Taurus shifts focus from initiative to consolidation while Pluto retrograde in Capricorn simultaneously triggers deep review of power structures and ambitions. This powerful combination demands authentic reassessment of material values and institutional systems, potentially revealing hidden motivations behind authority and resource management.

June 12: Partial solar eclipse, visible from much of Europe, northern parts of Asia, northern and western parts of North America, Pacific and Arctic. This partial solar eclipse catalyzes unexpected developments in security matters and resource management for the affected regions, particularly Europe and North America. The eclipse energy initiates a six-month cycle of adjustment to material foundations and values, with particular emphasis on economic systems and environmental resources.

June 13: Jupiter ends retrograde motion in Virgo. Jupiter turning direct in Virgo accelerates growth in health systems, workplace efficiency, and service methodologies after a period of internal review and refinement. This shift brings forward momentum to areas requiring practical expansion, with particularly beneficial effects for educational approaches to wellness and analytical problem-solving.

June 21: Sun moves from Taurus to Gemini. The Sun entering Gemini shifts collective focus from stability and resources toward communication, learning, and social connection. This transit energizes intellectual pursuits and diverse interests, supporting versatility and information exchange while potentially dispersing focus from material concerns.

June 21: Northern hemisphere summer solstice, southern hemisphere winter solstice. This solstice represents maximum light in the north and maximum darkness in the south, creating a powerful global polarity of energies affecting collective consciousness. Astrologically significant as the Sun enters Cancer, this transition marks a turning point in the annual cycle, emphasizing home, emotional security, and nurturing connections.

June 25 to 26: Total lunar eclipse, visible from Europe, western parts of Asia, Africa, North America, South America, Pacific, Atlantic, Indian Ocean and Antarctica. This total lunar eclipse in Capricorn dramatically illuminates the completion of emotional cycles related to career, authority, and public responsibility. The eclipse energy brings powerful culmination to matters of ambition and structure, potentially revealing emotional attachments to status and achievement that require release for authentic progress.

July 11: Partial solar eclipse, visible from South America, Pacific and Atlantic. This partial solar eclipse initiates unexpected shifts in emotional foundations and family dynamics, particularly affecting South American regions with its transformative energy. The eclipse marks the beginning of a six-month cycle of intuitive development and adjustment to security needs, potentially triggering important revelations about nurturing patterns and emotional roots.

July 15: Neptune begins retrograde motion in Pisces. Neptune's retrograde in Pisces fosters a period of spiritual realignment and emotional recalibration. Subtle undercurrents of illusion may be exposed, prompting a reassessment of personal ideals, creative visions, and intuitive insights. While the desire for escapism may increase, this transit ultimately supports deeper self-awareness, making it an ideal time for refining spiritual practices and reconnecting with authentic inspiration.

July 20: Sun moves from Gemini to Cancer. The Sun's ingress into Cancer shifts collective focus from intellectual variety toward emotional security and nurturing connections. This transit heightens sensitivity to home environments and family dynamics, emphasizing the importance of emotional roots and protective boundaries around vulnerability.

August 1: Pluto reaches opposition in Capricornus. Pluto at opposition intensifies transformative pressure on institutional structures and professional ambitions, bringing hidden power dynamics into stark visibility. This alignment forces confrontation with the shadow aspects of authority and achievement, potentially triggering profound crisis points that demand authentic reorganization of hierarchical systems.

August 10: Sun moves from Cancer to Leo. The Sun entering Leo shifts energy from protective nurturing toward creative self-expression and confident leadership. This transit illuminates opportunities for heartfelt generosity and dramatic display, supporting authentic sharing of talents while potentially intensifying ego-driven conflicts around recognition and attention.

August 24: Seasonal blue moon (third full moon in an astronomical season containing four full moons). This rare seasonal blue moon in Pisces amplifies emotional sensitivity and spiritual awareness, creating an unusual opportunity for intuitive breakthroughs and compassionate connection. The intensified lunar energy illuminates collective unconscious patterns, potentially bringing significant revelations about universal connections and dissolving artificial boundaries between self and other.

September 5: Saturn begins retrograde motion in Taurus. Saturn retrograde in Taurus initiates a serious review period of material security systems and resource management that will require careful restructuring. This transit turns disciplinary focus inward, potentially triggering anxiety around financial stability while offering valuable opportunities to strengthen foundations through thoughtful reassessment of what truly provides lasting value.

September 16: Sun moves from Leo to Virgo. The Sun entering Virgo shifts collective focus from creative self-expression toward practical improvement and analytical problem-solving. This transit illuminates opportunities for refining systems and developing skills, supporting methodical approaches to health and service while potentially intensifying critical perfectionism.

September 20: Mercury in retrograde until October 11 in Virgo. Mercury retrograde in its home sign of Virgo creates particularly challenging disruptions to analytical processes, daily routines, and health management systems. This retrograde invites meticulous review of details that may have been overlooked, with opportunities to perfect methodologies and communication systems before implementing improvements with greater precision.

September 22: Northern hemisphere autumn equinox, southern hemisphere vernal/spring equinox. This equinox represents perfect balance before tipping toward introspection in the north and outward growth in the south, marking a significant energy shift worldwide. Astrologically aligned with the Sun entering Libra, this transition emphasizes relationship harmony, justice, and the delicate balancing of opposing forces in all partnerships.

September 23: Uranus begins retrograde motion in Taurus. Uranus retrograde in Taurus turns revolutionary energy inward, potentially triggering internal resistance to necessary changes in material security systems. This transit invites innovative reimagining of

The Encyclopedia of Astrology

resources and values from within, with sudden insights about sustainable approaches that may need to be developed internally before manifesting externally.

October 22: Pluto ends retrograde motion in Capricornus. Pluto turning direct in Capricorn releases transformative energy into structures of power and authority after months of internal reassessment and purging. This shift accelerates profound changes in governmental, corporate, and societal hierarchies, potentially bringing to light corruption that was revealed during the retrograde period but now demands concrete restructuring.

October 30: Sun moves from Virgo to Libra. The Sun entering Libra shifts collective focus from analytical improvement toward balance, harmony, and relationship dynamics. This transit illuminates partnership opportunities and social justice concerns, supporting diplomatic negotiations while potentially highlighting indecision and people-pleasing tendencies that avoid necessary confrontation.

November 13: Saturn reaches opposition in Aries. Saturn at opposition intensifies tension between personal initiative and external limitation, creating pressure points where ambition meets structural reality. This alignment forces confrontation with authority figures and responsibility, potentially triggering significant tests of leadership capacity and the necessity to integrate discipline with authentic self-expression.

November 23: Sun moves from Libra to Scorpius. The Sun entering Scorpio shifts collective energy from balance-seeking harmony toward transformative intensity and emotional depth. This transit illuminates hidden motivations and power dynamics, supporting profound healing and regeneration while potentially intensifying psychological battles around control and vulnerability.

The Encyclopedia of Astrology

December 5: Partial solar eclipse, visible from South America, Pacific, Atlantic, Indian Ocean, Antarctica. This partial solar eclipse in Sagittarius initiates unexpected developments in philosophical understanding and belief systems, particularly affecting South American regions. The eclipse energy begins a six-month cycle of truth-seeking and horizon expansion, potentially triggering important revelations about educational systems and ethical frameworks.

December 8: Uranus reaches opposition in Taurus. Uranus at opposition creates maximum tension between revolutionary impulses and material security needs, potentially triggering unexpected disruptions in financial systems and resource management. This alignment forces confrontation with outdated values, bringing sudden breakthroughs or breakdowns that demand innovative approaches to stability and sustainability.

December 16: Venus in retrograde until January 27, 2030, in Sagittarius. Venus retrograde in Sagittarius prompts deep reassessment of relationships that expand horizons and philosophical values connected to love and resources. This retrograde invites review of cross-cultural connections and educational partnerships, potentially revealing misalignments between ethical ideals and actual expressions of affection or value exchange.

December 20 to 21: Total lunar eclipse, visible from Europe, Asia, northern and western parts of Australia, Africa, North America, South America, Pacific, Atlantic, Indian Ocean and Arctic. This total lunar eclipse in Cancer dramatically illuminates emotional patterns connected to home, family, and nurturing that have reached culmination points. The eclipse energy brings powerful revelation to matters of emotional security and protective boundaries, potentially trigger-

The Encyclopedia of Astrology

ing significant releases from ancestral patterns and attachment styles.

December 21: Northern hemisphere winter solstice, southern hemisphere summer solstice. This solstice represents maximum darkness in the north and maximum light in the south, creating a powerful global polarity affecting collective consciousness. Astrologically aligned with the Sun entering Capricorn, this transition marks a significant turning point emphasizing ambition, structure, and responsibility as the foundation for achievement.

December 22: Mercury in retrograde until January 11, 2030, in Sagittarius. Mercury retrograde in Sagittarius creates communication challenges around belief systems, higher education, and international connections during the holiday period. This retrograde invites reassessment of truth-seeking approaches and philosophical frameworks, with opportunities to correct misunderstandings about long-distance plans before implementing visions with greater clarity in the new year.

2030

January 21: Saturn ends retrograde motion in Aries. As Saturn stations direct in fiery Aries, restrictions will begin to lift, allowing for more decisive forward movement. This planetary shift marks a time when hard-earned lessons about self-assertion and leadership can be implemented with greater structural support.

The Encyclopedia of Astrology

February 3: Lunar new year, the Year of the Metal Dog. The Metal Dog brings a year of loyalty, integrity, and unwavering determination. While the Dog already values justice and protection, the Metal element enhances resilience and decisiveness. This year favors standing firm in one's principles, taking bold yet thoughtful action, and reinforcing long-term commitments. Challenges may arise that require moral clarity, but the steadfast energy of the Metal Dog supports perseverance and trustworthiness.

February 16: Sun moves from Capricornus to Aquarius. The Sun's movement into Aquarius signals a collective shift from structure-oriented thinking to innovative, community-minded awareness. This transition invites a break from conventional limitations and an opening to revolutionary possibilities for self and society.

February 21: Uranus ends retrograde motion in Taurus. Uranus stationing direct in Taurus brings sudden breakthroughs in financial matters and personal values that have been internally percolating for months. Expect unexpected developments in resource management and security concerns as the planet of disruption moves forward in this earth sign.

March 11: Sun moves from Aquarius to Pisces. As the Sun enters Pisces, the collective consciousness shifts toward greater compassion, spiritual connection, and creative inspiration. This watery, mutable energy dissolves boundaries and invites surrender to the mystical currents of life.

March 20: Northern hemisphere vernal/spring equinox, southern hemisphere autumn equinox. This powerful day of balanced light and dark heralds new beginnings in the north and completion in the south, creating a global energetic reset point. The equinox opens astrological doorways for initiating

The Encyclopedia of Astrology

fresh projects or harvesting the results of past efforts, depending on location.

April 18: Sun moves from Pisces to Aries. The Sun's entrance into Aries ignites a powerful surge of initiatory energy, marking the true astrological new year. This cardinal fire sign transition shifts the collective focus from dreamy introspection to decisive action, fueling courage and motivation for new ventures. Aries' dynamic influence encourages bold leadership, assertiveness, and a willingness to embrace fresh beginnings with confidence.

May 13: Sun moves from Aries to Taurus. As the Sun enters Taurus, the initial burst of spring energy settles into a more grounded, sensual approach to manifestation. This transition acts of deliberate patience, and savoring life's pleasures while establishing lasting security.

May 13: Jupiter reaches opposition in Libra. Jupiter's opposition in diplomatic Libra amplifies matters of justice, relationships, and balance, bringing them into full illumination. This expansive alignment offers extraordinary potential for breakthrough agreements and harmonious resolutions in partnerships, both personal and professional.

May 17: Supermoon, Pluto begins retrograde motion in Capricornus. This potent supermoon coinciding with Pluto's retrograde initiates a period of intense internal transformation regarding power structures and ambitions. The magnified lunar energies will expose shadow aspects of authority and achievement.

June 1: Annular solar eclipse, visible from Europe, Asia, much of Africa, northern and western parts of North America, Pacific, Atlantic and Arctic. This "ring of fire" eclipse catalyzes revolutionary new beginnings that will restructure foundational aspects of identity

The Encyclopedia of Astrology

and purpose. The eclipse's extensive visibility across multiple continents suggests collective paradigm shifts affecting global power dynamics and cross-cultural relationships.

June 15 to 16: Partial lunar eclipse of the supermoon full moon, visible from Europe, Asia, Australia, Africa, southern and eastern parts of South America, Pacific, Atlantic, Indian Ocean and Antarctica. This dramatic lunar event illuminates emotional patterns and subconscious programming that have reached culmination point, demanding release. The amplified supermoon qualities intensify the eclipse's revelatory nature, bringing heightened intuitive insights and profound emotional catharsis.

June 21: Sun moves from Taurus to Gemini. The Sun's movement into curious Gemini shifts collective focus from material concerns to intellectual exploration and social connection. This mutable air sign transition accelerates the pace of communication and learning, inspiring versatile thinking and adaptable approaches.

June 21: Northern hemisphere summer solstice, southern hemisphere winter solstice. This pivotal day of maximum light in the northern hemisphere and deepest darkness in the southern hemisphere establishes a powerful axis between creative expression and introspective wisdom. The solstice energies encourage a balance between external achievements and inner reflection, highlighting the cyclical nature of growth and renewal. This transition serves as a reminder of the interplay between action and contemplation, emphasizing the importance of both outward expansion and internal nourishment.

July 15: Jupiter ends retrograde motion in Libra. As Jupiter stations direct in Libra, the expansion of harmony, justice, and balanced partnerships accelerates after months of internal review. This forward movement breathes new life into relationship endeavors and legal matters, allowing external progress in areas that have been developing behind the scenes.

July 20: Sun moves from Gemini to Cancer. The Sun's entrance into nurturing Cancer shifts collective focus from intellectual curiosity to emotional security and familial connections. This cardinal water sign transition draws energy inward, prioritizing home sanctuary and ancestral roots as sources of strength and sustenance.

August 3: Pluto reaches opposition in Capricornus. Pluto's opposition illuminates the shadow aspects of societal structures and personal ambitions with transformative intensity. This powerful alignment brings subconscious power dynamics into conscious awareness, forcing a reckoning with outdated authority systems and catalyzing profound institutional metamorphosis.

August 10: Sun moves from Cancer to Leo. As the Sun enters its home sign of Leo, the collective energy shifts from protective nurturing to radiant self-expression and creative leadership. This fiery transition ignites the courage to shine authentically, celebrating one's unique gifts while inspiring others through generous heart-centered action.

September 16: Sun moves from Leo to Virgo. The Sun's movement into analytical Virgo channels the previous month's creative fire into practical, refined improvement and service. This transition encourages meticulous attention to detail and health-conscious choices, bringing a discerning energy that seeks efficient solutions and meaningful contribution.

September 23: Northern hemisphere autumn equinox, southern hemisphere vernal/spring equinox. This balancing point of equal day and night creates a harmonious portal for reassessing relationships and establishing new equilibrium between self and other. The equinox energies support harvesting the fruits of past efforts in the north while initiating fresh beginnings in the south, creating a global rhythm of completion and renewal.

October 5: Neptune reaches opposition in Pisces. Neptune's opposition in its home waters of Pisces brings spiritual revelations and creative inspiration to their most potent expression. This mystical alignment thins the veil between worlds, offering profound communion with the collective unconscious while potentially exposing illusions that have obscured higher truth.

October 24: Pluto ends retrograde motion in Capricornus. As transformative Pluto stations direct in Capricornus, deep internal revelations about power and authority begin manifesting as external changes in career and societal structures. This forward movement activates the evolutionary lessons absorbed during the retrograde period, empowering courageous steps toward authentic leadership.

October 30: Sun moves from Virgo to Libra. The Sun's entrance into harmonious Libra shifts focus from detailed analysis to balanced relationships and aesthetic appreciation. This cardinal air sign transition brings diplomatic energy that seeks equilibrium through cooperation, inspiring social harmony and refined judgment in matters of beauty and justice.

November 23: Sun moves from Libra to Scorpius. The Sun's plunge into mysterious Scorpius draws collective energy into the depths of transformation, passion, and psychological revelation. This intense transition invites profound emotional honesty and regenerative power, urging the surrender of superficial concerns in favor of authentic intimacy and spiritual rebirth.

The Encyclopedia of Astrology

November 25: Total solar eclipse, visible from southern parts of Asia, Australia, South/East Africa, Pacific, Atlantic, Indian Ocean and Antarctica. This potent total solar eclipse initiates a powerful reset in matters of personal power, shared resources, and psychological healing. The eclipse's wide visibility across the southern hemisphere suggests a collective evolutionary leap in consciousness that will reshape primal relationships with wealth, sexuality, and mortality.

November 27: Saturn reaches opposition in Taurus. Saturn's opposition in steadfast Taurus brings material limitations and financial responsibilities into sharp focus, demanding disciplined management of resources. This sobering alignment tests the sustainability of value systems and economic foundations, compelling necessary adjustments to ensure long-term security.

December 9 to 10: Penumbral lunar eclipse, visible from Europe, Asia, North/West Australia, Africa, North America, South America, Pacific, Atlantic, Indian Ocean and Arctic. This subtle lunar eclipse casts a gentle shadow across emotional patterns related to security, nourishment, and belonging that have reached completion. The widespread visibility suggests collective emotional processing that transcends cultural boundaries, creating space for evolved nurturing dynamics to emerge globally.

December 12: Uranus reaches opposition in Taurus. Uranus's opposition in steadfast Taurus brings revolutionary breakthroughs in material values and resource management to their fullest expression. This electric alignment catalyzes sudden insights regarding financial freedom and sustainable innovation, potentially triggering unexpected shifts in global economic systems.

The Encyclopedia of Astrology

December 21: Northern hemisphere winter solstice, southern hemisphere summer solstice. This profound turning point of maximum darkness in the north and light in the south creates a powerful portal for honoring both introspective wisdom and external achievement. The solstice energies support sacred communion and celebration of the cyclical nature of creation, dissolution, and rebirth.

TIMELINE OF ASTROLOGY

TIMELINE OF ASTROLOGY

The earliest human observations of celestial patterns can be traced back to carved bones and cave paintings from around 32,000 BCE, showing lunar phases and star positions. These observations evolved into the first calendars, with archaeological evidence from 8000 BCE showing communities tracking seasonal changes through astronomical markers such as the heliacal rising of certain stars. The need to predict seasonal changes for agriculture led to more systematic sky-watching, with sites like Nabta Playa in Egypt (*c.* 5000 BCE) and Stonehenge (*c.* 3000 BCE) serving as early astronomical observatories that aligned with solstices and other celestial events.

As agricultural societies developed, sky-watching became increasingly sophisticated, with early civilizations in Mesopotamia developing the first systematic celestial observations by 3000 BCE. The Babylonians created detailed clay tablets recording the movements of planets and stars, establishing the foundation for both astronomy and

LUNAR PHASES

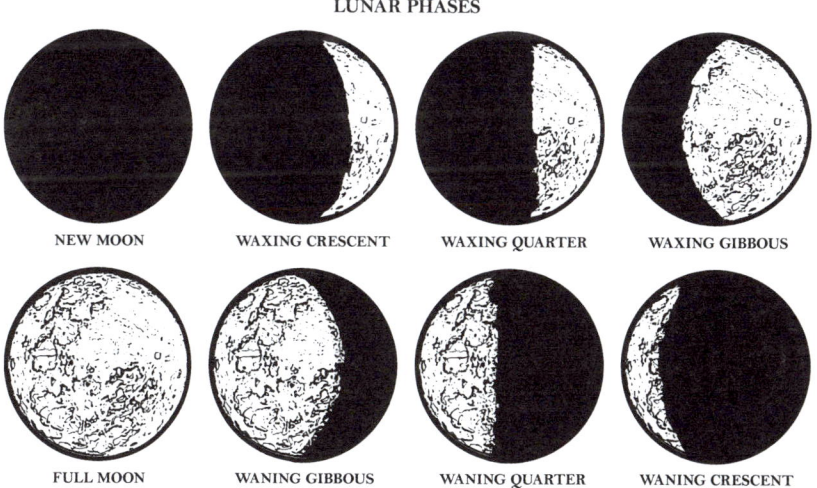

The Encyclopedia of Astrology

astrology. Their observations led to the recognition of patterns such as the 12-month calendar based on lunar cycles and the identification of five visible planets, which they associated with their deities.

Western astrology emerged as a distinct tradition when Greek scholars began translating and adapting Babylonian celestial knowledge around 600 BCE, adding their own philosophical framework and mathematical precision. This Hellenistic synthesis spread throughout the Mediterranean, where it was further developed by Roman scholars and eventually preserved by medieval European monasteries and Arab astronomers.

The Arabic preservation and development of astrology, often called the "Islamic Golden Age" of astrology, was crucial during the European Dark Ages (roughly 800–1200 CE). Arab scholars not only preserved ancient Greek texts by translating them into Arabic, but they also made significant original contributions. The House of Wisdom in Baghdad became a major center of learning where scholars translated works by Ptolemy and other Greek astrologers, while also developing new mathematical techniques for calculating planetary positions.

The knowledge eventually returned to Europe through Spain and Sicily in the 12th century, where Arabic texts were translated into Latin. This transmission restored much of the classical astrological knowledge that had been lost in Europe and introduced new techniques such as the Arabic Parts (mathematical points in a chart) and sophisticated systems for predicting weather and political events. The tradition that evolved in Europe, with its emphasis on the tropical zodiac and personal horoscopes, became what we now recognize as Western astrology.

30,000–10,000 BCE, PREHISTORIC OBSERVATIONS

Early humans created star maps long before maps of land or sea. Archaeological findings include cave paintings, mammoth tusks, and bones marked with lunar phases, indicating an early interest in celestial patterns.

ORION
constellation

MESOPOTAMIAN CONTRIBUTIONS

6000 BCE: The Sumerians in Mesopotamia began noting the movements of planets and stars, laying the groundwork for systematic celestial observations.

2400–331 BCE: The Babylonians (Chaldeans) advanced Sumerian practices, developing the first astrological system over millennia. They created the zodiac wheel used today, incorporating planets and houses around 700 BCE. The oldest known horoscope chart dates to 409 BCE.

2000 BCE–600 CE, THE AGE OF CLASSICAL ASTROLOGY

Classical astrology spans from approximately 2000 BCE–600 CE, originating in Mesopotamia and reaching its sophisticated peak during the Hellenistic period of Greece and Rome.

This foundational period established the core principles of horoscopic astrology, including the zodiac signs, houses, aspects between planets, and the significance of planetary movements. The era concluded with Ptolemy's influential work *Tetrabiblos*, which systematized astrological knowledge and remained the primary reference for Western astrology for over a thousand years.

The Encyclopedia of Astrology

300 BCE—200 CE, GREEK ASTROLOGICAL TEXTS

Greek astrological texts flourished between 300 BCE and 200 CE, marking the height of Hellenistic astrology and producing seminal works that blended Babylonian astronomical observations with Greek philosophy and mathematics.

140–170 CE: *Tetrabiblos* by Ptolemy

The most influential of all ancient astrological texts, systematically presenting the whole of ancient astrological knowledge. It established the fundamental principles of Western astrology, including detailed explanations of planets, signs, houses, and aspects that are still used today. Its rational, philosophical approach helped legitimize astrology as a field of study.

75 CE: *Carmen Astrologicum* by Dorotheus of Sidon

Critical for establishing predictive techniques such as annual progressions and electional astrology (choosing auspicious times for actions). Written in verse form to aid memorization, it heavily influenced Persian and Arabic astrology, and through them, medieval European practices. *Original Greek version lost; survives through Arabic translations, with the most complete copy in the British Library (Arabic manuscript Or. 3647).*

160 CE: *Anthology* by Vettius Valens

Notable for providing practical examples of chart interpretation and timing techniques. Contains the largest surviving collection of actual horoscopes from antiquity, offering invaluable insight into how astrology was practiced. Particularly influential for its teachings on length-of-life calculations and time-lord systems. *Most complete manuscript is in the Vatican Library (*Vaticanus graecus *191).*

8 CE: *Astronomica* by Marcus Manilius

The earliest comprehensive Latin text on astrology, written

in poetic form. Known for introducing the concept of decans (dividing each zodiac sign into three parts) to Western astrology and establishing connections between zodiac signs and various geographical regions. *Several manuscripts exist, with important copies in the Gembloux Abbey manuscript (now in Brussels Royal Library) and the Leipzig University Library.*

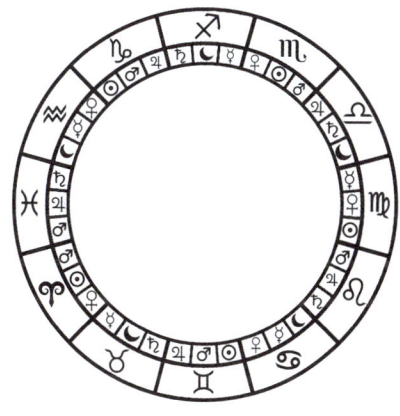

334–337 CE: *Mathesis* by Firmicus Maternus

The most extensive surviving Latin text on astrology from the classical period. Particularly influential for its detailed coverage of natal astrology and its attempt to reconcile astrological practice with emerging Christian beliefs. *Best preserved copy is in the Vaticanus Palatinus 1418 in the Vatican Library.*

380 CE: *Thesaurus* by Antigonus of Nicaea

Significant for preserving earlier Hellenistic techniques that would otherwise have been lost. Known for its detailed treatment of lunar astrology and timing techniques, though only fragments survive. *Fragments survive in various Byzantine manuscripts, primarily in the Vatican Library.*

ADVANCEMENTS IN ASTRONOMICAL CALCULATIONS

150 CE: Ptolemy's *Almagest*

Introduced sophisticated mathematical models for predicting planetary positions and established a geocentric model of the universe that would influence astronomical calculations for over a millennium.

The Encyclopedia of Astrology

825 CE: The House of Wisdom in Baghdad

Established around 800 BCE, made significant refinements to astronomical tables under Al-Khwarizmi, introducing more precise methods for calculating planetary positions and producing the first comprehensive set of astronomical tables (zij).

1252–1270 CE: The Alfonsine Tables

Commissioned by Alfonso X of Castile, provided more accurate planetary positions and became the standard astronomical reference in medieval Europe. These tables allowed for more precise astrological calculations and timing.

1543–1600s CE: The Copernican Revolution

Followed by Kepler's laws of planetary motion, dramatically improved the accuracy of planetary position calculations. While these developments challenged traditional astrological cosmology, they provided astrologers with more precise data for chart calculations.

100s–0 BCE DEVELOPMENT OF WHOLE SIGN HOUSE SYSTEM AND EQUAL HOUSE SYSTEM

Whole Sign Houses

Whole Sign, originating in Hellenistic astrology, assigns entire zodiac signs to each house, with the rising sign occupying the first house. The remaining houses follow in zodiacal order, creating clean, clear boundaries between houses. This system has seen a revival in recent years for its simplicity and historical accuracy.

Equal House

Equal House creates 12 houses of exactly 30 degrees each, starting from the ascendant degree. Its mathematical simplicity makes it one of the oldest systems, dating back to ancient Egypt. This system ensures every house has equal width and

The Encyclopedia of Astrology

influence, though planets may not be distributed evenly.

300s BCE DEVELOPMENT OF PORPHYRY HOUSE SYSTEM

Porphyry is a simple system that trisects the space between the angles in the ecliptic. Porphyry, named after the 3rd-century Greek philosopher Porphyry of Tyre, creates houses by taking the space between major angles (Ascendant, Midheaven, Descendant, and Imum Coeli) and dividing each quadrant into three equal parts. This means house sizes may vary within the chart depending on the spacing between these angles.

500—1500s CE MEDIEVAL EUROPEAN ASTROLOGY

Medieval European astrology, spanning roughly 500–1500 CE, merged Christian theology with classical astrological traditions, introducing angels and demons as celestial intermediaries while maintaining a strong focus on medical astrology and timing. Court astrologers became essential political advisors, while universities began teaching "astrologia" alongside astronomy and mathematics, leading to more sophisticated astronomical tables and calculation methods.

During this period, Arabic translations in the 12th century brought new techniques and terms into European practice,

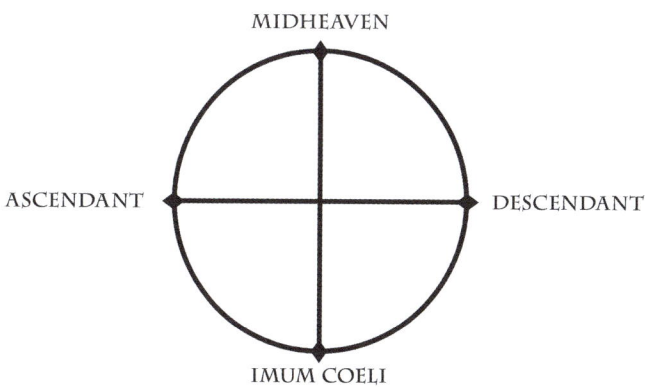

The Encyclopedia of Astrology

while influential texts like Alcabitius's *Introductorius admagisterium iudiciorum astrorum* and Bonatti's *Liber Astronomiae* standardized astrological education. The creation of detailed almanacs helped spread astrological timing concepts to the general population, combining practical agricultural advice with medical and political forecasting that would influence European society for centuries.

500–1200s CE MONASTIC PRESERVATION OF ASTROLOGICAL KNOWLEDGE

Between 500–1200 CE, monasteries served as crucial repositories for ancient astrological texts, with monks meticulously copying and translating Greek and Arabic manuscripts into Latin while adding their own interpretations and commentaries. The Benedictine monasteries were particularly important in this preservation effort, maintaining libraries that safeguarded classical works like Ptolemy's *Tetrabiblos* alongside astronomical calculation tables.

These monastic scribes often wrestled with reconciling astrological concepts with Christian doctrine, resulting in unique syntheses that emphasized astrology as a tool for understanding God's natural order rather than a form of divination. This preservation and interpretation work laid the groundwork for the later revival of astrology in medieval universities, where many texts that had been preserved in monasteries became standard academic references for both astronomical calculation and astrological interpretation.

325–1500s CE INTEGRATION WITH CHRISTIAN THEOLOGY

The integration of astrology with Christian theology primarily developed during two key phases—the early Christian period (325–600 CE) when Church fathers such as Augustine first addressed astrological concepts, and the High Medieval period

(1000–1500 CE) when scholastic theologians including Thomas Aquinas fully developed the theoretical framework for Christian astrology. During 1200–1500 CE, this synthesis reached its peak in European universities, where astrology was taught alongside theology as part of the standard curriculum.

Influential figures such as Thomas Aquinas argued that while the stars might influence physical matter and human inclinations, they could not override free will or divine providence. This created a theological framework that allowed for the practice of astrology within Christian contexts.

Saint Augustine's concept that God used the stars as a divine language, combined with the biblical reference to celestial signs in Genesis 1:14, helped legitimize the study of astrology as a means of understanding God's creation. This integration reached its peak in the medieval period, when church-sponsored universities taught astrology as part of their standard curriculum, and religious manuscripts often included astrological imagery, with Christ sometimes depicted as the Cosmic Man surrounded by zodiacal symbols.

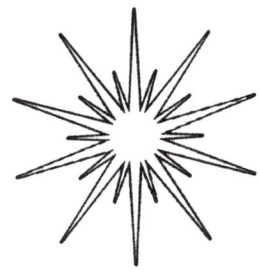

800–1700s CE THE RULE OF COURT ASTROLOGERS

Court astrologers wielded their greatest political influence during 800–1700 CE, reaching peak prominence in European courts during 1400–1600 CE. During this period, no major political decision, from marriage alliances to military campaigns, would be undertaken without consulting the court astrologer, who often held the formal title of "Mathematicus" or "Royal Astronomer."

The Encyclopedia of Astrology

Notable examples include Michel de Nostradamus (1503–1566), who advised Catherine de Medici and the French royal court; John Dee (1527–1608), who selected Elizabeth I's coronation date and advised on England's imperial expansion; and Johannes Kepler (1571–1630), who served as Imperial Mathematician to three Holy Roman Emperors while making his astronomical discoveries. The practice declined sharply after 1700 CE with the rise of Enlightenment thinking, though some courts, like the British monarchy, maintained royal astrologers well into the 18th century. The position of Royal Astronomer, which began as a role for court astrologers, gradually transformed into a purely astronomical position.

1000S CE ALCABITIUS HOUSE SYSTEM DEVELOPED

The Alcabitius house system, developed by 10th-century Arabic astrologer Al-Qabisi (Latinized as Alcabitius), was widely used throughout medieval Europe and remained popular until the 17th century when it was gradually replaced by the Placidus system. It uses a time-based method of house division similar to Placidus, but calculates the cusps by trisecting the diurnal and nocturnal semi-arcs in a different way, resulting in houses that can vary significantly in size. While rarely used in modern Western astrology, the system still maintains some following among traditional astrologers and those studying medieval astrological techniques, particularly those interested in working with historical source materials from the medieval period.

1400–1650S RENAISSANCE ASTROLOGY

Renaissance astrology flourished from approximately 1400–1650, characterized by a revival of classical astrological texts through new translations directly from Greek sources, rather than Arabic intermediaries. This period saw astrology

The Encyclopedia of Astrology

reach new heights of sophistication and social acceptance, with practitioners combining Hermetic philosophy, Neoplatonism, and Christian theology while developing more precise astronomical calculations and timing techniques.

Key figures like Marsilio Ficino (1433–1499) and Pico della Mirandola (1463–1494) established philosophical frameworks that integrated astrology with Renaissance humanism. The period reached its technical peak with practitioners like Gerolamo Cardano (1501–1576), who published detailed natal chart interpretations of famous figures, and William Lilly (1602–1681), whose work *Christian Astrology* marked both the pinnacle and approaching end of Renaissance astrological practice. This era began declining with the rise of the Scientific Revolution, though its influence extended into the early Enlightenment period.

1300s CAMPANUS HOUSE SYSTEM DEVELOPED

Campanus, developed by 13th-century mathematician Johannes Campanus, divides the celestial sphere using the prime vertical—an imaginary great circle passing through the east point, zenith, west point, and nadir.

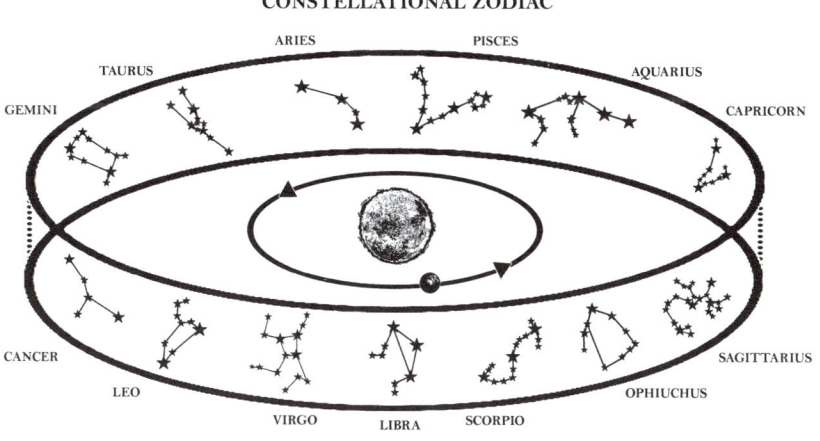

CONSTELLATIONAL ZODIAC

The Encyclopedia of Astrology

This creates houses of varying sizes but maintains mathematical elegance. Astrological research organizations often use Campanus for its geometric precision.

1500s REGIOMONTANUS HOUSE SYSTEM DEVELOPED

Regiomontanus, created by 15th-century German astronomer Johannes Müller von Königsberg, divides the celestial equator into 12 equal parts through great circles intersecting at the north and south points of the horizon. This system was widely used during the Renaissance and remains popular in horary astrology for its precision in timing events. The houses vary in size but maintain mathematical consistency around the equator.

1657—1658 PLACIDUS HOUSE SYSTEM DEVELOPED

The most widely used system in Western astrology. Placidus divides the ecliptic by time, calculating how long it takes a point to travel from the horizon to the midheaven. Developed by 17th-century Italian mathematician Placidus de Titis, it's particularly accurate for locations between 40 degrees north and 40 degrees south latitude. The system becomes less reliable in extreme northern or southern latitudes, where planets can sometimes skip houses entirely.

1600—1750s: THE SCIENTIFIC REVOLUTION AND ENLIGHTENMENT AND THE SEPARATION OF ASTRONOMY AND ASTROLOGY

As empirical observation and mechanical physics gained prominence through the work of Newton and others, astrology became increasingly separated from astronomy and natural philosophy. This period marked astrology's transition from a university subject to a more marginalized practice, though it remained popular among the general public.

The Encyclopedia of Astrology

Before the 17th century, astronomy and astrology were deeply intertwined disciplines, with most scholars practicing both the mathematical calculation of celestial movements and their interpretation for earthly meanings. Notable figures such as Tycho Brahe and Johannes Kepler worked as both astronomers and court astrologers, developing sophisticated mathematical models while also creating horoscopes for their patrons.

The split began gradually during the Scientific Revolution, marked by Copernicus's heliocentric model and Galileo's telescopic observations. The mechanistic worldview promoted by Newton's work (1687) and the emphasis on empirical evidence created an environment where astronomy increasingly focused on observable, measurable phenomena, while astrology's focus on symbolic interpretation and human experience became viewed as separate from scientific inquiry.

By the end of the 18th century, the separation was largely complete in academic and scientific circles. Astronomy had become firmly established as a natural science taught in universities, while astrology continued as a popular practice outside of academic institutions. This divide was reinforced during the 19th century as astronomy made major advances in understanding celestial mechanics, spectroscopy, and astrophysics.

1781 URANUS INCORPORATED INTO ASTROLOGY

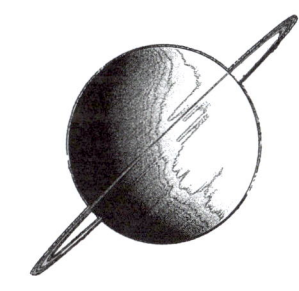

Uranus was the first outer planet to be incorporated into astrology following its discovery in 1781, though it took several decades before astrologers widely adopted it.

The Encyclopedia of Astrology

1846 NEPTUNE INCORPORATED INTO ASTROLOGY

Neptune was discovered in 1846 and began appearing in astrological interpretations by the 1870s.

19TH AND EARLY 20TH CENTURY REVIVAL

The revival of astrology in the 19th and early 20th centuries was largely sparked by the Theosophical movement, with Russian-American mystic Helena Blavatsky's 1877 publication of *Isis Unveiled* helping reframe astrology within a broader spiritual framework. English astrologer Alan Leo, often called the father of modern astrology, revolutionized the practice through his seven-book series published between 1898 and 1907, including *Astrology for All*, which made astrological concepts more accessible to the general public. The establishment of the Astrological Lodge of London in 1915 by Alan Leo and his wife Bessie, along with publications such as *Modern Astrology* magazine, helped create a formal structure for astrological education and practice that bridged traditional methods with contemporary psychological interpretations.

1900s DEVELOPMENT OF MERIDIAN HOUSE SYSTEM

Meridian divides the celestial sphere into 12 equal sectors using the local meridian as the starting point. The houses are created by great circles that pass through the north and south points of the horizon, similar to Regiomontanus, but using the meridian as the primary reference. This system is less commonly used but provides consistent results at all latitudes.

The Encyclopedia of Astrology

1930 PLUTO INCORPORATED INTO ASTROLOGY

Pluto, discovered in 1930, was quickly embraced by astrologers in the 1930s–40s, particularly as its discovery coincided with the rise of psychological astrology and depth psychology.

BLACK MOON LILITH

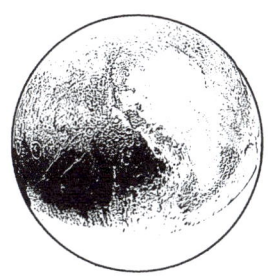

1937 BLACK MOON LILITH INTRODUCED TO ASTROLOGY

Black Moon Lilith is not a physical body but rather a mathematical point (the lunar apogee) that was first introduced into modern astrology by French astrologer Don Neroman in 1937, though it did not gain prominence in astrological practice until the 1970s–80s, alongside the feminist movement.

1960s DEVELOPMENT OF KOCH AND TOPOCENTRIC HOUSE SYSTEMS

Koch

Developed in the 1960s by German astrologer Walter Koch, the Koch house system uses a trisection of the quadrants of the ecliptic. The system calculates houses based on the birth time's relationship to the local space. It divides the quadrants of the sky into three equal portions of diurnal motion. The system works well in middle latitudes but, like Placidus, becomes problematic near the poles.

Topocentric

Topocentric, developed in the mid-20th century by Vendel Polich and Anthony Page, accounts for the observer's exact location on Earth's surface rather

The Encyclopedia of Astrology

than just the center of the Earth. This system attempts to correct the distortions that occur in other house systems at extreme latitudes, making it particularly useful for readings in places like Alaska or southern Argentina. Topocentric closely resembles Placidus but uses a more complex mathematical formula.

1977 CHIRON INCORPORATED INTO ASTROLOGY

The asteroid/comet Chiron was discovered in 1977 and popularized in astrology by American astrologer Zane Stein in the early 1980s.

CHIRON

1986 DEVELOPMENT OF EVOLUTIONARY ASTROLOGY

Evolutionary astrology emerged as a specialized branch of Western astrology, adapting traditional astrological concepts to focus specifically on spiritual development and soul growth, with a particular focus on Pluto's position and the lunar nodes in a birth chart. This approach, developed in the 1970s by American astrologer Jeffrey Wolf Green, views the birth chart as a map of past life experiences and current life purpose. The practice emphasizes understanding karmic patterns and evolutionary intentions, helping individuals identify their soul's trajectory and potential areas for spiritual growth. This modern interpretation gained prominence in the late 20th century, building upon Western astrological foundations while incorporating concepts of karma and reincarnation more commonly associated with Eastern philosophies. The system maintains Western astrology's familiar elements such as houses, aspects, and planetary placements, but reframes them through a lens of spiritual evolution and past-life influence.

The Encyclopedia of Astrology

ASTROLOGY AND SPIRITUAL PRACTICES

Astrology and Spiritual Practices

Astrological theories and planetary correspondences appear in a number of contemporary spiritual traditions that developed alongside and sometimes intertwined with mainstream religions. These alternative practices often preserved older mystical practices and alternative ways of understanding spirituality, including astrological principles. For example, Wicca incorporates planetary forces into ritual timing and spellwork, crystal healers use astrological knowledge for stone selection and gridwork, ceremonial magicians employ the concepts in ritual. Some traditional witchcraft paths work with planetary spirits as well.

The Hermetic arts flourished in ancient Alexandria, where Greek, Egyptian, and Middle Eastern wisdom traditions merged under the patronage of scholar-priests who worked in temple complexes equipped with laboratories and libraries. As these practices spread through the medieval world, they found homes in monasteries and universities where monk-scholars could study both sacred and scientific texts, though much work happened in secret due to religious persecution. Arab scholars preserved and expanded much of this knowledge during the Islamic Golden Age (8th–14th centuries), maintaining sophisticated laboratories and observatories where they integrated astrological timing with alchemical experiments and ritual practices—their texts later fueled a revival of Hermetic studies in medieval Europe, where wealthy patrons often maintained private laboratories for alchemists who combined practical experimentation with ritual magic and astrological timing.

The Encyclopedia of Astrology

ASTROLOGY: ONE OF THREE PRIMARY HERMETIC ARTS

Hermeticism is an ancient spiritual and philosophical tradition based on the core belief that there's a divine connection between the heavens and Earth, expressed in the famous principle "as above, so below," meaning patterns in the cosmos reflect and influence patterns on Earth.

Astrology is one of the three Hermetic arts, alongside alchemy (transforming one type of matter into another) and theurgy (sacred magic), and all three work together to create the foundation for spiritual practice.

Hermetic astrologers carefully select specific hours of the day when certain planets hold the most influence for their ritual work. They create personalized healing approaches by analyzing birth charts to identify areas of challenge, then use corresponding crystals, colors, and elemental forces to bring balance—for instance, someone with challenging Mars aspects might work with iron-rich stones like hematite during Mars hours, or incorporate red crystals and fire elements into their sacred spaces.

Beyond personal practice, these practitioners design talismans and amulets timed to specific planetary alignments, believing these moments infuse physical objects with celestial energy. This understanding of planetary correspondence adds depth to birth chart interpretation—rather than simply noting that Jupiter is in the second house, a hermetic astrologer might recommend working with tin or royal blue elements to strengthen Jupiter's abundance-bringing qualities in material matters.

Some of the modern applications of astrology in hermetic traditions include:

- Ritual timing: Choosing planetary days and hours for specific work.
- Crystal healing: Selecting stones based on planetary rulers.

The Encyclopedia of Astrology

- Herbal medicine: Using plants under their governing planets.
- Color therapy: Applying planetary colors for healing.
- Metalwork: Creating talismans from corresponding metals.
- Meditation: Visualizing planetary colors and energies.
- Spagyric medicine: Creating plant remedies using planetary timing.

Alchemy, the Art of Transforming Matter

Alchemy, alongside astrology and theurgy, is one of the three primary Hermetic arts. The practices of alchemy and astrology were deeply intertwined in ancient traditions, with alchemists believing that celestial bodies governed specific metals, elements on Earth, and that timing the creation of a talisman or a ritual could make it more powerful.

The seven classical planets corresponded to seven primary metals as shown in the chart below. These associations extended beyond physical materials to include colors, herbs, and energy patterns, creating a complex system of correspondences that alchemists used in their transformative work.

Celestial Body	Primary Metal	Color	Properties
Sun (☉)	Gold	Gold, yellow, orange	Representing perfection, vitality, and divine consciousness
Moon (☽)	Silver	Silver, white, pearl	Reflecting intuition, fluidity, and receptivity
Mercury (☿)	Quicksilver	Purple, iridescent, opalescent	Embodying transformation and communication
Venus (♀)	Copper	Green, pink, copper	Channeling love, harmony, and artistic expression
Mars (♂)	Iron	Red, crimson, scarlet	Carrying strength, courage, and dynamic energy
Jupiter (♃)	Tin	Blue, royal purple	Supporting expansion, wisdom, and good fortune
Saturn (♄)	Lead	Black, dark gray, deep brown	Grounding structure, discipline, and endurance

The Encyclopedia of Astrology

The term *Magnum Opus* (Latin for "Great Work") is the more historically accurate name for the alchemical transformation process. Medieval alchemists used this term to describe their ultimate goal of transmutation—both of physical matter and of the soul. The process involves intricate stages of transformation, each marked by distinct color changes and corresponding planetary influences, ultimately leading to the creation of the Philosopher's Stone.

While popularly associated with turning base metals into gold, serious practitioners viewed this process as a metaphor for personal transformation—the true "gold" being spiritual enlightenment and self-mastery. Each stage corresponds to specific psychological and spiritual developments, from the initial breaking down of ego (Nigredo) through various stages of purification and integration, culminating in illumination (Rubedo).

Ancient alchemists were often physicians, philosophers, and astronomers who worked in secret laboratories, documenting their work in cryptic texts filled with symbolic imagery. Today, while few practice physical alchemy, the psychological framework of the Great Work influences depth psychology (particularly Jungian analysis), various spiritual traditions, and some branches of alternative medicine. Modern practitioners might work through these stages through meditation, dreamwork, or ritual rather than with physical substances, viewing the planetary correspondences as guides for inner transformation rather than literal chemical processes.

The planets mark stages in the alchemical "Great Work," and at the same time reflects the soul's journey toward illumination:

1. Saturn (Nigredo): The blackening, decomposition
2. Jupiter (Growth): Expansion and development
3. Moon (Albedo): The whitening, purification
4. Venus (Citrinitas): The yellowing, dawning consciousness
5. Mars (Rubedo): The reddening, full manifestation
6. Mercury: Integration and fluidity
7. Sun: Final illumination and completion

Theurgy, Sacred Magic

Theurgy, divine magic or sacred ritual work, is also one of the three primary Hermetic arts. These disciplines were seen as interconnected paths to understanding divine mysteries, with practitioners often studying all three. The name "theurgy" comes from the Greek words *theos* (god) and *ergon* (work), literally meaning "divine-working" or "the work of the gods."

Theurgy differs from other forms of magic as it specifically focuses on connecting with divine powers for spiritual development rather than practical results. This could include rituals for divine communion, meditation practices, and ceremonies to purify the soul. Even today, these three arts continue to influence various esoteric traditions, though they're often practiced separately rather than as an integrated system.

In ancient and medieval practice, theurgy and astrology worked in close harmony: astrological timing was crucial for theurgic rituals, with practitioners carefully selecting specific planetary hours and alignments for divine invocations. Theurgists viewed the planets not just as celestial bodies, but as divine intermediaries, each associated with specific angels, spirits, or aspects of divine power that could be contacted through ritual. For example, a theurgist might perform a ritual designed to invoke nurturing, feminine divine energy during a Monday (the Moon's day), or during a full moon.

The Encyclopedia of Astrology

During these operations, practitioners would use planetary correspondences—specific incenses, colors, metals, and sacred names associated with each celestial body—to create the proper ritual conditions. This systematic approach to working with divine powers through celestial intermediaries distinguished theurgy from other forms of magical practice, as its goal was spiritual elevation and divine communion rather than practical results.

ASTROLOGICAL TALISMANS

Astrological talismans are physical objects created during precise celestial alignments to capture and store specific planetary energies. Traditional texts like the *Picatrix*, a medieval grimoire of astrological magic, provided detailed instructions for selecting materials, timing, and symbols, for example, a Jupiter talisman might be engraved on tin during a Thursday when Jupiter is well-dignified in the sky, incorporating both the planet's glyph and traditional seals.

Each planet governs different purposes in talisman creation: Venus talismans (made in copper) for love and harmony, Mars (in iron) for protection and courage, Mercury (in silver alloy) for communication and learning, Saturn (in lead) for binding and restriction, the Sun (in gold) for vitality and success, the Moon (in silver) for intuition and dreams, and Jupiter (in tin) for wealth and opportunity. Historical practitioners would calculate election times when the desired planet was at its strongest—often when well-placed by sign and house, free from challenging aspects, and during its assigned planetary hour and day.

The practice continues today, and many modern practitioners have shifted their focus from traditional metals and may incorporate crystals, herbs, or oils ruled by the relevant planet.

Chakras

Chakras are energy centers in the body, originating from ancient Indian spiritual traditions, particularly yoga and Ayurveda. There are seven primary chakras, each corresponding to specific physical, emotional, and spiritual aspects of a person.

These energy centers align along the spine, starting from the base (root chakra) to the crown (crown chakra), and are associated with colors, elements, and vibrations. In astrology, chakras are often linked to planets and zodiac signs, creating a bridge between cosmic and bodily energies.

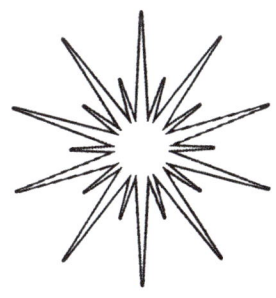

The Root Chakra (Muladhara) is associated with stability and survival and is often linked to Saturn and the earth signs (Taurus, Virgo, Capricorn).

The Sacral Chakra (Swadhisthana) governs creativity and emotions, resonating with Venus or Moon and water signs (Cancer, Scorpio, Pisces).

The Solar Plexus Chakra (Manipura) reflects personal power and confidence, connected to Sun or Mars and fire signs (Aries, Leo, Sagittarius).

The Heart Chakra (Anahata) relates to love and compassion, associated with Venus or the Moon and air signs (Gemini, Libra, Aquarius).

The Throat Chakra (Vishuddha) governs communication and truth, linked to Mercury and air or mutable signs.

The Third Eye Chakra (Ajna) represents intuition and wisdom, resonating with Jupiter or Uranus and water or mutable signs.

The Encyclopedia of Astrology

The Crown Chakra (Sahasrara) symbolizes spiritual connection and enlightenment, associated with Neptune or Pluto and the etheric elements.

Astrologers sometimes use chakra and planetary correspondences in holistic practices to align celestial insights with personal energy work, enhancing self-awareness and balance.

Sacred Plants and Astrology
Sacred plants played a vital role in theurgic rituals, with specific herbs corresponding to each planetary influence: frankincense for the Sun, lavender for Mercury, rose for Venus, and cedar for Jupiter, to name a few.

These plants were used with careful ritual preparation, often harvested during specific planetary hours and prepared with prayers or invocations to maintain their sacred nature.

- Plants should be harvested during their ruling planet's day and hour.
- The phase of the Moon was considered important for harvesting.
- Specific prayers or invocations were used during collection.
- Many plants were dried and used as incense.
- Some were prepared as oils or tinctures.
- Combinations of plants from complementary planets were common.
- Planetary hours and aspects were observed for preparation.

Sacred Plants and Their Celestial Correspondences
Solar Plants

Plants that track the Sun have golden flowers or fruits, or possess warming properties.

The Encyclopedia of Astrology

- Frankincense
- Sunflower
- Marigold
- St. John's wort
- Bay laurel
- Heliotrope
- Cinnamon

Lunar Plants

Qualities: Night-blooming plants, those with white flowers, or plants that respond to lunar cycles.

- Jasmine
- White willow
- Moonflower
- Evening primrose
- White lotus
- Mugwort
- Camphor

Mercury Plants

Qualities: Plants with quick growth patterns or fine, delicate leaves.

- Lavender
- Fennel
- Marjoram
- Parsley
- Dill
- Caraway
- Five-leaf grass

Venus Plants

Qualities: Sweet-smelling flowers, plants used in love magic, or those with soft textures.

The Encyclopedia of Astrology

- Rose
- Vanilla
- Violet
- Vervain
- Yarrow
- Apple blossom
- Damiana

Mars Plants

Qualities: Plants with thorns, sharp tastes, or red coloring.

- Dragon's blood
- Nettle
- Thistle
- Garlic
- Ginger
- Pepper
- Wormwood

Jupiter Plants

Qualities: Large, stately trees or plants associated with abundance and growth.

- Cedar
- Oak
- Sage
- Nutmeg
- Dandelion
- Hyssop
- Maple

Saturn Plants

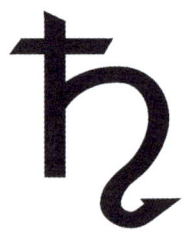

Qualities: Plants with dark colors, slow growth patterns, or binding properties.

- Myrrh
- Cypress
- Comfrey
- Mullein
- Solomon's seal
- Yew
- Black hellebore

The Encyclopedia of Astrology

ASTROLOGY AND NUMEROLOGY

Numerology is the study of the mystical relationship between numbers and events, names, or characteristics—specifically examining how numbers can reveal information about a person's personality, life path, and potentials.

Each number from 1–9, as well as master numbers 11, 22, and 33, carries distinct vibrational properties that can be discovered by analyzing birth dates, names converted to numerical values, and other significant numbers in a person's life. The practice dates back to ancient civilizations including Babylon, Egypt, and Greece, where philosophers like Pythagoras taught that reality itself could be understood through mathematical principles and relationships.

Astrology and numerology share ancient roots as symbolic systems for understanding patterns and cycles in human experience. While astrology focuses on celestial movements and their Earthly correspondences, numerology examines the vibrational qualities of numbers and their influence on character and destiny—both systems often work together, with astrological calculations incorporating significant numbers like 12 zodiac signs or seven classical planets.

The birth date numbers used in numerology can be mapped to corresponding astrological placements, creating a more complete picture of a person's cosmic blueprint.

ASTROLOGY AND SACRED GEOMETRY

Sacred geometry explores the mathematical principles and patterns found in nature, which are considered to reflect divine creation and cosmic order. Examples include shapes like the golden ratio, spirals, and platonic solids. These geometric forms were seen as blueprints of creation, demonstrating how mathematical harmony underlies the physical universe and connects all things.

The Encyclopedia of Astrology

The connection between sacred geometry and astrology emerged in ancient Greece, where Pythagoras and his followers (6th century BCE) saw numbers and geometric forms as the fundamental building blocks of both the cosmos and the physical world. They saw these patterns as key to understanding every aspect of life, including medicine, teaching that health resulted from mathematical harmony within the body, while illness came from discord. The Pythagorean school also applied these principles to psychology and ethics, believing that moral behavior followed the same mathematical order found in the cosmos.

This understanding heavily influenced how ancient astrologers mapped the heavens, with geometric aspects between planets (like the 60-degree sextile, 90-degree square, and 120-degree trine) being considered especially significant because they corresponded to sacred ratios and musical harmonies.

ASTROLOGY AND DIVINATION

The core divination systems that historically intertwined with astrology are geomancy, runes, cartomancy, and the ancient Chinese philosophy and text, the *I Ching*. Each system incorporated astrological timing and symbolism—for example, Viking rune casters considered planetary hours and moon phases for their divinations, while geomancers assigned planetary rulers to their figures and interpreted them partly through astrological associations.

I Ching

The *I Ching*'s connection to astrology centers on lunar timing and cyclical change. Traditional consultations often considered the Moon's phase and position, with readings during the waxing moon focused on growth and expansion while waning moon readings explored release and introspection. The philosophy mentions various celestial phenomena—including heaven, thunder, wind, and water—creating a system that mirrors astrological elements and qualities.

Geomancy

Geomancy, derived from the Greek words meaning "earth divination," developed a sophisticated connection to astrology during the medieval Islamic period. The 16 geomantic figures each have planetary and zodiacal rulers—for example, Via is ruled by the Moon and associated with Cancer, while Fortuna Major is governed by the Sun and linked to Leo. The geomantic houses mirror the 12 astrological houses in meaning and symbolism, allowing practitioners to create detailed readings that blend earthly divination with celestial wisdom.

Runes

The 24 Elder Futhark runes form an ancient alphabet used by Germanic peoples, but they were also deeply connected to celestial timing in divinatory practices. Norse practitioners often consulted these runes during specific moon phases and planetary hours, believing that cosmic influences shaped their meanings. The rune Dagaz, for example, symbolizes dawn and cycles of transformation, reflecting celestial rhythms, while Sowilo represents the Sun's power and vitality. Rune casters also took into account the positions of stars and constellations—such as Polaris—when timing their divinations, particularly during key seasonal transitions aligned with the solar calendar.

The Encyclopedia of Astrology

Cartomancy and Tarot

Cartomancy is the practice of using cards, such as tarot or playing cards, for divination to gain insight into the past, present, or future. In some systems of cartomancy, particularly tarot, astrological correspondences are assigned to the cards, blending the symbolic language of the stars with the archetypes of the cards. For example, the tarot's Major Arcana often align with zodiac signs or planets, such as the Lovers card representing Gemini or the Moon representing Pisces. Similarly, playing cards used in cartomancy can be associated with astrological elements: hearts with water, spades with air, diamonds with fire, and clubs with earth.

The Emperor: Aries
The Hierophant: Taurus
The Lovers: Gemini
The Chariot: Cancer
Strength: Leo
The Hermit: Virgo
Justice: Libra
Death: Scorpio
Temperance: Sagittarius
The Devil: Capricorn
The Star: Aquarius
The Moon: Pisces

Court cards are also often associated with zodiac signs based on their elemental qualities.

Scrying

Scrying is the practice of gazing into a reflective or translucent surface, such as a crystal ball, mirror, or water, to gain spiritual insight, receive intuitive messages, or predict the future. It often involves entering a meditative state to interpret the symbols, visions, or impressions that appear. An astrologer might choose specific times, such as a full moon or a planetary alignment, believed to enhance intuitive abilities, to conduct a scrying session, or use crystals associated with astrological signs or planetary energies, like lapis lazuli for Jupiter's wisdom or moonstone for lunar intuition. Astrological insights can also shape the focus of a scrying session, guiding questions about areas like love during Venus transits or career during Saturn influences.

Commonly used scrying crystals include:

Obsidian: A volcanic glass known for its deep, reflective surface, facilitating profound introspection and unveiling hidden truths. Obsidian is linked to Pluto, representing transformation and the uncovering of hidden aspects.

Clear Quartz: Renowned for amplifying energy and intentions, it promotes clarity and focus during scrying sessions and is often connected to the Sun for clarity and vitality.

Amethyst: Valued for its calming properties, it enhances spiritual awareness and intuition, aiding in connecting with higher realms. Connected to Pisces and the planet Neptune, Amethyst supports alignment with intuition and spiritual awareness.

Black Onyx: Tied to Capricorn and the planet Saturn, symbolizing grounding and protection. Black Onyx provides protection and grounding, creating a secure environment for scrying by shielding against negative energies.

Labradorite: Associated with Leo and the planet Uranus, reflecting transformation and heightened intuition. Known for its transformative qualities, Labradorite stimulates imagination and deepens intuitive insights during scrying practices.

Crystal Work

Crystal work is the practice of using crystals and gemstones for their energetic and metaphysical properties to promote healing, balance, and spiritual growth. In divination rituals, various crystals are employed to enhance intuitive abilities and spiritual insights. Each crystal is believed to resonate with specific planetary energies or astrological signs, amplifying their effectiveness in such practices.

Here are some commonly used crystals in divination and their associated celestial correspondences:

Moonstone: Known for its connection to the divine feminine, moonstone enhances intuition and insight, making it valuable in divination. It is associated with the Moon and the astrological sign Cancer, reflecting its lunar connections.

Lapis Lazuli: This deep blue stone is believed to enhance communication and spiritual insight, making it useful in divination. It is associated with the astrological sign Sagittarius and the planet Jupiter, aligning with wisdom and expansion.

Citrine: Known for its manifestation properties, citrine can be used in divination to attract abundance and clarity. It is associated with the astrological sign Sagittarius and the planet Jupiter, reflecting prosperity and growth.

OTHER SPIRITUAL TRADITIONS
Kabbalah

Kabbalistic astrology interprets an individual's birth chart by analyzing the positions of planets and their corresponding sephirot, or attributes, providing insights into one's spiritual journey, character traits, and potential life challenges. This system emphasizes personal growth and alignment with divine attributes, guiding practitioners toward spiritual fulfillment.

In Kabbalistic tradition, the Tree of Life serves as a profound symbol representing the structure of the universe and the human soul's journey toward divine connection. This intricate diagram comprises ten sephirot (singular: sephirah), each corresponding to specific divine attributes and planetary energies, interconnected by 22 paths that align with the energies of the zodiac signs.

Sephirot and their planetary correspondences:

Keter (Crown): Represents the divine will and pure consciousness; associated with the Primum Mobile or the divine source beyond the planets.

Chokmah (Wisdom): Embodies the initial spark of creation and intuitive insight; linked to the zodiac as a whole, symbolizing the entire celestial sphere.

Binah (Understanding): Signifies structure, form, and discernment; connected to Saturn, representing limitation and discipline.

Chesed (Mercy): Reflects expansive love, compassion, and benevolence; associated with Jupiter, the planet of growth and generosity.

Gevurah (Severity): Denotes strength, judgment, and discipline; aligned with Mars, symbolizing assertiveness and power.

Tiferet (Beauty): Represents harmony, balance, and spiritual beauty; connected to the Sun, the center of vitality and consciousness.

Netzach (Victory): Embodies endurance, ambition, and desire; linked to Venus, representing passion and creativity.

Hod (Glory): Signifies intellect, communication, and reverberation; associated with Mercury, the messenger of the gods.

Yesod (Foundation): Acts as the conduit between the spiritual and physical realms, governing subconscious and emotional energies; connected to the Moon, reflecting intuition and the inner self.

Malkuth (Kingdom): Represents the material world and physical manifestation; associated with Earth, the realm of tangible existence.

The 22 paths connecting the sephirot correspond to the 22 letters of the Hebrew alphabet and align with the 12 zodiac

The Encyclopedia of Astrology

signs and the seven classical planets, plus three elements (air, water, fire). Each path embodies specific spiritual lessons and astrological energies, facilitating the soul's ascent through the Tree of Life.

Rosicrucianism

Rosicrucianism is a spiritual and cultural movement that emerged in early 17th-century Europe, symbolized by the Rose Cross. It combines elements of mysticism, esoteric knowledge, and occultism, drawing from traditions such as Hermeticism, Jewish mysticism, and Christian Gnosticism. The movement was propelled by the publication of three anonymous manifestos between 1614 and 1617, which introduced the allegorical figure Christian Rosenkreuz and outlined the existence of a secret brotherhood dedicated to spiritual transformation and the advancement of knowledge.

Rosicrucian teachings emphasize the pursuit of esoteric wisdom, personal enlightenment, and the harmonious relationship between humanity and the divine. Over time, various organizations have drawn inspiration from Rosicrucian principles, contributing to its enduring influence on Western esoteric thought.

Central to Rosicrucian philosophy is the integration of astrology as a vital component of its esoteric teachings. Astrology is regarded as a divine science within Rosicrucianism, serving as a means to understand cosmic influences on human life and spiritual development. Rosicrucian organizations, such as the Rosicrucian Fellowship, offer structured courses in spiritual astrology, emphasizing its application in personal growth and esoteric studies. Astrology is interwoven with other esoteric disciplines within Rosicrucianism, including alchemy and symbolism, forming a comprehensive framework for spiritual transformation.

Through the study and application of astrology, Rosicrucians seek to align themselves with universal rhythms, facilitating a deeper connection between the microcosm (individual) and the macrocosm (universe). This alignment is believed to aid in the pursuit of spiritual enlightenment and the harmonious integration of the self with the cosmos.

Theosophy

Theosophy, derived from the Greek terms *theos* (god) and *sophia* (wisdom), is a spiritual movement that emerged in the late 19th century, primarily through the efforts of Helena Petrovna Blavatsky. It seeks to explore the divine mysteries of existence and the nature of the universe by synthesizing elements from various religious, philosophical, and scientific traditions, including Gnosticism, Neoplatonism, and Eastern philosophies. Central to Theosophical thought is the belief in an emanationist cosmology, positing that the universe is an outward reflection from the Absolute, and that the material world is illusory, a concept drawn from Asian religions.

Astrology holds a significant place within Theosophical teachings, serving as a tool to understand the cosmic influences on human life and spiritual evolution. Theosophists view astrology as a divine science that reflects the orderly and interconnected nature of the cosmos, aligning with the movement's emphasis on the unity between the macrocosm (universe) and microcosm (individual). Prominent Theosophists, such as Alan Leo, were instrumental in the resurgence of astrology in the West during the early 20th century, integrating Theosophical principles to provide a metaphysical foundation for astrological practices.

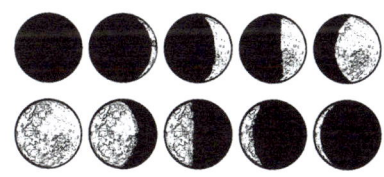

Wicca

Wiccan traditions intricately weave celestial timing and symbolism into their practices, aligning rituals with both solar and lunar cycles to harmonize with natural rhythms. The Wheel of the Year, comprising eight Sabbats, marks the Sun's journey through the seasons, reflecting the solar zodiac's influence. Complementing this, Esbats are rituals traditionally held during the full moon, though some practitioners also observe new moons or other significant lunar phases. These gatherings honor the Moon's cycles and are considered times for personal reflection, spiritual connection, and magical workings.

In Wicca, the Moon is often associated with the goddess, embodying femininity, intuition, and emotional depth. Esbats provide opportunities to commune with the divine feminine, harnessing the heightened spiritual energy believed to be present during these lunar phases. Rituals performed during Esbats may include meditations, invocations, and spellwork, all aimed at aligning practitioners with lunar energies.

Beyond Esbats, Wiccans often consider Moon phases, planetary hours, and zodiacal elements in their ritual work and spellcasting. For instance, specific Moon phases are believed to enhance particular types of magic—such as invoking growth during a waxing moon or banishing during a waning moon. Similarly, planetary hours, each ruled by a different planet, are selected to align with the desired outcome of a spell or ritual, thereby tapping into the associated planetary energies.

By integrating these celestial factors, Wiccans seek to synchronize their spiritual activities with the cosmos, fostering a deeper connection to the natural world and its cycles. This harmonious alignment is central to Wiccan practice, reflecting a profound respect for the interconnectedness of all existence.

ASTROLOGICAL TOOLS AND TECHNIQUES

ALMANAC

The almanac emerged from ancient Babylonian clay tablets that tracked planetary movements and omens. Medieval versions evolved to include weather predictions, astronomical data, and astrological forecasts for farming and daily life. Modern astronomical almanacs provide precise planetary positions and celestial events, while astrological almanacs incorporate interpretations and timing recommendations for magical and spiritual work.

The first almanacs were created by Babylonian scribes around 1800 BCE, who inscribed astronomical events and agricultural timing on clay tablets. By 1200 BCE, systematic records appeared in China during the Shang Dynasty, where oracle bones marked celestial patterns. The Roman *fasti* (calendar books) later evolved into medieval almanacs that guided both farming and church festivals. The English astrologer-physician Nicholas Culpeper published influential almanacs in the 1650s, combining medical and astrological advice, while Benjamin Franklin's *Poor Richard's Almanack* (1732–1758) brought the format to colonial America. Today's astronomical almanacs, like the comprehensive *Astronomical Almanac* published jointly by US and UK naval offices since 1849, provide highly precise data alongside historical tables.

ARMILLARY

Named from the Latin *armilla* meaning bracelet or ring, the armillary sphere was invented in ancient Greece around 250 BCE. This three-dimensional model uses rings to represent celestial circles including the equator, ecliptic, and meridians. The design spread through Islamic Golden Age astronomers to medieval Europe, where ornate versions served as both teaching tools and status symbols for wealthy patrons.

Eratosthenes of Cyrene (276–194 BCE) is credited with inventing the armillary sphere while serving as head librarian at

Alexandria. The device was further refined by Hipparchus (190–120 BCE), who added graduated rings for more precise measurements. During the Tang Dynasty (618–907 CE), the Chinese astronomer Yi Xing created an elaborate water-powered armillary sphere that demonstrated celestial mechanics. The Islamic astronomer Al-Zarqali (1029–1087) made significant improvements to the design in medieval Spain, adding equation mechanisms that showed planetary motions. The Danish astronomer and astrologer Tycho Brahe (1546–1601) used massive armillary spheres for his groundbreaking observations, including a 6-foot model at his Uraniborg observatory.

ASTROLABE

An astrolabe is a medieval astronomical instrument, essentially a handheld model of the known universe. Looking like an intricate brass disc with rotating parts, it helped calculate the positions of the Sun, Moon, planets, and stars at specific times and locations.

The astrolabe emerged in ancient Greece around the 2nd century BCE, with Hipparchus often credited for its invention, though similar instruments may have existed earlier. The device reached its peak sophistication during the Islamic Golden Age (8th–14th centuries CE), when scholars made significant improvements to its design and mathematical foundations. The word "astrolabe" comes from the Greek *astrolabos*, meaning star-taker or star-finder, reflecting its primary use in determining the positions of celestial bodies.

While often attributed to Hipparchus, the astrolabe's development was likely a gradual process involving many

Greek astronomers including Apollonius of Perga (262–190 BCE). The 6th-century philosopher John Philoponus wrote the earliest surviving treatise on astrolabe construction. During the Islamic Golden Age, the Baghdad mathematician Al-Khwarizmi (780–850) wrote extensively on astrolabe use, while the Andalusian craftsman Ibrahim ibn Sa'id al-Sahli created highly precise instruments in Toledo around 1050. Geoffrey Chaucer wrote the first technical manual in English, *A Treatise on the Astrolabe* (1391), for his young son. The instrument remained central to both astronomy and navigation until it was gradually replaced by more specialized tools in the 17th century.

EPHEMERIS

The ephemeris evolved from Babylonian clay tablets listing planetary positions to the sophisticated mathematical tables of the Hellenistic period. Medieval Islamic astronomers further refined these calculations, creating detailed *zij* (astronomical tables). Modern ephemerides provide precise planetary positions for any date, with both book formats and digital versions available.

Ptolemy created the first comprehensive ephemerides in his *Almagest* around 150 CE, building on Babylonian records from the MUL.APIN tablets (*c.* 1000 BCE). The medieval Syrian astronomer Al-Battani (858–929) significantly improved accuracy by correcting Ptolemy's calculations, publishing detailed tables of planetary motions. Johannes Müller von Königsberg (Regiomontanus) published the first printed ephemeris in 1474 in Germany, revolutionizing access to astronomical calculations. The 19th-century French astronomer Jean Meeus developed the mathematical algorithms still used in many modern ephemerides calculations. *Raphael's Ephemeris*, first published in 1819 by Robert Cross Smith, became a standard reference for astrologers, while the comprehensive

American Ephemeris series began publication in 1852.

See example chart on page 43.

FIXED STAR CALCULATOR

Originally developed in ancient Babylon to track significant stars, this tool evolved through Greek and Arabic innovations in spherical astronomy. Medieval astrologers used specialized tables to determine fixed star positions, while modern software can instantly calculate these positions alongside planetary placements. Traditional practitioners still value fixed star calculations for their connection to ancient timing practices.

The Babylonian MUL.APIN tablets (*c.* 1000 BCE) provided the first systematic fixed star calculations. Al-Battani created detailed star catalogs in the 9th century CE, significantly improving measurement accuracy with his innovative trigonometric methods. The 13th-century Persian astronomer Al-Tusi developed mathematical tools for tracking precession's effect on fixed star positions, building on work by Ibn al-Shatir. Tycho Brahe's star catalog (1598) set new standards for precision, while John Flamsteed's *Historia Coelestis Britannica* (1725) established the numbering system still used for many fixed stars. German astronomer Friedrich Wilhelm Bessel's 19th-century stellar position calculations created the foundation for modern fixed star tables.

HOUSE TABLES

House tables originated in Hellenistic Egypt as mathematical tools for dividing the sky into the 12 houses. Islamic astronomers refined these calculations during the medieval period, developing more precise methods. Modern house tables exist primarily in digital form, though some traditional astrologers maintain printed versions for their reliability and tangible connection to historical practice.

Early house division systems appear in Hellenistic texts by

The Encyclopedia of Astrology

Dorotheus of Sidon (1st century CE). The Persian astrologer Abu Ma'shar (787–886) developed sophisticated house calculation methods that spread throughout the Islamic world and medieval Europe. The mathematician Al-Biruni (973–1048) created detailed mathematical tables for house division at different latitudes. Regiomontanus (1436–1476) developed a new house system using great circles, while Placidus de Titis published his influential house system in 1650. Campanus of Novara's 13th-century system used the prime vertical for calculations, while Walter Koch developed his namesake system in 1962.

PLANISPHERE

The planisphere developed from Greek star maps as a two-dimensional representation of the celestial sphere. Medieval Islamic astronomers refined its design, adding rotating components to show the visible sky at

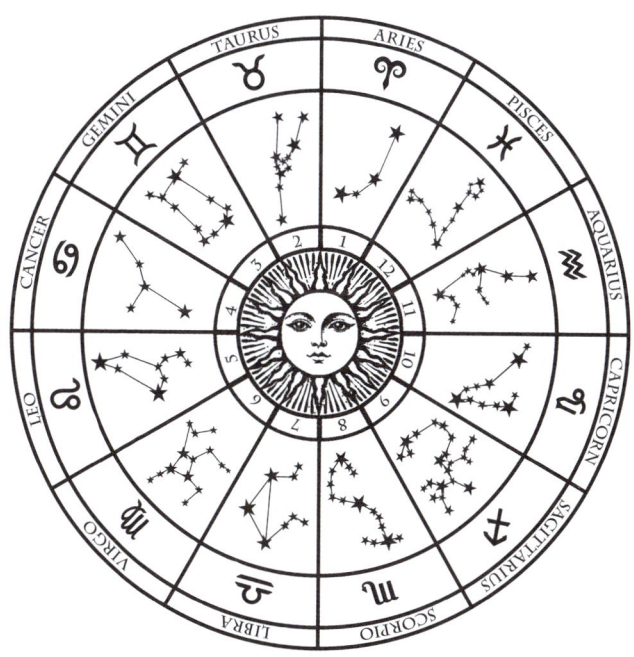

The Encyclopedia of Astrology

any time. Modern planispheres maintain this basic design, serving as educational tools and quick reference guides for celestial positions.

Greek astronomer Hipparchus (190–120 BCE) created early star maps that evolved into the planisphere concept. Al-Biruni (973–1048) developed a sophisticated planisphere design incorporating coordinate calculations for any latitude. In the 13th century, in Austria, Georg Purbach refined projection methods to reduce distortion in European planispheres. The Flemish astronomer Petrus Plancius (1552–1622) created detailed celestial maps incorporating newly discovered southern stars. English instrument maker John Bird (1709–1776) developed brass planispheres noted for their precision, while English Captain George Weymouth patented the modern rotating planisphere design in 1919.

PLANETARY HOUR CALCULATOR

Originating in Hellenistic Egypt, planetary hour calculators divided day and night into 12 temporal hours each ruled by different planets. Islamic astronomers refined these calculations with mathematical tables, while medieval European versions often took the form of specialized sundials. Modern digital versions automate these calculations while maintaining traditional correspondences.

The Egyptian Diagonal Calendar texts (*c.* 2300 BCE) first documented planetary hours. Hellenistic astrologer Vettius Valens (120–175 CE) provided detailed instructions for calculating planetary hours. The Persian astronomer Al-Khwarizmi (780–850) created mathematical tables to determine hours precisely. The Italian Peter of Abano (1257–1316) developed specialized sundials incorporating planetary hours. Johannes Angelus published comprehensive planetary hour tables in his 1494

ASPECT PATTERNS

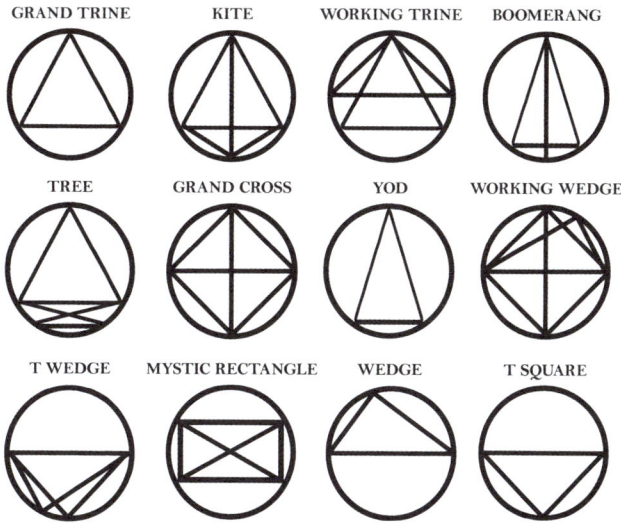

work *Astrolabium planum*, while William Lilly included practical calculation methods in his 1647 *Christian Astrology*.

TABLES OF ASPECTS

Tables of aspects emerged during the Hellenistic period as mathematical tools for determining angular relationships between planets. Islamic astronomers expanded these calculations during the medieval period, creating more detailed reference materials. Modern software has largely replaced manual aspect calculations, though some practitioners maintain traditional tables for their historical value.

Claudius Ptolemy established the first systematic aspect calculations in his *Tetrabiblos* (c. 150 CE). Roman astrologer Firmicus Maternus expanded aspect theory in his *Mathesis* (334–337 CE), adding detailed interpretations. The 9th-century Persian astrologer Masha'allah developed tables showing aspect patterns over time. Arabic astronomer

Al-Qabisi (died 967) created detailed mathematical tables for calculating aspects. Johannes Kepler revolutionized aspect theory with his 1619 work *Harmonices Mundi*, introducing new angular relationships. The 17th-century astrologer William Lilly standardized aspect calculations in his comprehensive tables.

TRANSIT CALCULATOR

Transit calculators evolved from ancient observational records to medieval predictive tables tracking planetary movements. Islamic astronomers developed sophisticated mathematical methods for predicting transits, while European astrologers created specialized tables. Modern transit calculators use computer algorithms to instantly determine planetary positions and aspects across any time period.

Ancient Babylonian priests developed the first transit prediction methods around 700 BCE. The Arab astronomer Ibn al-Shatir (1304–1375) created sophisticated mathematical models for calculating planetary transits. Johannes Regiomontanus published the first printed transit tables in 1474. Johannes Kepler's *Rudolphine Tables* (1627) enabled precise transit predictions. The 19th-century French astronomer Urbain Le Verrier developed mathematical methods still used in modern transit calculations. Heinrich Krüger published specialized astrological transit tables in 1907 that became standard references for early 20th-century astrologers.

MODERN ASTROLOGY: TECHNOLOGY AND NEW ADAPTATIONS

MODERN ASTROLOGY: TECHNOLOGY AND NEW ADAPTATIONS

Modern astrologers have evolved their techniques to meet today's needs by embracing digital platforms that offer instant chart calculations, daily horoscopes, and personalized readings. People have advanced tools at their fingertips and can access the movement of celestial bodies, regardless of their mathematical skills or ability to calculate astronomical events. These technological advances have made astrological wisdom more accessible than ever, allowing people to track planetary transits and connect with astrology communities all over the world.

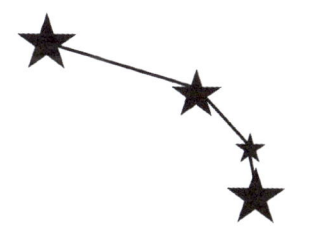

WEBSITES AND MOBILE APPS

Imagine how long the first birth chart took to make. Before it could even be considered, years if not decades of observation and study of the sky had to be recorded in an ephemeris, along with recordings of patterns of planetary and celestial movement over time. Then, a series of complicated mathematical equations tracking where the planets were at the exact moment of birth needed to be performed, followed by another series of calculations measuring the angles and relationships between the planets and celestial bodies. Only once this complex procedure was followed, could astrologers begin to make meaning from the data.

Astrological procedures were so complex and tools such as astrolabes or reference texts including copies of ephemerides so hard to get, that astrology was often reserved for the wealthy or elite. For example, in Aztec culture, astrological and astronomical study was reserved

The Encyclopedia of Astrology

exclusively for nobility and the upper classes. In the 19th and 20th centuries, as scientific innovations demystified the natural world, there was a decline in widespread astrological interest and innovation. The resurgence of interest in the late 20th and 21st centuries can likely be correlated to the increased accessibility of astronomical data becoming digitized and readily available online to all levels of astrologers, from professional and hobbyist.

Today you can get this level of detail from the click of a button. There are scores of websites that offer customized birth charts employing myriad different house systems. There are websites that feature Western birth charts, Chinese Rise and Fall charts, and Mayan day and number sign combinations. While this invites previously unknown levels of self-understanding and growth, there are some things to consider when using online tools to do astrological research.

Considerations

Cost

While some sites are free, others require a single payment for a birth chart or interpretation and some are subscription based. Ensure that you are opting in to only what you choose, and that you are intentional with payment information.

Data Privacy

It's not a safe idea to put your birth date and hometown into every website or app that offers a customized birth chart. Be sure to vet the privacy policies and online reviews of the website before entering your private information.

Features and Level of Detail

While some sites or apps simply give a daily horoscope based on a subscriber's sun sign, others focus on more detailed information about compatibility, celestial events, astrological season, and more. Get aligned with the information that serves you best, and make sure the site or app supports your needs.

House Systems and Cultural Context

Different cultural approaches to astrology and/or different house systems can result in very different birth chart results and interpretations. Make sure the website or app you choose aligns with the house system you'd most like to use. There is no "right" astrological system, so you may want to experiment with several different styles before choosing your favorite.

Online Communities

The rise of social media platforms and online forums has transformed astrology into a truly global conversation. Communities on sites like Reddit, Discord, and Facebook have created spaces where astrology enthusiasts, from curious beginners to seasoned practitioners, can gather to exchange ideas, ask questions, and share insights.

Astrology-focused forums offer real-time discussions, chart interpretations, and specialized study groups that cater to niche interests, such as Hellenistic astrology or synastry. Similarly, Reddit communities like r/astrology host threads for learning, discussing transits, and exploring astrological techniques, all while fostering a sense of connection among members from different cultural backgrounds. This accessibility has fostered a new era of collaboration, where users not only study but also co-create astrology, drawing from the diverse perspectives and experiences of its practitioners worldwide.

Modern technology has also brought creators and consumers together on sites like Etsy and eBay. From replicas of ancient astrology tools to customized gear that reflects someone's sun sign, people can find many ways to explore and celebrate their astrological identities.

The Encyclopedia of Astrology

Education and Learning

The digital era has revolutionized the way astrology is studied, with platforms like YouTube, podcasts, and online courses making astrological education more accessible than ever before. Whether you're a beginner seeking to understand your birth chart or an advanced practitioner exploring esoteric techniques, there's a wealth of resources tailored to every level.

YouTube channels dedicated to astrology provide free, visually engaging content on topics ranging from basic zodiac sign overviews to deep dives into complex aspects and transits. Popular creators often combine expert knowledge with vibrant visuals and relatable anecdotes, making astrology approachable for a wide audience.

Podcasts have also emerged as a popular medium for astrological learning. With episodes covering everything from weekly horoscopes to interviews with renowned astrologers, podcasts allow listeners to integrate astrology into their daily routines. Whether commuting, exercising, or relaxing at home, users can stay informed and inspired by the latest astrological insights.

For those seeking structured learning, online courses offer a more formalized approach. Platforms like Udemy, Teachable, and astrologer-specific websites feature classes on topics such as chart interpretation, predictive astrology, and specialized branches like evolutionary or Hellenistic astrology. These courses often include downloadable materials, interactive exercises, and access to professional astrologers for guidance, making them an invaluable tool for in-depth study.

This accessibility has opened doors for students from all walks of life, allowing them to explore astrology at their own pace and from the comfort of their own homes. As a result, astrology is no longer confined to the pages of books or the lecture halls of exclusive schools—it has truly become a global, inclusive learning experience.

The Encyclopedia of Astrology

Newer Astrological Practices
Esoteric Astrology

Esoteric astrology is a specialized branch of astrology that explores the relationship between celestial patterns and spiritual evolution. Rooted in the teachings of the English astrologer Alice Bailey and Tibetan master Djwhal Khul, this approach emphasizes soul development across multiple lifetimes. Unlike traditional astrology, which focuses on personality traits and life events, esoteric astrology seeks to understand the spiritual purpose and higher consciousness guiding an individual's journey.

Central to esoteric astrology is the concept of the seven cosmic rays, which are fundamental energies believed to shape consciousness, spiritual growth, and universal order. These rays influence planetary rulerships and provide a deeper layer of meaning beyond conventional interpretations. Esoteric astrology assigns planetary rulers to each zodiac sign based on three levels of spiritual development: personality (everyday traits), soul (higher purpose), and monadic (universal essence), offering profound insights into an individual's evolutionary path and their connection to the greater cosmic order.

Key concepts in esoteric astrology:

- Seven cosmic rays: Energies that govern the spiritual framework of the universe and influence personal and collective evolution.
- Soul-centered rulerships: Assigning planetary rulers based on spiritual stages rather than mundane characteristics.
- Three levels of development: Personality (outer self), soul (higher purpose), and monadic (universal consciousness).
- Spiritual purpose: Aligning natal chart interpretations with the individual's greater cosmic mission.

Cultural and philosophical variations in esoteric astrology:

- Western mysticism: Focuses on archetypal energies and connections to spiritual traditions like Theosophy.
- Eastern philosophies: Aligns planetary influences with karmic cycles and reincarnation themes.
- Tibetan wisdom: Incorporates meditative practices and insights from Buddhist teachings.
- Occult traditions: Blends esoteric astrology with practices such as alchemy, numerology, and sacred geometry.

Specific applications in esoteric astrology:

- Soul purpose analysis: Using natal charts to identify spiritual missions and karmic lessons.
- Spiritual evolution: Tracking planetary transits and progressions for insights into growth phases.
- Karmic patterns: Understanding unresolved energies and their influence on current lifetimes.
- Meditative practices: Aligning cosmic energies with meditation, visualization, and ritual work.
- Healing and energy work: Connecting astrological insights with chakra alignment and energy therapies.
- Cosmic alignment: Planning major life events during periods of heightened spiritual energy.
- Group dynamics: Analyzing collective charts to understand shared missions and spiritual synergies.
- Planetary cycles: Interpreting long-term influences like Saturn or Uranus cycles for profound transformation.

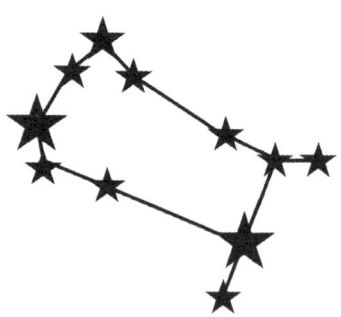

The Encyclopedia of Astrology

Evolutionary Astrology

Evolutionary astrology is a modern branch of astrology that focuses on spiritual development and soul growth, emphasizing the role of karma and reincarnation in shaping individual experiences. Emerging in the late 20th century, this approach builds on Western astrological foundations while integrating concepts from Eastern philosophies, particularly those related to past lives and karmic cycles. Evolutionary astrology interprets celestial patterns through the lens of soul evolution, offering profound insights into an individual's purpose, challenges, and spiritual trajectory.

Central to evolutionary astrology is the idea that the soul evolves through a series of lifetimes, each presenting opportunities to address unresolved karma and develop specific qualities. The natal chart is viewed as a map of the soul's journey, highlighting lessons from the past, current life themes, and potentials for future growth. Key elements include the lunar nodes (representing past-life karma and current life purpose), Pluto (indicating transformation and soul desire), and planetary aspects that reveal patterns of spiritual growth.

Key concepts in evolutionary astrology:

- Reincarnation: The belief in multiple lifetimes, with each life contributing to the soul's evolution.
- Karmic lessons: Challenges and experiences carried over from past lives, reflected in the natal chart.
- Soul purpose: The higher mission or evolutionary intent of the individual, often symbolized by the North Node.
- Transformation: The process of personal and spiritual growth, facilitated by planetary transits and progressions.

Cultural and philosophical variations in evolutionary astrology:

- Western traditions: Focus on psychological growth and the interplay of free will and destiny.
- Eastern influences: Integration of karmic principles from Hinduism and Buddhism.
- Mystical approaches: Incorporation of archetypal symbolism and spiritual practices to deepen understanding.
- Modern psychology: Use of depth psychology and Jungian concepts to explore unconscious drives and growth patterns.

Specific applications in evolutionary astrology:

- Karmic analysis: Identifying past-life influences through the South Node and Pluto placements.
- Life purpose guidance: Interpreting the North Node to uncover the soul's evolutionary goals.
- Relationship dynamics: Exploring karmic ties and growth opportunities in partnerships.
- Crisis and transformation: Using challenging transits (e.g., Pluto or Saturn) as catalysts for profound change.
- Career and creativity: Aligning professional paths with the soul's deeper intentions.
- Healing trauma: Addressing unresolved patterns through insight into past-life experiences.
- Spiritual practices: Incorporating meditation, journaling, and ritual work to align with evolutionary themes.
- Cycles of growth: Analyzing planetary returns (e.g., Saturn return) as key milestones in soul evolution.

APPLICATIONS OF ASTROLOGY

Applications of Astrology

Different cultures around the world use astrology to help make decisions and understand life events. In China, astrologers use the zodiac animals and Five Elements to guide choices about relationships, business timing, and important life changes, while some companies sometimes consider zodiac compatibility when hiring, and many people consult astrologers before choosing dates for weddings or business launches. In India, Vedic astrology remains deeply connected to daily life—practitioners advise on education choices, career moves, and marriage compatibility. Politicians in many countries consult astrologers about campaign timing, while some investors use planetary positions to make financial decisions.

Modern technology has created new ways to practice astrology, with apps and online services blending different traditions. Japanese fortune-telling combines Eastern and Western approaches, while Latin American astrologers often mix Western techniques with local traditions. Some international companies now employ corporate astrologers for business planning, though this practice remains disputed. Medical astrology continues in various forms—from its integration with Chinese traditional medicine to Western practitioners who study planetary positions at the start of illness, though medical professionals consistently advise against using astrology for health decisions. Across cultures, astrologers also offer relationship counseling, career guidance, and help with timing major life decisions.

This encyclopedia covers Western astrology in the most depth and astrological practices from around the world and practices that evolved over time.

Modern astrology encompasses many specialized branches and cultural traditions, each offering unique perspectives and interpretations. From timing-focused practices like electional astrology to specific applications like forensic astrology (the use of astrological techniques to analyze past events, crimes, or missing persons cases), these diverse approaches demonstrate how astrological wisdom has evolved for different cultures over time, and to serve different needs.

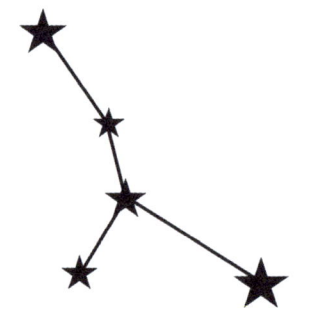

ASTROLOGY AND MENTAL HEALTH

Astrology has increasingly become a tool for introspection and emotional wellness in the modern era, particularly through the rise of psychological astrology. This branch of astrology integrates Jungian psychology with astrological principles to explore the relationship between the cosmos and the human psyche. Psychological astrology focuses less on prediction and more on understanding personality, behavioral patterns, and emotional needs. It offers a framework for self-awareness by interpreting the birth chart as a symbolic map of the unconscious, revealing personal strengths, vulnerabilities, and growth opportunities.

In the context of mental health, astrology can function as a non-clinical complement to traditional therapies. Many find value in using their natal charts to reflect on emotional dynamics or past experiences, uncovering insights that foster self-compassion and clarity. Digital tools and apps have made psychological astrology more accessible than ever, providing resources like journaling prompts, meditative practices tied to moon phases, and tailored insights during challenging planetary transits. While not a replacement for professional mental health care, astrology offers a reflective space where individuals can explore their inner landscapes in a structured yet personal way.

Specific uses of astrology for mental health:
- **Exploration of emotional patterns:** Using moon signs and aspects to understand subconscious drives and emotional responses.
- **Navigating life transitions:** Interpreting planetary transits (e.g., Saturn return) as opportunities for growth and restructuring.
- **Journaling and self-reflection:** Leveraging daily or monthly horoscopes to inspire introspective writing.
- **Building coping strategies:** Identifying challenges in natal charts (e.g., Saturn squares) and aligning them with psychological techniques for resilience.
- **Enhancing self-acceptance**: Understanding inherent personality traits through sun, moon, and rising signs.
- **Guidance for relationships:** Analyzing synastry charts to improve interpersonal understanding and empathy.
- **Connection to collective cycles:** Tuning into the phases of the Moon or retrograde cycles to feel a sense of rhythm and cosmic order.

ARCHETYPAL ASTROLOGY

Archetypal astrology emerged from the work of Swiss-American astrologer Richard Tarnas and Czech-American psychiatrist Stanislav Grof, combining Carl Jung's concept of archetypes with traditional astrological wisdom. This approach views planetary alignments as expressions of universal archetypal principles that manifest in both individual psyches and collective experiences throughout history. Rather than focusing on prediction, archetypal astrology examines how celestial patterns correlate with psychological, cultural, and historical cycles, suggesting that the cosmos reflects deeper patterns of meaning that shape human experience.

The Encyclopedia of Astrology

ASTROMETEOROLOGY

Astrometeorology is a specialized branch of astrology that explores the relationship between celestial phenomena and Earth's atmospheric conditions, providing insights into weather patterns, seasonal changes, and natural events such as storms and droughts. Rooted in ancient traditions and further developed by Islamic and medieval scholars, this practice integrates astrology, astronomy, and early meteorological science. Astrometeorologists analyze planetary alignments, lunar phases, eclipses, and solar cycles to interpret how cosmic rhythms might influence terrestrial weather.

Modern applications of astrometeorology have evolved to integrate traditional techniques with contemporary climate models, although it remains a niche practice. Practitioners often collaborate with historians, agricultural experts, and environmentalists to study historical weather patterns and their possible connections to celestial events. While mainstream meteorologists rely on atmospheric data and technology, some still consider astrometeorology as a supplementary tool for understanding long-term climatic trends.

Cultural variations in astrometeorology include:
- Islamic scholars: Developed advanced tables connecting planetary movements with seasonal forecasts.
- Chinese traditions: Incorporated lunar mansions and Five Elements into agricultural planning.
- European practices: Blended astrological and almanac-based predictions during the Middle Ages.

- Indigenous American cultures: Linked specific star clusters and celestial events with planting and harvesting seasons.

Specific applications in astro-meteorology:
- Agriculture: Predicting rainfall and frost timing to optimize planting and harvesting schedules.
- Disaster preparedness: Anticipating potential droughts, floods, or severe storms based on planetary alignments.
- Historical weather studies: Correlating major climatic events, such as famines or unusually warm winters, with celestial data.
- Seasonal forecasting: Using eclipses and lunar phases to guide long-term climate expectations.
- Marine navigation: Applying astrological insights to predict storm patterns and ocean conditions for sailors.
- Event planning: Choosing dates for outdoor activities or festivals based on weather expectations.

BUSINESS ASTROLOGY

Business astrology guides organizational decision-making through analysis of celestial patterns. The tradition emerged from ancient practices of timing trade routes by the stars and continues today in various forms worldwide. Modern business astrologers often combine traditional timing techniques with contemporary management theory, offering consulting services to corporations and entrepreneurs.

Cultural variations in business astrology include:
- Japanese companies consider zodiac compatibility in team building.

The Encyclopedia of Astrology

- Indian businesses consult Jyotish astrologers for launch timing.
- Chinese corporations align major decisions with lunar new year energies.
- Middle Eastern businesses observe lunar phases for contracts.

Specific applications in business astrology:
- Company incorporation: Selecting auspicious dates for business launches.
- Contract timing: Choosing favorable moments for agreements.
- Hiring decisions: Assessing team compatibility through charts.
- Product launches: Timing releases with beneficial aspects.
- Marketing campaigns: Aligning promotions with planetary energies.
- Expansion planning: Using Jupiter cycles for growth timing.
- Crisis management: Navigating challenging transits.

COURT ASTROLOGY

Court astrology was a prestigious practice where astrologers provided guidance to rulers and nobility on matters of state, personal decisions, and military strategy. Predominantly practiced between the 8th and 17th centuries CE, this tradition combined astronomical observation with predictive techniques to advise on critical issues like marriage alliances, treaty negotiations, and military campaigns. Court astrologers often held official titles such as "Royal Mathematician" or "Imperial Astronomer," emphasizing their influence in both scientific and mystical domains.

As centers of power and culture, royal courts across the world cultivated astrology as a tool for governance. Kings, queens, and emperors consulted astrologers for coronation timing, economic forecasts, and insights into the fates of their realms. The practice waned during the Enlightenment, as scientific paradigms overtook mystical interpretations, but

The Encyclopedia of Astrology

echoes of court astrology persisted in some royal households well into the 18th century.

Cultural variations in court astrology:
- European monarchies: Astrologers such as John Dee and Michel de Nostradamus served as trusted advisors to rulers such as Elizabeth I and Catherine de' Medici.
- Islamic empires: Astrological insights were integrated into statecraft, with scholars developing advanced astronomical tables.
- Chinese imperial courts: Astrologers influenced dynastic decisions through a combination of lunar calendars and celestial interpretations.
- Indian kingdoms: Jyotish astrologers advised maharajas on military campaigns, political alliances, and religious rituals.

Specific applications in court astrology:
- Military strategy: Choosing auspicious dates for battles or defense plans based on planetary alignments.
- Marriage alliances: Evaluating compatibility between royal families to ensure political and astrological harmony.
- Treaty negotiations: Timing agreements during favorable celestial configurations.
- Succession planning: Assessing the astrological charts of heirs to determine suitability for leadership.
- Coronation timing: Selecting propitious moments for ceremonies to align rulers with cosmic forces.
- Economic predictions: Forecasting agricultural yields or trade prospects using planetary cycles.
- Diplomatic decisions: Advising rulers on timing and strategy for negotiations with foreign powers.
- Crisis management: Interpreting eclipses or comets as omens and providing guidance for mitigating perceived threats.

The Encyclopedia of Astrology

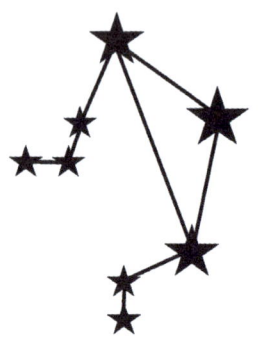

- Jyotish employs muhurta for precise timing of actions.
- Chinese agricultural almanacs track lunar mansions for farming.
- Indigenous American traditions follow corn-planting stars.
- Islamic astrology considers lunar mansion influences for elections.

ELECTIONAL ASTROLOGY

Electional astrology selects optimal moments to initiate activities by analyzing celestial patterns. The practice emerged from ancient agricultural societies tracking stellar and lunar cycles for planting and harvesting, later evolving to encompass all types of endeavors. Contemporary practitioners adapt these traditional timing methods for modern needs while maintaining core principles about planetary dignity and lunar phases.

Different cultural approaches to timing include:
- Hellenistic katarchic astrology emphasizes planetary sect and dignity.

Specific applications in electional astrology:
- Planting and harvesting: Selecting optimal periods based on lunar phases.
- Crop selection: Matching plants to their ruling planets and elements.
- Land assessment: Choosing favorable times for purchasing farmland.
- Irrigation planning: Timing water management with lunar phases.
- Seed saving: Harvesting seeds during beneficial aspects.
- Animal husbandry: Timing breeding and veterinary care.

The Encyclopedia of Astrology

- Business launches: Choosing favorable times for new ventures.
- Wedding timing: Selecting auspicious dates for ceremonies.
- Surgery scheduling: Identifying beneficial periods for procedures.
- Travel planning: Determining optimal departure times.
- Contract signing: Selecting favorable moments for agreements.
- Project initiation: Beginning ventures under supportive aspects.
- Product launches: Timing releases for maximum impact.
- Moving dates: Choosing beneficial times for relocations.

FINANCIAL ASTROLOGY

Financial astrology applies celestial patterns to understand market cycles and economic trends. This practice dates back to Babylonian commodity price tracking and remains influential in modern trading, particularly in Asian markets. Recent technological advances have enabled sophisticated software that combines astrological timing with technical analysis, though traditional interpretation remains important for long-term forecasting.

Different cultural approaches to financial astrology include:

- Western astrology focuses on planetary cycles and market timing.
- Chinese astrology emphasizes zodiac years for business cycles.
- Vedic astrology uses muhurta (electional timing) for transactions.
- Islamic astrology considers lunar phases for financial decisions.

Specific applications in financial astrology:

- Market timing: Identifying potential turning points in financial markets.
- Currency trading: Tracking planetary influences on exchange rates.

- Commodity cycles: Following Venus-Jupiter patterns for price trends.
- Economic forecasting: Using longer planetary cycles to predict economic shifts.
- Investment planning: Aligning portfolios with favorable planetary positions.
- Risk assessment: Analyzing challenging planetary aspects.
- Cryptocurrency timing: Examining Uranus cycles for digital currency trends—Uranus is associated with sudden change, innovation, and technological advancements.

FORENSIC ASTROLOGY

Forensic astrology applies astrological techniques to investigate crimes, locate missing persons, or recover lost objects. Dating back to horary astrology's roots in ancient Mesopotamia, this branch has evolved to incorporate modern investigation methods. Contemporary practitioners often work with historical cold cases or missing persons situations, though they emphasize their work should complement, never replace, traditional investigative methods.

Different cultural approaches to investigative astrology include:
- Western horary astrology focuses on planetary hour charts.
- Jyotish uses prashna (question) charts for location and timing.
- Chinese astrology employs flying star techniques for location.
- Persian astrology uses degree-based interrogation methods.

Specific applications in forensic astrology:
- Missing persons: Analyzing charts to suggest possible locations.
- Cold cases: Examining event charts for new insights.
- Lost objects: Using horary techniques for recovery.
- Timeline analysis: Reconstructing event sequences through planetary positions.
- Location mapping: Applying directional indicators from charts.
- Perpetrator profiling: Identifying possible timing and characteristics.
- Evidence discovery: Suggesting promising search areas.
- Pattern recognition: Linking related events through astrological signatures.

HORARY ASTROLOGY

Horary astrology answers specific questions by analyzing the celestial positions at the moment a question is asked. The word "horary" derives from the Latin *hora* meaning "hour," emphasizing how this ancient practice treats each question as a unique moment in time.

Different cultural approaches to question-based astrology include:
- Persian astrology pioneered complex horary timing methods.
- Jyotish uses prashna (question) charts with nakshatras.
- Chinese astrology employs time-based divination with *I-Ching*.
- Arabic astrology developed specialized rules for planetary dignity in questions.

Specific applications in horary astrology:
- Relationship questions: Understanding undisclosed intentions.
- Career decisions: Evaluating potential opportunities.
- Property matters: Assessing real estate transactions.
- Health concerns: Timing medical consultations.
- Travel plans: Determining favorable journey times.

The Encyclopedia of Astrology

- Legal outcomes: Predicting possible case results.
- Business decisions: Evaluating partnership potential.

MEDICAL ASTROLOGY

Medical astrology, also known as iatromathematics, connects celestial patterns with health and healing practices. This ancient tradition appears in Egyptian medical papyri and Greek physicians' texts, and continues in various forms today. Modern practitioners emphasize preventive health insights while clearly stating that astrological guidance should complement, never replace, professional medical care.

Different cultural approaches to medical astrology include:
- Greek medicine links body systems to planets and signs.
- Chinese medical astrology aligns with Five Elements.
- Jyotish associates body parts with nakshatras.
- Tibetan medicine integrates astronomical timing with pulse diagnosis.

Specific applications in medical astrology:
- Constitutional analysis: Understanding innate health tendencies.
- Timing treatments: Selecting favorable periods for procedures.
- Preventive care: Identifying potential vulnerable periods.
- Dietary guidance: Aligning nutrition with planetary patterns.
- Stress management: Recognizing challenging transit periods.
- Recovery timing: Understanding healing cycles.
- Herb selection: Choosing remedies by planetary rulers.

- Exercise planning: Optimizing physical activity timing.

MUNDANE ASTROLOGY

Mundane astrology interprets celestial patterns to understand collective events and societal trends. The term comes from the Latin *mundus* meaning "world," reflecting its focus on global rather than personal matters. Modern mundane astrologers track long planetary cycles while incorporating rapid changes in technology and society, often using software to analyze multiple chart layers simultaneously.

Different cultural approaches to world astrology include:
- Western mundane astrology focuses on planetary cycles and ingresses.
- Jyotish examines raja yogas for political leadership.
- Chinese astrology uses stem-branch combinations for national forecasting.
- Persian astrology developed specialized techniques for weather and agriculture.

Specific applications in mundane astrology:
- Political transitions: Analyzing leadership changes and elections.
- Economic cycles: Tracking market and financial patterns.
- Social movements: Understanding collective behavior trends.
- Weather patterns: Forecasting climate and natural events.
- Cultural shifts: Identifying emerging social changes.
- Geopolitical relations: Examining international dynamics.
- Technological developments: Tracking innovation cycles.
- Mass psychology: Understanding public mood and reaction.

The Encyclopedia of Astrology

PSYCHOLOGICAL ASTROLOGY

Psychological astrology merges traditional astrological symbolism with modern psychological concepts, particularly Jungian archetypes and depth psychology. This approach emerged in the 20th century through pioneers such as American author Dane Rudhyar and American-British author Liz Greene, transforming astrology from prediction-focused readings to a tool for self-understanding and personal growth. Contemporary practitioners often combine birth chart analysis with counseling techniques and dream work.

Different cultural approaches to psychological understanding through astrology include:
- Western psychological astrology emphasizes Jungian archetypes.
- Jyotish explores karmic patterns and soul development.
- Chinese astrology examines personality through element balance.
- Evolutionary astrology focuses on soul intention and growth patterns.

Specific applications in psychological astrology:
- Personal development: Understanding core personality patterns.
- Shadow work: Exploring unconscious material through chart symbols.
- Family dynamics: Analyzing inherited psychological patterns.
- Life transitions: Navigating major developmental phases.
- Dream analysis: Connecting celestial symbols with dream imagery.
- Trauma processing: Understanding challenging aspects as growth opportunities.
- Relationship patterns: Identifying recurring emotional themes.
- Career guidance: Aligning work with authentic self-expression.
- Inner child work: Exploring early life influences through chart placements.

The Encyclopedia of Astrology

- Crisis intervention: Using transits to understand psychological challenges.

SPORTS ASTROLOGY

Sports astrology analyzes celestial influences on athletic performance and competition outcomes. This specialized field combines traditional timing techniques with modern statistical analysis. While controversial in mainstream sports, it has gained followers among athletes and teams, particularly in Eastern countries where astrological timing is more culturally accepted.

Cultural approaches to sports astrology include:
- Greek Olympic traditions of timing competitions with celestial events.
- Chinese martial arts schools consulting lunar calendars.
- Indian wrestling matches scheduled by Jyotish timing.
- Japanese sumo tournaments aligned with seasonal points.

Specific applications in sports astrology:
- Performance timing: Identifying peak athletic periods.
- Team dynamics: Analyzing player compatibility.
- Competition scheduling: Selecting favorable match times.
- Injury prevention: Noting challenging transit periods.
- Training optimization: Aligning workouts with lunar phases.
- Career planning: Mapping favorable periods for advancement.
- Tournament strategy: Understanding planetary influences on outcomes.

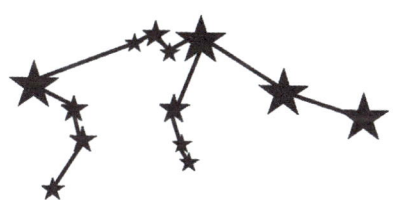

SYNASTRY ASTROLOGY

Synastry astrology examines the interaction between two or more birth charts to understand

The Encyclopedia of Astrology

compatibility in love, friendship, family, and other relationships, along with potential dynamics.

This branch of astrology integrates ancient wisdom about planetary relationships with modern psychological insights to provide guidance about partnerships. It can be used to find and focus on compatible romantic relationships, get marriage advice, or evaluate potential business partnerships.

Different cultures approach relationship astrology through unique frameworks:

- Western astrology focuses on planetary aspects between charts and composite charts.
- Indian Jyotish astrology uses a points-based system called Guna Milan or Koota matching.
- Chinese astrology examines zodiac sign compatibility and element harmony.
- Mayan astrology considers day sign energies and their sacred timing.

Specific applications in synastry:

- Partnership evaluation: Analyzing potential strengths and challenges in romantic relationships.
- Business compatibility: Examining dynamics between business partners or teams.
- Family dynamics: Understanding parent-child relationships and sibling connections.
- Timing relationships: Identifying favorable periods for initiating or developing relationships.
- Conflict resolution: Recognizing sources of tension and paths to harmony.
- Group dynamics: Assessing team compatibility in professional settings.
- Past life connections: Exploring karmic ties and soul contracts (in evolutionary astrology).

The Encyclopedia of Astrology

RESOURCES

Glossary

Almanac—a yearly calendar that tracks astronomical and astrological events, including moon phases, planetary movements, eclipses, and seasonal changes.

Ascendant—the zodiac sign rising on the eastern horizon at the exact time of a person's birth.

Aspect—an aspect in astrology refers to the angular relationship between two planets in a birth chart, which is measured in degrees along the zodiacal circle. These angles are believed to create specific energy patterns that influence how the planets' energies interact and manifest in a person's life.

Astrology—the ancient and contemporary practice of interpreting the movements and positions of celestial bodies to understand and interpret their influence on the daily life of humans.

Astronomical precession—the gradual shift in Earth's rotational axis over an approximately 26,000-year cycle, causing the apparent position of stars and constellations to drift relative to Earth's seasonal markers.

Astronomy—the scientific study of celestial objects, phenomena, and the universe as a whole. It encompasses the observation and analysis of stars, planets, moons, comets, galaxies, and cosmic events like supernovas and black hole mergers.

Axis (plural Axes)—an axis on an astrological birth chart represents a pair of opposite houses or points in the zodiac wheel that work as complementary forces, creating a dynamic polarity in a person's birth chart.

Birth chart—a personalized map of the sky at the exact moment and location of a person's birth. It represents the positions of the planets, Sun, Moon, and other celestial points within the twelve astrological houses, each governing specific areas of life.

Celestial spheres—an ancient cosmological model that envisioned the universe as a

The Encyclopedia of Astrology

series of concentric, transparent spheres centered around a stationary Earth, with each sphere carrying celestial bodies such as the Moon, Sun, planets, and stars.

Chart patterns—occur in birth charts when planets form distinct geometric shapes or configurations that create significant meaning. These patterns tell a story of how planetary energies interact and flow within a person's life, with each shape suggesting different dynamics, some harmonious and some filled with tension.

Constellational zodiac—the constellational zodiac system follows the actual star patterns along the ecliptic. The system reflects what we actually see in the night sky, with planets moving through both the star patterns and the empty space between them. This system includes thirteen constellations of varying sizes rather than twelve equal divisions.

Cusps—people whose birthday falls within one day of the boundary between two adjacent zodiac signs fall on the cusp, or transition, between the two signs and are sometimes said to have traits of both signs.

Cycles—a sequence of events or processes that repeat in a specific order, often returning to the initial state. The zodiac itself is a cycle, and other examples of important and influential cycles in astrology include: lunar phases of the Moon, planetary returns and transits retrograde periods, astrological ages, and more.

Decans—a division of an astrological sign into three equal parts, each spanning 10 degrees of the 30-degree zodiac sign.

Degree—a specific point within the 360-degree zodiac wheel. These degrees help astrologers pinpoint the exact position of planets, stars, and other celestial bodies at any given moment, allowing for more precise astrological interpretations.

Ecliptic—the apparent path that the Sun, Moon, and planets trace across the sky over the course of a year, as viewed from Earth.

The Encyclopedia of Astrology

Elements—the four elements —fire, earth, air, and water— represent fundamental energies that shape the zodiac signs' core qualities and behaviors.

Equinox—an equinox occurs twice a year when the Sun is directly above Earth's equator, resulting in nearly equal day and night lengths worldwide. These events mark the start of spring around March 21 and autumn around September 23 in the northern hemisphere.

Glyphs—a symbolic character or pictograph that represents an element of astrology, such as a planet, zodiac sign, or aspect. These simplified drawings evolved from ancient astronomical notations and sacred symbols, allowing astrologers to efficiently record complex cosmic information.

Houses—there are twelve houses in the zodiac. As Earth rotates, the planets and stars in each house shift. Each house represents a specific area of our lives—a section of the sky as seen from Earth and mapped in a birth chart.

Luminaries—shorthand for the Moon and the Sun, derived from the Latin word *luminare*, meaning "light-giving body." Together, they represent the two most visible and influential celestial bodies in traditional astrology, with the Sun ruling conscious, outer expression and the Moon governing inner emotions and subconscious patterns.

Lunar phases—the changing appearances of the Moon as observed from Earth, resulting from the Moon's orbit around Earth and the varying angles of sunlight illuminating its surface.

Meridian (local meridian or celestial meridian)—the imaginary line that arches across the sky from the northern point of the horizon, traveling directly overhead, and then down to the southern point of the horizon.

Planetary positions—indicate where celestial bodies are located within the zodiac at any given moment, measured in degrees along the 360-degree zodiac wheel.

The Encyclopedia of Astrology

Retrograde (Rx)—retrograde motion occurs when a planet appears to move backward through the zodiac from the perspective of Earth, although it is actually an optical illusion caused by differences in orbital speeds.

Rulership—describes the natural affinity between planets and zodiac signs, where a planet is said to express its energy most purely through its ruled sign. Each planet traditionally rules one or two signs where its influence is strongest and most harmonious.

Sidereal zodiac—primarily used in Jyotish and Vedic astrology, sidereal zodiac bases zodiac sign placements on the actual current positions of the constellations, accounting for the precession of the equinoxes over time.

Solstice—when the Sun reaches its highest point in summer, or lowest point in winter, in relation to the celestial equator, marking the longest and shortest days of the year in each hemisphere.

Tropical zodiac—a zodiac system that defines the twelve signs of the zodiac based on Earth's seasonal cycles and the Sun's apparent movement relative to Earth's equator, rather than the fixed positions of the constellations.

Zodiac—a beltlike section of the sky that follows the annual path of the Sun as it appears from Earth (called the ecliptic). This belt extends about 8 degrees on either side of the ecliptic and is divided into twelve equal 30-degree sections. Each section of the zodiac is named after the major constellation that historically appeared within it.

Zodiac wheel—represents the continuous cycle of the twelve astrological signs as they move through the sky. This circular diagram maps the Sun's apparent path through the constellations over the course of a year, with each sign occupying a 30-degree segment of the 360-degree circle. The wheel begins with Aries at the spring equinox and progresses counterclockwise through the developmental phases of each sign.

The Encyclopedia of Astrology

INDEX

Page references in *italics* indicate images.

Adams, Evangeline 159–60
Age of Aquarius 13, 25, 46
Age of Pisces 13, 26, 26, 46
Ages of Man 21
Al-Andalus (Islamic Spain) 246
al-Biruni, Abu Rayhan 249, 479, 480; *Elements of Astrology* 248
al-Qabisi, Abd al-Aziz 137, 249–50, 440, 482; *Introduction to Astrology* 249
Alcabitius house system 137, 250, 440
alchemy 48, 194, 452, 453–4, 453, 468, 492
Aldebaran 44, 85, 86, 366
Ale's Stones (*Ales Stenar*), Sweden 315–16
Alexandrinus, Paulus: *The Astrological Treatises* 321
Alfheim 313
Alfonsine Tables 22, 436
almanacs 21–2, 42, 79, 124, 164, 166, 222, 264, 475, 502, 506, 518; five-year almanac of upcoming celestial events 381–427
Amaterasu Cave 200
American Federation of Astrologers 156
Andromeda and Perseus, story of 231
animal cycle interpretation 206
animal signs 12 174–9, *175*, 185, 213
Anishinaabe (Ojibwe) Nation 297, 299
Antigonus of Nicaea: *Thesaurus* 435

Antioch Academies (Antioch, Syria) 236
Antiscia 22–3, *23*
Apache 298–9
applications of astrology 495–514
Aquarius: Age of 13, 25, 46; season 120–1, *120*; western zodiac sign 105–7, *105*, *106*
archetypal astrology 501
Aries: constellation *83*; season 111–12, *111*; western zodiac sign *80*, 81–3, *81*
Aristotelian cosmology 32, 232, 233, *234*, 250
armillary sphere *23*, *123*, *126*, *193*, 475–6
around the world, astrology 170–323
ascendant 15, 24, *24*, 27, 57, 64, 66, 122, 124, 127, 129, 138, 139, 154, 155, 232, 233–4, *234*, 256, 319, 320, 328, 332, 336, 339, 342, 345, 348, 352, 355, 358, 361, 364, 436, 437, 518
Ascendant-Descendant (ASC-DESC) Axis 27, *27*
Asgard 312, 313, 314, 315
Asia, cultural variations in 197
aspect 8, 24–5, *24*, 30, 38, 46, 49, 57, 60, 69, 122, 124, 125, 126, 128, 129, *132*, 140, 141–50, 152, 164, 226, 234, 249, 458, 462, 508, 512, 514, 518, 520; applying 153–4; patterns 24, *141*, *481*; separating 155–6; tables 154, 481–2, *481*; theory 164, 291, 481, 482, 520
astrocartography 25
astrolabe 123, 229, 476–7, *476*, 487
astrological ages 25–6, 35, 46, 520
Astrological Association 156, 462

astrological prophecy 168, 323
astrological talismans 456–8
Astrologer's Guide, The (*Anima Astrologiae*) (Lilly/Coley) 158
astrometeorology 502–3
astronomical diaries 291, 293
astronomical precession 13, *14*, 16, 47, 62, *62*, 70, 71, 72, 229, *242*, 251, 518, 522
astronomy 26, 34, 156, 160, 161, 164, 187, 191, 193, 196, 197, 199, 202, 203, 218, 220, 221, 222, 237, 246, 247, 248, 249, 252, 260, 263, 264, 279, 289, 290, 291, 293, 294, 300, 303, 312, 431, 437, 477, 478, 502, 518; and astrology, separation of 442–3
autumnal equinox 26, 518
axis 26–7, 28, *28*, 52, 519

Babylonian zodiac system 290
benefic planets 30, *30*, 384, 519
Berossus 293
Bhavas (Houses) *253*, *253*
Biboonikeonini (Wintermaker) 299
Big Dipper 188, 205, 299, 300, 311, *312*
Bimaristans (Islamic hospitals) 244
birth chart 4, 5, 6, 24, 25, 26–8, 30–1, 33, 34, 36, 38, 40, 42, 45, 46, 47–8, 49, 54, 57, 60, 63, 64, 65, 66, 67, 79, 80, 109, 121–33, *123*, 135, 136, 141, 143, 148, 154, 162, 167, 174, 203, 218, 225, 232, 234, 235, 236, 242, 247, 261, 282, 290, 446, 452, 466, 487, 488, 489, 490, 500, 512, 513–14, 518, 519, 521; celestial bodies and 327, 328, *328*, 329, 332, 335–6, 338–9, 342, 345, 348, 351–2, 355, 358; creating 122–6, *124*, *125*; reading 126–9, *127*
birth totems 304–8

The Encyclopedia of Astrology

522

Black Moon Lilith *131*, 360–3, *360*; introduced to astrology 445, *445*
Blackfoot or Siksika nation 299–300
blue moons 371, *371*, 385, 396, 409, 416
Bonatti, Guido 160, 438
Book of Nut, The 220, 221
Borsippa, Temple Observatory at 292
Börte Chino, the Blue Wolf 208
business astrology 503–4

Cairo Calendar (Ramesseum Papyrus IV), The 221–2
Callisto and the Bear constellations 230–1
Calmecac (Priestly Schools) 276–7
Campanus house system 137, 441–2, 479
Campion, Nicholas: *The Dawn of Astrology* 157–8
Cancer: season 114–15, *114*; western zodiac sign 88–90, *88*
Capricorn: season 119–20, *119*; western zodiac sign 102–4, *102*
cartomancy 462, 464
Castor 367
Cat 214, *214*
celestial equator 26, 31, *31*, 36, 57, 63, 65, 70, 138, 139, 373, 375, 442, 518, 522
celestial events 368–427; five-year almanac of upcoming 381–427
celestial spheres 31–2, *32*, 44, 49, 79, 80, 137, 138, 161, 203, 233, 244, 320, 441, 444, 467, 479, 519
celestial tablets, creation of 295–6
centers of learning in Western astrology 156–7

Centre for Psychological Astrology 156
Ceres 95, 366, 367
Chaldean order 32, 33, *33*, 227, 433
Chang'e 194–5, 348
chart patterns 33, 65, 66, 146, *147*, 519
Cheonmun Ryucho 203
Cheonsang Yeolcha Bunyajido 203
Cherokee astrology 297–8, 308–11
Chinese astrology 44, 173–97, *173*, *175*, *180*, *181*, *182*, *183*, *184*, *185*, *188*, *189*, *190*, *194*, 201, 507, 508, 509, 511, 512, 514; centers of learning 191; festivals that celebrate the zodiac 189–90; key texts 192–7
Chiron 33–4, 68, *131*, 363–6, *363*; incorporated into astrology 446, *446*
Christian theology, integration of astrology with 438–9
classical astrology, age of 433–4
Codex Borbonicus 275, 278
Codex Borgia 278
Codex Fejérváry-Mayer 278
Codex Mendoza 278
codices 268, 275, 277
combustion 34, 38
conjunctions 13, 25, 35, 38, 67, 124, 129, *132*, 140, *140*, 145, 146, 153, 154, 155, 210, 226, 234, 269, 290, 291, 371, *371*
constellational zodiac 71, 72, *441*, 519
contra-antiscia 22–3, *23*
Copan (Honduras) 283–4, 285
Copernican Revolution 436
Copernicus, Nicolaus 160–1, 436, 443
Cornelius, Geoffrey: *The Moment of Astrology* 158

Corona Borealis 300, *300*
cosmic determinism 232, 235
cosmology 34
court astrologers 79, 160, 161, 162, 168, 191, 200, 202, 291, 437, 439–40, 443, 504
court astrology 161, 168, 204, 504–5
Coyote 303
creation of the world 287
Cree Nation 297, 300
crystal work 452–3, 465–6
cusps 34, *35*, 50, 51, 57, 64, 67, 124, 136, 137, 138, 440, 519
cycles 35, *35*, 520

Đắc Bằng, Lương 215
dashas 252, 253–4, 261
daykeeper 309
day signs 20 268, 269–72, *270*, 273, 274, 276, 278, 283, 308
decans 36, *36*, 217, 218–20, *218*, 221, 222, 224, 435, 520
declination 36
Dee, John 161–2, 440, 505
degree 36, 520
Delphi 227
Dendera zodiac 217–18, *218*, 221, 222
developmental phases 21, 36–7, 70, 73, 512, 522
Dhanu (Sagittarius) 259, *259*
dignity 37–9, 236, 250, 254, 506, 509
direct motion 39, 331, 361, 410
Directorate of Astronomy, The (Qintian Jian) 191
dispositor 39–40
diurnal arc 40
divination systems 192, 462–3
Đoàn, Trần 215
Dorotheus of Sidon 237–8, 232, 237–8, 479; *Carmen Astrologicum* 228–9, 232, 238, 434

The Encyclopedia of Astrology

Dresden Codex 284–5
Dunhuang Manuscripts 192

Eanna Temple, Uruk 291
earthly branches 174, 184–6
eclipse 6, 21, 22, 35, 111, 212, 213, 218, 264, 266, 268, 285, 288, 292, 318, *371*, 398, 414–15, 502, 503, 505, 518; lunar 218, 372, *372*, 383–4, 388, 394, 398, 400, 405, 409, 415, 419, 423, 426; solar 200, 290, 371–2, *372*, 382, 388, 393, 397, 401, 405, 410, 419, 422, 426; tracking 290
ecliptic 23, 28, 29, 31, 40, 44, 51, 69, 70, 71, 73, 80, 138, 139, 218, 252, 260, 288, 290, 437, 442, 445, 475, 519, 520, 522
Egyptian astrology 216–24, *216, 218, 219*, 225, 228, 231, 232, 233, 238, 239, 240, 480
Ekur, Temple of, Nippur 291
El Caracol, Chichen Itza (Mexico) 284
electional astrology 160, 232, 237, 434, 506–7
elements 40–1, *40, 41*
Enheduanna 293–4
Enlightenment 440, 441, 442, 454, 458, 468, 469, 504
ephemerides 42, 129, 243, 477, 487
ephemeris 22, 42, *43*, 123, 124, 125, 477–8, 487
Equal House 15, 138, 436–7
equinoxes 13, 26, 31, 42–4, *42*, 49, 64, *65*, 260, 268, 277, 279, 281, 284, 312, 373, *373*, 520, 522; autumnal 26, 117, 389, 398, 417, 424–5, 518; precession of the 62, *62*, 72, 229, 261, 522; spring 49, 62, 70, 71, 73, 111, 112, 251, 375, 384, 389, 395, 398, 403, 407, 412, 417, 421–2, 424–5, *522*; vernal 64, 69–70, 73, 112, 122, 251, 373, 395, 403, 407, 412, 421–2, 522

Eratosthenes of Cyrene 475–6
Eris 366, 367
Erkhii Mergen and the Seven Suns 207–8
Esagila, Temple of, Babylon 291–2
esoteric astrology 165, 491–2
ethnoastrology 44, 296
Eudoxus of Knidos 229
evolutionary astrology 162–3, 366, 446, 493–4, 512, 514

Faculty of Astrological Studies 156, 169
Feather Woman 299–300
Fifth Sun, creation of 280
Figulus, Nigidius 318, 321
financial astrology 507–8
Five Elements 44, 174, *175*, 179–81, *180, 181*, 182, 183, 185, 197, 199, 203, 499, 502, 510
Five Suns 275–6
five-year almanac of upcoming celestial events 381–427
fixed star calculator 478
fixed stars 17, 44, 183, 252, 260, 366, 478
Flint Boys 302
forecasting 45, 49, 187, 226, 290
forensic astrology 500, 508–9
Four Humors 427
Four Pillars of Destiny (*Saju Palja*) 183, 201, 202
Four Pillars System (*Ba Zi*) 185–7, *185*
Fourth World 303
Frawley, John: *The Real Astrology* 158
free will versus determinism 5, 13–14
full moon 53, 112, 113, 114, 115, 116, 117, 118, 119, 120, 121, *133*, 302, 371, 372, 373, 377, 385, 396, 402, 403, 409, 413, 416, 423, 455, 464, 470

Galdrabók 316
Gemini: season 113–14, *113*; western zodiac sign 86–8, *86*
geocentric model of the universe 32, *43*, 45, 48, 161, 233, 239, 435
geomancy 192, 198, 203, 462, 463
gibbous moon 45–6, *46*, 52, *52, 53, 133*, 376, 377, *377*
glossary 518–22
glyphs 46, 129, 520
Gondishapur, Academy of 246
Gonggong 367
Goseck Circle, Germany 315
grahas (planets) 254, 260
great ages. *See astrological ages*
Great Bear 230, 300
great turning 25, 46–7
Greek astrology 225–31, *225, 230*, 318; astrological texts 156, 434–5
Green, Jeffrey Wolf 162–3, 446
gunghap 202
Guo Pu 192–3
Gyatso, Desi Sangye 210–11
Gyatso, Phugpa Lhundrub 211

Haab calendar 267, 269, 274, 282, 284, 285
Harran University 246
Harut and Marut 251
Hati 312, 317
Haumea 367
Hearthstones, the Three 287
heavenly stems 174, 184–5
Helgason, Oddi 316
Helheim 312, 314
helical rising 47
heliocentric model 32, 45, 47–8, 161, 239, 443

Hellenistic astrology 21, 67, 74, 140, 157, 173, 216, 217, 220, 222, 223, 225, 228, 229, 231–41, *234*, *235*, *239*, *241*, 248, 250–1, 256, 289, 293, 294–5, 311, 319, 432, 433, 434, 435, 436, 477, 478–9, 480, 481, 489, 490, 506

hemispheric differences 14–15

Hephaistio of Thebes 237, 238; *On Inceptions* 237

Heracles and the zodiac, myth of 240, *240*

Hermeticism 48, *48*, 161, 166, 441, 451, 452–3, 455, 468

Hero Twins 286–7

High Priests of Heliopolis 223

Hikoboshi 200–1

Hipparchus 229, 476, 480

historical accuracy 15, 140, 436

horary astrology 139, 160, 166, 238, 442, 508–10

horoscope 5, 12, 16, 48–9, 66, 79, 159, 162, 164, 165, 168, 169, 201, 225, 226, 234, 235, 236, 264, 265, 288, 317, 432, 434, 443, 487, 488, 490, 501, 520; horoscopic astrology 173, 290, 294, 433

House of Wisdom, Baghdad 156, 241–2, 247, 432, 436

house systems 49, 51, 124, 125, 136, 137, 138, 139, 154–5, 233, 250, 253, 322, 329, 332, 336, 339, 342, 345, 348, 352, 355, 358, 361, 364, 436–7, 440–42, 444–6, 479, 488, 489; validity 15. *See also individual house system name*

house tables 478–9

Hwang, Yi 204

I Ching 192, 462–3, 509

Imhotep 222

Imperial Observatory, The (Guanxiang Tai) 191

Imum Coeli 27, 28, 139, 437

Inanna 288, 289, 295

ingress 49–50

intercepted signs 50

International Academy of Astrology 156–7

Iroquois 301

Ishbaljir 207

Isis and Osiris, love of 223–4

Islamic astrology 233, 241–52, *242*, *245*, 506, 507

Islamic Golden Age (8th–14th centuries CE) 241, 243, 245, 247, 432, 451, 475, 476, 477

Jade Emperor 175, 195–6

Jamshid, King 251–2

Japanese astrology 197–201, *198*, *200*, *201*

Jotunheim 313

Jumong, Prince 204

Jung Tsi 208–9

Jung, Carl Gustav 6, 163–4

Jupiter 13, 21, 30, 33, 35, 36, *39*, 46, 50, 59, *60*, 61, 63, 68, 100, 101, 102, 107, 109, 125, *131*, *136*, 142, 146, 218, 225, 227, 241, 254, 259, 260, 319, 320, 323, 452, *453*, 455, 456, 457, 458, 460, 464, 466, 467, 504, 508; celestial events 371, 381, 384, 391, 394, 395, 401, 403, 404, 411, 412, 414, 422–4; planets and celestial bodies 328, 331–4, *331*, 354, 357, 367; return 50, *50*

Jyotish astrology 71, 252–66, *253*, *265*, *266*, 504, 505, 506, 508, 509, 510, 511, 512, 513, 514, 522

Kabbalah 466–8

Kalachakra (Wheel of Time) 211–12

Kanya (Virgo) 258, *258*

Karka (Cancer) 257, *257*

karma and karmic patterns 67, 254–5, *255*, 262, 266, 446, 493

Karnak, Temple of 220–1

Kashi (Varanasi) 263

Kepler, Johannes 22, 164, 436, 440, 443, 482

Kepler College 157

Kerala 263

Ketu 212, *213*, 254, *255*, 258, 260, 263, 265–6

Kidinnu 294

Kin'ugyokuto-shū 199

Kituwah Mound 309

Koch, Walter 164–5, 479

Koch house system 15, 126, 138, 164–5, 445, 479

Koch tables 51

Korean astrology 201–5, *201*, *204*

Kumbha (Aquarius) 259, *259*

Lạc Long Quàn 215–16

Lady Six Sky 286

Lakota 301–2

Lantern Festival (15th Day of First Lunar Month) 190

Leo, Alan 165, 444, 469

Leo: season 115–16, *115*; western zodiac sign 90–2, *90*

Li Chunfeng 193

Libra: season 117, *117*; western zodiac sign 94–7, *95*

Library of Alexandria 157, 216, 220, 228

Library of Pergamon 236–7

Life-Force Calculations (Srog) 209–10

Life's Rise and Fall Chart (Ming Gong) 187

Lilly, William 158, 166, 441, 481, 482

Liu Xin 193

Long Count Calendar 282, 287

Long Man 311

Lord of the Dance 310–11

lot astrology 319–20
luminaries 51, 521
lunisolar calendar 53–4, 207, 211, 223

Ma Danyang 194
Ma'shar, Abu 247, 248, 250–1, 479; *The Book of Thousands* 248
Madrid Codex, The 285
Makara (Capricorn) 259, *259*
Makemake 367
malefic planets 38, 54, 521
Manilius, Marcus: *De Astronomica* 158, 321–2, 434–5
Mantreswara: *Phaladeepika* 264, 265
Maragheh Observatory 243, 247
Mars 21, *33*, 38, *39*, 46, 54, 58, *60*, 61, 63, 64, 68, 81, 83, 97, 99, 125, *131*, 136, 142, 143, 144, 146, 218, 225, 227, 254, 257, 258, 260, 323, 452, *453*, 455, 456, 457, 460, 467; celestial events 374, 392–4, 395, 411–13; planets & celestial bodies 334–7, *334*, *335*, 351, 367
Masha'allah 250, 481
Maternus, Julius Firmicus: *Matheseos Libri VIII* 158, 237–9, 435, 481
mathematical astronomy 247, 290, 291, 293, 294
Mayan astrology 281–7, *282*, *285*, *286*, 514
medical astrology 54, 168, 195, 210, 243–4, 437, 499, 510–11
medicine wheel 303–8
medieval European astrology 248, 250, 437–8
Meena (Pisces) 256, 259, *259*
melothesia 54–5, 227
mental health 500–1

Mercury 6, 21, *33*, *39*, 58–9, *60*, 63, 68, 86, 87, 93, 94, 125, *131*, 136, 218, 225, 254, 257, 258, 260, *453*, 455, 456, 457, 458, 459, 467; celestial events 374, 383, 386, 394, 396, 399, 401, 404, 407, 410, 413, 417, 420; opposition 145–6; planets & celestial bodies 327, 344–7, *344*, *345*; retrograde 55
meridian 23, 28, 55, 63–4, 138, 475, 521
meridian house system 444
Mesha (Aries) 256, 257, *257*
Mesoamerican astrology 267–80, *268*, *270*, *272*, *276*, *280*, 281, 298, 308
Mesopotamian astrology 5, 58, 173, 217, 225, 226, 231, 232, 239, 240, 287–96, *290*, 361, 431, 433, 508
meteor showers 374
Mid-autumn Festival (15th Day of 8th Lunar Month) 190, 195
Midgard 312, 313, 315
midheaven 27, 28, 63, 122, 124, 139, 154, 233, 235–6, *235*, 437, 442
Midheaven-Imum Coeli (MC–IC) Axis 27, 28
Milky Way 101, 196, 201, 298, *298*, 311
Mirandola, Pico della 166–7, 441
Mithuna (Gemini) 257, *257*
Moctezuma II 279
modalities 56
modern astrology 54, 138, 159, 165, 168, 169, 289, 312, 351, 444, 445, 483–94, 499
monastic preservation of astrological knowledge 438
Mongolian astrology 205–8, *208*

Moon: Black Moon Lilith *131*, 360–3, *360*, 445, *445*; blue 371, *371*, 385, 396, 409, 416; eclipse 218, 372, *372*, 383–4, 388, 394, 398, 400, 405, 409, 415, 419, 423, 426; full 53, 112, 113, 114, 115, 116, 117, 118, 119, 120, 121, 133, *133*, 302, 371, 372, 373, 377, 385, 396, 402, 403, 409, 413, 416, 423, 455, 464, 470; gibbous 45–6, *46*, 52, *52*, 53, *133*, 376, 377, *377*; lunisolar calendar 53–4, 207, 211, 223; mansions 183–4, *184*, 195, 252, 255, 261, 502, 506; new 52, *52*, 53, *53*, 66, 67, 112–20, 133, *133*, 175, 302, 372–5, 470; nodes 29, 51–2, *51*, 255, 260, 266, 446, 493; phases 35, 52–3, *52*, *53*, 57–8, *58*, *60*, *133*, 210, 243, 244, 302, 309, 316, 431, *431*, 433, 470, 502, 503, 504, 506, 507, 513, 520, 521; sign 55–6, 66; supermoons 375–6, 392, 393, 402, 403, 412, 413, 422, 423; waning phase 44, 45, 46, 53, *53*, *133*, 376, *376*, 463, 470; waxing phase 44, 45, 46, 52, *52*, *133*, 377, *377*, 463, 470
Mooney, James: *Myths of the Cherokee* 309–10; *The Sacred Formulas of the Cherokees* 310
Morin de Villefranche, Jean–Baptiste 167
Morning Star 280–1, 287, 295, 299–300
Mouseion 220
MUL.APIN 292–3, 477, 478
mundane astrology 229, 238, 291, 511
Muspelheim 314

Nabta Playa, Egypt 431
Nabu-rimanni 294
nakshatras, or lunar mansions 252, 255–6, *256*, 261, 509, 510

Nalanda University 263

natal astrology 15, 16, 29, 30, 44, 56–7, 68, 69, 141, 144, 147, 150, 154, 155, 158, 167, 189, 228, 229, 232, 237, 238, 249, 253, 254, 255, 261, 319, 321, 435, 441, 491, 492, 493, 500, 501

Navajo 302, *302*

Nechepso 239

Neptune 15, 50, 54, 63, 68, 107, 109, 125, *131*, 146, 444, 458, 465; celestial events 386, 389, 391, 396–400, 408–9, 415, 425; incorporated into astrology 444; planets & celestial bodies 354–7, *354*, *355*, *358*

new moon 52, *52*, 53, *53*, 66, 67, 112–20, 133, *133*, 175, 302, 372–5, 470

newborns, assignment of day and number signs to 309

newspaper/app horoscopes 16

Nezahualcóyotl 279

Nicholas, Chani: *You Were Born for This: Astrology for Radical Self-Acceptance and Living Your Purpose* 159

Nidavellir 313

Niflheim 314

Nine Star Ki 187–8, *188*

Nine Worlds System 313

Ninth Sphere 244

nodal axis 28, *29*, 52, 163

nodal return 29–30

Norse astrology 311–17, *312*, *314*, 335, 341, 344, 463

North American Indigenous astrology 296–308, *297*, *298*, *299*, *300*, *302*

North Node 28–9, 52, 134, 254, 259, 493, 494

Nostradamus, Michel de 168, 440, 505

notable figures: around the world 192–3, 199–200, 203–4, 207, 211, 215, 222–3, 229, 237–8, 249–51, 264–5, 279, 285–6, 293–4, 316, 321–2; of western astrology 159–69

numerology 187–8, 215, 461, 492

oblique ascension 57

Obstacle Year Calculations (Keg-Tsi) 210

Ojiig Anang (Fisher Star) 299

omen readings 276

Onmyōdō 198–200

Ophiuchus 16

Orcus 367

Orihime 200–1

Orion 216, 224, 230, 287, 299, 396

Pakal, K'inich Janaab 285–6

Palenque, Temple of the Sun at (Mexico) 284, 285

Pan Gu 196–7

Parashara, Sage: *Brihat Parashara Hora Shastra* 264–5

Part of Fortune 57, *134*

Petosiris 239

phases of the moon. *See lunar phases*

Pisces: Age of 13, 25, 26, *26*, 46; season 121, *121*; western zodiac sign 107–11, *107*, *108*

Placidus house system 15, 126, 137–40, 165, 440, 442, 445, 446, 479

planetary days 33, 57–9, *58*, 452

planetary dignity 232, 236, 250, 506, 509

planetary hours 33, 59–60, *60*, 244, 445, 458, 462, 463, 470; calculation 16, 480–1

planetary periods 252–4, 261, 264, 290

planetary positions 60

planetary rulership 15, 21, 33, 39, 54, 64, 67, 154, 236, 321, 351, 354, 357, 491, 521; integration of 226–7

planetary sect 61, 506

planets and celestial bodies 324–67

planisphere 479–80, *479*

Platonic Academy, Athens 228

Pleiades 86, 206, 302, *302*, 367

Pluto 6, 15, 50, 54, 63, 68, 97, 99, 125, *131*, 146, 162, 163, 458, 465, 493, 494; celestial events 384–5, 387, 390, 395, 397, 399, 403, 404, 406, 407, 413–14, 416, 418, 422, 424, 425; incorporated into astrology 445; planets and celestial bodies 354, 357–60, *357*, *358*

Poetic Edda 316

polarities 61, *61*

Pollux 367

Popol Vuh 285, 286

Porphyry house system 139, 437

Porphyry of Tyre 322

prehistoric observations 433

professional standards 16

psychological astrology 156, 163, 168, 445, 450, 512–13

Ptolemy, Claudius 32, 157, 220, 223, 225, 238, 432, 477; *Almagest* 435, 477; *Tetrabiblos* 140, 158, 223, 225, 229, 232, 237, 239, 245, 317–18, 433, 434, 438, 481

Pueblo 303

Purple Mountain Observatory (*Zijin Shan*) 191

Purple Star Astrology (*Zi Wei Dou Shu*) 188–9, 194, 213, 214

The Encyclopedia of Astrology

527

Quaoar 367

Ra 216, 222, 224, 338
Rahu 212, *212*, 254, 255, 259, 260, 265–6
Rao, K.N. 265
Rashi chart 252, 256, 257, *257*, 262
Ray Observatory 247–8
Regiomontanus house system 138, 139, 442, 444, 477, 479, 482
Regulus 44, 367
religious opposition 16
Renaissance 139, 160, 162, 166, 167, 209, 239, 243, 294, 440–1, 442
retrograde (Rx) 6, 35, 39, 55, 62–3, 128, *134*, 326, 331, 335, 341, 345, 351, 354, 357, 361, 364, 366, 374, *374*, 375, 382–425, 501, 520, 521
revival of astrology, 19th and early 20th centuries 444
Rhodes, Astronomical Center of 228, *229*
Right Ascension of Midheaven (RAMC) 63–4
rising sign. *See* ascendant
ritual calendar, 260-Day 267, 268–9, 275, 276
Roman astrology 79, 158, 217, 223, 237, 238, 239, 240, 294, 317–23, *323*
Rome, founding of 322–3
Romulus 322–3
Rosicrucianism 468–9
Rudhyar, Dane 168–9, 512
rulership 15, 21, 33, 39, 54, 64, 67, 154, 236, 321, 351, 354, 357, 491, 521; integration of 226–7; modern versus traditional 15
runes 314–15, 462, 463

sacred days, birth of 224
sacred geometry 320, 461–2

sacred plants 458–61
Sagittarius: season 118–19, *118*; western zodiac sign 100–2, *100*, *101*
Sago, Nam: *Prophecies* 203
Saju Gilui 203
Sasportas, Howard: *The Twelve Houses* 158
Saturn 11, 13, 21, 33, 34, 35, 38, 39, 50, 54, 59, 60, 61, 63, 64, 68, 102, 104, 125, *131*, *136*, 143, 144, 146, 218, 225, 227, 241, 254, 255, 259, 260, 266, 290, 320, 371, 375, 387, 453, 455, 456, 457, 460, 465, 467, 492, 494, 501; celestial events 397, 399, 400, 406, 408, 410, 416, 418, 420, 426; planets and celestial bodies 327–31, *327*, 332, 351, 363, 364; return 64, *64*
scientific falsifiability 17
Scientific Revolution 32, 441, 442, 443
Scorpio: season 117–18, *117*; western zodiac sign 97–9, *97*
scrying 464–5
seasonal divination (Улирлын зурхай) 206
Sedna 366, 367
Seimei, Abe no 199–200; *Senji Ryakketsu* 199
Senenmut 221, 223; astronomical ceiling of Senenmut's tomb 221
Seven Birds 300, *300*
Seven Star Spirit (Chilseong) 204–5
Shani, myth of 266
Sibylline Books 323
sidereal 62, 71–2, 252, 260–1, *260*, 522; versus tropical zodiac 17
Simha (Leo) 258, *258*
Sirius, the Dog Star 47, 217, 219, *219*

Sköll 312, 317
Sky Woman 301
solar calendar, 365-Day 269, *270*, 275, 282, 284–5
solar eclipse 200, 290, 371–2, *372*, 382, 388, 393, 397, 401, 405, 410, 419, 422, 426
solstice 5, 23, *42*, 65, *65*, 113, 114, 115, 119, 120, 175, 221, 277, 279, 281, 284, 300, 304, 312, 315, *373*, 375, 386, 392, 396, 400, 404–5, 414–15, 420, 423, 427, 431, 522
South Node 28, 29, 52, *134*, 254, 258, 260, 494
Spica 367
spirit animals 304–8
spiritual practices, astrology and 447–70
sports astrology 513
spring equinox 49, 62, 70, 71, 73, 111, 112, 251, 375, 384, 389, 395, 398, 403, 407, 412, 417, 421, 424, 522
Spring Festival (Lunar New Year, late January to early February) 189–90
Star Boy 299–300
star clocks 219–20
Star Woman 310
stations 375
statistical studies 17, 163
Stellium 65–6, *65*, 153, 155, 381
Stonehenge 431
Sturluson, Snorri 316
Sudines 294
Sufi astrology 244, 251
Sun: celestial events 381, 382, 383, 384–90, 393–408, 410–25; planets and celestial bodies 327–8, *331*, 335, 338–41, *338*, *343*, 344, 347, 350, 351, 353, 354, 356, 357, 359, 362, 363, 365

Sun-ji, Lee 203
sunstone navigation 315
Surya Siddhanta 264
synastry astrology 11, 489, 501, 513–14
synodic month 52, 66–7

tables of aspects 481–2
tables of houses 67, 123, 124
Taeun 202–3
talismanic magic 245
tarot 464
Taurus: season 112–13, *112*; western zodiac sign 84–6, *84*, *85*
Taxila University 157, 263
Tegus Buyantu Zurkhai 207
Templo Mayor (Great Temple) 268, 277
Tenger (Sky) Observations 206–7
terms, astrological 19–75
texts, key 157–9, 192, 199, 203, 207, 210–11, 214–15, 221–2, 228–9, 237, 248–9, 264, 278, 284–5, 292–3, 308, 309–10, 316, 321
theosophy 67, 469, 492
theurgy 48, 452, 453, 455–6
Thrasyllus of Mendes 322
Thunderbirds 301, *301*
Tibetan astrology 205, 207, 208–13, *210*, *212*, 510
time lords 21, 67
time zones and birth time accuracy 17
timeline of astrology 428–46
Titanomachy, or Battle of the Titans 240–1
Tlacaelel 279
Tlillan Tlapallan (House of Darkness and Light) 277–8
Tompkins, Sue 6, 169
Tonalamatl 276

Tonalpohualli 276
tools and techniques 471–82
Topocentric house system 445–6
transits 33–4, 35, 45, 50, 60, 64, 66, 67–8, 69, 261, 266, 465, 487, 490, 492, 493, 494, 500, 501, 504, 510, 513, 520; calculators 482
translation movement 243, 245
translation of light 69
Treatise on Astrology of the Kaiyuan Period (Kaiyuan Zhanjing) 192
Tử Vi Chỉ Nam (*Guide to Tử Vi*) 215
Tử Vi Đẩu Số Toàn Thư 214
Tử Vi Hàm Số (*The Functions of Tử Vi*) 215
Tula (Libra) 258, *258*
Twins Paradox 17
Tzolk'in calendar 267, 268, 273, 274, 282, 283–5, *283*

Ujjain 263–4
University of Bologna 157, 160
Uranus 11, 15, 34, 50, 54, 63, 68, 104, 105, 106, 107, 125, *131*, 146, 457, 465, 492, 508; celestial events 382, 388, 391, 394, 398, 399, 402, 407, 408, 411, 417–19, 421, 426; incorporated into astrology 443; opposition 69, *69*; planets and celestial bodies 350–3, *350*, 363, 364
Uxmal Observatory (Mexico) 284

Valens, Vettius: *Anthology* 157, 228, 434, 480
Vanaheim 313–14
Varahamihira 264, 265; *Brihat Jataka* 264, 265

Vedas 5, 262
Venus; as the Morning Star, birth of 280–1, *280*; celestial events 374, 390, 403–4, 419; descent and ascent of 287; planets and celestial bodies 335, 341–4, *341*, *342*; Venus Tablet of Ammisaduqa 292
vernal equinox 64, 69–70, 73, 112, 122, 251, 373, 395, 403, 407, 412, 421–2, 522
Vietnamese astrology 213–16
Virgo: season 116, *116*; western zodiac sign 93–4, *93*, *94*
Vrishabha (Taurus) 257, *257*
Vrishchika (Scorpio) 258, *258*

Water Buffalo 214
websites and mobile apps 487–90
week, planetary 290
Western astrology 76–169; birth charts 121–33; centers of learning 156–7; key texts 157–9; notable figures 159–69; Western zodiac 80–1; Western zodiac houses 134–55; Western zodiac seasons 109–21; Western zodiac signs 81–109
wheel of life 70, 73
White Beryl (Baidurya Karpo) 210–11
White Cloud Temple (Baiyun Guan) 191
whole sign houses 436
Wi and Hanwi 301–2
Wicca 451, 469–70
World Tree, or Ceiba tree 282–3, 312, 313, 315

Xook, Ah 285

Yasunori, Kamo no 200
Yeong-sil, Jang 203–4
Yggdrasil, or the World Tree 312, 313, 315, 316
Yin-Yang Polarity 189, *189*
yogas 262–3, 511

Zanabazar 207
Zheng Xiaoyun 194
Zij-i Ilkhani 249
zijes 245, 247, 249
zodiac 70
zodiac division 70–1, *71*
zodiac releasing 74–5
zodiac season 71
zodiac system 71–3, *71*, *72*, *73*
zodiac wheel 27, 36, 60, 70, 73–4, *73*, *74*, 109, 134, 138, 304, 433, 519, 520, 521, 522

Further Reading and Resources

Alice-astro. (2023, February 16). Colorized reconstruction of the Dendera Zodiac. *World History Encyclopedia*. https://www.worldhistory.org/image/17053/colorized-reconstruction-of-the-dendera-zodiac/

Ask the Astrosofa oracle – astrosofa.com. (n.d.-a). https://www.astrosofa.com/esoterism/Oracle/astrosofa-oracle

Astrodienst Astrowiki. (2023, February 5). *Myth of Heracles*. https://www.astro.com/astrowiki/en/Myth_of_Heracles

Astrologer. (2017, April 5). Ascendant and midheaven. Astrology Cafe. https://www.astrologercafe.com/2020/12/ascendant-and-midheaven.html

The astrological side of Rome: 6(+1) locations in the capital where the stars are reflected in architecture. (n.d.-j). https://www.elledecor.com/it/best-of/a61802685/astrological-curiosities-rome/

Astronomy calendar of celestial events for calendar year 2025. Astronomy Calendar of Celestial Events 2025 – Sea and Sky. (n.d.). http://www.seasky.org/astronomy/astronomy-calendar-2025.html

Astronomy. Palenque. (n.d.). https://archeoastronomyofpalenque.weebly.com/astronomy.html

AstroTwins, T. (2022, May 27). History of astrology: A timeline: Astrostyle: Astrology and daily, weekly, monthly horoscopes by the Astrotwins. Astrostyle. https://astrostyle.com/astrology/history/

What is My Spirit Animal. (2024, June 29). Native American Zodiac & Astrology: Birth Signs & Totems. What Is My Spirit Animal. https://whatismyspiritanimal.com/native-american-zodiac-astrology/

Aveni, A. F. (2001). *Skywatchers*. University of Texas Press.

Ballinger, G. (2022, October 2). Abu ma'shar: Persian prince of Astrology. Satya Astrology. https://satyastrology.com/abu-mashar-persian-prince-of-astrology/

Bhattacharjee A. S. (2023, March 30). Medical Astrology – Planets & Diseases. AstroSanhita. https://astrosanhita.com/astrology-medical-astrology-medical-astrology-planets-diseases/

Borealis, A. (2024, November 22). History of astrology: From its early days to the present. History of Astrology: From Its Early Days to the Present. https://morinus-astrology.com/history-astrology

Brennan, C. (2020). *Hellenistic astrology: the study of Fate and fortune*. Amor Fati Publications.

Burnett, C. (2015, May 1). East (and south) Asian traditions in astrology and divination as vi... Extrême-Orient Extrême-Occident. https://journals.openedition.org/extremeorient/293

The Encyclopedia of Astrology

Campos, S. (2023). *Seasons of the zodiac: Love, Magick, and manifestation throughout the astrological year.* Fair Winds.

Cartwright, M. (2024b, December 31). The Aztec calendar. *World History Encyclopedia.* https://www.worldhistory.org/article/896/the-aztec-calendar/

Chen, Y., Xu, L., & Xu, G. (2019). *Introduction to chinese culture: Cultural history, arts, festivals and rituals.* Palgrave Macmillan.

Cherokee stories. Native History Association - Origin of the Pleiades and the Pine. (n.d.). https://www.nativehistoryassociation.org/pleiades.php

Cherokee stories. Native History Association – The Milky Way. (n.d.). https://www.nativehistoryassociation.org/milkyway.php

Chesnokova, N. (2023, March 28). The Jeong Gam Nok Prophecy Book and its influence on the Korean history in the late Joseon period. St. Petersburg University Studies in Social Sciences & Humanities. Vol. 1: Proceedings of the 9th International Conference Issues of Far Eastern Literatures. https://www.academia.edu/99230698/The_Jeong_Gam_Nok_Prophecy_Book_and_Its_Influence_on_the_Korean_History_in_the_Late_Joseon_Period

Chinese 28 lunar mansions astrology. (n.d.-b). https://benebellwen.com/wp-content/uploads/2023/06/the-28-lunar-mansions-chinese-astrology.pdf

Decans. (n.d.). https://ib205.tripod.com/decans.html

Deciphering the symbols and symbolic meaning of the Maya World Tree. Society of Ethnobiology. (1970, January 1). https://ethnobiology.org/deciphering-symbols-and-symbolic-meaning-maya-world-tree

Dendera Zodiac. Greco-Roman Period Monuments. (n.d.). https://egyptianmuseum.org/explore/greco-and-roman-period-monuments-dendera-zodiac

The Dendera Zodiacs as narratives of the myth of Osiris, Isis, and the child horus, Gyula Priskin, Enim 8, 2015, p. 133-185 " enim – une revue d'égyptologie sur internet. ENIM. (n.d.). http://www.enim-egyptologie.fr/index.php?page=enim-8&n=9

Did you know? the influence of astrology on the science of astronomy along the Silk Roads. Silk Roads Programme. (n.d.). https://en.unesco.org/silkroad/content/did-you-know-influence-astrology-science-astronomy-along-silk-roads

Egyptian decans. Occult Encyclopedia. (n.d.). https://www.occult.live/index.php/Egyptian_decans

Encyclopædia Britannica, inc. (2024, December 25). Encyclopædia Britannica. https://www.britannica.com/topic/Islam/Islamic-myth-and-legend

Encyclopædia Britannica, inc. (2024, December 5). Al-Bīrūnī. Encyclopædia Britannica. https://www.britannica.com/biography/al-Biruni

Encyclopædia Britannica, inc. (n.d.-a). Alexandrian Museum. Encyclopædia Britannica. https://www.britannica.com/topic/Alexandrian-Museum

The Encyclopedia of Astrology

Encyclopædia Britannica, inc. (n.d.-b). Berosus. Encyclopædia Britannica. https://www.britannica.com/biography/Berosus

Encyclopædia Britannica, inc. (n.d.-c). Borsippa. Encyclopædia Britannica. https://www.britannica.com/place/Borsippa

Encyclopædia Britannica, inc. (n.d.-d). Esagila. Encyclopædia Britannica. https://www.britannica.com/topic/Esagila

Encyclopædia Britannica, inc. (n.d.-e). Hipparchus. Encyclopædia Britannica. https://www.britannica.com/biography/Hipparchus-Greek-astronomer

Flint boys. Flint Boys, Navajo Myth about Pleiades – Windows to the Universe. (n.d.). https://www.windows2universe.org/mythology/flintboys_pleiades.html

Foundations of Tibetan astrology (Jung-tsi) – shrīmālā: Consulting, media, and Education. Shrīmālā | Consulting, Media, and Education. (n.d.). https://www.shrimala.com/tibetan-elemental-calculations

Garcia, E. S., & Pringle, V. (2006). *Coyote and the sky: How the sun, Moon, and stars began.* University of New Mexico Press.

Gautschy, R. (n.d.). The star Sirius in Ancient Egypt and Babylonia. Sirius. https://www.gautschy.ch/~rita/archast/sirius/siriuseng.htm

Gill, N. S. (2020, January 3). The Library of Alexandria and the famous people who worked there. ThoughtCo. https://www.thoughtco.com/geniuses-of-the-library-of-alexandria-118080

Google. (n.d.). The book of instruction in the elements of the art of Astrology. Google Books. https://www.google.com/books/edition/The_Book_of_Instruction_in_the_Elements/7jTdDsBklc4C?hl=en

Hail, R. (2008). *Cherokee astrology: Animal Medicine in the stars.* Bear & Co.

Heyworth, R. (2015, July 12). Quiriguá: The Maya Creation Stones. Uncovered History. https://uncoveredhistory.com/guatemala/quirigua/the-maya-creation-stones-of-quirigua/

History of astrology and astronomy in Islamic medicine. (n.d.-d). https://hrmars.com/papers_submitted/6293/History_of_Astrology_and_Astronomy_in_Islamic_Medicine.pdf

History, M. and A. (2024, December 27). Inanna and Enki: The giving of the sacred measures. Mythology and History. https://www.historyandmyths.com/2024/11/enki-giving-inanna-sacred-measures.html

Holden, J. H. (2013). A history of horoscopic astrology: From the Babylonian Period to the modern age. American Federation Of Astrologers, Inc.

Home "NineStar" 9 Star Ki Astrology. NineStar. (n.d.). https://www.9starkiastrology.com/

Indian astrology – jyotish. Numerologist PRO. (n.d.). https://www.numerologistpro.com/astrology/indian-astrology-jyotish/

The Encyclopedia of Astrology

Introduction to Tibetan Astrology – Tibetan Buddhist Encyclopedia. (n.d.). https://tibetanbuddhistencyclopedia.com/en/index.php?title=Introduction_to_Tibetan_Astrology

The Islamic perspective on astrology. Astrozodiac-harmony. (2023, November 3). https://astrozodiacharmony.com/the-islamic-perspective-on-astrology

Jamie. (2024, September 27). Chinese Lunar Mansions – 宿 xiù. Astrology King. https://astrologyking.com/chinese-lunar-mansions/

Jeni. (2022, June 17). Shani Deva – one of the Navagraha & Hindu god of justice. VedicFeed. https://vedicfeed.com/shani-deva/

Jyotish | Vedic astrology | the science of light. (n.d.-e). https://qatoqi.com/ayurveda/jyotish.htm

Kendy and Daisy. (n.d.). Chinese zodiac signs compatibility: Love, marriage, Relationship Calculator and Chart. Your Chinese Astrology. https://www.yourchineseastrology.com/zodiac/compatibility/

Keçelioğlu, F. (2021, October 4). The directions of the Mayan signs - my Mayan sign. Mayan Horoscope Blog. https://mymayansign.com/blog/directions-mayan-signs/

King, A. (2023, February 17). Hellenistic astrology. World History Encyclopedia. https://www.worldhistory.org/Hellenistic_Astrology

King, A. (2024a, July 11). Ptolemaic egypt. World History Encyclopedia. https://www.worldhistory.org/Ptolemaic_Egypt

King, A. (2024b, July 12). Ptolemaic dynasty. World History Encyclopedia. https://www.worldhistory.org/Ptolemaic_Dynasty/

King, A. (n.d.). Astrology and Imperial legitimacy in Ancient Rome. Ancient World Magazine. https://www.ancientworldmagazine.com/articles/astrology-imperial-legitimacy-rome

King, Jerry. (2011). *Four pillars of destiny a guide to relationships.* iUniverse Inc.

Korean Culture and Information Service (KOCIS). (n.d.). Jumong: Founder of Goguryeo Kingdom is man of legend, history: Korea.net: The Official Website of the Republic of Korea. Korea.net. https://www.korea.net/NewsFocus/Culture/view?articleId=121572

Kukulcan. Kukulcan and Mayan Myths about Venus – Windows to the Universe. (n.d.). https://www.windows2universe.org/mythology/Kukulcan_venus.html

Lady six sky and the definition of ritual space at Naranjo | vanderbilt undergraduate research journal. (n.d.-f). https://ejournals.library.vanderbilt.edu/index.php/vurj/article/view/2709

Lau, T., Lau, L., & Lau, K. (2019). *The handbook of Chinese horoscopes.* North Atlantic Books.

Learn your mayan sign. MyMayanSign. (n.d.). https://mymayansign.com/

Legend of the twelve zodiac animals. International Dunhuang Programme. (n.d.). https://idp.bl.uk/exhibition/chinese-astronomy/articles/astrology-and-myth/legend-of-the-twelve-zodiac-animals/

León Portilla, M. (1990). *Aztec thought and culture: A study of the ancient nahuatl mind*. University of Oklahoma Press.

The light of the Equinox. The Gardens of Babylon. (2024, August 27). https://thegardensofbabylon.com/event/the-gardens-of-babylon-the-light-of-the-equinox/

Maestri, N. (2020, December 1). The Mayan myth of the hero twins - stories from the Popol Vuh. ThoughtCo. https://www.thoughtco.com/hunahpu-xbalanque-maya-hero-twins-171590

Manilius, M., & Liuzzi, D. (1991). *Astronomica*. Libro II. Congedo.

Mark, E. (2024, April 17). Oracle Bones. World History Encyclopedia. https://www.worldhistory.org/Oracle_Bones/

Mark, J. J. (2022, September 14). Library of Pergamon. World History Encyclopedia. https://www.worldhistory.org/Library_of_Pergamon

Mark, J. J. (2024, December 31). Imhotep. World History Encyclopedia. https://www.worldhistory.org/imhotep/

Mask of the black god: The Pleiades in Navajo cosmology. (n.d.-g). https://nhmu.utah.edu/sites/default/files/attachments/pleiades.pdf

Mayan day signs. (n.d.). https://alabe.com/daysigns.htm

Milky way myths from all over the world. (n.d.). https://native-science.net/Milky_Way_Myths.htm

Modgia, E. (2023, October 24). Aztec astrology: Exploring the influence of celestial bodies on personality and destiny. Astrology Blog. https://astrolozy.com/uncategorized/aztec-astrology/

Mongol odon zurhai | endangered archives programme. (n.d.-h). https://eap.bl.uk/archive-file/EAP529-1-51

Native American legends: Star-boy (poia). Star-Boy (Scar-Face or Poia). (n.d.). https://www.native-languages.org/star-boy.htm

Iroquois Legends (Haudenosaunee Folklore, Myths, and Traditional Indian Stories). (n.d.). https://www.native-languages.org/iroquois-legends.htm

Nechepso and Petosiris. The Hellenistic Astrology Website. (2016, February 5). https://www.hellenisticastrology.com/astrologers/nechepso-and-petosiris/

Nicholas. (2009). *History of western astrology*. Bloomsbury Academic.

Nick. (2024, February 27). Unveiling the mysteries: Your ultimate tzolkin calculator guide. Mayan Day. https://mayanday.com/unveiling-the-mysteries-your-ultimate-tzolkin-calculator-guide/

Norse zodiac signs: How to find your birth rune - norsemythologist. (n.d.-i). https://norsemythologist.com/norse-zodiac-signs/

Person. (2018, December 3). A brief history of 郭璞 Guo Pu, the founding father of Feng Shui – read this story on Magzter.com. Magzter. https://www.magzter.com/stories/Lifestyle/BaziChic-Feng-Shui-Chinese-Astrology/A-Brief-History-Of-Guo-Pu-The-Founding-Father-Of-Feng-Shui

The Encyclopedia of Astrology

Philippe Lepoivre de Vesle – Brice Joly – Astrotheme. (n.d.). Planetary rulerships, dignities and Debilities. Astrotheme. https://www.astrotheme.com/astrology_planetary-rulerships.php

Pothos.org. Astronomical Diaries. (n.d.). https://www.pothos.org/content/indexaf77.html?page=astronomical-diaries

Reading a chart using Hellenistic methods. Kepler College Research Library. (n.d.). https://library.keplercollege.org/reading-a-chart-using-hellenistic-methods/

Sancho, B. (2024, November 18). Roman sacred rituals: The influence of Astrology. Roman Mythology. https://roman.mythologyworldwide.com/roman-sacred-rituals-the-influence-of-astrology-3

Saq' be': Organization for Mayan and Indigenous Spiritual Studies. Welcome to Saq' Be'. (2024, August 30). http://sacredroad.org/

Sardar, M. (1AD, January 1). Astronomy and astrology in the medieval Islamic world: Essay: The Metropolitan Museum of Art: Heilbrunn timeline of art history. The Met's Heilbrunn Timeline of Art History. https://www.metmuseum.org/toah/hd/astr/hd_astr.htm

Selvadurai, S., Patnaik, E., & Kazmi, A. (2022). *Mansions of the Moon*. Knopf Canada.

Sever, A. (2024, June 9). Visions in the crystal: A practical guide to crystal gazing. Occultist. https://occultist.net/crystal-gazing-guide/

Shams al-ma'arif – the sun of wisdom. (n.d.). https://renaissanceastrology.com/shamsalmaarif.html

Skinner, S., & Lin, C. P. (2016). The original Eight mansions formula: A classic Ch'ing dynasty Feng Shui text. Createspace Independent Publishing Platform.

Skyscript astrology. Skyscript Astrology. (n.d.). https://www.skyscript.co.uk/

Sopdet. Ancient Egypt Online. (n.d.). https://ancientegyptonline.co.uk/sopdet/

Suchandra. Suchandra – Tibetan Buddhist Encyclopedia. (n.d.). https://www.tibetanbuddhistencyclopedia.com/en/index.php?title=Suchandra

Sun, X. (2014). Chinese armillary spheres. Handbook of Archaeoastronomy and Ethnoastronomy, 2127–2132. https://doi.org/10.1007/978-1-4614-6141-8_223

Titanomachy. Greek Mythology. (n.d.). https://www.greekmythology.com/Myths/The_Myths/Titanomachy/titanomachy.html

TOI Astrology / Jul 11, 2024. (n.d.). Story of Rahu and Ketu – Times of India. The Times of India. https://timesofindia.indiatimes.com/astrology/others/story-of-rahu-and-ketu/articleshow/111650701.cms

Tomasz. (2024a, May 12). Mongolian astrology: The ancient art of divination on the steppes. Knowledge Voyager. https://knowledgevoyager.com/mongolian-astrology-the-ancient-art-of-divination-on-the-steppes

Tomasz. (2024b, May 12). Vietnamese astrology: The spiritual connection between the stars and the elements. Knowledge Voyager. https://knowledgevoyager.com/vietnamese-astrology-the-spiritual-connection-between-the-stars-and-the-elements

The tomb of k'inich Janaab Pakal. (n.d.-k). https://www.mesoweb.com/articles/guenter/TI.pdf

Translation of light. The Astrology Dictionary. (2013, April 10). https://theastrologydictionary.com/t/translation-of-light/

Tzolkin. (n.d.). https://www.mayan-calendar.com/ancient_tzolkin.html

Understanding the art of scrying with crystals. All Crystal. (2024, February 22). https://www.allcrystal.com/articles/scrying-crystals/

The venus tablets of Ammizaduga (1928): Langdon, Stephen and Fotheringham, John Knight: Internet Archive. (n.d.). https://archive.org/details/TheVenusTabletsOfAmmizaduga1928

Vietnam.com. (n.d.). Lạc long quân and âu Cơ – the legend of ancient Vietnam. https://www.vietnam.com/en/culture/art/fairy-tales/lac-long-quan-and-au-co-the-legend-of-ancient-vietnam.html

Vietnamese zodiac. Vietnamonline.com. (n.d.). https://www.vietnamonline.com/culture/vietnamese-zodiac.html

Văn nghệ TP.HCM. (1970, January 1). Giai Thoại VÀ Sấm Ký Trạng Trình: Phạm đan quế: Internet Archive. https://archive.org/details/giai-thoai-va-sam-ky-trang-trinh-pham-dan-que

Warnock, C. (2019). Mansions of the moon: A lunar zodiac for Astrology and magic 2nd edition with 2019-2033 mansion ... ephemeris. Lulu.com.

Waxman, O. B. (2018, June 21). Are zodiac signs real? here's the history behind horoscopes. Time. https://time.com/5315377/are-zodiac-signs-real-astrology-history/

Welcome to Astrology.com. Tarot, Zodiac, Astrology & Horoscopes – Astrology.com. (n.d.). https://www.astrology.com/

Wen, B. (2016). *The Tao of Craft: Fu talismans and casting sigils in the Eastern Esoteric Tradition*. North Atlantic Books.

Wikimedia Foundation. (2023, September 13). Enuma Anu Enlil. Wikipedia. https://en.wikipedia.org/w/index.php?title=Enuma_Anu_Enlil

Wikimedia Foundation. (2024a, January 22). Chandramauli Upadhyay. Wikipedia. https://en.wikipedia.org/wiki/Chandramauli_Upadhyay

Wikimedia Foundation. (2024b, April 3). Brihat Jataka. Wikipedia. https://en.wikipedia.org/wiki/Brihat_Jataka

Wikimedia Foundation. (2024c, May 25). Indigenous astronomy. Wikipedia. https://en.wikipedia.org/wiki/Indigenous_astronomy

Wikimedia Foundation. (2024d, November 9). Zanabazar. Wikipedia. https://en.wikipedia.org/wiki/Zanabazar

Wikimedia Foundation. (2024e, November 13). Tetrabiblos. Wikipedia. https://en.wikipedia.org/wiki/Tetrabiblos

Wikimedia Foundation. (2024f, November 30). Five Suns. Wikipedia. https://en.wikipedia.org/wiki/Five_Suns

Wikimedia Foundation. (2024g, December 6). Platonic Academy. Wikipedia. https://en.wikipedia.org/wiki/Platonic_Academy

Wikimedia Foundation. (2024h, December 18). Book of nut. Wikipedia. https://en.wikipedia.org/wiki/Book_of_Nut

Wikimedia Foundation. (2024i, December 20). Eanna. Wikipedia. https://en.wikipedia.org/wiki/Eanna

Wikimedia Foundation. (2024j, December 20). Harut and Marut. Wikipedia. https://en.wikipedia.org/wiki/Harut_and_Marut

Wikimedia Foundation. (2024k, December 22). Jang Yeong-sil. Wikipedia. https://en.wikipedia.org/wiki/Jang_Yeong-sil

Wikimedia Foundation. (2024l, December 25). Astrological symbols. Wikipedia. https://en.wikipedia.org/wiki/Astrological_symbols

Wikimedia Foundation. (2024m, December 26). Academy of gondishapur. Wikipedia. https://en.wikipedia.org/wiki/Academy_of_Gondishapur

Wikimedia Foundation. (2024n, December 29). Wolves in folklore, religion and mythology. Wikipedia. https://en.wikipedia.org/wiki/Wolves_in_folklore%2C_religion_and_mythology

Wikimedia Foundation. (2024o, December 31). Humorism. Wikipedia. https://en.wikipedia.org/wiki/Humorism

Wilkinson, R. H. (2003). *The complete gods and Goddesses of Ancient egypt.* Thames & Hudson.

Wu, S. (2005). *Chinese astrology: Exploring the eastern zodiac.* New Page Books, a division of the Career Press, Inc.

Yang, L., An, D., & Turner, J. A. (2008). *Handbook of Chinese mythology.* Oxford University Press.

Zhao, R. (2023, August 23). Chinese zodiac. Chinese Zodiac: 12 Animal Signs and 2025 Horoscope Predictions. https://www.chinahighlights.com/travelguide/chinese-zodiac/